National Socialist Extermination Policies

WAR AND GENOCIDE
General Editor: Omer Bartov, Rutgers University

NATIONAL SOCIALIST EXTERMINATION POLICIES

Contemporary German Perspectives and Controversies

Edited by
Ulrich Herbert

Berghahn Books
New York • Oxford

Published in 2000 by Berghahn Books
www.berghahnbooks.com
Reprinted in 2004
© 2000, 2004 English-language edition, Berghahn Books
© 1998 Fisher Taschenbuch Verlag GmbH, Frankfurt am Main
Originally published as *Nationalsozialistische Vernichtungspolitik,
1939-1945: Neue Forschungen und Kontroversen*

Library of Congress Cataloging-in-Publication Data

Nationalsozialistische Vernichtungspolitik, 1939-1945. English
    National-Socialist extermination policies : contemporary German
perspectives and controversies / edited by Ulrich Herbert ; [with
texts by Götz Aly ... et al.].
        p.   cm. — (War and genocide ; v. 2)
    Revised and expanded essays based on a series of lectures given
during the 1996/97 winter semester, sponsored by the History Dept.
at the Albert-Ludwigs University in Freiburg.
    Includes bibliographical references.
    ISBN 1-57181-750-6 (alk. paper)
    ISBN 1-57181-751-4 (pbk. : alk. paper)
    1. Holocaust, Jewish (1939-1945)—Influence. 2. Germany—
History—1933-1945—Moral and ethical aspects. 3. World War,
1939-1945—Atrocities. 4. National socialism—Historiography.
5. National characteristics, German. I. Herbert, Ulrich, 1951- .
II. Aly, Götz, 1947- . III. Title. IV. Series.
D804.3N3813 1999   99-25765
940.53'18—DC21   CIP

British Library Cataloguing in Publication Data

A catalogue record for this book is available from the British Library.

Printed in the United States on acid-free paper.

Contents

FOREWORD

In the winter semester of 1996/97, the History Department at the Albert-Ludwigs University in Freiburg sponsored a series of lectures on the history of National Socialist extermination policy that aroused uncommon interest among both students and members of the general public. Its purpose was to leave behind the stale and rigid terms of Holocaust scholarship and public discussion of the issue. In the preceding years, several young historians, removed from the increasingly agitated but uninformed public controversies, had produced new studies based on a wealth of empirical evidence which had both significantly broadened our knowledge and revised it in many ways. In this context "revision" does not mean, as is periodically proclaimed, that the history of the National Socialist regime must now be "written anew." On the contrary, we are now in a position to state that hitherto we have lacked any knowledge of entire aspects of this period of history. This is especially true of the Germans' concrete activities in the individual regions of central and eastern Europe.

The texts published in this volume deal with developments in Poland, the Soviet Union, Serbia, and France. They aim primarily at identifying the impulses that drove German activities in the individual occupation regions. Here the vigorous twenty-year-old discussion about whether the Holocaust was the "culmination of an ideology" or the result of a process of "cumulative radicalization" proves to be of little help. What emerges rather is a general picture in which elements of particular situations and gradual processes of radicalization are joined, in a multiplicity of ways, with equally varied goals and basic ideological convictions. National Socialist extermination policy thus proves not to have been a secret event but part of the policy of conquest and occupation throughout Europe.

The aim of this volume is to present these findings and to discuss the issues, contradictions, and areas of confusion that remain or have recently emerged. With two exceptions, the essays published here originated in the papers presented in the Freiburg lecture series, although they have been revised and, to some extent, significantly expanded.

Ulrich Herbert
Freiburg im Breisgau
August 1999

Bundesrepublik

ı Politik

d
ıania pryeciwko
ⁱ der
suchung der
arschau

AHR	American ɪ ɪɪ...
A	Armeekorps
AMV	Archiv Ministerstva vnitra a České republiky (Archiv des tschechischen Innenministeriums, Prag)
AO	Auslandsorganisation
AOK	Armeeoberkommando
AoStKom	Außerordentliche Staatskommission zur Untersuchung der deutsch-faschistischen Verbrechen
APL	Archiwum Państwowe w Lubline
APMO	Archiwum Państwowego Muzeum w Oświęcimiu (Archiv des staatlichen Museums in Auschwitz)
Art.	Artillerie
Aufl.	Auflage
AV	Aktenvermerk
Az.	Aktenzeichen
AZIH	Archiwum Żydowskiego Instytutu Historycznego
b.	bei(m)
BA	Bundesarchiv

BAB	Bundesarchiv Berlin
BA D-H	Bundesarchiv Zwischenarchiv Dahlwitz-Hoppegarten
BAK	Bundesarchiv Koblenz
BAK VV	Bundesarchiv Koblenz ErblaßsammlungVorbeugende Verbrechensbekämpfung
BA-L	Bundesarchiv Außenstelle Lichterfelde
BA-MA	Bundesarchiv-Militärarchiv Freiburg i. Br.
BAP	Bundesarchiv Abteilung Potsdam
BBC	British Broadcasting Company
Bd.	Band
BDC	Berlin Document Center
BdO	Befehlshaber der Ordnungspolizei
BdS	Befehlshaber (Beauftragter) der Sicherheitspolizei und des SD
BdW	Befehlshaber der Waffen-SS
Bearb.	Bearbeitung
Begl.Btl.	Begleitbatallion
Berück	Befehlshaber des rückwärtigen Heeresgebiets
Bes.Ano.	Besondere Anordnung
Betr.	Betrifft
BGBl	Bundesgesetzblatt
BGH	Bundesgerichtshof
BGKBZ	Biuletyn Głównej Komisji Badania Zbrodni Hitlerowskich w Polsce [jetzt: przeciwko Narodowi Polskiemu]
Bgm.	Bürgermeister
Bl.	Blatt
BLI	Bulletin Leo Baeck Institute
BRABAG	Braunkohle-Benzin AG
Brif./Brig.F.	SS-Brigadeführer
BRT	Bruttoregistertonnen
BT	Berliner Tageblatt
Btl.	Bataillon
BuF	Bevölkerungswesen und Fürsorge
BZIH	Biuletyn Żydowskiego Instytutu Historycznego w Polsce
CDAHO	Central`nyj Deržavnyj Archiv Hromads`kych Orhanizaciï Ukraïny
CDAVO	Central`nyj Deržavnyj Archiv Vysšych Orhanov Ukraïny
CDIA	Central`nyj Deržavnyj Istoryčeskyj Archiv L`viv
CDJC	Centre de Documentation Juive Contemporaine, Paris
CdO	Chef der Ordnungspolizei
CdS, CSSD	Chef der Sicherheitspolizei und des SD
ChdA	Chef des Amtes
CdZ	Chef der Zivilverwaltung

CV	Centralverein deutscher Staatsbürger jüdischen Glaubens
DAF	Deutsche Arbeitsfront
DAIFO	Deržavnyj Archiv Ivano-Frankivs`koï Oblasti
DALO	Deržavnyj Archiv L`vivs`koï Oblasti
DALO-PA	Deržavnyj Archiv L`vivs`koï Oblasti - Partyjnyj Archiv
DAW	Deutsche Ausrüstungs-Werke
DAZ	Deutsche Allgemeine Zeitung
Dez.	Dezernat
DFG	Deutsche Forschungsgemeinschaft
DGFP	Documents on German British Foreign Policy
DG IV	Durchgangsstraße IV
DiM	Dokumenty i Materialy
Distr.	Distrikt
Div.	Division
DNSAP	Dänische Nationalistische Arbeiterpartei
Dok.	Dokument
Dok.-Slg.	Dokumenten-Sammlung
DP	Displaced Person
DUT	Deutsche Umsiedlungs-Treuhand GmbH
DVL	Deutsche Volksliste
DVP	Deutschnationale Volkspartei
DWB	Deutsche Wirtschaftsbetriebe GmbH
DÖW	Dokumentationsarchiv des österreichischen Widerstands, Wien
EG	Einsatzgruppe
EK	Eisernes Kreuz
Eko	Einsatzkommando
EM	Ereignismeldung (UdSSR)
Erl.	Erlaß
EWZ	Einwanderer-Zentralstelle
f./ff.	folgende Seite/n
FHA	Führungshauptamt
FHO	Fremde Heere Ost
FKO	Feldkommandantur
FHQ	Führerhauptquartier
Flak.-Abt.	Flugabwehrkanonenabteilung
FRUS	Foreign Relations of the United States
fr.	frame
FS/FSchr.	Fernschreiben
FZ	Frankfurter Zeitung
FZH	Forschungsstelle für Zeitgeschichte Hamburg
Gaul.	Gauleiter
GBA	Generalbevollmächtigter für den Arbeitseinsatz
GB Rüst.	Generalbevollmächtigter für die Rüstung
GBV	Generalbevollmächtigter für die Reichsverwaltung

GDG	Gouverneur des Distrikts Galizien
GDG	Gouverneur des Distrikts Lublin
Gdp.	Gendarmerie-Posten
GDR	German Democratic Republic
Geb.Div.	Gebirgsdivision
GedOb.	Generaldivision der Ostbahn
Gen.	General
Gend.	Gendarmerie
Gen.Dir.	Generaldirektor
Gen.Insp.	Generalinspekteur
Gen.Lt.	Generalleutnant
Gen.Maj.	Generalmajor
GenStH	Generalstab des Heeres
Gestapa	Geheimes Staatspolizeiamt
Gestapo	Geheime Staatspolizei
GFP	Geheime Feldpolizei
GG	Generalgouvernement
GGr	Generalgouverneur
GK	Gebietskommisar(iat)
GKBZHwP	Głowna Komisja Badania Zbrodni Hitlerowskich w Polsce (Hauptkommission zur Untersuchung der Naziverbrechen in Polen)
g.Kdos.	geheime Kommandosache
G.L.	Gauleiter
GmbH	Gesellschaft mit beschränkter Haftung
GPK	Grenzpolizei-Kommissariat
GPP	Grenzpolizei-Posten
GPU	Gosudarstvennoe Političeskoe Upravlenie [bis 1934 Staatssicherheitsdienst der UdSSR]
GQu	Generalquartiermeister des Heeres
Gr.	Grenadier/Gruppe
Gr.F./Gruf.	SS-Gruppenführer
gRS	geheime Reichssache
GSR	German Studies Review
GstA	Generalstaatsanwalt
GstAB/GStAPK	Geheimes Staatsarchiv Preußischer Kulturbezirk, Berlin
GuG	Geschichte und Gesellschaft
GVBl	Gesetz- und Verordnungsblatt
HA	Hauptamt/Hauptabteilung
Hg.	Herausgeber
HGS	Holocaust and Genocide Studies
HGr.	Heeresgruppe
Hipo	Hilfspolizei
HJ	Hitler-Jugend
Hptm.	Hauptmann
Hptstf./Hstuf.	SS-Hauptsturmführer

Hscharf.	SS-Hauptscharführer
HöSSPF	Höchster SS- und Polizeiführer
HSSPF	Höherer SS- und Polizeiführer
HStAD	Hauptstaatsarchiv Düsseldorf
HTO	Haupttreuhandstelle Ost
Ia	Erster Generalstabsoffizier
Ic	Dritter Generalstabsoffizier
ID	Infanterie Division
IdO	Inspekteur der Ordnungspolizei
IdS	Inspekteur der Sicherheitspolizei
IfZ	Institut für Zeitgeschichte
IG	Industriegruppe
IHK	Industrie- und Handelskammer
IKG	Israelitische Kultusgemeinde
IKL	Inspektion der Konzentrationslager
IMT	Internationales Militär-Tribunal (Nürnberg)
Inf.	Infanterie
Inf.Reg	Infanterieregiment
Insp.	Inspekteur
I.V.	Innere Verwaltung
JA	Jahrbuch für Antisemitismusforschung
JHK	Jüdisches Hilfs-Komitee
JR	Jüdische Rundschau
JSS	Jüdische Soziale Selbsthilfe
JUS	Jüdische Unterstützungsstelle
Kav.	Kavallerie
Kav.Rgt.	Kavallerieregiment
KdGend	Kommandeur der Gendarmerie
KdO	Kommandeur der Ordnungspolizei
Kdo.	Kommando
Kdo.Stab	Kommandostab
Kdr.	Kommandeur
KdS	Kommandeur der Sicherheitspolizei und des SD
KdSch	Kommandeur der Schutzpolizei
Kdt.	Kommandant
KGB	Kommissariat Gosudarstwennoj Besopasnosti (Kommissariat für Staatssicherheit)
KHm	Kreishauptmann
KK	Kriminal-Kommissariat
Kommand.	Kommandierender
Korück	Kommandant des rückwärtigen Armeegebiets
Kp.	Kompanie
KPP	Kriminalpolizei-Posten
Kp(b)U	Kommunističeskaja Partija Ukrainy (bol'ševiki)[KP der Ukraine]
Kripo	Kriminalpolizei
Krs.	Kreis

KTB	Kriegstagebuch
KVK	Kriegsverdienstkreuz
KZ, KL	Konzentrationslager
LAH/LSSAH	SS-Division "Leibstandarte Adolf Hitler"
LBIY	Leo Baeck Insitute Yearbook
LCVA	Lietuvos Centrinis Valstybinis Archyvas (Litauisches Zentrales Staatsarchiv)
LdKom	Landkommissar
Leg.	Legion(s)
LG	Landgericht
LKA	Landeskriminalamt
LO	Leitz-Ordner
LV	Landesverband
LVA	Latvijas Valsts Arhivs (Staatsarchiv Lettlands)
LVVA	Latvijas Valsts Vestures Arhives (Latvian Historical State Archive)(Historisches Archiv Lettlands)
MBF	Militärbefehlshaber Frankreich
MBliV	Ministerialblatt der inneren Verwaltung
MdI	Minister des Inneren
MdR	Mitglied des Reichstages
MGB	Ministerstvo Gosudarstvennoj Bezopasnosti [Ministerium für Staatssicherheit]
MGFA	Militärgeschichtliches Forschungsamt
MGM	Militärgeschichtliche Mitteilungen
MHA	Militärhistorisches Archiv, Prag
MiG	Militärbefehlshaber im Generalgouvernement
Min.	Minister
MinDir	Ministerialdirektor
Mio.	Millionen
mot.	Motorisiert
MVD	Ministerstvo Vnutrennich Del [Ministerium für Inneres]
MVerw.	Militärverwaltung
NA	Nationales Archives, Washington
Napola	Nationalpolitische Erziehungsanstalten
Nbg.Dok.	Nürnberger Dokument im IMT
NKGB	Narodnyj Komissariat Gosudarstvennoj Bezopasnosti [Volkskommissariat für Staatssicherheit]
NKVD/NKWD	Narodnyj Komissariat Vnutrennich Del [Volkskommissariat für Inneres]
NL	Nachlaß
NPD	Nationaldemokratische Partei Deutschlands
NPL	Neue Politische Literatur
NS, ns	Nationalsozialismus, nationalsozialistisch
NSB	Nationaal-Socialistische Beweging der Nederlanden
NSDAP	Nationalsozialistische Deutsche Arbeiterpartei
NSFK	Nationalsozialistische Fliegerkorps

NSG	Nationalsozialistische Gewaltverbrechen
NS-Hago	Nationalsozialistische Handels-, Handwerks- und Gewerbeorganisation
NSKK	Nationalsozialistische Kraftfahrkorps
NSM	Nordrhein-Westfälisches Staatsarchiv Münster
NSNAP	Nationaal-Socialistische Nederlandsche Arbejder partij
NSV	Nationalsozialistische Volkswohlfahrt e.V.
NSZ	Narodowe Sily Zbrojne [Nationale Streitkräfte]
NYT	New York Times
NZZ	Neue Zürcher Zeitung
OA	Oberabschnitt
OB	Oberbefehlshaber
OBD	Ostbahn-Direktion
OBdH	Oberbefehlshaber des Heeres
OBdM	Oberbefehlshaber der Marine
Oberf.	SS-Oberführer
Oberfr.	Oberfranken
Oberpräs.	Oberpräsident
Oberstgruf.	SS-Oberstgruppenführer
OBOst	Oberbefehlshaber Ost
o. D.	ohne Datum
Offz.	Offizier
OFK	Oberfeldkommandantur
Ogruf./OGruf./ OgruF.	SS-Obergruppenführer
o.J.	ohne Jahresangabe
OK	Ortskommandantur
OKH	Oberkommando des Heeres
OKW	Oberkommando der Wehrmacht
OLG	Oberlandesgericht
OQu	Oberquartiermeister
Orpo	Ordnungspolizei
OS	Osobi-Archiv
OSAF	Oberste SA-Führung
Oscharf.	SS-Oberscharführer
OStA	Oberstaatsanwalt
Ostubaf.	SS-Obersturmbannführer
Ost-Dok	Ost-Dokumentation
Ostuf.	SS-Obersturmführer
OT	Organisation Todt
OUN	Orhanizacija Ukraïns'kych Nationalistiv [Organistation ukrainischer Nationalisten]
OUN-B	Bandera-Flügel der OUN
OUN-M	Melnyk-Flügel der OUN
PA-AA/PAA	Politisches Archiv des Auswärtigen Amtes
Pers.Stab.RF-SS	Persönlicher Stab Reichsführer-SS

PKW	Personenkraftwagen
Pol.	Polizei
Pol.Abt.	Politische Abteilung
Pol.Btl.	Polizeibataillon
Pol.Regt.	Polizeiregiment
PPR	Polska Partia Robotnicza [polnische Arbeiterpartei]
pr.	preußisch
Präs.	Präsident
PRO	Public Record Office, London
Prot.	Protokoll
Prof.	Professor
Pz.	Panzer
Pz.Div	Panzerdivision
Pkzl.	Parteikanzlei
Qu	Quartiermeister
RA	Rechtsanwalt
RAF	Royal Air Force
RAM	Reichsaußenminister
RdErl.	Runderlaß
RdSchr.	Rundschreiben
Ref.	Referat/Referent
RegBez.	Regierungsbezirk
RegGG	Regierung des Generalgouvernements
RegPräs.	Regierungspräsident
Res.	Reserve
RFM/RMdF	Reichsminister der Finanzen
RFSS/RF-SS (uChdDtPol)	Reichsführer-SS (und Chef der Deutschen Polizei)
RG	Record Group
RGBl.	Reichsgesetzblatt
Rgt.	Regiment(s)
RHF	Rassenhygienische Forschungsstelle
RMdF	Reichsminister der Finanzen
RK	Ritterkreuz
RKF/RKFDV	Reichskommissar für die Festigung deutschen Volkstums
RKO	Reichskommissariat Ostland
RKPA	Reichskriminalpolizeiamt
RKU	Reichskommissariat Ukraine
RKW	Reichskuratorium für Wirtschaftlichkeit
R.L.	Reichsleiter der NSDAP
RLM	Reichsluftfahrtministerium
RM	Reichsmark
RMBliV	Ministerialblatt des Reichsministeriums des Innern
RMdI	Reichsminister des Innern
RMdJ	Reichsminister der Justiz
RMEL	Reichsminister für Ernährung und Landwirtschaft

RMO/RMfbO	Reichsministerium für die besetzten Ostgebiete
RMRK	Reichsministerium für Rüstung und Kriegsproduktion
RMVP	Reichsminister für Volksaufklärung und Propaganda
RSD	Reichssicherheitsdienst
RSHA	Reichssicherheitshauptamt
RuSHA	Rasse- und Siedlungs-Hauptamt
Rükdo	Rüstungskommando
Rüln	Rüstungsinspektion
RVerwBl	Reichsverwaltungsblatt
RVM	Reichsverkehrsministerium
RVK	Reichsverteidigungskommissar
RWM	Reichswirtschaftsministerium
SA	Sturmabteilung/Sammelakte
SBU	Služba Bezpeki Ukraïny [Sicherheitsdienst der Ukraine]
SBZ	Sowjetische Besatzungszone Deutschlands
Scharf.	SS-Scharführer
Schupo.	Schutzpolizei
SD	Sicherheitsdienst
SHm	Stadthauptmann
Sich.Div.	Sicherungsdivision
Sipo	Sicherheitspolizei (Gestapo/Kripo)
Sk	Sonderkommando
SLF	Staatsanwaltschaft beim Landgericht Frankfurt
Slg.	Sammlung
SMT	Sowjetisches Militärtribunal
Sog.	Sogenannte(r)
Soko	Sonderkommando
SOPADE	Sozialdemokratische Partei Deutschlands
SS	Schutzstaffel der NSDAP
SS-Brif.	SS-Brigadeführer
SS-FHA	SS-Führungshauptamt
SSFP	SS- und Polizeiführer
SS-Gruf.	SS-Gruppenführer
SSHA	SS-Haptamt
SSO-Akte	SS-Officer-Akte
SS-OStubf.	SS-Obersturmbannführer
SSPF	SS- und Polizeiführer
SSPHA	SS-Personalhauptamt
SS-TV	SS-Totenkopfverbände
SSÚA	Štátny slovenský ústredný archív (Staatliches slowakisches Zentralarchiv), Bratislava
SS-VT	SS-Verfügungstruppe
StA	Staatsanwalt(schaft)
StA	Staatsarchiv
Staf./Stand.F.	SS-Standartenführer

StaL/StL	Staatsarchiv Ludwigsburg
StdF	Stellvertreter des Führers
StGB	Strafgesetzbuch
StKom	Stadtkommissar
StS	Staatssekretär
Stv.	Stellvertret(end)e
Stubaf.	Sturmbannführer
SUA	Státný ústrední archív (Staatliches Zentralarchiv), Prag
SZH	Sonderzug Heinrich
SZP	Slużba Zwyciestwa Polskiego [Dienst für den polnischen Sieg]
Tgb.	Tagebuch
TK	Taschenkalender
TÜP	Truppenübungsplatz
u.	und
UAbt.	Unterabteilung
UdSSR	Union der Sozialistischen Sowjetrepubliken
UIŽ	Ukraïns'kyj istoryčnyj žurnal
ukr.	ukrainisch
Ukr.Pol.kdo.	Ukrainisches Polizeikommando
Uscharf.	SS-Unterscharführer
USHMM/USHM	United States Holocaust Memorial Museum
Ustuf./Unterst.F.	SS-Untersturmführer
UWZ	Umwanderer-Zentralstelle
UWZ/P	Umwanderer-Zentralstelle Posen
UZK	Ukrainisches Zentral-Komitee
VAA	Vertreter des Auswärtigen Amtes
VB	Völkischer Beobachter
VdA	Volksbund für das Deutschtum im Ausland
Vern.	Vernehmung
Verw.	Verwaltung
VfZ	Vierteljahrshefte für Zeitgeschichte
vgl.	vergleiche
VJPL	Vierjahresplan
Vm.	Vermerk
VO	Verordnung
VOBl.	Verordnungsblatt
VOBlGG/VOGG	Verordnungsblatt des Generalgouvernements
vol.	volume
VoMi	Volksdeutsche Mittelstelle
VSWG	Vierteljahrschrift für Sozial- und Wirtschaftsgeschichte
VZ	Vossische Zeitung
WFSt	Wehrmachtsführungsstab
WIG	Wehrkreisbefehlshaber im Generalgouvernement
WiRüAmt	Wehrwirtschafts-Rüstungsamt des OKW

WiSt(ab) Ost	Wirtschaftsstab Ost
WL	Wiener Library
WPH	Wojskowy Przegląd Historyczny
W-SS	Waffen-SS
WVHA	Wirtschafts- und Verwaltungs-Hauptamt
YIVO	Yidischer Visenschaftlikher Institut
YV	Yad Vashem
ZAL	Zwangsarbeiterlager
ZASM	Zentrum zur Aufbewahrung historisch-dokumentarischer Sammlung (früher Sonderarchiv), Moskau
z.B.	zum Beispiel
z.b.V.	zur besonderen Verwendung
ZfG	Zeitschrift für Geschichtswissenschaft
ZGO	Zeitschrift für die Geschichte des Oberrheins
ŻIH	Żydowski Instytut Historyczny
zit.	zitiert
ŻSS	Żydowski Samopomoc Społeczny (JSS)
ZStA/ZStL	Zentrale Stelle der Landesjustizverwaltungen zur Aufklärung nationalsozialistischer Verbrechen, Ludwigsburg
ZUV	Zentraler Untersuchungsvorgang
z. Wv.	zur Wiederverwendung

CONTRIBUTORS

Götz Aly was born in 1947. He studied at the German School for Journalists in Munich, and political science and history in Berlin, earning his Ph.D. and admission to the teaching faculty at the Otto-Suhr-Institute (Free University of Berlin). Editor of the *Berliner Zeitung* since 1997, his publications include: *Vordenker der Vernichtung. Auschwitz und die deutschen Pläne für eine europäische Ordnung* (Frankfurt am Main, 1995 [co-author Susanne Heim]); *Cleansing the Fatherland. Nazi Medicine and Racial Hygiene* (Baltimore, London: JHUP, 1994 [co-authors Peter Chroust and Christian Pross]); *"Final Solution". Nazi Population Policy and the Murder of the European Jews* (New York, London: Arnold, 1999).

Christoph Dieckmann was born in 1960. He studied history, economics, and sociology in Göttingen, Hamburg, and Jerusalem, and is presently earning his Ph.D. at the University of Freiburg on German occupation policy in Lithuania. He is a member of the editorial board of the *Beiträge zur nationalsozialistischen Gesundheit- und Sozialpolitik*. Publications include: *Die nationalsozialistischen Konzentrationslager, 1933-1945. Entwicklung und Struktur* (Göttingen 1998 [co-editor with U. Herbert and K. Orth]).

Christian Gerlach was born in 1963. He studied history, German language and literature, sociology, and pedagogy at Technological University in Berlin, and earned his Ph.D. doing research on German occupation policy in White Russia. Publications include: "Männer des 20. Juli und der Krieg gegen die Sowjetunion" in Hannes Heer and Klaus Naumann (eds.), *Vernichtungskrieg: Verbrechen der Wehrmacht 1941-1944* (Hamburg, 1995): 427-447; *Krieg, Ernährung, Völkermord. Studien zur deutschen Vernichtungspolitik im Zweiten Weltkrieg* (Hamburg, 1998).

Ulrich Herbert was born 1951. He studied history, German language and literature in Freiburg. From 1980 to 1992 he was assistant professor and Research Fellow at the universities in Essen, Hagen and Tel Aviv. From 1992 to 1995, he was Director of the *Forschungsstelle für die Geschichte des Nationalsozialismus* in Hamburg. Since 1995 he is Professor of Modern History at the University of Freiburg. His publications include: *A History of Foreign Labor in Germany, 1880-1980* (Ann Arbor: Michigan UP, 1990); *Hitler's Foreign Workers. Enforced Foreign Labor in Germany under the Third Reich* (New York: Cambridge UP, 1997); *Arbeit, Volkstum, Weltanschauung. Über Deutsche und Fremde im 20. Jahrhundert* (Frankfurt am Main, 1995); *Best. Biographische Studien über Radikalismus, Weltanschauung und Vernunft, 1903-1989* (Bonn, 1996); *Die nationalsozialistischen Konzentrationslager, 1933 bis 1945. Entwicklung und Struktur* (Göttingen, 1998, co-edited with K. Orth and C. Dieckmann).

Walter Manoschek was born 1957. He studied political science and sociology at the University of Vienna. Since earning his doctorate in Vienna in 1992, he has been Assistant Professor an the *Institut für Staats- und Politikwissenschaft* (Vienna), and active in arranging the exhibition "Vernichtungskrieg. Verbrechen der Wehrmacht. 1941-1944." Winner of the Fraenkel Price of the Institute of Contemporary History and Wiener Library, London. Publications include *"Serbien ist judenfrei". Militärische Besatzungspolitik und Judenvernichtung in Serbien*, Volume 38 of *Schriftenreihe des Militärischen Forschungsamtes* (Munich, 1995, 2nd edition). *"Es gibt nur eines für das Judentum: Vernichtung". Das Judenbild in deutschen Soldatenbriefen, 1939-1944* (Hamburg, 1995) (ed.); *Die Wehrmacht im Rassenkrieg. Der Vernichtungskrieg hinter der Front* (Vienna, 1996) (ed.).

Karin Orth was born in 1963. She studied history, political sciences, and sociology in Frankfurt am Main and Berlin. From 1994 to 1996, she worked as Research Fellow at the *Forschungsstelle für die Geschichte des Nationalsozialismus* in Hamburg. Since 1996, she is Assistant Professor at the University of Freiburg. Her publications include *"Nur weiblichen Besuch". Dienstbotinnen in Berlin 1890-1914* (Frankfurt am Main, 1993); *Überlebensgeschichten. Gespräche mit Überlebenden des KZ-Neuengamme* (Hamburg, 1994, co-author with U. Jureit); *Die nationalsozialistischen Konzentrationslager 1933 bis 1945. Entwicklung und Struktur* (Göttingen, 1998, co-edited with U. Herbert and C.

Dieckmann); *Das System der nationalsozialistischen Konzentrationslager. Eine politische Organisationsgeschichte* (Hamburg, 1999); *Die Konzentrationslager-SS. Sozialstrukturelle Analysen und biographische Studien* (Göttingen, 2000).

Dieter Pohl was born in 1964. He studied history and political science in Munich and is currently a Fellow of the *Institut für Zeitgeschichte*, in Munich. Publications include: *Von der "Judenpolitik" zum Judenmord. Der Distrikt Lublin des Generalgouvernements 1939-1944* (Frankfurt am Main, 1993); *Nationalsozialistische Judenverfolgung in Ostgalizien. Organisation und Durchführung eines staatlichen Massenverbrechens* (Munich, 1996).

Thomas Sandkühler was born in 1962, and studied history, German language and literature, and philosophy in Bochum and Freiburg im Breisgau, earning his Ph.D. in 1994. He is Associate Professor at the University of Bielefeld; from 1997-99 he was consultant for the Independent Commission of Experts: "Switzerland—Second World War." Publications include: *"Endlösung" in Galizien. Judenmord in Ostpolen und die Rettungsinitiativen von Berthold Beitz* (Bonn, 1996).

Sybille Steinbacher was born in 1966. She studied history and political science in Munich; was from 1994-1996 grant holder at the *Institut für Zeitgeschichte*; and earned her Ph.D. in 1998 on extermination policy in East Upper Silesia and the history of the city of Auschwitz. She is a research fellow at the history department of the Ruhr University in Bochum. Publications include: *Dachau—Die Stadt und das Konzentrationslager in der NS-Zeit. Die Untersuchung einer Nachbarschaft* (Frankfurt am Main, 1993).

Michael Zimmermann was born in 1951; studied history, social science, and Latin language and literature in Bochum. He is a Lecturer at the University of Jena and consultant with the Ruhrland Museum in Essen. Publications include: *Schachtanlage und Zechenkolonie. Leben, Arbeit und Politik in einer Arbeitersiedlung 1880 bis 1980* (Essen, 1987); *Verfolgung und Widerstand in Essen* (Essen, 1991); *Rassenutopie und Genozid. Die nationalsozialistische "Lösung der Zigeunerfrage"* (Hamburg, 1996); *Geschichte der Juden im Rheinland und in Westfalen* (Cologne, 1998).

Chapter 1

EXTERMINATION POLICY
New Answers and Questions about the History of the "Holocaust" in German Historiography

Ulrich Herbert

In Germany, the public discussion of National Socialist extermination policy has changed significantly due to the debate surrounding Daniel Goldhagen's book.[1] As always in such cases, this debate was not lacking in shrillness and absurd exaggerations. But despite all the criticism of Goldhagen's book, it is certainly a positive development if the discussion about National Socialism and the "Holocaust" is at last being refocused on the actual event—the mass murder itself, the motives of the perpetrators, and the suffering of the victims. By contrast, questions such as whether or not the murder of the Jews is a phenomenon peculiar to modernity, or whether it was a kind of putative self-defense against the Bolsheviks' apprehended murderous intent toward the European bourgeoisie, as well as other issues that have defined public debate in past years—have faded into the background.[2]

Even so, the book has not stood up well to expert scrutiny. All professional historians who hitherto have spoken out, in Israel and the United States as well as in Germany or England, have criticized Goldhagen's study as inadequate in scholarship and simplistic.[3] In addition to charges that his methodology does not meet accepted standards, Goldhagen has been faulted chiefly for severing the German genocide of the Jews from its intimate connection to the German war effort in general and, in particular, to the brutal extermination policy directed against the Soviet population, as well as other ethnic and social groups.

Furthermore, Goldhagen understands the mass murder of European Jews as the culmination of a centuries-long pent-up obsession, and depicts it, shorn of its historical context, as a unique, Manichaean conflict without direct connection to other historical events. According to this analysis, the event no longer offers the potential for enhanced historical and political understanding because the root of the trouble lay in the German people, and if the Germans—as is repeatedly postulated—have "changed," then the danger has been eliminated.

And finally, his attempts to represent the cases he describes as symptomatic and the behavior of the Germans as absolutely typical are especially unconvincing because he is unable to deploy conclusive arguments that would justify such generalizations.

As scholarship, Goldhagen's book must indeed be regarded as a failure. But why then, one must ask, has it provoked such a surprising, at times enthusiastic, public response, at least in the United States and Germany? In the course of the debate, some of the reasons have become clear. First, Goldhagen has broken an unwritten taboo. Specifically, he describes the act of murder itself with such a wealth of detail that, confronted with the emotional impact of the horrors described, intellectual criticism of Goldhagen's conclusions sounds like little more than quibbling. Traditional Holocaust research, by contrast, while investigating the origins and effects of mass murder, has depicted murder itself only in distanced terms— out of respect for the victims of course, but also to avoid charges of sensationalism. Furthermore, to an ever increasing degree academic scholarship has concentrated on theoretical disputes about how the Holocaust should be interpreted. For that reason alone it could not match Goldhagen's graphic presentation for popular appeal.

Second, Goldhagen answered questions about the causes of genocide in an extremely simple way. He matched the magnitude and monumentality of the crime with an equally monumental and simple explanation: The Holocaust was the Germans' national project. Here he strikes a responsive chord in the children of the victims. Given the dimension of the crime and its repercussions in virtually every European-Jewish family, the yearning both for a clear and identifiable motive and for an equally identifiable group of perpetrators large enough to be worthy of the crime is natural, even inevitable. An explanation that traces the murder of parents and siblings to impersonal authority structures specific to the regime is, by contrast, hard to convey—and hardly bearable.

In contrast to increasingly complex scholarly approaches, which, for all their more evenhanded and accurate analyses, no longer can provide explanations that are emotionally satisfying and, as it were, politically transferable, Goldhagen's explanation offers the possibility of identifying with the victim even to Germans striving thus to circumvent or reject the discomfiting demands of post-Holocaust society. To put it bluntly, Goldhagen suggests, especially to Germans of the younger generation, a way of satisfying an understandable desire: By applauding his book, they need no longer be lumped with the vilified but can stand on the side of the vilifiers.

And yet, aside from such considerations, the significance of Goldhagen's book derives in part from its theses and from the challenge they pose for scholarship. For the book has refocused discussion on that basic question that was repressed for so long, was hardly discussed, and not even thoroughly researched: What role did Germans, "ordinary Germans," play in the National Socialist persecution of the Jews? How important was the behavior of the broad masses of the population in their murder?

It is to Goldhagen's lasting credit that he has posed these questions because they move beyond political structural analysis and philosophical truisms to the core historical and moral problem of the genocide of the Jews—and because they reflect the viewpoint of the victims. After all, it was known even before 1933 that Hitler and the National Socialist Party, along with its functionaries and thugs, were rabid antisemites. Only the worst was to be expected from them. But that the repression of the Jews meant disparagement, humiliation, mockery, and open hatred in a wide variety of forms, even by those Germans who were not part of the SS or other political units; or that even army units and—almost without exception—the regular police would be actively involved in mass executions; or that the occupation authorities in 1941, to give one example, might confidently count on the German employees of local savings banks to lend a hand in cleaning out the ghettos in Poland whenever there were insufficient policemen available—these are scenarios that German Jews did not consider possible. The horror they evoke remains embedded in the collective memory of the surviving victims.

Goldhagen explains these phenomena by supposing that Germans had, for decades if not for centuries, been driven by a shared obsessive belief that they had to "eliminate" the Jews—and that the

Germans chose Hitler as their leader because he offered the most likely realization of that burning desire. These answers are indeed very provocative, but clearly not very convincing. But even if the answers are both false and far too simple, the questions posed remains valid, even urgent.

I

Scholarly research on the murder of the European Jews began late in West Germany (as well as in the German Democratic Republic, which I shall treat but peripherally). Initially, it concentrated primarily on those aspects that related to the "thesis of collective guilt,"[4] which arose after the war: the conservative opposition against Hitler, in order to demonstrate the existence of the other (i.e., the non-nazi) Germany, and the SS, which was, so to speak, interpreted out of German society and, as a residual category of abnormality, was made solely responsible for the mass crime. At the same time, stressing the omnipotence of the SS and the security police helped to explain the absence of popular resistance and acted as a protective shield against all accusations against the Germans, either actually leveled or anticipated.[5] Beyond that, in those years the Germans were portrayed as victims of historical developments—of air attacks and "ethnic cleansing"—but also of a dictatorship that had been imposed on the Germans just as it had been imposed on enemy nations.[6]

In the first phase of the process that I shall sketch here, extending from the end of the war until roughly 1957, publications by West German historians were dominated by individual editions of source material as well as short articles and essays about the extermination of the Jews.[7] Public perception, however, made connections with the images of the liberation of the concentration camps Bergen-Belsen, Buchenwald, or Dachau—and not with the mass shootings in Riga or the mass gassings in Auschwitz. In this way, the process of mass murder was construed as a series of secret events that occurred in specially cordoned-off zones in "the east" to which no witnesses were granted access.

The second phase extends roughly from 1958 to 1972. Two developments marked its beginning. First, as a result of the desecration of Cologne synagogues, the Einsatzgruppen trial in Ulm, the Eichmann trial in Jerusalem, and the Auschwitz trial in Frankfurt, the relevance of Nazi mass crimes to West German culture quickly became a controversial issue. Within a few years, the mass crimes of the National Socialists had become an important subject in the Fed-

eral Republic—one of the most important by the early 1960s—
thanks to lengthy and detailed reports on the above-mentioned trials in the press and in popular books, but also due to continuously
erupting scandals concerning the involvement of leading West German politicians in the National Socialist regime, which had been set
in motion in no small measure by the publication of the "brown
books" in the GDR.[8] Second, a new generation had grown up
whose demands for knowledge about the history of National
Socialism, especially the National Socialist extermination policy,
were becoming more insistent and which was not bound to the
older generation's conspiracy of silence. At the same time, a new
generation of historians was coming on the scene, which, in Munich
and elsewhere, had intensively researched the Nazi regime and its
crimes and were now appearing as expert witnesses in court and
publishing their findings in books appearing in the early 1960s.[9]
This development first culminated in the publication of documents
relating to the Auschwitz trial under the title *Anatomie des SS-
Staates* (*Anatomy of the SS-State*).[10] The studies included in that
volume by Krausnick on the National Socialist persecution and
extermination of the Jews, by Broszat on the system of concentration camps, by Buchheim on the SS and the police, as well as by
Jacobsen on the "Commissar Directive" provided analyses of the
motives, structure, and methods of the leaders of the National
Socialist regime that were as sobering as they were impressive.
Those studies set the level of knowledge of National Socialist extermination policy for decades, and it would be a long time before an
equivalent standard of scholarship would again be attained.

The year 1969 saw the publication of Karl Dietrich Bracher's
book *The German Dictatorship*—the first comprehensive scholarly
description of the Nazi Regime.[11] In previous years, it had been due
largely to Bracher that West German treatments of the period
desisted in their concentrated attempts to refute real or ostensible
accusations of collective guilt and began producing critical studies
of the regime's structure and policies based on original documents
that were rapidly becoming available. That those studies concentrated on the late Weimar Republic and the early phase of the
National Socialist regime was a natural response to West German
society's need for historical orientation. In Bracher's presentation,
National Socialist anti-Jewish policy was treated quite thoroughly;
but in its analysis of developments following the pogroms of
November 1938, the commentary, which had been so clear and
impressive up until then, amounted to little more than recording the
steps in an apparently automated process. The policy of mass exter-

mination characteristic of the war years was merely noted rather
than actually investigated—the murder of the Jews claiming a mere
twelve of 580 pages (in the 1979 edition). This marginalization of
the mass murders, which is found in virtually all comprehensive
treatments of the Third Reich published in German up to the late
1980s, reflects scholarly and public preoccupation with the search
for the causes of the "seizure of power," to which for many years
the subjects of war and genocide took a back seat. At the same
time, those treatments provide a record of the comparatively low
level of detailed knowledge about how mass murder originated and
evolved, because the "Holocaust" was never a focal point of German histories of the period up to the mid-1980s. At the end of this
phase, Adam's *Judenpolitik* (published 1972) represented a significant and innovative work, the first in which a West German author
examined in such detail the process of political decision-making
leading up to the murder of the Jews and called into question the
universally accepted notion that the murder of the Jews resulted
from Hitler's long-term calculation and specific orders.[12]

It is no wonder that the best works of the years between 1962
and the early 70s are still in print, because in the next phase,
stretching until the beginning of the 1980s, little was published that
reflected the same depth of knowledge and quality of analysis. On
the other hand, the shortcomings of that period of research soon
became undeniable; the search on the part of state attorneys for
specific deeds and perpetrators, for orders and their execution—for
guilt and responsibility that was measurable at the individual
level—also led many historians who were cooperating with prosecutors to concentrate on painstaking reconstructions of the
processes of decision-making and the conflicts within the regime's
leadership. Of course, many important areas remained unexamined, among them the perspective of the victims, especially victims
from outside of Germany—Jews from all countries occupied by the
German army, the population of eastern Europe, as well as those
groups, such as "Gypsies" or Russian prisoners of war, who had
hitherto been perceived or recognized as victims neither by the public nor by scholars. Thus, the political and ideological connections
between the persecution and murder of the various groups of victims of the Nazi regime went undetected.

Second, researchers were keeping the events they were studying
at a safe distance. The thousands of individual acts of murder, massacre, shooting, and gassing that were carried out by German personnel and German authorities in the cities and villages of eastern
Europe were not being presented as individual events with unique

preludes and identifiable perpetrators and victims. In this way, the mass murders assumed the characteristics of a process that was uniformly and centrally directed, but at the same time abstract and inaccessible to traditional reason and experience.

Finally, it was striking that even pioneering studies of German occupation policy in Europe barely treated the fate of the Jews, even peripherally—as if it represented an independent process lacking any direct connection to German occupation policy.[13] Thus, the importance of the civil and military administrators of the occupation in initiating and carrying out the "Final Solution of the Jewish question" was exempted from examination, as was the role of industry, the Wehrmacht in general, and academia. Consequently, connections between the extermination policy directed against the Jews and such matters as the administration of the occupation in western and eastern Europe, the manifold schemes for a "re-ordering" of Europe, and the various goals pursued in the name of those aims went unexamined for decades.

These were the major shortcomings at the end of the second phase that required intensive research. But that did not happen at once.

In the decade from the early 1970 to the early 1980s, interest in empirical research on the mass crimes of the Nazis declined dramatically both among professional historians and the general public. If one considers that the period between the completion of a manuscript and its appearance in book form is usually a year or two, or even longer, then one can see that in the third phase, between roughly 1969/70 and the early 1980s, there is a hiatus in empirical research on National Socialism in general, and an especially large and unmistakable one in the research on the extermination of the Jews. The only large monographs on National Socialist extermination policy published in those years are Hans G. Adler's study of the deportation of German Jews (1974), Falk Pingel's *Häftlinge unter SS-Herrschaft*, and Christian Streit's major study of the deaths of millions of Russian prisoners of war in German hands (1978).[14]

After the onset of the student revolts in the late 1960s, objective study of the Nazi regime gave way to a strongly politicized debate over Fascism engendered first by the younger generation's personal preoccupation with its parents' past, and then by the debate over the culpability of the society of the Federal Republic due to the continuation of the old elitist power structures. But soon the demonstrable reality of the Nazi regime was upstaged by an increasingly abstract and synthetic concept of "fascism," the chief characteristic of which was no longer the genocide of the Jews, but rather—in the trivialized popular form of the thesis—an alliance between monopolistic capitalism and the dictatorship that aimed at eliminating the workers' movement.

This interpretation was strikingly similar to the dominant theme in GDR historiography, which traced even National Socialist racist terror to German imperialism's—hence German capitalism's—plans for conquest and domination, so that antisemitism was regarded as merely an instrument for manipulating the German population; the extermination of European Jews, was something of a peripheral phenomenon—a mere "manifestation" of German imperialism.[15]

But even the serious scholarly controversy at the time over whether the Nazi regime should be regarded as a fascist or totalitarian regime ultimately produced few valuable results, because, with few exceptions, it was not grounded in empirical, comparative studies but remained on the level of system theory.[16]

Initially, using the concept of "fascism" as a basis for comparing the radical right, popularly supported regimes of the period between the wars made perfectly good sense. In the long run, however, it had serious consequences for the study of Germany. For although the term "fascism" might be stretched to fit important elements of the National Socialist movement before 1933 and the Nazi dictatorship up until 1938-1939, a term that had been coined for conditions in Italy under Mussolini, which emphasized the suppression of domestic opposition and the restoration of the authority of traditional elites with the aid of mass violence and pseudo-rallies and events, could not account for German occupation policy in Europe, the policy of "ethic cleansing" in almost all of Europe, or especially for the million-fold mass murder of Jews and inhabitants of the occupied regions in Poland, the USSR, and southeastern Europe. Thus the left—and not only in Germany—was conceptually unable to confront the phenomena of National Socialist mass murder, and unable to approach the subject analytically rather than merely with moral outrage.

Generally speaking—at least as far as public perception is concerned—the 1970s and early 1980s can be designated as a phase in which memories of the past were repressed a second time. Perpetrators and crime scenes, accomplices and opportunists, but most of all the victims themselves were rendered anonymous. On the Left-Right continuum, the debate over the interpretation of National Socialism became once more a Cold War battlefield and the object of an increasingly hypocritical ritual of mutual recrimination. In the meantime, numerous scholarly works on National Socialist extermination policy, some outstanding, that had appeared in the United States, Israel, and Poland went unpublished and unread in the Federal Republic. Disregarding international scholarship can actually be viewed as characteristic of German publications on contemporary history—especially, but not limited to, studies of the National Socialist dictatorship—and this deficiency has not been completely overcome even today. The same can also be said of other countries (France, for example, but also Italy or Great Britain), and yet the criticism is more telling with regard to the writings of German historians inasmuch as it reflects a perception of the Nazi dictatorship and the Holocaust as an episode in German history. A German translation of Raul Hilberg's pioneer study *The Destruction of the European Jews*, for example, did not appear until 1982, more than twenty years after it first appeared in the United States. Now Hilberg's book, along with the first scholarly study of the Einsatzgruppen in the Soviet Union, increased several fold the information potentially available to both the West German public and historians.[17] And, especially after the 1980s, the Holocaust increasingly became the subject of public debate, at least in conjunction with attempts to define German identity, but then only as a metaphor. It was not knowledge about genocide that increased but the number of people talking about it. In German scholarship the Holocaust remained the preserve of a few specialists. Compared to other countries, especially the United States, Israel, and Poland, the German contribution to empirical research on the persecution and destruction of the Jews was paltry in sum.

Nevertheless, beginning in the early 1980s, new trends arose, especially in scholarly writings, not least of all in reaction to the period just described. First, scholarly discussions about "Fascism or Totalitarianism" and "Hitlerism or Polyocracy," which had concentrated primarily on the internal structure of the regime, the role of the traditional elites, the processes of decision-making within the regime's leadership, and, last but not least, on the regime's foreign policy, now shifted to the decision-making process that initiated the "Final Solution." Already in the 1970s serious doubts had arisen here and there—especially in the works of Adam, Broszat, Mommsen, who from then on came to be known as "structuralists"—about whether tracing the decision-making process that led to the destruction of the Jews to the Nazi world-view, will, and authority of Hitler alone—as had been done by those historians who were now labeled "intentionalists"—corresponded to historical reality.[18] Now a debate arose that had lasting significance for both the discipline of history and the public perception of the Holocaust. Specifically, the structuralists demonstrated that numerous departments and interest groups outside the government were involved in the policy of the destruction of the Jews and that the one-sided emphasis on Hitler was not only false but also served to excuse others who were involved, directly or indirectly. The genocide was not set in motion by a single, unique cause, and certainly not by a *Führerbefehl* (order from Hitler), but rather took shape gradually in the course of a dynamic process that played out in the years 1941 and 1942—a process of "cumulative radicalization."[19] By virtue of that thesis, the structuralists set the causes and effect of the National Socialist policy of mass destruction in a different, sharper, and simultaneously broader focus. Of course, they were not entirely free from dogmatism either. They remained unaware of how important a role racist, even antisemitic, ideologies played in determining the thoughts and actions both of large population groups and of the National Socialist ideological elite. They viewed the process of mass murder as arising automatically, without human involvement, most of all without perpetrators. We should note also that these theses led not to intensified research efforts but merely to a war over how to interpret the same old scanty facts.[20]

This obvious deficiency did not, however, result from a lack of source material, as is sometimes assumed. It is true, of course, that most of the archives in the states of the East Bloc were closed to Western historians until 1990 and 1991, but accessible archival material in the West, especially documents relating to West German criminal proceedings against Nazi criminals, would have been sufficiently voluminous to make intense research possible. Publications such as those of Wolfgang Scheffler and Adalbert Rückerl, as well as often extraordinarily lengthy and detailed legal verdicts, also offered important leads.[21] And yet, in the rapidly spreading disputes between "internationalists" and "structuralists," it was even asserted that enough was already known about the murders themselves and that the real problem lay in politically categorizing and interpreting them in layman's terms. That view, which indeed reflected broad public opinion then and is still widely held today, does in fact reveal a persistent refusal to come to grips candidly and directly with events. In that respect, concentrating on the implications of genocide, on conclusions that might be drawn from it, has significantly exculpatory effects—a process that became readily apparent in 1986/87 during the scholarly fruitless *Historikerstreit*.[22]

Beginning in the mid-1980s, criticisms of the already sterile debates between intentionalists and structuralists began yielding new inquiries and approaches—especially a turn to the concrete, to the empirical, which resulted in studies of everyday life and mentalities under the Nazi dictatorship.[23] The significance of those approaches for the study of National Socialist Jewish policy lay in a kind of reconstruction of the factual history of the Nazi regime, primarily by attempting to focus on the victims of National Socialist policies of terror and extermination themselves—and to an increasing extent on *all* the victims. That was manifested in an increasing number of studies of "gypsies," the handicapped, "asocials," homosexuals, prisoners of war, forced laborers, and other persecuted groups.[24] It was now gradually becoming possible to expose the regime's racist policy as a unified entity and trace its traditions in German history. Persecutions motivated by concerns for racial hygiene against various classes of victims in Germany, actions taken against members of Slavic ethnic groups, and especially measures implemented against Jews were slowly being recognized and investigated as phenomena that were closely interconnected even on a conceptual level.[25]

Typically, those important new approaches were not promoted by those who had been playing leading roles in the disputes over the interpretation of the Holocaust. Clearly, the distanced perspective of outsiders was required to recognize that the debate had wandered down a blind alley. The new impetus arose primarily from four sources: first, from the studies of everyday life and mentalities already mentioned; second, from an increasing awareness of research in foreign countries, which was promoted most of all by the project for a comprehensive study of the murder of the Jews initiated by the *Institut für Zeitgeschichte*;[26] and third, from the efforts promoted by a group associated with the Berlin historian Wolfgang Scheffler to exploit German legal documents for purposes of Holocaust research. In that way, the narrow focus on the centers of the regime's authority in Berlin was broken, and a multiplicity of perpetrators, crimes scenes, details of the crimes, and victims came under scrutiny.[27]

The fourth source of renewed scholarly activity was the publication of the series *Beiträge zur nationalsozialistischen Gesundheits- und Sozialpolitik* and its promoter, the Berlin historian Götz Aly.[28] Aly and his co-editors were interested originally in the regime's euthanasia policy and the roles played by physicians, health institutions, and "population experts" in connection with it. Attention was now being focused on those ostensibly non-political research institutions that served in advisory capacities, whose roles in various policy areas were now examined more closely. Thus, the study of National Socialist racial and social policy was broadened gradually to include more than merely Party and SS institutions; the importance of the traditional elites in administration, science, and industry was being recognized increasingly. In the volume *Vordenker der Vernichtung* (1991), Susanne Heim and Götz Aly attempted to apply this approach to the origins of the mass murder of the Jews.[29] Their research turned up many writings and programs that had originated in universities and institutes in which the underdevelopment of central and eastern Europe was attributed to overpopulation, and population reduction was proclaimed as a necessary precondition for sustained economic improvement in those countries, which was to be implemented under German hegemony. After the outbreak of the war, quite a few of those experts were to be found on administrative staffs directing the German occupation of eastern Europe. Here, Aly and Heim concluded, lay the rational starting point of National Socialist Jewish policy beginning in 1939/40, especially in Poland, and from it they derived their theory of the "economy of the Final Solution," which was greeted with both enthusiastic approval and much criticism.[30]

What was truly sensational in the book was the revelation that such schemes and scholarly proposals existed at all, even if one were not inclined to accept Aly's and Heim's inference that they provided the actual momentum that set the Holocaust in motion. But the question of how these economic and population schemes fit into the entire process that initiated the "Final Solution" remained unsettled. Despite much criticism of Aly's and Heim's theory, the process cannot be unraveled without taking into account such projects, which reveal clearly how many, especially younger, German social scientists embraced the goal of a policy of imperialistic German expansion in central and eastern Europe. What remained unclear is in what way those allegedly extra-ideological schemes linked up generally with the political attitudes of the National Socialists and the German right-wing. Was antisemitism merely *mass suggestion* behind which lurked the sober and dispassionate calculation of the scholarly elite? Was the National Socialists' widespread hatred of the Jews merely exploited so that, as the authors assumed, the goals of population policy might be achieved by acting against a group that was being deprived of its rights in any event?

In his book, *Endlösung. Völkerverschiebung und der Mord an den europäischen Juden* (1995), Aly significantly modified his theory.[31] Where he had previously postulated a direct connection between economic and population planning and its "translation" into the reality of mass murder, he now turned the relationship

around: The precondition for starting up the machinery of destruction was not the development of the various schemes and plans but
their repeated and unalloyed failure. Aly now takes as his starting
point the "resettlement" of the "ethnic Germans" (*Volksdeutsche*)
from eastern and southeastern Europe, which had been stipulated in
the Hitler-Stalin pact. With the arrival in German-controlled territory of the first few tens of thousands of this group, Aly contends, an
ominous chain-reaction was set in motion: In order to make room
for the resettled Germans, large numbers of Poles and especially
Jews were deported from the Warthegau and other regions without
provisions having been made for them. Now began a process of
increasingly extensive deportation schemes embodied in the utopian
notion of the "ethnic cleansing" of central Europe. At the center of
these plans for "expulsion" and deportation stood the Jews, whom
the Germans wanted to push out of their sphere of influence entirely,
into the eastern regions of the Government General, to Madagascar,
or to the Arctic Ocean in northern Russia. Since no one in a position
of authority in the National Socialist regime was prepared to accept
the Jews in "his" area, a system of stop-gap measures and compromises developed that, because of the attendant and universally
lamented "untenable conditions," created pressure for a long-term—
or "final"—solution. The murder of the Jews, who had become
superfluous and could not be resettled, began as a consequence of
the failures of the various plans for deportation. As Aly points out,
the same men who had been responsible for relocating Germans
from the Soviet Union—Adolf Eichmann, for example, along with
many other experts in the RSHA—subsequently organized the
deportation and murder of the Jews.[32]

Aly's analysis represented an important step forward in that it
provides an empirical basis for the thesis, hitherto merely asserted,
that Jewish policy gradually became more radical due to the failure
of alternative plans. The beginning of the murder of the Jews is thus
placed within the context of German efforts to carry out an "ethnic
cleansing" of central and eastern Europe, which began in Poland
immediately after the outbreak of the war and was seen as comprising a re-ordering of Europe reaching as far as the Urals and
involving the "shifting" (*Verschiebung*) of millions of people—all
of which was conceptualized in the various versions of *Generalplan
Ost*, which Himmler ordered developed in his capacity as *Reichskommissar für die Festigung des deutschen Volkstums* (RFK; Reich
Commissar for the Strengthing of the German Nation).[33]

To be sure, a range of questions remains open. The radicalization of Jewish policy was no longer understood as a manifestation of

long-term schemes, but rather as the result of the failure of plans for
the deportation of the Jews that were always being revised and
extended—a process that proceeded in fits and starts and was
always tailored to decisions designed to deal with the problems of
the moment. Moreover, such plans, ultimately culminating in *Generalplan Ost*, never embraced the Jews alone but also involved
Poles, Russians, even entire populations of countries lying to Germany's east. But one is compelled to point out that the failure of the
deportation plans metamorphosed into the practice of genocide only
in the case of the Jews—hence only against precisely that group that
National Socialist ideology had branded as the implacable enemy,
and which, within a few years of the National Socialists' assumption
of power in Germany, had been massively persecuted and deprived
of its rights. What role then did antisemitism play here? In what way
did the dilemmas—real or contrived—arising in specific situations
link up with long-standing attitudes and aims? What was the relationship between ideological factors, such as racism and hatred of
Jews, to goal-oriented, "rational" motives, such as economic modernization or dealing with food scarcity? How did the motives—
both individual and situationally determined—of the murderers and
those who bore responsibility for their actions relate to a general
dynamic of violence directed against Jews?

Considering these question together enables us to distinguish
two main lines of development leading to genocide. First, there
were those programmatic schemes that, when implemented as a
continental imperialistic policy, regarded the fates of independent
ethnic populations as quantitatively negligible, embraced an amoral
utilitarianism, and manifested themselves in a myriad of ways
according to the circumstances. Second, there was that racist brand
of antisemitism that set as its goal the expulsion (or in Goldhagen's
words, the elimination) and ultimately the murder of some or all
Jews. Although each of these two factors has its own traditions,
their histories are closely intertwined, involving, on the one hand,
policies pursued by Germany and the other great powers in their
(especially African) colonies and the long tradition of planning for
a German, quasi-colonial *Hinterland* in eastern and southeastern
Europe, and, on the other hand, the tradition of modern antisemitism. Both began in the 1880s and reached their zeniths after
the turn of the century and again during the First World War.

In order to answer these questions, it was necessary for scholars
to turn their attention away from the politicians in Berlin and Cracow and to study in detail how genocide was implemented in specific occupied areas. This has been the starting point for a series of

new studies, the results of which raise the analysis of the entire process of genocide to a new level.

That is true first of all of Michael Zimmermann's imposing study of the National Socialist policy of persecution directed against "Gypsies."[34] Zimmermann is able to demonstrate that National Socialist "Gypsy Policy" drew on traditional anti-Gypsy prejudices, but managed to radicalize them at decisive points by representing them as scientifically sound with the aid of social and biological theories. Here there is no evidence of a unified process of decision-making, certainly not one that can be traced back to Hitler (who consistently showed his thorough indifference to the "Gypsy question")—nor of a corresponding chain of command for the murder of "Gypsies." On the contrary, the radical stigmatizing of this group became so widespread and virulent that Einsatzgruppen on their sweeps in the Soviet Union always killed any "Gypsies" they came across without being specifically ordered to do so—always with the justification (which seemed somehow reasonable under the circumstances) that "Gypsies" were spies, posed a threat to troops or the native population, spread pestilence and disease, and so forth. Zimmermann establishes how a widely held prejudice was provided with a "scientific basis" in order to form a racist construct that was promulgated by many experts and became part of the belief system at the leadership levels of the Criminal and Security Police (inaccurately known as "Gestapo"), with those making specific operational decisions in units operating at the local level.

In the publications by Dieter Pohl and Thomas Sandkühler dealing with the murder of the Jews of Galicia, those by Walter Manoschek on Serbia, by Christian Gerlach on White Russia, and in other studies, some still in progress, it is becoming possible to make out the relationships between the regional German authorities (civilian bureaucracies, military commands, the upper leadership of the SS and police, as well as the entire leadership of the Security Police and the SD) and the central Berlin authorities at Hitler's headquarters, in the RSHA, and in the office of the Reichsführer SS—hence to connect concrete events in the individual regions to reactions in Berlin.[35] Moreover, it is becoming apparent that, in the German-occupied regions of eastern Europe as late as the early weeks of 1942, there was no unified general process in motion but rather specific developments, each with its own unique prelude. The "fateful months" from June to December 1941 were thus the phase of the constitution and gradual standardizing of the genocide.

Recent research also stresses the modus operandi, motives, world-view, and biographical backgrounds of the perpetrators themselves—both the murderers at the scene who actually did the killings, held the rifles, or closed the doors to the gas chambers, as well as those who were responsible in the strict sense. It is obvious that these issues have now become central to any discussion of the murder of the Jews.

In his book *Ordinary Men*, Christopher Browning studied the members of Police Battalion 101, which carried out mass shootings in occupied areas in the East for months on end.[36] The results of his analysis of one of those units, of which there were many, are sobering. These men were not remarkable for their ideological conditioning, extreme hatred of Jews, or other ideological motivations. Other factors proved more important: a numbing atmosphere of brutality, a remarkable *esprit de corps*, considerable group pressure, excessive alcohol consumption—all combined with a growing insensitivity to violence in all its forms. For Browning it was not the specifically antisemitic motives of the killers that proved most important but rather a propensity for violence that, under political direction, was unleashed against the Jews.

Goldhagen judges precisely the same group quite differently. That the propensity for violence was directed against the Jews was, in Goldhagen's view, hardly a coincidence but rather the manifestation of the "eliminationist" antisemitism that was widespread in Germany.[37] If those policemen were normal, then they were normal in the sense that they represented a radical hatred of Jews that was the norm in Germany.

To be sure, those policemen took orders. What was important to them was their mission, and whether their mission seemed legitimate and justified within the social and political environment as they perceived it. Quite apart from their individual motivations, which can hardly be discerned in hindsight, they were living in a context in which the expulsion, even the extermination, of entire peoples was publicly discussed, a readiness to indulge in brutality and fanaticism was ubiquitously demanded, and the actions of individuals were legitimized by history and politics. Browning is surely correct in saying that group pressure, a propensity to violence, and desensitization are in no way peculiar to the situation in Germany. But the political and social context in which those policemen operated and accepted orders to kill thousands of men, women, and children was indeed quite peculiar to National Socialist Germany, where the readiness for violence received a specific ideological and political charge and underwent a dynamic of de-inhibition.

Studies of the Nazi perpetrators that relied on detailed biographies rather than generalizations concerning the history of social structures had for decades been one of the great taboos of German contemporary history; this was especially true for members of the traditional elites whose careers, with few exceptions, continued after 1945. That these constraints no longer apply is one of the major advances in German scholarship, which have implications beyond the Nazi period and have led to questions concerning the structure of German society in the twentieth century in general. The victims of the National Socialist policy of mass murder, by contrast, have hitherto not been studied by German scholarship in that way; the starting points and the range of inquiry was concentrated on Germany and Germans. There are, to be sure, numerous studies in which the victims' fate is described with both empathy and sympathy. But there are almost no studies by German historians that not only describe sympathetically and with regret the fate of the victims but exploit heuristically the victims' point of view; almost none that do not present and analyze events merely from the perspective of German policemen, bureaucrats, and officers; almost none from the standpoint of the Jewish councils and forced laborers, deported "gypsies" and inmates of the camps; almost none that break the perpetrators' interpretive monopoly that derived from the surviving documents.[38] That holds true for this volume, which in that sense continues the German tradition.

II

It is clear that, whatever starting point one adopts in studying the process by which genocide was set in motion—whether one begins with the schemes of the population-planners, the failure of deportation schemes, the investigation of events in specific occupied areas, or an analysis of the motives of the National Socialist "direct perpetrators"—the questions that remain always point in the same direction: What was the relationship between ideological factors, such as racism and hatred of Jews, to goal-related, "rational" motives, such as economic modernization and solving food shortages? What was the importance of antisemitism in that complex of events? How were the individual and situational motives of the killers and those responsible connected to the general dynamic of violence directed against Jews? What specific ideological concepts and aims drove the commanders of the Einsatzgruppen and thus (since the two groups overlapped) the leadership of the Security Police and the SD? These questions stand at the center of the following discussion. In the following we shall examine more closely the development of antisemitism in Germany in general, then specifically among the leaders of the police and the SS. Finally, based on several examples, we shall discuss the connections between ideological and non-ideological factors in setting the genocide in motion.

That the antisemitism rampant in Germany was an essential, perhaps even the decisive, factor in setting the National Socialist policy of murder in motion was largely taken for granted in the research published on into the 1960s. To be sure, the degree and significance of the German population's anti-Jewish attitudes remained unclear. Of course, it was undeniable that anti-Jewish attitudes began to spread anew, especially after the 1880s, first in relatively small antisemitic political parties, then in nationalist organizations that rapidly gained influence—from the *Bund der Landwirte* [Union of Landowners] to the *Deutschnationaler Handlungsgehilfen Verband* [German Nationalist Association of Business Trainees]. This trend grew in strength during and especially after World War I, when the radical antisemitic alliances and political parties experienced rapid growth. For example, the *Deutschvölkischer Schutz- und Trutzbund* had more than 200,000 members.[39] But this increase in the number of Jew-haters also appeared to have been a passing phenomenon. As of the mid-1920s, the public lost interest in the subject; after 1930, the election propaganda of the rising National Socialists mentioned antisemitism only peripherally.[40] Those observations led many historians, beginning in the 1970s, to conclude that antisemitism during the Weimar Republic was a marginal phenomenon. The radical *völkisch* groups did not influence the masses, and National Socialism achieved power, not because of, but in spite of its antisemitic slogans, which were viewed correctly as expressions of social rejection, above all directionless protests against a loss of social status, whether suffered or feared, rather than as a long-term political orientation.[41]

There are, however, no studies that would permit us to draw firm conclusions about how widespread anti-Jewish attitudes were in the German population in the 1920s and 1930s. Here too, scholarly neglect of the subject has led to a radical swing of the pendulum in the opposite direction. Thus the notion that antisemitism was a "marginal phenomenon" in the Weimar Republic has turned into the thesis that all of German society was infected by a kind of antisemitism that aimed at "elimination"—both theses resting admittedly on insufficient empirical evidence.

The current scholarly consensus can be summarized as follows:[42] There existed a certain hardcore of radical Jew-haters, which attracted attention, primarily in the early years of the Weimar Republic. It drew its members, first, from the old anti-Jewish groups (names such as Pudor and Fritsch were again prominent), and, second, from both the traditional right and, above all, from young people, who were as yet politically uncommitted. These young people responded to their disappointment, bitterness, and confusion at events between 1918 to 1920 simply and effectively by identifying a definable group as the biological embodiment of catastrophic political and social changes. Beginning in the early 1920s, and especially in the early 1930s, the NSDAP and SA became receptacles for these elements.

At the same time, however, we must not forget that there were relatively few cases of physical violence against Jews in the early Weimar years. Even in the years from 1930 to 1933, while there were various assaults on Jews as Jews, even those were exceptions, and they did not come close to the forms of violence that were occurring every day in clashes between the Communist Party and the National Socialists.[43] Rather the 1920s were characterized by lengthy campaigns of defamation and abuse, the best known of which were launched in connection with the publication of the "Protocols of the Elders of Zion" or propaganda alleging ritual murders, along with nightly desecrations of Jewish cemeteries and synagogues—certainly not isolated events, but quite the opposite of an aggressive antisemitism on the march.[44] As a rule, those arrested for these offenses were young, and only in some cases could a direct link to the political right be established. But, of course, desecrating cemeteries suggests not so much conscious political action as subconscious death fantasies, a potential for aggression toward Jews that was a social taboo and thus unleashed only stealthily under the cover of darkness. To this extent, such phenomena might well be interpreted as symptoms of barely repressed fantasies of violence against the Jews, who were felt to be an alien, mystical force.

One should not underestimate such developments, but it is still difficult to connect them directly to National Socialist anti-Jewish policy, especially after 1938. The radical antisemites with a propensity for violence were generally a marginal group during the Weimar years. They were certainly not insignificant, but their rowdy behavior, often accompanied by riots, was indignantly rejected by the public, and even at times within the NSDAP. At the same time, it is probably right to view the potential for violence that was vented in these cases as symptomatic of a widespread propensity for violence against the Jews, which was held in check in the Weimar years by social ostracism and legal prosecution—a potential that would only become significant when the pressure of ostracism and social restraint was lifted.

Far more significant, however, were those forms of passive anti-semitism that had already spread during the Second Reich and again, more virulently, during the Weimar years. That antisemitism had fed upon developments during the First World War and the postwar period but had not manifested itself in open displays of enmity or public brawls. Many in Germany were convinced that Jews represented an alien element in the German *Volk*, that they possessed especially unattractive traits, that they were allied with Germany's enemies from the First World War, that they controlled the press, and that they had profited both from the war and from economic inflation and depression. And, if one considers enmity toward the Jews in all its nuances, one cannot exclude the possibility that people holding such views were in the majority. That applies, in the first place, to those who supported and voted for the NSDAP. Of course, not all, and perhaps not even most of those, who cast their votes for the NSDAP were antisemites, but they were ready to accept the party's program of depriving Jews of their rights, were prepared even blindly to lend a hand, if only they were provided with bread and jobs.[45] The *Deutschnationale Volkspartei* was notoriously antisemitic, its right wing even radically so; even in Stresemann's DVP such attitudes were not rare; and the same was true of the large paramilitary groups, such as the *Stahlhelm*; and most conspicuously in the Protestant church.[46] In 1924, the *Stahlhelm*, with almost 400,000 members, adopted an "Arian Clause," which denied admission to all Jews, including Jews highly decorated for front-line action. Similar provisions were adopted by the *Jungdeutscher Orden* (Order of Young Germans) for its 200,000 members, the *Deutschnationaler Handlungsgehilfen Verband* for its 400,000 members, the *Reichslandbund* with a million members, the German *Burschenschaften*, the *Turnerbund*, and many other organizations.[47]

This was, nevertheless, not a truly fanatical, aggressive species of antisemitism. On the contrary, its most salient feature was precisely that it kept its distance from the much maligned "shrill anti-semitism" with its voyeuristic campaigns alleging Jewish ritual murder and Jewish involvement in the female slave trade, its desecration of cemeteries, and its hooliganism. The more forthrightly one criticized such excesses, the greater was one's conviction when one pointed to one's own serious intentions and to the actual existence of an ostensibly "unsolved Jewish question." This passive antisemitism, moreover, was not committed to a specific goal or "solution," and certainly did not unanimously support a solution involving the "elimination" of the Jews, although there were many such ideas and projects in circulation[48] that had not lent themselves to incorporation in any imaginable party platform. This brand of antisemitism was reactive rather than proactive. And yet, for all its criticism of "excesses," it was ready to accept even a radical program against the Jews when, after 1933, such was provided not by vulgar antisemites but legally, by the government. And to the extent that such acceptance spread, so did the conviction that there must be something correct about the persecution of the Jews, because no doubt no one who was so punished could possibly be completely innocent.

But before 1933 there were also opposition forces, almost as strong as the antisemites themselves, which combated them openly, especially in the workers parties but also among the Catholics and left-liberals. However widespread antisemitism may have been before 1933—whether embracing 30, 40, or 50 percent of the population—it always had its determined opponents. The most important point in this regard is frequently overlooked: The Weimar Republic was a constitutional state under the rule of law. Certainly there were scandalous jury verdicts in cases involving Jews, in which sympathy with the antisemites was clearly perceptible; but the point is that such verdicts provoked scandal; they were the exception, not the rule. Legal action against assault, defamation, and abusive propaganda remained until the end of the republic the most important defense of Jewish organizations against the antisemites, and the *Central-Verein* was tireless in taking recourse to that remedy, and not without success.[49]

The second factor was the public. Throughout the Weimar years, there were numerous waves of outright indignation against antisemitism in all newspapers ranging along the political spectrum all the way from the respectable right-wing to the far left—after, for example, the riots in the Scheunen-viertel in Berlin, the murder of Rathenau, the increase in cemetery desecrations in 1924 and 1925, attacks on Jews by the SA, and especially after the "Kurfürstendamm Riot" organized by the Berlin NSDAP under Count Helldorf.[50] The reactions were not the least important cause for the hope, even the conviction, shared by many German Jews that, viewed historically, antisemitism was a gradually disappearing relic of a darker past and thus, as it were, had no future.[51]

In their confidence regarding the future, Jews who were relatively moderate politically found themselves agreeing with the left's estimation of the importance of antisemitism, especially with the views of leftist intellectuals. In the famous left-wing journal *Die Welt-bühne*, for example, antisemitism and antisemites were the object of either biting scorn or at least head-shaking contempt. The most dangerous aspects of the radical right in the Weimar period were thought to be militarism and the continuing ties to the traditional elites; organized hatred of Jews, by contrast, had about it something of fading moronic folklore.[52] Yet the left lacked the analytical tools required to gauge the effectiveness and persuasiveness of radical right-wing ideologies. While that did not lessen its rejection of antisemitism, it does make clear the degree to which antisemitism was underestimated. That may strike us as surprising today. But if one examines statements on antisemitism by such prominent and critical minds as Kurt Tucholsky and Carl von Ossietzky, one gains the paradoxical impression that the more intelligent the observers were, the more they underestimated the political significance of antisemitism.

After 1933, however,—this is a simple but nonetheless important statement—anti-antisemitism could no longer be expressed in public. To be sure, there were ways in which one could continue to express one's disgust at anti-Jewish measures in private—by ostentatiously greeting one's Jewish acquaintances, by maintaining old contacts to the point of offering direct help, which was not without risk after a few years. But the point is that these were private, not public actions. Meanwhile the public stage was reserved for anti-semitism in its various nuances. Even so, the notion that a considerable fraction of those who had spoken out against antisemitism before 1933 now changed their stance and mutated into antisemites is not very credible.[53] But after 1933, speaking out against the suppression of the Jews in public was frowned upon. Assaults on Jews were no longer prosecuted but rather permitted, even approved of, by the new government. Discrimination against Jews was no longer forbidden but decreed as policy. The antisemites dominated the field, and, precisely because they did not represent a small minority, it was not easy to speak out or mobilize against them publicly.

In recent years, numerous new studies have shown that support for National Socialist policies among the German population was probably somewhat greater than had long been considered possible, whether support is defined as agreeing with the National Socialist regime's war policy, which enjoyed its highest public support following the defeat of France, or with the repression of specific marginalized groups, such as "Gypsies," homosexuals, or forced laborers from abroad. The time-honored image of a regime controlling the German population primarily through "seduction and violence" is untenable. Rather it is becoming clear that even in the case of those who had rejected the Nazis before 1933, disapproval came to be tempered by approval, due not least of all to the regime's ostensibly extraordinary success in economic matters, foreign policy, and military strategy.[54]

Based on available sources, this approval seems to have extended to National Socialist policy regarding the Jews, but only to a small degree. Of course, what is often overlooked is the fact that the regime's anti-Jewish policy was a matter of public discussion and concern in Western nations, but not in Germany. This is especially clear in the documents that have survived from the labor movement, for example in analyses of the SPD in exile or the reports of the Communist Party. The left surely was aware of discrimination against the Jews, and even made note of it. But the left considered it a manifestation of a kind of violence in another sphere, not as a clear manifestation of itself. In the summer of 1938, leftists were deeply worried about political repression in the country and about the clear danger of war. The importance of the persecution of Jews, on the other hand, was grossly underestimated. It was regarded, if at all, as a symptom of the regime's general propensity for violence or as an attempt to intimidate labor. Until November 1938 at the earliest, it was not regarded as an autonomous, highly dynamic political factor.[55]

In society's mainstream, this editing out or ignoring of the regime's anti-Jewish policy was even more pronounced—and it increased to the degree that support for the policies of the National Socialist regime grew in the German population. Presumably, the regime's Jewish policy was not popular among large segments of the population. But neither was it a subject of primary concern; there was after all much that disposed people to excuse Hitler and his crowd their "mistakes" or "excesses" in other areas. Given the constant stream of great political events and the rapid improvement of the social and economic lot of most Germans, the regime's policy toward the Jews seemed an aspect that was, though unattractive, still marginal and perhaps unavoidable, in any case a matter of a little importance in the face of the Nazis' successes. More than anything else, this indifference and readiness to accept the persecution of the Jews, and to ignore it as unimportant, characterized the attitude of the "normal Germans" toward the Jews in those years.[56] This suggests that the generally accepted principles of what today is called civil society—protection of the individual, the universality of human rights, the protection of minorities—did not have deep roots in Germany.

This became obvious to everyone following the pogroms of 9 November 1938. There was, to be sure, much criticism of that night's "excesses," but the regime was not especially discomfited by it—in marked contrast to its reaction to growing criticism of the practice of killing the mentally ill a year and a half later.[57] The difference is obvious: Germans were deeply concerned about the fate of their own relatives, even if they were handicapped; faced with mounting protests, the regime found itself compelled to change, or at least to modify, its actions. But attitudes were quite different in the case of the Jews. When it became clear to everyone in the autumn of 1938 with what degree of violence the policy toward the Jews could and would be pursued, there was no comparable outcry. The criticism that was expressed related primarily to rioting, the plebian character, the form of the excesses of November 9, and— stereotypically—to the "unnecessary destruction of property." Hardly anyone, however, spoke of the ninety-one Jews who had been murdered, and when the legal proceedings against the murderers were quashed without exception, there was neither outcry nor criticism from either the judiciary or the public. When the regime subsequently modified the form of its antisemitic policy by replacing the riots of street gangs with a quiet policy against the Jews that, while observing legal niceties, produced much harsher results, beginning with the detention of more than 20,000 male Jews in concentration camps after 9 November, the uproar quickly died down. The signal that these events sent to the leadership of the regime was that the murder of Jews would no longer involve legal repercussions. And evidently, as long as one avoided public sensations, uproar, and property damage, nothing was to expected from the German population other than indifference.[58]

III

A relatively small, very radical, but active anti-Jewish movement; an equally strong movement in opposition to antisemitism; a still functioning legal system and public opinion that despite all its shortcomings protected the Jews up until 1933, along with a broad area of passive antisemitism—this pattern runs throughout the entire society during the Weimar years. But there was one area in which radical antisemitism gained acceptance quite early, met with only limited opposition, and remained dominant up until 1933, and of course from then on. That was, of all places, the universities, where the generation that would assume leading positions in state and society during the National Socialist period, and especially during the war years, was being trained.[59] With the rise of the *Deutschen Hochschulring* in 1921, the agenda was already being set by an organization that was uniting most of the traditional student organizations and in which, within a brief period, radical, that is, racist, antisemitism had already asserted itself. In those years, the *Hochschulring* won on average more than two-thirds of the seats in student parliaments at German universities, where the "Jewish Question" was not a peripheral theme but rather a central issue in university political debates. True, the aim of the *Hochschulring* of excluding students who were Jewish by descent (not religion) from the union of *German* students, hence violating the principle of civil rights at a leading state institution and placing the Jews under legal restrictions for aliens, was rejected by the Prussian government. But in a referendum in 1926, which had a high turnout, 77 percent of the Prussian students voted to retain the membership requirements that excluded Jews.[60]

The antisemitism spreading through the *völkisch* student movement in the universities was radical and racist, but at the same time expressly elitist and strictly opposed to the "vulgar antisemitism" (*dumpfen Radau-Antisemitismus*). The Jewish problem was to be solved quickly, in a manner as radical as it was "dispassionate"; instead of pogroms and riots, Jews would be forced out of Germany through legal and government measures.

According to this line of thinking, Jewishness represented the immediate and underlying cause of Germany's unprecedented decline during and after the war—a decline that was neither accepted nor understood. Jewishness embodied the principles of the enemy, such as universalism and internationalism, to which Germany was thought to have fallen victim. For many, political developments in the postwar years thus served as empirical confirmation of all that the radical right had been preaching for many years before the war: that the forces of internationalism on the domestic front together with the powers committed to universalism in the world at large comprised the greatest threat to Germany and the Germans—and that Jewry was the "racial" expression of precisely that association.

Such lines of reasoning, which are to be found again and again in the writings of the student right-wing in the 1920s, make it clear that any attempt to detect radical antisemitism in German society by looking for wild-eyed fanatics misses the point. Antisemitism among university students was a significant and an increasingly important factor in German politics from the early 1920s precisely because it provided a link between socially acceptable, passive anti-semitism and the antisemitic *völkisch* extremists. Radical, race-based antisemitism thus achieved something like respectability and was no longer identified solely with the abusive and pogrom anti-semitism that even radical *völkisch* students held in contempt.

This linkage is immediately detectable in the leadership of the Security Police and the SD—which we can recognize as the genocide's active core—those men who, after the outbreak of war, directed the police forces and Einsatzgruppen in the conquered countries, were responsible for initiating the deportation and ghet-toization of Jews, and, from the summer of 1941, bore responsi-bility for the organization of the mass murders themselves. Of the several hundred men in this group—including *Gruppenleiter*, *Referatsleiter*, and *Amtsleiter* in the RSHA, leaders of Einsatzgrup-pen and *Einsatzkommandos*, chiefs and commanders of the Secu-rity Police and the SD, as well as the directors of regional Gestapo stations—approximately two-thirds belonged to the generation born roughly between 1903 and 1915.[61]

Four-fifths of those men had earned the *Abitur*, two-thirds had earned university degrees, and nearly a third a doctorate, almost always in law. The leadership of the Security Police and the SD was thus considerably younger than the leaders of the administration, economy, and the military, and were clearly better educated than the party leadership, including the leaders of the Waffen SS and the Höhere SS- und Polizeiführer, Himmler's regional representatives. The group was therefore relatively homogenous both in age and social origins. They came not from the fringes or the dregs of Ger-man society but rather from its middle and upper strata—the uni-versity-educated middle-class youth, which had been politically socialized in the years of the Weimar Republic.[62]

Those men had typically been active in one or several radical *völkisch* or nationalistic groups, federations, parties, and circles, since the early 1920s. Before 1933 they had undergone a political socialization that synthesized generational self-consciousness and political radicalism (which meant particularly: radical, race-based antisemitism) into a formative world-view.

By the outbreak of war at the latest, these maxims attained an unprecedented relevance for the leadership of the Security Police and the SD, and were a kind of legitimizing self-image for leaders of the special task forces and organizers of the mass deportations, who had been socialized by the ideals of firmness and "objectivity" and were now being put to the test. This ready frame of reference for the acts they were committing not only secured them against

external interference but also provided a de-inhibiting and exculpatory discourse by which the individual could justify his own
actions as the necessary means to attain a higher goal, the rightness
of which was a given, not an object of reflection, and so acquired
humanitarian principles were suspended. Here it became clear that
ideological intensity on the one hand and the lack of consistency
and any grounding in values of the ideological doctrines on the
other were connected closely to a symbolic coalescing of the com-
mitment to a "stance" and "mentality" that enabled individuals to
do "the right thing" at the critical moment without reflection or
discussion, but also without benefit of direct orders, and thus select
the most radical among various available courses of action in any
given situation.[63]

That did not mean that all, or even most, of the men who led
the Einsatzgruppen on their murderous sweeps through occupied
countries worried much about such elaborate ideological niceties.
But the ability to relate their behavior to an established ideological
principle not only gave them political cover against authorities that
may have been inclined to intervene; it also it enabled them also to
justify themselves both to themselves and to their unit in that their
deeds were seen as a necessary means to a higher end, the justification of which was a given, no longer a matter of reflection.

It would be wrong to assume that the ideas described here set
forth a clear political aim. The significance of these factors becomes
clear when one views them in the context of National Socialist
extermination policy as a gradually radicalizing process. The urge
to take increasingly radical options in order to escape from self-created dilemmas, the impulse to resort to measures that would have
been unthinkable one short year before, does not indicate an automatically unfolding program but rather presupposes the removal of
inhibitions and legitimation by the men holding responsible positions in the Security Police. The necessary precondition for such
developments was not the formulation, sooner or later, of an intention to murder all Jews. What was required was rather a framework
of ideological justifications that ruled out a humane solution in
every case and was explicitly prepared to brush aside all opposing
points of view whether pragmatic, political, or ideological in nature.
It is precisely when we recognize the process that set the genocide in
motion as one of cumulative radicalization that the issue of the ideological justifications and motivations of the perpetrators becomes
especially acute, because it is not the pursuit of a predetermined
goal that needs explaining but rather the continuous, persistent
readiness repeatedly to represent one's actions to others and to one-

self as "harsh, but unavoidable" given the ostensibly urgent circumstances. Appealing to the world-view and mentality of the
responsible perpetrators is not a substitute for an investigation of
the political process; rather it constitutes such an investigation.

IV

But how are the various shadings of antisemitism in the German
population and the ideological elite related to the mass murder of
millions? We shall now consider these issues in greater detail based
on several examples taken from recent publications.

The first case has to do with "aryanization." The Hamburg historian Frank Bajohr has asked who profited from the seizure of
Jewish property, and in what manner.[64] Before 1939, the businesses
and property of Jews who were dispossessed, whether they emigrated or stayed in Germany, were claimed not only by the state
and the large banks but frequently by their immediate neighbors. In
Berlin alone, there were roughly 25,000 such cases of dispossession
by 1939. What was not known, however, was to what degree this
practice continued after the war broke out. By 1945, in Hamburg,
more than 3,000 pieces of real estate belonging to Jews had been
confiscated as "enemy property" or "aryanized." Especially prized
in Germany were the dwellings of German Jews who were deported
after the fall of 1941 and then murdered immediately or very
shortly thereafter in Poland or the Soviet Union.

Especially noteworthy in this connection are the activities of
Gauleiters, such as Karl Kaufmann of Hamburg, who petitioned
Hitler to have the Jews deported from a given city or region in
order to relieve the housing shortage affecting the "German" population. The sequence of events makes it clear that Hitler's decision
of September 1941 to deport German Jews was also a response to
such interventions. In such cases, the connection between the antisemitic and materialistic motives of the protagonists is clearly recognizable. In the climate of an ongoing state of emergency in
Germany during the war, appeals to Germany's housing shortage
were used to justify the demand for the deportation of the Jews.[65]
The few houses and apartments occupied by Jews—at this point
there were fewer than 200,000 Jews living in all of Germany, and
the housing units they occupied amounted to less than 0.3 percent
of the total number of units available—could not actually have
solved or even ameliorated the housing problem in Germany. In
that respect, the demands of the Gauleiters amounted to a counter-

feit solution—proof that they were doing something at the cost of a group that had already been marginalized in any event. The notorious radical antisemitism of the National Socialist leaders had so lowered the threshold for aggression against the Jews that even trivial, or merely intimated, transgressions sufficed to provoke actions so radical that they would have been inconceivable if directed against another group at the time. The confiscation of apartments presented just such a utilitarian motive for demanding the deportation of Jews "to the east." But such a utilitarian connection was obviously necessary in order to justify such action

The example of "aryanization" in Hamburg also shows how public these events were. Each week in the Hamburg harbor, beginning in 1941, huge quantities of household goods belonging to Jews of Hamburg, then of all Germany, and ultimately from throughout western Europe, were sold or auctioned; furs, carpets, and period furniture were especially in demand. But linen, lamps, tableware, and children's toys were also sold at bargain-basement prices. In Hamburg alone during the war years, linens and furnishings totaling 60,000 metric tons were sold. At least 100,000 residents of Hamburg bought something at the auction of "Jewish goods." That the objects had belonged to Jews was widely known.

The same is true of the "fur sales." Before the Jews in the East were taken away for shooting or deportation, they were relieved of their warm coats. Most went to the tailor shops of the Wehrmacht (which, incidentally, were staffed by Jewish forced laborers). A smaller number of coats came into the Reich, where they were distributed or sold, especially in cities that were coming under air attack. There, too, word quickly spread about who the original owners were. The dispossession of first the German Jews and then the Jews of Europe was not a secret, compartmentalized process. On the contrary, a not inconsiderable number of Germans managed to profit from it. As is clear from the available sources, this knowledge did not cause unease in the population. Certainly most Germans did not know, or at least not precisely, what was going on "in the east." But where were the Jews whose dwelling one now occupied, or whose business one had taken over? What had become of the people on whose sofa one was sitting, or whose fur coat one was wearing, in which was sewn the label reading "Fashion House Hirsch, Cracow"? People did not want to know. And it was better not to ask.

The extant sources, especially biographical documents of a private nature, give many indications of what information about the fate of the Jews "in the East" seeped into the Reich, about how

much, and how much precisely, soldiers home on leave told or
merely hinted at.[66] But there are almost no indications that such
knowledge occasioned any concern in Germany. Most people, faced
with their own concerns, were indifferent, especially since their
own wartime worries had begun to loom larger. Why, with one's
own son or father at the front and one's hometown exposed to air
attack, should one worry about the fate of a small group that,
rightly or wrongly, had always been accused of bad things and with
which one as a rule had hardly any personal contact? The anti-Jewish policy was not an important subject for the German population
before the war, and still less after war came. And *not* following up
on one's own many observations, or reports, or rumors about what
was happening to the Jews; *not* allowing them to coalesce into a
mental image and *not* drawing the obvious conclusions—that
describes precisely the process of verdrängung, repression.

My second example has to do with Lithuania in the late summer and fall of the year 1941, and with the research efforts of the
Freiburg historian Christoph Dieckmann.[67]

About forty thousand Jews lived in the city of Kaunas. As soon
as the Germans marched into town, a dreadful bloodbath began
that all but defies description. At the behest of the Einsatzgruppen
of the Security Police and the SD, Lithuanian nationalists chased
the Jews through the streets, shooting or otherwise slaying hundreds of them. Afterwards, the Germans brought about 7,000 into
Fort No. 7—a barracks located in town.[68] In the next few days
most of them—all men—were shot by German police and Lithuanian auxiliary units, who claimed that the prisoners were Jewish
Bolshevists. In subsequent weeks, the surviving men, along with the
women and children, were confined in a ghetto in a sealed-off
section of Kaunas. Eight weeks later, in early September 1941,
German authorities began preparing to clear out a section of the
ghetto. As in the other occupied regions of the Soviet Union, the
Jews, who were declared superfluous, were to be shot—women and
children included.

How the genocide of the Jews began in the Soviet Union was
for a long time a matter of dispute. The fact that German Einsatzgruppen, together with other police units, began mass shootings of
Jewish men, especially in the Baltic countries, only days after the
outbreak of war seemed to suggest that they had been sent into the
Soviet Union with orders to slaughter the Jews en masse.[69] Dieckmann, however, is able to show that such was not the case. The task
of the Einsatzgruppen and police commando units was rather to
establish security behind the front, which was assumed to be

threatened primarily by Communists and Jews—Bolshevism being regarded as the political expression of Jewish power. The first mass shootings of Jewish males in July 1941 were justified on those grounds, which the leaders of those units seem clearly to have found personally convincing. To put it bluntly: in this situation Jewish men were murdered because the leaders of the German police units were convinced that Jews threatened the safety of German occupation forces. It did not matter whether that was actually proven; it was taken as an established fact requiring no additional proof. That in any case something had to be done with the Jews in the East was part and parcel of the general, antisemitic conviction. The threshold of inhibitions regarding them was already at the lowest level imaginable. But a specific reason was required to unleash and justify actions such as mass shooting.

In mid-August 1941, following a tour by Himmler of police and SS units in occupied areas of the northern Soviet Union, Einsatzgruppen and Waffen SS units began systematically murdering Jewish women and children.[70] Two factors, not mutually exclusive, were decisive. First, there were the long-term plans for resettlement and the shifting of ethnic populations. If the newly occupied territories in the East, specifically the Baltic region, were to be controlled and settled by Germans, as was foreseen in the numerous plans developed by the *Reichskommissar für die Festigung deutschen Volkstums* and in other agencies, then the Jews had to vanish from those areas. At the same time, all ideas about where "in the East" Soviet Jews were to be sent had become obsolete when a quick victory against the Red Army appeared unlikely—that is, after the late summer of 1941. From that point on, "vanish" could only mean "die." But now that tens of thousands of Jewish men had already been killed, killing the women and children did not appear to be a major step.

A second motivation also came into play: Jewish women and children could not be productively employed; the phrase "useless eaters" (*nutzlose Esser*) soon became common currency. In view of the serious and worsening food shortages in the newly conquered territories, about which even Wehrmacht units were beginning to complain, the pressure mounted to reduce further the number of mouths to feed. Thus there arose yet again that situational motivation, allegedly utilitarian, which suggested—even seemed to mandate—that Jewish women and men no longer be fed but shot instead.[71]

In Kaunas, however, another factor intervened. Several thousand Soviet prisoners of war were being housed at the town's partly

destroyed airport. As was the case throughout the Soviet Union in
that period, prisoners of war received either no or quite insufficient
provisions so that many of them died. In early September, the death
rate rose from 50 to over 300 per day. By the end of the month
nearly all of the soldiers housed at the airport had died. But that
meant that the German occupation authorities had no workers to
rebuild the airport. So the responsible official in the labor office,
which had been established in Kaunas by then, asked his colleagues
in the civilian administration who were responsible for the Jews to
stop the "partial clearing" of the Jewish ghetto because he needed
the Jews to replace the Soviet soldiers as workers at the airport.

The request was granted, and roughly 3,000 Jews began cleaning up the Kaunas airport. Nevertheless, the civilian authorities still
agreed with the Security Police that the number of Jews in the Kaunas ghetto who were unfit for work was too high and had to be
decimated. Accordingly, the inhabitants of the ghetto were selected
according to their ability to work. Two thousand mostly elderly
men, about 3,000 women, and 5,400 children were moved to Fort
No. 9 and, in the course of two days, shot by members of *Einsatzkommando* 3 and the 11th Police Battalion—thus by German
order police—as well as by Lithuanian auxiliary policemen.

No attempt was made to keep the matter secret. All these
events took place in full public view— the starvation of the Soviet
prisoners, the pogroms, and finally the mass shootings of the Jews.
The responsible parties were, first of all, the local military commander and the Security Police, then, following the establishment
of the German civilian administration, the civilian authorities. The
responsibility for guarding the Jews was first assumed by police
units, later by a unit of the NSKK—the National Socialist Drivers'
Corps—which happened to be available. The Wehrmacht command, in this case the regional commander, was responsible for
caring for war prisoners. All German authorities in Kaunas were
involved in discussions relating to the fate of the Jews. This process
was played out in those weeks in all the larger cities in Lithuania,
in the Baltic, and in the occupied areas of the Soviet Union. The
process of the mass murder of millions of people—and this
becomes increasingly evident the more one examines the matter in
detail—was not an aberration in the overall administration of the
occupation but was a component of German occupation policy in
the East.

Moreover, setting mass murder in motion in no way required
any peculiar anti-Jewish sentiment on the part of, say, the participating policemen. The police were probably not unanimous in their

attitudes toward Jews. But that did not matter. Decisive was the fact that humanitarian, humane attitudes toward the Jews no longer had any meaning even for those Germans who did not consider themselves committed antisemites at all, perhaps not even as Nazis. By then indifference, desensitization, and roughness meant more than merely accepting what others were doing. Often they were sufficient to motivate participation in the murders. Certainly many were motivated by hatred and fanaticism. But in many others such motives were clearly lacking, at least in the beginning. Jan-Philipp Reemtsma has formulated the fateful implication as follows: "Many were doing it because they wanted to. But the others wanted to because they were doing it."[72]

The incident in Kaunas also shows that there is something quite arbitrary about drawing distinctions among the various groups that fell victim to the National Socialist extermination policy. On the one hand, the Jewish Holocaust was unique by virtue of its aim, its radical nature, and its order of magnitude; and yet, on the other hand, in its execution the Holocaust was closely related to, at times virtually interchangeable with, the campaigns of mass murder carried out against other groups. This suggests that an assumption that the motivations of any of the perpetrators toward the various groups of victims can always be clearly sorted out is at least dubious.

The incident described also shows the linkage between utilitarian and ideological elements. For one thing, the different varieties of antisemitism become clearly visible. A barbaric, but in a certain sense traditional, hatred of the Jews confronts us in some of the German protagonists, but also in the Lithuanians. Their frame of reference was basically the pogrom; and yet they willingly carried out actions that went far beyond a pogrom, and that they did not initiate.

On the other hand, the intellectual antisemitism, so to speak, is detectable, especially in the leaders of the Security Police and the Einsatzgruppen. Here, in genocide's hard core, enmity toward the Jews is recognizable as a manifestation of a radical *völkisch* world-view. To repeat, seeing their own actions within the context of such a world-view not only insulated them against interference by other agencies, it also provided that exculpatory discourse that lessened inhibitions and offered an avenue of self-justification by representing one's own actions as the necessary means to a higher end, thus suspending acquired humanitarian principles.

And finally, we can also detect a widespread lack of interest on the part of an undetermined, but obviously considerable, number of Germans, especially among civilian officials and military officers who did not personally promote or even desire the campaign against the Jews, but who by then quite lacked the moral substance to be outraged by it. These men, presumably the largest group of Germans in the occupied areas of the East, were ultimately willing even to accept the murder of the Jews when it was justified, not as the outgrowth of hatred of Jews, but by the exigencies of intractable dilemmas, as an essentially incidental side-effect of the pursuit of a larger, important goal, opposition to which was regarded as unpatriotic even by people who did not think much of the National Socialists—whether that goal was the German mission and settlement of the East, victory over Bolshevism, or simply victory.

This already suggests the importance of the utilitarian motivations that surfaced as the process played out. First, there was the security aspect—the murder of Jewish men as a means of pacifying the hinterland. Of course, a readiness to regard the murder of thousands of Jewish men as a security measure already presupposed that both resistance to Germany and Bolshevism were essentially the work of the Jews. In that sense, justifications on security grounds alone represent a specific manifestation of a basically antisemitic mindset from which the objective argument involving security concerns derives. And yet that argument is obviously necessary because it implies an empirical justification for antisemitic prejudice. The killing of Jews as putative saboteurs confirms the original assumption that they are enemies of Germany; otherwise they would not be so severely punished. Through the deed, the prejudice becomes a fact.

On the other hand, there is the line of argument relating to food shortages, which was pursued mostly by the Wehrmacht: Since there is insufficient food for all, women and children who are considered unable to work are killed. The demand for a reduction in the number of mouths to feed consciously singles out a specific group—precisely the group whose right to exist, which has already been disqualified by tradition and outbreaks of antisemitism, is recognized to a lesser degree than that of other groups. Food shortages mandated reducing the number of those at the bottom of the ideological hierarchy—the Jews. But once that argument was accepted, murdering Jews as a problem-solving strategy became an option in other emergencies, and thus the idea of killing ever larger groups of Jews gradually became detached from the specific case in which it was pursued on utilitarian grounds and gains a degree of abstraction.

It must also be stressed that these justifications are very change-able. A large number of Soviet prisoners of war fell victim to the policy of restrictive rationing on grounds that sufficient food was simply not available for such masses of people. But in fact the death of Soviet war prisoners was part and parcel of the general policy of starving the Soviet population, which had been worked out before the war began and was now being implemented in stages.[73]

Our third example: In the first days of October 1941, the civilian authorities of the district of Galicia decided to gather the Jews in the small border town Stanislau into their own residential district—a ghetto. Similar decisions had already been made in Lemberg as well as in other cities and districts. The ghetto was designed to absorb far fewer people than there were Jews in Stanislau. Thus, *Höherer SS- und Polizeiführer* Katzmann and the commander of the Security Police, Tanzmann, ordered the director of the Stanislau border police, Krüger, to reduce the number of the Jews in Stanislau.

The decimation was to take place on Sunday, 12 October, which was a Jewish holy day. On the same day, the Jewish council was required to provide city maps to aid in planning evictions. The German police ordered Ukranian auxiliary police under their command to dig two ditches on the grounds of the Jewish cemetery, which lay some distance outside of Stanislau. On the morning of 12 October, Companies 1 and 2 of Police Battalion 133 showed up for roll call and were given orders for the "Jewish Operation." Several assembly points were set up in town, from which the arrested Jews were marched in columns of 250 to the Jewish cemetery.

The shootings began between ten or eleven in the morning. The victims were driven through a large gate onto the cemetery grounds. There they were forced to sit down on the ground next to the gate, where they were watched by a machine-gun post. Small groups of victims were then driven to one of the large ditches, where the executioners were lined up. On the way to their execution, the Jews had to pass by spread-out blankets, where they placed their valuables and furs. Then, in groups of five, they had to step to the edge of the ditches, where they were shot, small children in the arms of the adult.

When the shootings began, panic broke out among the waiting Jews. They rushed by the hundreds to the cemetery gate. Some were trampled to death. Policemen and their assistants, probably including on-lookers, forced the Jews back onto the cemetery grounds. Between fifteen and twenty shooters, Security Police and members of the police battalion, were posted on each side of the ditches.

There is evidence that a shortage of personnel resulted in railroad guards being recruited, presumably also as executioners. Many gawkers had gathered at the cemetery, especially members of the Wehrmacht, railroad workers, and police, who followed the whole proceeding and took numerous photographs.

The number of victims cannot be precisely determined even today. We may assume that at least 20,000 persons, two-thirds of the Jewish community, were forced to set out for the execution grounds. The Jewish Council estimated that about 10,000 to 12,000 people had been killed before the onset of darkness forced the police units to call a halt to the "operation."

That same evening Krüger, who had led the unit, held a "victory celebration" with members of his staff. The next day a unit from the police battalion searched the cemetery grounds for survivors, whom they shot. Krüger sent a summary report of the "operation" complete with photographs to the RSHA in Berlin. For weeks the massacre was the major topic of conversation in Stanislau and the surrounding area. Numerous curiosity-seekers passed by the cemetery hoping to catch sight of the remaining evidence of what had transpired there; the dead had been buried only haphazardly. One may assume that Governor General Frank was informed since he paid Stanislau a visit ten days after the event.

This report on the Bloody Sunday of Stanislau of 12 October 1941 is found in studies of the "Final Solution" in Galicia by Thomas Sandkühler and Dieter Pohl.[74] It describes the everyday reality of murdering Jews. There were many such massacres in Galicia long before the German authorities arranged to have most of the Jews killed in the extermination station in Belzec beginning in the spring of 1942. The report is symptomatic in several ways. For one thing, it shows how publicly all this took place, how many non-participants watched or visited the scene later. There are numerous eye-witness accounts of the massacre. As in most other cases, numerous photographs were taken; in some postwar trials, there were reports of home movies made by members of the civilian authorities and shown back home in Germany.

Above all this case makes it clear that the number of those involved directly or indirectly in the National Socialist policy of murder reaches far—*very far*—beyond those who held the rifles or locked the gas chamber doors. In contrast to the situation in the Reich, the mass murder of Jews in the East was by no means secret. Too many officials of the German occupation administration, representatives of the party and government offices, members of police and Wehrmacht units, employees on economic staffs and in industrial ventures, from organizations such as the railroad and the labor department, were devoting their time and energy to—or were direct involved in the process of—deporting, classifying, forcing into ghettoes, recruiting for forced labor, and ultimately carrying out the murders themselves. From these groups knowledge, or suspicions, of mass murder spread rapidly.

Anyone who has read how various German authorities and representatives of industries, in an all-but-incredible fashion, haggled over 1,000 Jews here, 200 there, another 3,000 somewhere else—all in the implicit knowledge that those who could not work would be killed immediately, and those who could probably not much later—will surely view the notion of a secret plan for murder with some cynicism.

Regarding the number of people involved in the murders, the widespread conception of mass murder as a quasi anonymous process, or as "factory-like" killing, is misleading. The number of Jews gassed in the large killing centers account for about 60 percent of the six million murdered Jews. And even in Auschwitz, Treblinka, Majdanek, many officials, party representatives, military personnel, and police were required to apprehend, round up, deport, and send the Jews into forced labor, and to feed them, move them to one of the extermination camps, and finally to murder them. The image of a "clean" death by gassing does not apply to much of the genocide. On the contrary, the Holocaust meant, to a considerable degree, exterminating human beings in very traditional, even archaic, ways, with a correspondingly high number of direct perpetrators. The notion of a modern "industrial" genocide, in which the victim-perpetrator structure is replace by anonymous relationships, is clearly an attempt to represent the mass murder as an abstract, even metaphysical, mass death of nameless victims.

The report of the massacre in Stanislau reveals also how anti-Jewish policy became radicalized in the fall of 1941. In September of that year, the future course of Jewish policy in the Government General was quite unclear. The administrative staff of Governor General Hans Frank in Cracow was relying on relevant commitments by Hitler to the effect that Polish Jews and Jews who had been deported to Poland would not remain there permanently but would be shifted "to the east" in the foreseeable future. In order to keep stressing the urgency of those deportations, it was advisable for Frank to ensure that the stay of Jews in the Government General was temporary and that any action that might stabilize the situation be avoided. The administration of the Government General was thus at pains to present the living conditions of the Jews as "untenable" in as dramatic a manner as possible. Forming new ghettos had already been prohibited for that reason; and moreover, ghettos had proven very problematic arrangements for the Germans. If the ghettos were to support themselves financially, then a corresponding infrastructure of productive jobs needed to be developed. But that would have meant significant investment, which could only be pay off in the long term, thus contradicting the maxim of a "temporary stay" in the Government General.[75]

Local civilian authorities in Galicia, on the other hand, were pressing for the establishment of self-contained Jewish residential districts. Given the proximity of the Hungarian border, they viewed the Jews as a security risk. Thus it was agreed—presumably on the initiative of Schöngarth, the commander of the Security Police in the Government General, Tanzmann, commander of the Security Police in Lemberg, along with Katzmann, the leader of the SS and police in Galicia—to establish relatively small, inexpensive ghettos in the southern districts of Galicia.[76] But since many more Jews lived there than there were places in the ghettos, the extra Jews were to be killed.

There are indications that during October 1941 Hitler, Himmler, and Heydrich agreed to "solve" the Jewish question, at least in eastern Europe, by murder rather than by deportations—although in what orders of magnitude and time-frames they were thinking cannot be established.[77] Establishing ghettos and killing the Jews for whom there was no room, which continued on into late December 1941, would have made no sense if a general order for a "Final Solution" had already been issued. Obviously some legitimation for mass murder was still required. Here the reciprocal interplay between the central government in Berlin and the regions becomes clear: the Berlin authorities reacted to reports of "untenable conditions" coming in from everywhere, and to urgent inquiries about what was to be done with the Jews, by consistently ordering, or sanctioning post facto, increasingly radical measures, which in turn anticipated operations in the regions.

While, on the one hand, the Berlin leadership found itself under constant pressure from the regional occupation authorities, especially from the Security Police, to "remove" the Jews from the individual regions, there was, on the other hand, no center of opposition to the policy on the German side. Where the Wehrmacht, for example, had sharply criticized the actions of the Einsatzgruppen in the fall of 1939, there was a complete absence of any such resistance after the outbreak of war against the Soviet Union. Even the indigenous populations of the occupied zones put up no resistance to the constantly expanding campaign of murder directed at Jews. Ludolf Herbst has described this process as "uncoupling": "A leadership considering extermination without having ordered extermination could progress to extermination because it encountered no opposition."[78]

Justifications of the mass murder were always linked with hazards or threats that allegedly could be averted through the "liquidation" of Jews: "purging the hinterland" on the East Front, or "routing the partisans," eliminating the black market or disease, punishing sabotage or attacks on German soldiers—or the extermination of Bolshevism. Antisemitism found its specific expression in the fact that the persecution, repression, and murder of the Jews was always justified on utilitarian grounds—and in the fact that the perpetrators found such rationalizations convincing: Jews as the carriers of Bolshevism, spreaders of disease, or as spies or partisans. Or, it was said, there was no space left where the Jews might live, so they must be decimated, or, continuing to feed Jews who could not work endangered the care of troops. In this way, genocide was linked to the pursuit of political, military, security, population, health, or food supply–related concerns that were supported on patriotic grounds even by people who believed they maintained an inner distance from the National Socialists.

At the same time, this process did not function automatically. On the contrary, the end result of the procedure of always creating new "dilemmas" that required increasingly radical measures eventually culminating in mass murder was perfectly clear to players such as Schöngarth, Tanzmann, and Globocnik. Moreover, to assume that the perpetrators were focused exclusively on their individual areas of responsibility would miss the point. Knowledge of what was going on at the fronts and in other occupied areas, especially on the part of the uncommonly well-informed leadership of the Wehrmacht and Security Police, was much greater and much more detailed than is usually assumed. Reports of mass shootings spread like wildfire in the individual occupation zones, and even beyond, not least when men went on leave or were transferred. One must then assume that anyone who insisted on the deportation of Jews in either western or eastern Europe in the fall of 1941 had knowledge of the rapidly circulating reports of mass shootings by the Einsatzgruppen in the Soviet Union; demands for deportations can, therefore, not be construed as mere "emergency solutions" to ostensibly sticky situations. It is becoming clear that the regional authorities tried to represent their actions against the Jews as resulting from "dilemmas" and "untenable conditions," as the consequences of dispassionate decisions, but were in fact well informed about what was happening in other regions and thus knew that in this context their recommendations and decisions meant more than what they appeared to signify.

The intensification of the situation and the radicalization of anti-Jewish policy did not arise on their own but were willfully initiated. In that sense, the justifications of harsh or radical treatment of the Jews based on "expediency" turn out to have been neither "rational" justifications camouflaging by antisemitism nor euphemisms concealing outright hatred of Jews. Rather they prove to have been the practical application, the situational manifestation, of a fundamentally antisemitic attitude.

In this context, the racist mindset, specifically antisemitism, lays the groundwork by providing definitions. It establishes a hierarchy of groups based on their relative worth and their right to exist, and it represses the reservations of the humanist or Christian tradition about brutal forms of problem-solving, even including extermination. This, of course, presupposes a pressing set of problems that is initially limited to a given situation, the solution of which is viewed as absolutely necessary for achieving a higher goal. Thus radical antisemitism seizes on real individual situations that, without exception, take the form of emergencies requiring emergency measures, indeed the most radical measures conceivable, and which override all reservations—even (especially) regard for the lives of such groups whose right to life has already been assigned a low priority. At the same time, such situational considerations of practicality also function as empirical evidence for the validity of the a priori ideological premise. The very fact that so many different situations in the individual regions, though arising independently, always led to the same result, i.e., the murder of Jews, powerfully suggests this connection. And yet, already implicit was the effort, which began in late 1941 and early 1942, to free the policy toward the Jews from such situational and utilitarian constraints after the sheer number of various immediate causes seemed to make compelling the need for a "Final Solution to the Jewish question."

In this regard, it is also possible to gauge more precisely the significance of the Wannsee conference.[79] Given the numerous complaints and inquiries from the occupied areas, in the West as well as in the East, in the fall of 1941, the plan that Heydrich presented at the conference (which had originally been planned for December 1941) should be understood as a recommendation to pull together the manifold versions of anti-Jewish policy into a single policy and expand it to include the Jews of *all* European countries. In view of the events leading up to the conference that we have sketched in these pages, the notion that Heydrich managed to establish himself as "Commissar of Jews for All of Europe" against the resistance of other competing agencies is not very convincing.[80] On the contrary, the considerable knowledge about Jewish policy in the individual regions derived from recent research suggests that Heydrich's offer to take full responsibility for the "Jewish problem" met with relief in the occupied areas, because it now seemed assured that the aim of the regional authorities of making "their" territories "free of Jews" would soon be achieved without their having to lend a hand.[81] In addition, Heydrich's suggestion that the Jews be employed in "building roads into the east" amounted to adopting practices already in effect in Galicia.[82] Henceforth, "putting the Jews to work" became the dominant "practical consideration" of the policy of the "Final Solution."

Christian Gerlach has argued recently that the shift from the former policy of successive mass murder campaigns, each justified on the basis of individual situations, to the "Final Solution of the Jewish question," i.e., the murder of all European Jews with no consideration for specific local conditions, can be traced to a speech that Hitler made in Berlin to the leadership of the NSDAP on 12 December 1941.[83] Gerlach regards the speech, the text of which has not survived, as representing a "fundamental decision" on Hitler's part, based on notes made by several National Socialist leaders. Gerlach believes that Hitler was reacting to the entry of the United States entry into the war, which had confirmed his "announcement" of January 1939 that an expansion of the European war to a world war would be the work of the Jews and would be answered with the destruction of the Jewish race. Now, based on our knowledge of Hitler's habit of avoiding giving explicit orders on such occasions in favor of suggesting radical measures in general terms or designating them as "inevitable," it does not seem all that certain that Hitler actually gave an "order" to implement the "Final Solution of the Jewish question" or announced an explicit decision. But it is quite obvious that the speech had that effect on the leadership of the Security Police and the authorities in the occupied regions. Where earlier extermination campaigns had been limited to specific regions and had always been undertaken in pursuit of such concrete aims as combating Bolshevism, eliminating the black market, freeing up housing, and eliminating "unproductive eaters," etc., from this moment on such compulsive justifications fell away. Leaving behind individual motivations and regional limitations, the "Final Solution of the Jewish question" now took the form of a general project.

V

In summary, the studies in this volume reveal a multiplicity of factors that contributed to setting the genocide in motion: a process of increasing brutality in pursuit of continental-imperialist expansionist goals, especially the "resettling" of central and eastern Europe and starving out some of the indigenous populations, and directly related to that, various kinds of individual and ideological motivations; opportunism; a widespread lack of positive values; fatalism and submission to authority; sadism and complete desensitization. Nevertheless, it cannot be denied that many of the protagonists, if not all, were antisemites, although obviously the term obviously encompassed very diverse attitudes that functioned differently in the playing out of historical events. In the case of a not inconsiderable part of the German population, especially those on the political right before 1933, one must take manifest antisemitism as a given, although that had not been the sole or even a major factor in the political orientation of such Germans. That is something quite different from a conviction dating from time immemorial that Jews should be "eliminated." The gradual introduction of the systematic extermination policy cannot be explained as the direct result of the spread of anti-Jewish attitudes in the German population, however that is presented. On the contrary, one of the prerequisites for setting the policy of murder in motion was an extraordinary indifference toward the fate of the Jews on the part of a considerable portion of the German population. That does not indicate a society lusting to drive out or eliminate Jews—in any sense of the word. But it does suggest a growing lack of moral concern in German society for human rights and the protection of minorities, which grew rapidly during the years of the dictatorship, and which led to a profound moral brutalization in Germany. This brutalization became equally characteristic of the elites and white- and blue-collar workers, of the Wehrmacht and the churches—its effects can be found even in the circles of conspirators comprising the conservative and military resistance, for whom, even as late as 1943, the Jewish question was still of secondary interest.[84]

What proved decisive was the fact that the groups of anti-semites urging action were operating in a political space to which the majority of the population attached no significance. Both among

the common people and in many government ministries, we dis-
cover, after 1933, and even more so after 1939, a general attitude
that the treatment of the Jews was an issue of secondary importance
compared to political developments—an issue one could safely
leave to the Nazis. Especially significant after the war began was the
frequently encountered notion that the persecution of Jews was all-
in-all a manifestation of the politics of war and conquest that was
justified by exceptional war-time conditions. To oppose that view
would have required, not indifference and reserve, but explicit rejection based on principle. But few were yet prepared to express opposition, especially when Jews were the victims.

The conclusion to which this insight compels us is that no
widespread ideological fanaticism, no mass hysteria, no "national
project" was needed for the developing National Socialist extermination policy to be tolerated or even approved. General disinterest,
the pronounced absence of a canon of values in which the protection of minorities was regarded as a central ethical norm in a civi-
lized society, indifference, brutalization, repression—these proved
to be quite sufficient. In a certain sense, the discovery that an escalating indifference was typical of German society's attitude toward
National Socialist extermination policy is far more alarming than
the discovery of a thoroughly antisemitic, hate-filled population for
whom the policy toward the Jews represented their dearest expectations and most fervent demands. For, of course, viewing the
requirements for genocide as limited to the special case of Germany, to the historically uniqueness of the Germans' warped ideas
about Jews, is somehow reassuring; it seems to exclude the possibility of genocide in the future as long as someone makes sure that
this German delusion either is repressed or, as was recently asserted,
has completely disappeared in the postwar years.

If, however German society was largely characterized not so
much by active, ideologically grounded, fanatical behavior, but
rather by indifference, disinterest, and a striking lack of moral values, then genocide does not refer merely to that historically unique
situation, that specific German society, of the 1930s and 1940s but
becomes oppressively current and urgent, not only, but certainly,
here in Germany.

These matters will continue to concern us long after all of
today's disputes and emotional involvements are forgotten. To
stress the incomprehensibility of the event is as unhelpful as mono-
causal and superficially radical arguments that are said to have
some kind of cathartic effect for the public.

Thus, publications on the history of the Holocaust will not be judged on the attitudes they display—the degree of empathy or outrage they exhibit—but solely on their quality, on the breadth of their grounding in the literature and source material, on the rigor of their analysis, and on the persuasiveness of their findings—that is, on professional standards subject to proof. Now, of course, that is certainly more difficult with this topic than with any other because even after fifty years the subject has lost none of its capacity to shock and cause pain; indeed it may appear all the more incomprehensible the more accurately we perceive it. But without painstaking historical research into the events themselves, without the specific enlightenment that historical treatments offer, repression of the memory of the Holocaust throughout society is inevitable.

Historical research into National Socialist mass extermination policy has brought to light a process that was so complex, so multilayered in terms of the perpetrators, so characterized by competition, ambitions, private interests, banality, lust for murder, and petit bourgeois hypocrisy, as well as by political utopianism and ostensibly scientific systems for interpreting the world, that this extraordinarily multifaceted image is ill-suited as a metaphor for political education and, in a sense, cannot even be identified with. And yet the didactic challenge of the history of the Holocaust lies precisely in the fact that it does not lend itself to explanations involving pithy formulations and simple, readily digested concepts or theories.

And because the Holocaust possesses no theory or redemptive formula, our need to understand can only be satisfied by continuing to wrestle with the subject.

Notes

1. Daniel Jonah Goldhagen, *Hitler's Willing Executioners: Ordinary Germans and the Holocaust* (New York, 1996); in German: *Hitlers willige Vollstrecker. Ganz gewöhnliche Deutsche und der Holocaust* (Berlin, 1996).
2. Michael Prinz and Rainer Zitelmann (eds.), *Nationalsozialismus und Modernisierung*, (Darmstadt, 1994); for a critical evaluation of the modernity thesis, see Norbert Frei, "Wie modern war der Nationalsozialismus?," in *GuG* 19 (1993): 367-387; Ernst Nolte, *Der europäische Bürgerkrieg 1917-1945. Nationalsozialismus und Bolschewismus* (Frankfurt a.M./Berlin, 1987); *"Historikerstreit". Die Dokumentation der Kontroverse um die Einzigartigkeit der nationalsozialistischen Judenvernichtung* (Munich, 1987).
3. See Julius H. Schoeps, *Ein Volk von Mördern? Die Dokumentation der Goldhagen-Kontroverse um die Rolle der Deutschen im Holocaust* (Hamburg, 1996); Dieter Pohl, "Die Holocaust-Forschung und Goldhagens Thesen," in *VfZ* 1 (1997): 1-48; Reinhard Rürup, "Viel Lärm um nichts? D.J. Goldhagens 'radikale Revision' der Holocaust-Forschung," in *NPL* 4 (1996): 357-363; Ruth-Bettina Birn, "Revising the Holocaust," in *Historical Journal* 40 (1997): 195-215. Of the many approaches to criticizing Goldhagen, I have found most convincing Omer Bartov's article "Ordinary Monsters," in *The New Republic*, 29 April 1996.
4. See Norbert Frei, "Von deutscher Erfindungskraft oder: Die Kollektivschuldthese in der Nachkriegszeit," in *Rechtshistorisches Journal* 16 (1997).
5. Concerning the historiography of the Holocaust, see Ian Kershaw, *The Nazi Dictatorship: Problems and Perspectives of Interpretation* (London, 1993); Yisrael Gutman and Gideon Greif (eds.), *The Historiography of the Holocaust Period* (Jerusalem, 1988); Bernd Jürgen Wendt, "Der 'Holocaust' im Widerstreit der Deutungen," in Arno Herzig et al. (eds.), *Verdrängung und Vernichtung der Juden unter dem Nationalsozialismus* (Hamburg, 1992), pp. 29-74. The following is based on the thoughts I presented in "Der Holocaust in der Geschichtsschreibung der Bundesrepublik Deutschland," in Ulrich Herbert and Olaf Groehler, *Zweierlei Bewältigung. Vier Beiträge über den Umgang mit der NS-Vergangenheit in den beiden deutschen Staaten* (Hamburg, 1992), pp. 7-27.
6. For general presentations, Norbert Frei, *Vergangenheitspolitik. Amnestie, Integration und die Abgrenzung vom Nationalsozialismus in den Anfangsjahren der Bundesrepublik* (Munich, 1996); Ulrich Herbert, "Zweierlei Bewältigung," in Herbert and Groehler, *Zweierlei Bewältigung*, pp. 193-212.
7. See for example, "Der Gerstein-Bericht," in *VfZ* 1 (1953): pp. 185ff; Himmler's memorandum on the treatment of alien ethnic elements in the East (May 1940), Helmut Krausnick (ed.), in *VfZ* 5 (1957): 194-198; Helmut Heiber (ed.), "Der Generalplan Ost" [General Plan for the East], in *VfZ* 6 (1958): 281-325; Gerald Reitlinger: *The Final Solution: The Attempt to Exterminate the Jews of Europe* (London, 1968).
8. Ulrich Herbert: "Rückkehr in die Bürgerlichkeit? NS-Eliten in der Bundesrepublik," in Bernd Weisbrod, *Rechtsradikalismus in der politischen Kultur der Nachkriegszeit: Die verzögerte Normalisierung in Niedersachsen* (Hanover, 1995), pp. 157-173; Ulrich Brochhagen, *Nach Nürnberg. Vergangenheitsbewältigung und Westintegration in der Ära Adenauer* (Hamburg, 1994).
9. Gutachten des Instituts für Zeitgeschichte [Documents of the Institute for Contemporary History], 2 vols., (Munich 1958 and 1966); Wolfgang Scheffler, *Judenverfolgung im Dritten Reich 1933-1945* (Berlin, 1960); Eberhard Kolb,

Bergen-Belsen. Geschichte des Aufenthaltlagers 1943-1945 (Hanover, 1962; new revised edition Göttingen, 1985).

10. Helmut Krausnick et al., *Anatomy of the SS State* (New York/London, 1968).

11. Karl Dietrich Bracher, *The German Dictatorship: The Origins, Structure, and Effects of National Socialism* (New York, 1970).

12. Uwe Dietrich Adam, *Judenpolitik im Dritten Reich* (Düsseldorf, 1972).

13. See for example, Alexander Dallin, *German Rule in Russia, 1941-1945: A Study of Occupation Policies* (New York, 1980); Eberhard Jäckel, *Frankreich in Hitlers Europa. Die deutsche Frankreichpolitik im Zweiten Weltkrieg* (Stuttgart, 1966); Hans Umbreit, *Der Militärbefehlshaber in Frankreich 1940-1944* (Boppard, 1968).

14. Hans G. Adler, *Der verwaltete Mensch. Studien zur Deportation der Juden aus Deutschland* (Tübingen, 1974); Falk Pingel, *Häftlinge unter SS-Herrschaft. Widerstand, Selbstbehauptung und Vernichtung im Konzentrationslager* (Hamburg, 1978); Christian Streit, *Keine Kameraden. Die Wehrmacht und die sowjetischen Kriegsgefangenen 1941-1945* (Stuttgart, 1978).

15. Representative of this approach: Dietrich Eichholtz et al. (eds.), *Faschismus-Forschung: Positionen, Probleme, Polemik* (Berlin, 1980); critical appraisals of the approach: Olaf Groehler, "Der Holocaust in der Geschichtsschreibung der DDR," in Herbert and Groehler, *Zweierlei Bewältigung*, pp. 29-40; Jürgen Danyel, *Die geteilte Vergangenheit: zum Umgang mit Nationalsozialismus und Widerstand in beiden deutschen Staaten* (Berlin, 1995). The problematic nature of this approach is especially clear in Reinhard Kühnl, *Der deutsche Faschismus in Quellen und Dokumenten* (Köln, 1977), pp. 283f.

16. *Totalitarismus und Faschismus: Eine wissenschaftliche und politische Begriffskontroverse. Kolloquium des Instituts für Zeitgeschichte* (Munich, 1980); Kershaw, *The Nazi Dictatorship*, pp. 43-87.

17. Raul Hilberg, *The Destruction of the European Jews* (Chicago, 1961); Helmut Krausnick, Hans-Heinrich Wilhelm, *Die Truppe des Weltanschauungskrieges: Die Einsatzgruppen der Sicherheitspolizei und des SD 1938-1942* (Stuttgart, 1981).

18. Martin Broszat, *The Hitler State: The Foundation and Development of the Internal Structure of the Third Reich* (London, 1981); Hans Mommsen, "Nationalsozialismus," in *Sowjetsystem und demokratische Gesellschaft*, Vol. 4 (Freiburg, 1971), pp. 695-713; idem, "Der Nationalsozialismus: Kumulative Radikalisierung und Selbstzerstörung des Regimes," in *Meyers Enzyklopädisches Wörterbuch* (Stuttgart, 1976), pp. 785-790; idem, "Ausnahmezustand als Herrschaftstechnik des NS-Regimes," in Manfred Funke (ed.), *Hitler, Deutschland und die Mächte. Materialien zur Außenpolitik im Dritten Reich* (Düsseldorf, 1976), pp. 30-45; Karl A. Schleunes, *The Twisted Road to Auschwitz. Nazi Policy toward German Jews 1933-1939* (London, 1972); Adam, *Judenpolitik*.

19. Martin Broszat, "Hitler und die Genesis der 'Endlösung.' Aus Anlaß der Thesen von David Irving," in *VfZ* 25 (1977): 739-775; Christopher Browning, "Zur Genesis der 'Endlösung.' Eine Antwort an Martin Broszat," in *VfZ* 29 (1981): 97-101; Hans Mommsen, "The Realization of the Unthinkable," in idem, *From Weimar to Auschwitz* (Princeton, 1991).

20. Eberhard Jäckel and Jürgen Rohwer (eds.), *Der Mord an den Juden im Zweiten Weltkrieg. Entschlußbildung und Verwirklichung* (Stuttgart, 1984); for a summary presentation, see Kershaw, *The Nazi Dictatorship*.

21. Wolfgang Scheffler, Helge Grabitz, *Der Ghetto-Aufstand Warschau 1943 aus der Sicht der Täter und Opfer in Aussagen vor deutschen Gerichten* (Munich,

1993); Adalbert Rückerl, *NS-Verbrechen vor Gericht. Versuch einer Vergangenheitsbewältigung* (Heidelberg, 1984); Adelheid L. Rüter-Ehlermann, *Justiz und NS-Verbrechen: Sammlung deutscher Strafurteile wegen nationalsozialistischer Tötungsverbrechen, 1945-1966*, revised by Rüter-Ehlermann, C. F. Rüter et al., Amsterdam 1968-1976ff.

22. Ernst Nolte, *Der europäische Bürgerkrieg 1917-1945. Nationalsozialismus und Bolschewismus* (Frankfurt a.M./Berlin, 1987); *"Historikerstreit"*. *Die Dokumentation der Kontroverse um die Einzigartigkeit der nationalsozialistischen Judenvernichtung* (Munich, 1987); also Richard J. Evans, *In Hitler's Shadow: West German Historians and the Attempt to Escape from the Nazi Past* (New York, 1989); Hans-Ulrich Wehler, *Entsorgung der deutschen Vergangenheit? Ein polemischer Essay zum "Historikerstreit"* (Munich, 1988).

23. Martin Broszat et al. (eds.), *Bayern in der NS-Zeit*, 6 vols., (Munich/Vienna, 1977-1983); Lutz Niethammer (ed.), *Lebensgeschichte und Sozialkultur im Ruhrgebiet 1930 bis 1960*, 3 vols., (Bonn/Berlin, 1983-1985); in Peukert's influential book, the comparison of the persecution of the Jews to the persecution of other groups of victims is presented only peripherally, as Peukert himself later conceded: Detlev Peukert, *Inside Nazi Germany: Conformity, Opposition and Racism in Everyday Life* (New Haven, 1987); Detlev Peukert, Jürgen Reulecke (eds.), *Die Reihen fast geschlossen: Beiträge zur Geschichte des Alltags unterm Nationalsozialismus* (Wuppertal, 1981).

24. For example, Hans-Walter Schmuhl, *Rassenhygiene, Nationalsozialismus, Euthanasie. Von der Verhütung zur Vernichtung "lebensunwerten Lebens", 1890-1945* (Göttingen, 1987); Michael Zimmermann, *Verfolgt, vertrieben, vernichtet. Die nationalsozialistische Vernichtungspolitik gegen Sinti und Roma* (Essen, 1989); Burkhard Jellonek, *Homosexuelle unter dem Hakenkreuz. Die Verfolgung der Homosexuellen im Dritten Reich* (Paderborn, 1990); Ulrich Herbert, *Hitler's Foreign Worker Enforced Foreign Labor in Germany under the Third Reich* (Cambridge, 1997); Herbert, *A History of Foreign Labor in Germany, 1880-1980* (Ann Arbor, 1990); Wolfgang Ayaß, *"Asoziale" im Nationalsozialismus* (Stuttgart, 1995).

25. Ulrich Herbert, "Traditionen des Rassismus," in idem, *Arbeit, Volkstum, Weltanschauung*, pp. 11-30; Hans-Walter Schmuhl, "Rassismus unter den Bedingungen charismatischer Herrschaft. Zum Übergang von der Verfolgung zur Vernichtung gesellschaftlicher Minderheiten im Dritten Reich," in Karl Dietrich Bracher, Manfred Funke, Hans-Adolf Jacobsen (eds.), *Deutschland 1933-1945. Neue Studien zur nationalsozialistischen Herrschaft* (Vol. 23 of *Bonner Schriften zur Politik und Zeitgeschichte*) (Düsseldorf, 1992), pp. 182-197; Michael Burleigh, Wolfgang Wippermann, *The Racial State: Germany 1933-1945* (Cambridge, 1991).

26. Benz (ed.), *Dimension des Völkermords*; Dieter Pohl, "Nationalsozialistischer Judenmord als Problem von osteuropäischer Geschichte und Osteuropa-Geschichtsschreibung," in *Jahrbücher für die Geschichte Osteuropas* 60 (1992): 96-119.

27. Scheffler, Grabitz, *Ghetto-Aufstand*; Helge Grabitz, Wolfgang Scheffler, *Letzte Spuren. Ghetto Warschau—SS-Arbeitslager Trawniki—Aktion Erntefest. Fotos und Dokumente über Opfer des Endlösungswahns im Spiegel der historischen Ereignisse* (Berlin, 1988); an overview can be found in Klaus Bästlein, Helge Grabitz, Johannes Tuchel (eds.), *Die Normalität des Verbrechens. Bilanz und Perspektiven zu den nationalsozialistischen Gewaltverbrechen. Festschrift für Wolfgang Scheffler zum 65. Geburtstag* (Berlin, 1994).

28. Götz Aly et al. (eds.), *Beiträge zur nationalsozialistischen Gesundheits- und Sozialpolitik*, Berlin 1985ff.

29. Götz Aly and Susanne Heim, *Vordenker der Vernichtung. Auschwitz und die deutschen Pläne für eine neue europäische Ordnung* (Hamburg, 1991; Frankfurt a.M., 1994); Aly and Heim, *Sozialpolitik und Judenvernichtung. Gibt es eine Ökonomie der Endlösung?*, Vol. 5 of *Beiträge zur nationalsozialistischen Gesundheits- und Sozialpolitik* (Berlin, 1987); Aly and Heim, *Bevölkerungsstruktur und Massenmord. Neue Dokumente zur deutschen Politik der Jahre 1938 bis 1945*, Vol. 9 of *Beiträge zur nationalsozialistischen Gesundheits- und Sozialpolitik* (Berlin, 1991); See also similar arguments by Zygmunt Baumann, *Modernity and the Holocaust* (Cambridge, 1989).

30. For criticism of Aly's and Heim's approach, see the contributions in Wolfgang Schneider (ed.), *Vernichtungspolitik. Eine Debatte über den Zusammenhang von Sozialpolitik und Genozid im nationalsozialistischen Deutschland* (Hamburg, 1991); in that volume, see Christopher R. Browning: "Vernichtung und Arbeit. Zur Fraktionierung der planenden deutschen Intelligenz im besetzten Polen," pp. 37-52; Ulrich Herbert: "Racism and Rational Calculation. The Role of 'Utilitarian' Strategies of Legitimation in the National Socialist 'Weltanschauung,'" in *Yad Vashem Studies* XXIV (1994): 131-147; also Dan Diner, "Rassistisches Völkerrecht. Elemente einer nationalsozialistischen Weltordnung," in *VfZ* 37 (1989): 23-56; and Norbert Frei, "Wie modern war der Nationalsozialismus?," in *GuG* 19 (1993): 367-505.

31. Götz Aly: *"Endlösung". Völkerverschiebung und der Mord an den europäischen Juden* (Frankfurt a.M., 1995); see also Alys contribution in this volume.

32. See on this point, Hans Safrian, *Die Eichmann-Männer* (Vienna/Zürich, 1993).

33. Czeslaw Madajczyk (ed.), *Vom Generalplan Ost zum Generalsiedlungsplan* (Munich, 1994); Mechthild Rössler, Sabine Schleiermacher (eds.), *Der "Generalplan Ost". Hauptlinien der nationalsozialistischen Planungs- und Vernichtungspolitik* (Berlin, 1993); Bruno Wasser, *Himmlers Raumplanung im Osten. Der Generalplan Ost in Polen 1940-1944* (Basel/Berlin/Boston, 1993); on the beginning of "ethnic reordering" [*Volksverschiebung*] as a defining moment in setting genocide in motion, see Hans Mommsen, "Umvolkungspläne des Nationalsozialismus und der Holocaust," in Bästlein et al. (eds.), *Die Normalität des Verbrechens*, pp. 68-84.

34. Michael Zimmermann, *Rassenutopie und Genozid. Die nationalsozialistische "Lösung der Zigeunerfrage"* (Hamburg, 1996); see Zimmermann's contribution in this volume.

35. Dieter Pohl, *Nationalsozialistische Judenverfolgung in Ostgalizien, 1941-1944. Organisation und Durchführung eines staatlichen Massenverbrechens* (Munich, 1996); idem, *Von der "Judenpolitik" zum Judenmord. Der Distrikt Lublin des Generalgouvernements 1939-1944* (Frankfurt a.M., 1993); Thomas Sandkühler, *"Endlösung" in Galizien. Der Judenmord in Ostpolen und die Rettungsinitiativen von Berthold Beitz, 1941 bis 1944* (Bonn, 1996); Walter Manoschek, *"Serbien ist judenfrei". Militärische Besatzungspolitik und Judenvernichtung in Serbien 1941/1942*, Vol. 38 of *Schriftenreihe des Militärgeschichtlichen Forschungsamtes* (Munich, 1995); Christian Gerlach, *Die deutsche Wirtschafts- und Vernichtungspolitik in Weißrußland 1941-44*, published 1998; see also the contribution of the authors in this volume.

36. Christopher Browning, *Ordinary Men: Reserve Police Battalion 101 and the Final Solution in Poland* (New York, 1992); see the collected individual contributions by Browning, *Fateful Month: Essays on the Emergence of the Final*

Solution (New York, 1985); idem, *The Path to Genocide. Essays on Launching the Final Solution* (Cambridge, 1992).

37. Goldhagen, *Hitlers willige Vollstrecker*, pp. 285-312.

38. That is effectively accomplished only rarely even in non-German scholarship; most treatments approach the issue from the point of view either of the perpetrators or the victims. See as an exception to this rule, Saul Friedländer: *Nazi Germany and the Jews: The Years of Persecution, 1933-1939*, Vol. 1 (New York, 1997).

39. Shulamit Volkov, *Jüdisches Leben und Antisemitismus im 19. und 20. Jahrhundert* (Munich, 1990); idem; *Die Juden in Deutschland 1780-1918* (Munich, 1994); Werner Jochmann, *Gesellschaftskrise und Judenfeindschaft in Deutschland 1870-1945* (Hamburg, 1988); Uwe Lohalm, *Völkischer Radikalismus: Die Geschichte des Deutschvölkischen Schutz- und Trutzbundes, 1919-1923* (Hamburg, 1970); Helmut Berding, *Moderner Antisemitismus in Deutschland* (Frankfurt a.M., 1988).

40. Gerhard Paul, *Aufstand der Bilder: Die NS-Propaganda vor 1933* (Bonn, 1992), pp. 85-88, 144f., 236-239.

41. Hans Mommsen, *The Rise and Fall of Weimar Democracy* (Chapel Hill, 1996); Martin Broszat: *Hitler and the collapse of Weimar Germany* (Leamington Spa, 1987).

42. Friedländer, *Nazi Germany and The Jews*; Moshe Zimmermann, *Die deutschen Juden 1914-1945* (Munich, 1997); pp. 9-45; Daniel L. Niewyk, *The Jews in Weimar Germany* (Louisiana, 1980); idem, "Solving the 'Jewish Problem': Continuity and Change in German Antisemitism, 1871-1945," in *Leo Baeck Year Book 35* (1990): 335-370; for a general survey, see Heinrich August Winkler, "Die deutsche Gesellschaft der Weimarer Republik und der Antisemitismus," in Bernd Martin and Ernst Schulin (eds.), *Die Juden als Minderheit in der Geschichte* (Munich, 1981), pp. 271-289; Trude Maurer, "Die Juden in der Weimarer Republik," in Dirk Blasius and Dan Diner (eds.), *Zerbrochene Geschichte. Leben und Selbstverständnis der Juden in Deutschland* (Frankfurt a.M., 1991); see for a current treatment A. Kauders, *German Politics and the Jews—Düsseldorf and Nürnberg 1910-1933* (Oxford, 1996).

43. Here I am relying on conclusions in Dirk Walter, *Antisemitische Kriminalität und Gewalt Juden Feindschaft in der Weimarer Republik* (Bonn, 1998).

44. Norman Cohn, *Warrant for Genocide: The Myth of the Jewish World-conspiracy and the Protocols of the Elders of Zion* (Harmondsworth 1970; London 1996).

45. There are no in-depth studies on the role of antisemitism in NSDAP before and after 1933; Peter Pulzer, *The Rise of Political Anti-Semitism in Germany and Austria* (Cambridge, Mass., 1988).

46. See Werner Jochmann, "Die Ausbreitung des Antisemitismus in Deutschland 1914-1923," in Jochmann, *Gesellschaftskrise und Judenfeindschaft in Deutschland* (Hamburg, 1988), pp. 99-170; Otto D. Kulka and P.R. Mendes-Flohr (eds.), *Judaism and Christianity under the Impact of National Socialism* (Jerusalem, 1987); Kurt Nowak and Gérard Raulet (eds.), *Protestantismus und Antisemitismus in der Weimarer Republik* (Frankfurt/New York, 1994); Eberhard Röhm and Jörg Thierfelder, *Juden—Christen—Deutsche*, Vol. 1: 1933-1945 (Stuttgart, 1990).

47. Werner Jochmann, "Der Antisemitismus und seine Bedeutung für den Untergang der Weimarer Republik," in Jochmann, *Gesellschaftskrise*, pp. 171-194.

48. Merely as an example Daniel Fryman (i.e., Heinrich Claß): *Wenn ich der Kaiser wär—Politische Wahrheiten und Notwendigkeiten* (Leipzig, 1912).

49. For details, see Walter, *Antisemitische Kriminalität*.

50. See Ted Harrison, "Der 'Alte Kämpfer' Graf Helldorff im Widerstand," in *VfZ* 3 (1997): 385-424, especially 391f.

51. "Fantastic Middle Ages: 'We'—the threatened Jews. I actually feel more shame than fear—shame for Germany. I have really always felt myself to be German. And I have always imagined that the twentieth century and central Europe would be different from the fourteenth century and Romania. Wrong." Victor Klemperer: *I Will Bear Witness: The Diaries of Victor Klemperer* (New York, 1998); Entry of 30 March 1933.

52. For example the series of articles on "Grotesque or Mob Anti-Semitism" by Arnold Zweig in *Weltbühne*, No. 15, 1919ff., in which Zweig writes that, in the eyes of antisemites, a Jew is an "amusing fairy-tale animal" and the Aryan Siegfried will not rest until "the Judaized world has been cured by the German spirit. Simply stated: we are dealing with the eternal puberty fantasies of immature, pot-bellied fans of [Felix] Dahn and Wagner who achieve ecstasy by doing battle with bogey-men of their own creation, thus distorting their very natures into something repulsive." Here No. 15 (1919): 384f.

53. David Bankier, *The Germans and the Final Solution: Public Opinion under Nazism*, (Oxford, 1992); for the earlier opposing view, see Daniel L. Niewyk, *Socialist, Anti-Semite and Jew* (Baton Rouge, 1971).

54. Ulrich Herbert, "Arbeiterschaft im 'Dritten Reich'," in idem, *Arbeit, Volkstum, Weltanschauung*, pp. 79-119.

55. *Deutschland-Berichte der Sozialdemokratischen Partei Deutschland* (Frankfurt a.M., 1980), "Sopade-Berichte," for example December 1938.

56. Regarding the issue in general, the contributions in Wolfgang Benz (ed.), *Die Juden in Deutschland, 1933-1945. Leben unter nationalsozialistischer Herrschaft* (Munich, 1988); Ursula Büttner (ed.), *Die Deutschen und die Judenverfolgung im Dritten Reich* (Hamburg, 1992); Ian Kershaw, "The Persecution of the Jews and German Popular Opinion in the Third Reich," in *Leo Baeck Institute Year Book* 26 (1981): 261-289; idem, "Antisemitismus und Volksmeinung. Reaktionen auf die Judenverfolgungen," in *Bayern in der NS-Zeit*, Martin Broszat et al. (eds.), Vol. 2 (Munich, 1979), pp. 281-348.

57. Hans-Walter Schmuhl, *Rassenhygiene, Nationalsozialismus, Euthanasie. Von der Verhütung zur Vernichtung "lebensunwerten Lebens", 1890-1945*, Göttingen, pp. 211ff; Henry Friedlander, *The Origins of Nazi Genocide: From Euthanasia to the Final Solution* (Chapel Hill, 1995).

58. Friedländer, *Nazi Germany and The Jews*, pp. 269-305; Ulrich Herbert, "Von der 'Reichskristallnacht' zum 'Holocaust.' Der 9. November und das Ende des 'Radauantisemitismus'," in Herbert, *Arbeit, Volkstum, Weltanschauung*, pp. 137-156; Herbert Graml, *Antisemitism in the Third Reich* (Oxford, 1992).

59. Ulrich Herbert, *Best. Biographische Studien über Radikalismus, Weltanschauung und Vernunft, 1903-1989* (Bonn, 1996); Herbert, "'Generation der Sachlichkeit'. Die Völkische Studentenbewegung der frühen zwanziger Jahre," in Herbert, *Arbeit, Volkstum, Weltanschauung*, pp. 31-58; regarding the following, see Michael Grüttner, *Studenten im Dritten Reich* (Paderborn, 1995).

60. See Herbert, *Best*, pp. 68f. Regarding the constitutional battles among the students, see Wolfgang Zorn, "Die politische Entwicklung des deutschen Studententums 1918-1931," in Kurt Stephanson et al. (eds.), *Darstellung und Quellen*

zur Geschichte der deutschen Einheitsbewegung im neunzehnten und zwanzig-sten Jahrhunderts, Vol. 5 (Heidelberg, 1965), pp. 223-307.

61. Regarding the following, Herbert, *Best*, pp. 191ff; Herbert, "Weltanschau-ungseliten. Ideologische Legitimation und politische Praxis der Führungs-gruppe der nationalsozialistischen Sicherheitspolizei," *Potsdamer Bulletin für zeithistorische Studien* 9 (1997): 4-18; Michael Wildt (ed.), *Die Judenpolitik des SD, 1935-1939* (Munich, 1995).

62. On this point, see Jens Banach, *Heydrichs Elite. Das Führerkorps der Sicher-heitspolizei und des SD 1936-1945* (Paderborn, 1998); this study is based on an evaluation of the largest sampling to date.

63. Hermann Lübbe, "Rationalität und Irrationalität des Völkermordes," in Hanno Loewy (ed.), *Holocaust. Die Grenzen des Verstehens. Eine Debatte über die Besetzung der Geschichte* (Reinbek, 1992), pp. 83-92; Herbert, *Best*, pp. 196ff.

64. Frank Bajohr, *"Arisierung" in Hamburg. Die Verdrängung der jüdischen Unternehmer 1933-45* (Hamburg, 1997).

65. Peter Witte, "Zwei Entscheidungen in der 'Endlösung der Judenfrage': Depor-tation nach Lodz und Vernichtung in Chelmno," in *Theresienstädter Studien und Dokumente 1995*, pp. 38-68.

66. Walter Manoschek (ed.), *"Es gibt nur eines für das Judentum: Vernichtung." Das Judenbild in deutschen Soldatenbriefen* (Hamburg, 1995); Hans Momm-sen, "Was haben die Deutschen vom Völkermord an den Juden gewußt?," in Walter H. Pehle (ed.), *November 1938: from 'Reichskristallnacht' to Genocide* (New York, 1991); Walter Laqueur, *The Terrible Secret: Suppression of the Truth about Hitler's "Final Solution"* (Boston, 1980); for an individual exam-ple, see Herbert and Sibylle Obenaus (eds.), *Schreiben, wie es wirklich war. Die Aufzeichnungen Karl Dürkefäldens aus der Zeit des Nationalsozialismus* (Hanover, 1985).

67. See Christoph Dieckmann's article in this volume, as well as Dieckmann, "Das Getto und das Konzentrationslager in Kaunas 1941-1944," in Ulrich Herbert, Karin Orth, and Christoph Dieckmann (eds.), *Die nationalsozialistischen Konzentrationslager—Entwicklung und Struktur* (Göttingen, 1998).

68. See the descriptions and photographs of these pogroms in Ernst Klee, Willi Dressen, and Volker Riess (eds.), *"The Good Old Days": The Holocaust as Seen by its Perpetrators and Bystanders* (New York, 1991).

69. See the debate in Jäckel and Rohwer, *Der Mord an den Juden*; Peter Longerich, "Vom Massenmord zur 'Endlösung'. Die Erschießung von jüdischen Zivilisten in den ersten Monaten des Ostfeldzuges im Kontext des nationalsozialistischen Judenmords," in Bernd Wegner (ed.), *Zwei Wege nach Moskau. Vom Hitler-Stalin-Pakt zum "Unternehmen Barbarossa"* (Munich, 1991); Ralf Ogorreck, *Die Einsatzgruppen und die "Genesis der Endlösung"* (Berlin, 1996).

70. On Himmler's trip, see Ogorreck, *Einsatzgruppen*, pp. 176-209; Aly, *Endlö-sung*, p. 78.

71. On the subject of food shortages, see the contributions by Dieckmann and Ger-lach in this volume; also Aly, *Endlösung*, pp. 165f; for a broad treatment of National Socialist food policy, though with emphasis on the prewar period, see Gustavo Corni and Horst Gies, *Brot, Butter, Kanonen. Die Ernährungswis-senschaft in Deutschland unter der Diktatur Hitlers* (Weinheim, 1996).

72. Jan-Philipp Reemtsma, "Individuelle und kollektive Tötungsbereitschaft," lec-ture of 20 March 1997 at the conference "Neuere Tendenzen der Holocaust-forschung," at the Kulturwissenschaftliches Institut in Essen.

73. See the contributions by Gerlach and Dieckmann in this volume, along with Rolf-Dieter Müller's studies in *Germany and the Second World War*, edited by the Office of Military Research (Oxford, 1990-1995); see also the references concerning *Generalplan Ost* in note 33.

74. Pohl, *Judenverfolgung in Ostgalizien*, pp. 144ff; Sandkühler, *"Endlösung" in Galizien*, pp. 150ff.

75. See Ulrich Herbert, "Labor and Extermination: Economic Interests and the Primacy of "Weltanschauung" in National Socialism," in *Past and Present* 138 (1993): 144-195; Aly, *Endlösung*, pp. 317-357.

76. Pohl, *Judenverfolgung in Ostgalizien*, pp. 154ff; Sandkühler, *"Endlösung" in Galizien*, pp. 155ff.

77. Aly, *Endlösung*, pp. 358 ff.

78. Ludolf Herbst, *Das nationalsozialistische Deutschland 1933 bis 1945. Die Entfesselung der Gewalt: Rassismus und Krieg* (Frankfurt a.M., 1996), pp. 378f.

79. Kurt Pätzold: "Die Wannsee-Konferenz—zu ihrem Platz in der Geschichte der Judenvernichtung," in Werner Röhr (ed.), *Faschismus und Rassismus: Kontroversen um Ideologie und Opfer* (Berlin, 1992), pp. 257-290; Kurt Pätzoldt and Erika Schwarz, *Tagesordnung: Judenmord. Die Wannsee-Konferenz am 20. Januar 1942* (Berlin, 1992); Götz Aly and Susanne Heim, *Vordenker der Vernichtung. Auschwitz und die deutschen Pläne für eine europäische Ordnung* (Hamburg, 1991).

80. Eberhard Jäckel, "'Die Konferenz am Wannsee. Wo Heydrich seine Ermächtigung bekanntgab'—Der Holocaust war längst im Gange," in *Die Zeit*, 17 January 1992, p. 33.

81. See Sandkühler's contribution to this volume.

82. This was especially the case with work on "Durchgangsstraße IV" (DG IV); Sandkühler, *"Endlösung" in Galizien*, pp. 154-165; Pohl, *Judenverfolgung in Ostgalizien*, pp. 165-174, 338-344.

83. Christian Gerlach, "Die Wannsee- Konferenz, das Schicksal der deutschen Juden und Hitlers politische Grundsatzentscheidung, alle Juden Europas zu ermorden," in *Werkstatt Geschichte* 18 (1997): 7-44; See my criticism: "Eine 'Führerentscheidung' zur 'Endlösung.' Neue Ansätze in einer alten Diskussion," in *Neue Zürcher Zeitung*, 14 March 1998, p. 69; also Gerlach's reply in *Krieg. Ernährung, Völkermord. Forschungen zur deutschen Vernichtungspolitik im Zweiten Weltkrieg* (Hamburg, 1998), pp. 258-300.

84. Christoph Dipper, "Der deutsche Widerstand und die Juden," in *GG* 9 (1983): 349-380.

– Chapter 2 –

"JEWISH RESETTLEMENT"
Reflections on the Political Prehistory
of the Holocaust

Götz Aly

O ne of the great achievements of historians after the Second
World War is that in the face of the German crimes they have
adopted the perspective of the victims.[1] Therefore, the view from
the perpetrator's perspective must be irritating. However, the question of the decision-making process leading to the Holocaust forces
us into the interior perspective of the administrators and planners.
Only then can we see the extent to which common state-bureau-
cratic procedures were applicable to the so-called "Final Solution
of the Jewish Question" (Endlösung der Judenfrage). Most of these
procedures do not seem so remote to us as to make them inde-
scribable by ordinary historiographical means.

The findings of the investigation into the German resettlement
policy between September 1939 and September 1941, presented
here in condensed form, allow us to comprehend more precisely the
prolonged formative processes creating the political will that eventually resulted in the murder of the European Jews. Those processes
involve the "interactions" (Wechselwirkungen)—described as such
quite early by Eichmann—of a dual policy. On one hand, the policy was aimed at the deportation of the Jews to the periphery of

German dominion. On the other hand, it was both personally and institutionally—and thus apart from all programs and plans—closely tied to the daily politics of the "Home into the Reich" (*Heim ins Reich*) program for more than 500,000 ethnic Germans. The analytical reconstruction of the settlement of one group and the expropriation, ghettoization, and deportation of the other is indispensable for those who take a closer look at the dynamics forming the political will that preceded the decisions—or perhaps one could better speak of alignments—for genocide. With that, however, we have by no means explained everything. It also does not clarify how, in retrospect, the events of the resettlement ought to be weighted in relation to other factors. Presumably, it was also impossible for the actors to discern the overlapping of prejudice, political program, practical benefits, and self-inflicted military and economic predicaments, and finally, the unleashed homicidal urges.

The inner logic of the political processes in the National Socialist state evolved in the tension of vast plans geared toward change and expansion, unstable intermediary solutions, and, measured against the objectives, extremely limited resources. This constellation precipitated the pressure of expectations and the necessity for action. However, the framework for decisions was crucially changed and expanded in two respects. On the one hand, the racist value system, enforced by the state and widely accepted by German society, and the militaristic imperial expansion, deliberately escalated from the outset, made it possible to shift blame for any problems to "inferior" ethnicities or groups. On the other hand, this value system allowed a "project-based" elimination of topical problems by means of further conquests. The possibility of a great, and in its totalitarian perfection also utopian, solution (in retrospect always illusory) made it possible both to do without compromises as well as to operate without establishing any fixed priorities.

Political decisions are generally neither made on one day nor implemented in a straight line. They are also not positively determinate. What remains decisive for the result is which options prove feasible or unfeasible during the experimental phase of trial and error. Viewed in this way, the course of the formation of political will—even under the conditions of the Nazi dictatorship—can be understood as a more or less open process: The transitions between schemes, pre-emptory actions and decisions are always malleable; the boundaries between the numerous participating and interested institutions, between the various administrative levels, remain porous. There was no single order by Hitler for genocide; there is only the mistaken assumption of later analysts that the monstrous deed must have been decided upon in a completely extraordinary way.[2]

Jewish Policy and the SD

The "Guidelines for the Jewish Question" (*Richtlinien zur Judenfrage*) were issued by Heydrich on 21 September 1939 for the German-occupied part of Poland. Aimed at expropriating approximately two million people and forming "Jewish reservations" (*Judenreservate*), they stated: "It goes without saying that the impending tasks cannot be delineated from here in all their detail"; rather the guidelines "aimed simultaneously at encouraging the commanders of the *Einsatzgruppen* to entertain practical considerations."[3] Every active participant was supposed to formulate his own concrete practices and thus contribute to adjustments of the continuously provisional instructions for action. Moreover, Heydrich always distinguished between a "short-term plan" (*Nahplan*) and a "long-term plan" (*Fernplan*): This way the practitioners of Jewish policy could act with the assurance that their improvisations were provisional elements of a "planned comprehensive scheme," a "Final Solution."

Of course, the high degree of practical liberties in the implementation of anti-Jewish state terror also applied for the local command posts of the Gestapo and the SD. The second volume of Victor Klemperer's diaries reveals the particular cruelty of the responsible figures in Dresden. As early as 1936 in the protocol of the annual "Training Session of Experts on Jewish Affairs" (*Schulungstagung der Judenreferenten*), the Dresdeners received honorable mention among the regional offices—in contrast to Munich: "Section II Dresden: Here the Jews are not treated as a small matter but have a major division assigned to them. The branch offices also work very well, their staff is first-class."[4]

In part, the functionaries of the *Führerstaat* cultivated an open, cooperative leadership style. For example, the lecturers of the SS training school for SS-officer candidats (SS-*Junkerschule*) in Bad Tölz abandoned overly simplistic indoctrination in favor of challenging the intellectual and undoubtedly destructive inventiveness of each individual graduate. In the spring of 1937, some topics among the choices of final exam questions were: "Which measures would you take in order to check and prove the Jewish ancestry of a person?"; "Compile a report for the entire Reich on 'Jews in the livestock trade' and make your own proposals to rectify the evils described"; or "How do I envision the solution of the Jewish question?"[5] All of these issues were still undecided then, but they preoccupied those who had formulated the questions.

Among the members of the SD's Jewish Department II/112 (Surveillance of Ideological Opponents/Jewry) in the Berlin headquarters of the SD were, from quite early on, men like Adolf Eichmann, Herbert Hagen, and Theodor Dannecker. Subsequently, after several re-organizations of the security apparatus, they became representatives of the bureaucracy of death; the bureaucratic abbreviation then read: RSHA (Reich Security Main Office) IVB4. As early as May 1934, one of these SD men warned that the long-term goal of "complete emigration" might turn into a "standstill of Jewish deportation" and thus into a "permanent condition." In order to prevent this, it was imperative to restrict the options of existence for the Jews, to reinforce their fear and the feeling of hopelessness, "even by means of the otherwise objectionable street methods," that is, with the help of state-administered doses of "popular wrath." "Germany must be a country without a future for them," the expert concluded his strategic point.[6]

In the diary entries of Klemperer in the summer of 1935 the same topic is portrayed as follows: "I believe I have already written that a policeman asked me recently for how long I have been 'naturalized'; they had to be informed about the non-Aryans in their municipality. I swear I expect that one day they will set fire to my little house or beat me to death. We said farewell to the Blumenfelds between the boxes in their already emptied apartment ..."[7] Among the assignments of the SD Department "Jewry" was also the surveillance and intimidation of those "Aryans" who put up resistance against or at least exhibited passivity toward antisemitism. This included the "clerically indoctrinated Catholic population in the country," or those Protestants who half-openly observed "with shame and anguish" that "there are parish councils refusing to baptize Jews."[8]

The lords of the SD did everything possible to impede Jewish organizations' freedom of action. They controlled the selection of chairmen for the "orientation of the Jewry"; they strove for the establishment of an "intellectual ghetto"; early on they began to finance the apparatus of persecution (and later, the machinery of extermination) with funds extorted from the victims—"through a contribution to be paid by every Jew."[9] Theodor Dannecker, who later organized the deportation of the French, Greek, and Hungarian Jews, demanded in 1937 on the occasion of a training session of regionally responsible experts on Jewish affairs: "Never give them a minute's rest, always keep the leading Jews on tenterhooks through constant reprimands."[10] Adolf Eichmann reinforced: "In most cases you will only be successful if you play the Jews against each other in a Jewish-political way."[11]

Nevertheless, this was never enough for the SD's experts on Jewish affairs. "So far, a systematic view of the work has been lacking," they complained internally in 1937, and there was supposedly a danger of "losing sight of the larger direction" in the face of numerous details. They grumbled about the fact that state bids were still tendered to Jewish firms; that the anti-Jewish propaganda of the NSDAP after 1935 had "almost completely petered out"; and that party orators were lacking in specific training.[12] They perceived themselves as the pioneers of systematic segregation, whether it be the brainchild of the exact individual registration of German Jews by means of a census, the criminalization of "race defilement" (*Rassenschande*) or—long before the Swiss government asked for it—the special marking of Jewish passports and finally the visual stigmatization of the persecuted persons themselves. This measure was considered by the SD—along with graphic sketches and cost estimates—as early as 1938, a full three years before the introduction of the Jewish badge in Germany. In occupied Poland, beginning in the autumn of 1939 Jews were already forced to wear white arm badges with the Star of David.

The experts on Jewish affairs in the SD coordinated, checked, altered, alleviated or advocated ideas aimed at the escalation of antisemitic policies issued by other authorities, so that "as soon as possible a uniform direction on the Jewish question will be established in the various ministries." They reported to the worried minister of economics how the increased discrimination was directly affecting the easing of the foreign boycott; for reasons of survival, it was forcing the German Jews—whom they considered in this respect as a "pawn" (*Faustpfand*)—"to intervene with the responsible American Jews for a change of course."[13]

In 1938 Klemperer made a note of the individual repercussions of the state terror: "Again greatly increased antisemitism. I have written to Blumenfelds about the surtax on Jewish property. In addition, prohibition of certain trades, yellow registration card at health spas. The *Weltanschauung* now also rages scientifically. In Munich an academic society for research into Jewry is convening."[14] In the report of the SD for the same year all of these details appear, substantiated and deliberately annotated: "In summary it can be noted that the Jews ... are thus finally excluded from all spheres of German communal life."[15] Klemperer: "Incredibly deep loneliness."[16]

Before this backdrop, it is only consistent that Göring in his internal
speech of 6 December 1938 emphasized the "good aspect" of the
November pogroms (*Reichskristallnacht*). He perceived in this the
fact that "the entire question of emigration has become acute, the
other peoples realize: The Jew cannot live in Germany."[17]

War and Resettlement

As much as anti-Jewish policy since 1933 was already directed
toward expulsion and, parallel to this, toward social strangulation
and annihilation of civic existence, nevertheless the most important
prerequisites in the Holocaust were only created during the war. To
start with, the German leadership destroyed all possibilities of
forced emigration favored until then—an option that had at any
rate been problematic in foreign political terms. It was replaced by
plans of deportation of the German, and then the European, Jews
to an actual or only imagined periphery of the rapidly expanding
German empire. The ideas of a Jewish reservation (*Judenreservat*)
around Lublin, subsequently the Madagascar deportation plan,
and soon thereafter the *Ostraumlösung*—projecting resettlement
to the icy northeast of the Soviet Union—followed within the next
eighteen months.

At the same time, due to the conquest of ever more countries,
more and more Jews came under German rule. After the conquest
and division of Poland, Jews no longer numbered in the hundreds of
thousands but in the millions. After the campaign against France
there were four million Jews in the German-occupied countries of
Europe. In late autumn of 1940, Eichmann noted under the heading
"Final Solution of the Jewish question" 5.8 million Jews who were
supposed to be evacuated from the "*Lebensraum* of the German
people."[18] The term *Lebensraum* encompassed more than the occupied countries already mentioned in the Madagascar plan: it implied
all continental European Jews west of the Soviet-German demarcation line including those living in the French colonies of Tunisia,
Algeria, and Morocco. At the start of the campaign against the Soviet
Union in the summer of 1941, Eichmann counted 11 million Jews in
all of Europe whom he now considered for the "Final Solution."[19]

Far beyond what was achieved during the first six years of the
Nazi dictatorship, the war fostered an atmosphere of secrecy,
atomized the Germans, and increasingly destroyed their clearly
existing commitments to religious and judicial traditions. Because
foreign political considerations also hardly weighed in any more, a

situation arose that in the perpetrator's language was called a "unique opportunity."[20]

A close associate of Heydrich's justified the mass deportation of one million people from the occupied west of Poland, planned for 1941, thus: It was necessary to carry out "the action" now, "because during the war the opportunity" presents itself "to proceed relatively rigorously without consideration for world opinion."[21] Using the same argument, Hitler had already in 1935 postponed the murder of the mentally handicapped to the time of a possible war. Eventually, Goebbels made a note in March of 1942 on the operation of the first gas chambers: "... of the Jews themselves not much remains.... Thank God that now during the war we have a whole range of opportunities barred to us in peacetime. We must take advantage of them."[22]

During the initial two years of the Second World War most European Jews also became victims of the discriminatory policy that had been tested before in Germany and Austria. In occupied Poland, the Netherlands, and France, and in the dependent states of Slovakia, Romania, and Hungary, the Jewish minorities were expropriated after the German model, and robbed of their political and social rights. In addition, the Jews also became victims of that comprehensive political project that envisaged the resettlement and deportation, the "ethnic disentangling," of many millions of people, and which soon began to be realized in large parts of German-dominated Europe.

In his Reichstag speech of 6 October 1939, Hitler proclaimed the new principles of "a farsighted ordering of European life." He viewed as the "most important task" the creation of "a new order of ethnographic constellations, meaning a resettlement of nationalities so that at the conclusion of this development better lines of division arise than exist today." The speech continues: "In this context the attempt" ought to be made to achieve "an ordering and settlement of the Jewish problem."[23]

In addition to his role as Reichsführer SS and Chief of the German Police, Himmler was assigned on the following day a second, less well known duty: that of Reich Commissiar for the Strengthening of the German Nation (*Reichskommissar für die Festigung des deutschen Volkstums*; RKF). In this capacity, he implemented during the following years the "Home into the Reich" resettlement of about 500,000 ethnic Germans (so-called *Volksdeutsche*). For this endeavor, he relied on the help of several thousand collaborators and a dozen newly created institutions—such as the ethnic German Liaison Office (*Volksdeutsche Mittelstelle*), the Main Trust Company Office East (*Haupttreuhandstelle Ost*), the German Resettlement and Trust Company Ltd. (*Deutsche Umsiedlungs- und Treuhandgesellschaft m.b.H.*), and the Headquarters of the RKF. The ethnic Germans came from the Baltics or South Tyrol, Volhynia or Bessarabia, from Bukovina, the Dobruja and other regions. In contrast to what Hitler's speech suggests, the resettlements did not primarily result from ethnopolitical objectives, but arose rather inadvertently—and without any preparation—from the same military and wartime economic considerations that resulted in the German-Italian and the Soviet-German alliance pacts.[24]

No matter how much many of the forced settlers of German origin may have sympathized with the Third Reich, they were merely objects of power politics. Because of higher political priorities they were uprooted within only a few weeks, relocated, and subjected to a "modern migration of peoples,"[25] as Himmler preferred to euphemize the state-administered violent act of displacement. The Finance Ministry of the German Reich traded their possessions, amounting to more than three billion reichsmarks for deliveries of oil and foodstuffs from Soviet Union, Romania, and Italy—in the interest of the foreign trade balance. For their part, the resettlers were supposed to receive the homes, the farms and businesses, the tools, the livestock and the household effects of those Poles and Jews that had been systematically expropriated, expelled, and ghettoized from December 1939 onward. This procedure was called "*Naturalrestitution.*"[26]

The connection between the resettlement of the ethnic Germans and the deportations becomes obvious in the example of Lodz, which became the trading center and storage place of ethnic policy. In addition to the ghetto, where 160,000 Jews were locked up, perennially overcrowded deportation camps for approximately 30,000 Poles and settlers' camps for an equal number of ethnic Germans were located there.[27] As well, the connection between the task distribution plans and the careers of the organizers becomes evident. Like Himmler, Heydrich had a dual role. His special responsibility for the "Jewish question" is well known and has been described many times. Less well researched are his dual jurisdictions for the Main Office for Immigrants (*Einwandererzentralstelle*; EWZ) and the Main Office for Resettlers (*Umwandererzentralstelle*; UWZ) under his direction. On one hand, Heydrich was active in the "Home into the Reich" resettlement of the ethnic Germans from eastern and southern Europe; on the other hand, he organized the "deportations" necessary for their settlement.[28] For this reason he created Eichmann's Department IVD4. Responsible for the resettlement of Poles, and subsequently, of Serbs, Croatians, and Slovenes, it also oversaw the deportation of the Jews: In 1940 the Department had the rather general designation "Matters of emigration and evacuation" (*Auswanderungs- und Räumungsangelegenheiten*).[29]

A man like Oswald Pohl was not only in charge of the entire concentration camp administration. At the same time, he was confronted with all the delays of the entire resettlement policy in his capacity as the rather active chairman of the *Deutsche Ansiedlungsgesellschaft*. Hermann Behrends had been Eichmann's superior in the SD in 1936/37; from 1939 to 1941 he organized the "Home into the Reich" resettlement of German minorities abroad as Deputy Leader of the Ethnic German Liaison Office. It was not a matter of biographical coincidences when those figures who had been in charge for months of the expulsion of the Poles subsequently organized the extermination of the European Jews from central positions. It is well known that the head of the UWZ for Lodz, Hermann Krumey, traveled to Hungary together with Eichmann in 1944 in order to coordinate the deportation of the Hungarian Jews to Auschwitz.[30] Since December of 1941 both tasks simply belonged to the "competence of the UWZ": the resettlement of Poles and the "implementation of practical measures against Jews and asocial elements,"[31] as one of the SS men employed there described the mass gassings in Chelmno. If from autumn of 1941 onward the German administration used the terms "*Judenaussiedlung*" (emigration of the Jews), "*Judenumsiedlung*" (resettlement), and "*Judenevakuierung*" (evacuation) and really meant murder, this should not be understood only as a camouflaging device but also as an indication of how the program evolved.

In September 1939 Poland had been divided in three parts: Germany annexed the western part, the Soviet Union the eastern part, and in the middle—between Warsaw, Cracow, Radom, and Lublin a German-occupied zone was created, the "Government General" under the control of Hans Frank. Initially, all Jews and about half of the Poles from the west were supposed to be deported there. In total more than five million people, deprived beforehand of all their means of survival, were to be deported into an economically truncated area that already contained twelve million inhabitants and was about as big as Bavaria and Baden-Württemberg together.

Ethnic Domino Policy

The policy of resettlement, however, affected the Jews in their entirety far more severely than the Poles. Not only were they col-

lectively expropriated from the very start, which was usually only
the case for individual Poles and only if they were actually expelled
in favor of resettled families of German ethnicity; at the destination
of the expulsion, too, that is, in the Government General, the Jews
were forced in turn to retreat from displaced Poles. Wherever problems arose during the following months in the course of the "Home
into the Reich" resettlement of more than half a million ethnic Germans—when homes, money, household effects, and employment
for "resettled" Germans or for "relocated" Poles were lacking, or
"exchanged" Romanians had to be accommodated—the members
of the Jewish minority in Europe were robbed, squeezed, and driven even faster to the periphery of the respective cities and regions.
The situation was exactly as the Hungarian newspaper *Magyarság*
observed on 24 October 1939: By means of this resettlement
scheme and through the transfer of assets from the resettlers, Germany would be able "to secure for some time the procurement of
foodstuffs and raw materials" and to relocate without substantial
cost those resettlers in Poland "who take over the extensive area
that had previously been in Jewish hands for the most part."[32]

Originally, the region of Lodz was not intended to be ceded to
the German Reich; after all, in 1939 more than 500,000 Poles and
about 300,000 Jews lived there. The annexation occurred—belat-
edly, on 9 November 1939—solely in terms of the "Settlement of
Baltic Germans" (*Baltenansiedlung*), because the urban background
of these resettlers required that they receive a second major city
besides Posen (Poznán).[33]

For entirely different reasons, because of the coal mines there,
the region of Sosnowitz/Dombrova in the east of Upper Silesia was
also annexed. Approximately 70,000 Jews were living there. On 21
September 1939 Heydrich had assumed that he would have to
deport about 180,000 Jews from the newly annexed territories to
the Government General. Three weeks later, because of additional
annexations which had nothing to do with Jewish policy, that number had risen threefold to a total of 550,000.

At the same time, the Government General, where the deportees were headed, had been reduced in size and disproportionately
weakened economically as well. However, this was not all. If the
organizers of the mass deportations had initially based their plans
on the assumption that central Poland was a "deportation territory"—intended to be only controlled by the German occupiers in
terms of policing but otherwise "left to its own devices"—this now
changed rapidly. Before the spring of 1940, Göring, in his capacity
as Commissioner for the Four-Year Plan (*Beauftragter für den Vier-*

jahresplan), prohibited, for economic and military reasons, any more deportations beyond those already authorized. This occurred on 12 February 1940 on the request of the Governor General in Cracow, Frank, but against the will of the seemingly omnipotent Reichsführer SS. At an early stage, therefore, a stalemate arose in which the various occupying and resettlement concepts obstructed each other.[34]

Even in the first concrete steps toward forming the ghetto in Lodz, the connection to the resettlement of the Baltic Germans becomes apparent. For instance, in January of 1940, the representative of the Reich Commissar for the Strengthening of the German Nation in Posen wrote to his colleague in the UWZ: "The Baltic Germans destined for Lodz are already on their way to Posen, so that in a few days homes must be available there. The evacuation of Jewish residences and the transport of the home owners to the [not yet closed, G.A.] ghetto must therefore take place immediately."[35] At the beginning of March the Gestapo reported from Lodz: "At dawn on 2 March a peripheral section of the ghetto was surrounded. The Poles living there were arrested and, after police checks by the criminal and state police, one part was handed over to drumhead court martials and the others directed by the municipal authorities to their new living quarters in the Polish area. We will evacuate the rest of these persons on 4 March. Jews will be transported into the entire area cleared through this operation on Monday, 4 March, so that a substantial residential area for the accommodation of Baltic Germans will be created."[36]

These examples show how the "Home into the Reich" resettlement of the ethnic Germans, the dispossession of the Poles, and the Jewish policy were interdependent. For instance, in mid-October 1939 Eichmann had been forced to end the deportation of Jews from Vienna, Katowice, and Moravian Ostrava, because the settlement of the Baltic Germans and the evictions necessary for it suddenly received priority status. The deportation of about 1,000 Jews, on the other hand, from Stettin (Szczecin) to the area of Lublin, carried out on 11–12 February 1940 against the protest of the German occupying authorities, also appeared in a new context: On the request of the Baltic German leadership, Himmler had ordered residences cleared for those resettlers from Mitau (Jelgava, Mitava), Riga and Reval (Tallinn) who pursued "maritime occupations."[37]

The project of the deportation of the German and west Polish Jews to a "Jewish reservation Lublin" failed rapidly for the reasons indicated above. The practitioners of resettlement saw as a preliminary last resort the formation of the Lodz ghetto. During the night

of 30 April to 1 May 1940, they sealed it off. The city administration received the "firm promise" that by 1 October, that is,
within five months, the Jews would be "completely removed from
the Lodz ghetto."[38]

But how? As early as 24 January 1940 Goebbels had noted in
his diary: "At the moment Himmler is shifting peoples. Not always
successfully."[39] The difficulties of resettlement and the closely related
deportation of the Jews resulted not from a unified strategy but precisely from those diverging interests pursued by the various centers
of power in Germany at this time. Frank not only demanded a stop
to the deportations, because they would inevitably destroy his ambitious plans for the creation of a model colony, "*Nebenland des
Reiches,*"[40] but soon also the deportation of the one and a half million Jews living in the Government General. He demanded this for
racist as well as demographic-economic reasons, because even in
their first evaluations his economic experts had declared the territory
"overpopulated."[41] No compromise of the differences, however, ever
came to pass; instead, those involved began to overcome their conflicts on a per project basis by means of larger, ever expanding plans.
Thus in late May 1940, even before the surrender of France, the project of the "Madagascar insular solution" emerged.[42]

In retrospect, this scheme appears completely bizarre. Consequently, it is quite often interpreted as a metaphor for the supposedly already intended genocide. If one recalls, however, that
the Axis powers already stood in Addis Ababa and Mogadishu in
the form of Italian soldiers; that Algeria, Morocco, and Tunisia
belonged to the defeated France; and that the German Foreign Ministry tried everything to prompt Fascist Spain to enter the war, then
it becomes rather clear, why during the summer of 1941, Hitler was
already at work on personnel options for the position of a future
governor of the still fictitious "German East Africa"; why the
walling of the Warsaw Ghetto was stopped with reference to the
Madagascar plan; and why some of Eichmann's colleagues enrolled
in courses on the tropics and were even vaccinated against malaria.

The project fell through after a few weeks due to the superiority of the British Mediterranean Fleet. And exactly for that reason
the Warsaw Ghetto was cordoned off for good in November of
1940, after a further resettlement plan had proven unworkable. This
ghetto, too, just like the Lodz Ghetto, was supposed to exist for only
a short time. However, for just how long remained entirely unclear.

"Liquidation of the Jewry?"

Because the Reich Finance Minister was worried at the time that the moment approached "when the maintenance of the Jews poses a burden to the official coffers," he commissioned the Reich Audit Office to review the ghetto administration in Lodz.[43] The auditors observed in their final report dated January 1941: "The responsible local German authorities realized that the problem of the pacification and Germanization as well as the economic build-up of the city could only be solved in connection with the total eviction or, temporarily, also the isolation of the Jewry." "Nothing final could be said" on how the situation would evolve further. This much, however, was clear to the auditors: The maintenance of the Jews in Lodz, calculated on the basis of prison fare, required at least 2.5 million reichsmarks per month. In order to reduce this amount, they counted on the supposed possibility "that a greater part of the incapacitated ghetto inmates will be evacuated in spring of 1941 to the Government General,"[44] and on the prospect of detailing those fit for work, about one quarter of 160,000, to forced labor.

While the auditors of the Reich Auditing Office reckoned with deportation in the direction of Warsaw and wished simply to banish a fiscal problem from their jurisdiction, a similar occurrence took place in Warsaw. There the director of the *Dienststelle Generalgouvernement* of the *Reichskuratorium für Wirtschaftlichkeit* (RKW) was commissioned in January of 1941 to compile a business management assessment of the local ghetto.[45] He concluded that for mere survival the approximately 400,000 ghettoized people would require a monthly subsidy close to 4.6 million reichsmarks, provided the ghetto was not regarded "as a means to liquidate the Jewish people."[46] If one wanted to avoid the burden on the public purse, three courses could be taken in the opinion of this expert on rationalization, either individually or parallel: First, the "better exploitation of Jewish labor" could be attempted, which presupposed investment funds and secondly "a certain relaxation" of the confinement—or: "One lets insufficient supplies occur without consideration for the consequences."

The coolly calculating formulation of both assessments speak for themselves. In practice they precipitated the distinction between "work-able" and "work-unable" Jews, not customary until then, that became characteristic for the initial phase of the subsequent mass murders in the gas chambers. Viewed thus, it appears to be a specific reply to the fiscally justified considerations about "undersupplying" of hundreds of thousands of people, when Eichmann's

liaison officer in Posen, the administrative jurist Rolf Heinz Höppner, wrote six months later: "It will have to be seriously considered
if the most humane solution is not to finish off those Jews who are
not fit for work with some kind of effective method. That would at
least be more agreeable than letting them starve to death."[47]

Still in the context of the Madagascar plan, a second wave of
resettlement had been prepared in the summer of 1940. The Germans from Lithuania, from Bessarabia, and from northern Bukovina
were brought "Home into the Reich" between October of 1940 and
March of 1941 under the provisions of further but clearly mutually
negotiated annexations by the Soviets. Some of the Romanian Germans were also moved. They too had to leave their homeland
because of considerations of pure power politics. It constituted a
concession to Romania (important due to its raw materials), which
at the instigation of Germany lost a substantial part of its territory
to the Soviet Union. Additionally, Romania had to cede the southern
Dobruja to Bulgaria and northern Transylvania to Hungary—once
again, due to the scheming of the Germans. The resettlement of parts
of the ethnic German population was intended to facilitate the integration of Romanian refugees and forced settlers.

The new settlement was conceptually always linked with economic rationalization as well. With this logic, for every ethnic German family two, or often three, "foreign ethnic" (fremdvölkische)
families—thus the technical term—had to give way. In addition, the
Wehrmacht intended to set up huge troop exercise grounds. The
Ministry of Agriculture planned to "transplant" at least 300,000
small farmers' families—about one and a half million people—
from the poor rural regions of the Reich to the newly conquered
East; there they would be allotted 20-hectare farms. They were supposed to originate from the southern and southwestern areas with
shared inheritance of estates. For example, in the Gau Mainfranken, statisticians had calculated that in Röhn 84.1 percent of
agricultural operations would have to be closed and the acreages
subsequently amalgamated into more profitable units.

Based on these considerably different projects, the "deportation quota" by the winter of 1940/41 already amounted to at least
five million people. The staff of the UWZ was lagging far behind.
In fact, by March 1941 Eichmann's Department "Deportation Matters" (Räumungsangelegenheiten) had "only" deported 408,525 persons. As a result, as early as the winter of 1940/41, a quarter of a
million ethnic German "homecomers" were stuck in 1,500 resettlement camps that had to be put up in the eastern and southern
regions of the German Reich. Moreover, the contract with Italy,

stipulating the resettlement of 200,000 South Tyroleans, could not be fulfilled at all or only very slowly.[48] Thus a continually mounting pressure for ever more comprehensive expropriation and deportation plans accumulated, precipitated by Himmler and his staff themselves.

Practicing Murder

By autumn of 1939 and during the following winter, 10,000 to 15,000 mentally ill had already been murdered in Pomerania, West Prussia, and in occupied Poland. This did not take place in the context of the so-called "euthanasia," the *"Aktion T-4,"* which began somewhat later. The institutional inmates were either shot by two commandos of the SS or murdered in mobile gas chambers.

The background can easily be documented: Between October and December 1939, within only six weeks, 60,000 Baltic Germans had arrived in the port cities of Danzig (Gdansk), Stettin, and Swinemünde; in January and February 1940, 120,000 Germans from Volhynia and Galicia followed by horse or railway. In this context, on 29 October 1939, the functionaries of the Main Office for Immigrants (EWZ), part of the Reich Security Main Office (RSHA), spoke in Gdingen about the evacuation of sanatoriums and care facilities for the purpose of "caring for the sick and frail Baltic Germans." In Danzig alone 1,000 hospital beds had to be set aside immediately. As a precaution, the discussion went on, mental institutions were to be "cleared" near the Pomeranian ports where the next ships with resettlers were expected, and made available for the "persons in need of care" arriving on these transports. In summary, the teletype to the RSHA read: "The question of the transportation of the frail to the accommodations in Pomerania and Mecklenburg will be dealt with by the Central Office Gotenhafen (i.e., Gdingen/Gdynia)."[49]

Four days later, on 3 November, the same office was already organizing the removal of mentally ill Poles in West Prussia: "These are 700 mentally ill patients, who are to be re-routed from the mental institution Schwetz to the mental institution Konradstein near Pr. Stargard. The beds made available thus are to be newly occupied on Saturday, 11 November 1939, by 200 frail Baltic Germans from Neustadt (West Prussia) and 500 from Danzig."[50] Konradstein was one of the centers where the men of the Sonderkommando "Kurt Eimann" shot Polish and Pomeranian psychiatric patients.

In January 1940 SS units murdered 500 patients at the Chelm institution near the Soviet-German border in order to make the facility available as a transit camp for Germans from Volhynia. Simultaneously, hundreds of inmates of the Tiegenhof institution near Gnesen were murdered in the gas vans prepared for this purpose in the automotive shops of the Sachsenhausen concentration camp. At the time, Dieter Wisliceny, a close associate of Eichmann's, headed the emigration staff in Gnesen. In the summer of 1940, with a view to the Madagascar plan and on orders of the RSHA, all mentally ill German Jews who were patients in psychiatric clinics were collectively murdered. This stands in contrast to the Aryan patients, only some of whom were determined to be "unworthy of life" (*lebensunwert*), and then only based on diagnostic criteria, however superficial these may have been.[51]

After Himmler had been forced twice to postpone the resettlement of the 50,000 Lithuanian Germans due to the overload of his resettlement machinery, it seemed to him to be close at hand in May 1941. Transit camps were to be prepared in East and West Prussia. In the period of 21 May to 8 June, 1,558 German and about 400 Polish mentally ill patients, who had been transported there from a larger catchment area, were killed in the East Prussian sanatorium and care facility Soldau. The institution later served as a central transit camp for Lithuanian German resettlers. The SS unit that organized the mass murders by means of gas van and was assigned to the resettlement staffs called itself the Sonderkommando "Lange." It was the same commando that operated the first extermination camp beginning in December 1941—Chelmno (Kulmhof) near Lodz.[52]

How such practical experiences influenced subsequent actions can be illustrated by a small example. Soon after the deportation of "cripples, the disabled, the sick, those unfit for transport, etc."[53] from the region of Posen/Lodz into the Government General had been halted in June 1940—owing to the protests by Frank—the district administrators (*Landräte*) of the Warthegau complained: Those left behind apparently "become a burden to public welfare," and thus in the long run "impossible conditions"[54] would arise. Eichmann's local expert, Höppner, who knew that he was not allowed to evacuate patients and frail persons, noted at the margins of the report: "Possibly, other measures will have to be taken against those persons unfit for transport." This marginal note is dated 22 October 1940. On 27–30 October, 290 old and sick Jews were hauled from Cracow to a forest nearby, under the pretext that they would be taken to "a sanatorium for recovery,"[55] and shot.

At the same time, the resettlement authorities in the south of Germany began confiscating church-operated sanatoria and care facilities in order to accommodate temporarily a few tens of thousands of resettlers from South Tyrol. The memoranda, letters, and teletypes of the organizers speak a clear language. Two examples may illustrate this.

In September 1940 the commissioner of the ethnic German Liaison Office in Würzburg reported to his superiors in Berlin: "For the purpose of accommodating the ethnic Germans destined for the Gau Mainfranken, I have, among other things, confiscated several housing units from the psychiatric clinic Werneck and effected evacuation through resettlement of the mental patients."[56] A leading expert on resettlement in the SS noted about the institution Attl near Wasserburg at the Inn River: "This monastery belongs to lay brothers who had thus far put up lunatics. A part of this staff has already 'departed.' The *Kreisleiter* has put the sanatorium at the disposal of the Reichsführer SS for the purpose of accommodating resettlers."[57]

Even these first mass murders stood in close connection with the general resettlement policy. A concrete order to kill the mental patients did not exist. Obviously, the participants acted on a tacit understanding, which only required a vague expedient direction. By autumn of 1941, a total of 30,000 people had already been murdered for the purpose of "making space for the ethnic German resettlers." Before the functionaries of resettlement built the camps for the extermination of the European Jews, they had practiced mass murder for two years and gained the certainty that many of the participating German officials and the German public as well condoned these practices.[58]

Intermediary Solution and Radicalization

By November 1941, Himmler had obviously maneuvered himself into a dead end with his policy of "*völkische Flurbereinigung*" (ethnic cleansing).[59] Instead of the announced ethnic and economic new order, instead of the rapid "removal" of millions of "non-Aryans" ("*Fremdvölkische*"), the reality looked completely different. By late autumn of 1940, hundreds of thousands of people were stranded in resettlement camps or crowded into ghettos, deprived of their economic means. Depending on whether they were Jews, Poles, or ethnic Germans, they had to be kept alive starving, with meager or adequate sustenance, but in any case in an unproductive manner— in the middle of war, in a state of acute scarcity of food, lack of accommodations, and scarcity of labor.

On 10 December 1940, Himmler tried to defend this fiasco before the *Reichsleiter* and *Gauleiter* with his "*Vortrag über Siedlung*" (Talk on Settlement). The details can be disregarded here; they merely confirm the close interconnection of the settlement schemes already shown. The last sheet of the extant lecture notes is crucial. Because Frank persistently refused to admit any deported Poles, Himmler announced for the Government General: "Resettlement of the Jews and thus even more space for Poles." He therefore expressed the expectation to himself and his audience that the deportation of the million and a half Jews from central Poland would create room for the removal of Polish farmers from the annexed west Poland. Thus, it would free space for the settlement of ethnic German resettlers (mainly from southeastern Europe).[60]

As he presented this intention, Himmler was probably already thinking of the war with the Soviet Union and assumed a victorious outcome. In the short term, however, he had to fall back on the method of ghettoization, which he always regarded as a provisional arrangement, never a permanent situation, but a sort of mass custody prior to deportation. As early as 20 January 1941 the head of the Department for Resettlement in Warsaw announced what subsequently occurred in the following weeks: "Resettlement" of an additional 72,000 Jews into the Warsaw Ghetto would occur because, in the western part of the district, room had "to be made for 62,000 Poles [resettlers to be removed from the annexed west, G.A.]," who in turn had to give way to the Germans from Bessarabia, Bukovina and Dobruja.[61]

The logic of the ethnic domino policy precipitated, on one hand, the further impoverishment and ghettoization of the Polish Jews. During the first months of 1941, tens of thousands of additional Jews were pressed between the ghetto walls of Warsaw at the end of a long chain of resettlements. These had not originated with the "Jewish question" but had been set in motion in 1939 by the Soviet-German treaties and the military as well as by economic projects for the reordering of Europe. Apart from the plight of the newcomers themselves, they would necessarily decrease even further the chances for survival of those already incarcerated there.

On 25 March 1941, the Chief of the General Staff of the Army, Franz Halder, noted a discussion by his General Quartermaster, Wagner, "with Heydrich on imminent eastern questions."[62] Generally, this exchange is assumed to have concerned exclusively the freedom of action for the subsequent *Einsatzgruppen*. However, one day later, immediately after a discussion with Göring, Heydrich noted: "With respect to the Jewish question I reported briefly

to the Reich Marshall [Göring] and submitted to him my new blueprint, which he authorized with one modification concerning
Rosenberg's jurisdiction and then ordered for resubmission."[63] The
document has been found only recently in the Moscow Special
Archive. It relativizes the assumption of many historians that the
famous letter by Göring of 31 July 1941, represented the major
caesura on the path to the Holocaust. In this document, he commissioned Heydrich "to submit a comprehensive blueprint of the
organizational, subject-related, and material preparatory measures
for the execution of the intended Final Solution of the Jewish question."[64] This note of 26 March 1941 must be understood as a confirmation, possibly an expansion, of an assignment "for the Final
Solution of the Jewish question"—an order Heydrich had received
informally at the turn of 1940/41 and had already developed it further. The official written form probably became necessary only to
extend Heydrich's room for maneuver vis-à-vis other authorities. In
any case, Heydrich subsequently used it in exactly this way.

The "jurisdiction of Rosenberg" mentioned by Göring is an
indication of this direction, for at that time Rosenberg has already
been designated Minister for the Civilian Administration of the
Soviet territories occupied later. Furthermore, the head of the
Department IV, Heinrich Müller, received a copy of the letter "for
the notification of Eichmann," the head of the Department IVB4
responsible for all deportations.[65] Accordingly, since at least March,
Heydrich had been preparing in the same context—parallel to the
conceptual formation of the subsequent *Einsatzgruppen* of the
Security Police and of the SD—the deportation of all European Jews
who lived west of the Soviet-German demarcation.

Since then Eichmann, too, reckoned with "further deportation
to the east"; this idea was hardly fixed yet in terms of geographical
targets but it was increasingly understood as a dynamic option.
Certainly, the genocidal principle of "natural decimation through
resettlement"[66] already characterized the Madagascar plan; yet the
object had not been the complete extermination of the deportees.
The new plan, however, included genocide, envisioning the separation of the deportees according to gender or, optionally, mass ster-
ilizations, murderous slave labor for those deportees fit for work,
and "attritional reservations" (*Absterbereservate*) for the children
and the aged. In view of this projected mass resettlement, especially
in the face of the deliberate, unimaginable cruelty of its circumstances, the moral sense will revolt against differentiating further
with respect to terminology. Yet the difference from the subsequent
industrial extermination is evident: The deportees were still sup-

posed to die of a "natural" death. For one part, they were to starve and freeze to death in ghettos and camps, and for the other, they would work themselves to death under a barbaric police regime.

Like previous deportation projects, this new scheme was also tied to narrow time projections. Like the previous ones, this plan also presupposed military success—rapid victory over the Soviet Union. However, in National Socialist Germany that which had not been achieved served nevertheless already as the basis for further action. Now things were really handled as if the Jews had already been deported. And from this resulted exactly those concrete prerequisites that lead to the last steps toward the murder of the European Jews by means of gas chambers.

Practical Options and Command Structure

As early as January 1940, Eichmann had complained about "the difficulties that arise from the reciprocal action between the settlement of the ethnic Germans and the evacuation of the Poles and Jews."[67] One and a half years later, in September 1941, when the central questions already revolved around mass deportations into the newly conquered Soviet "spaces," Höppner inquired of Eichmann "what should eventually happen to these resettled segments of the population that were undesirable for the German settlements areas; whether the goal consisted of securing a measure of permanent existence for them, or whether they ought to be completely wiped out?"[68]

The query occurred on 3 September. As early as 15 August, Eichmann knew that Hitler had "rejected an evacuation *during* the war."[69] On 16 September, Himmler discussed the topic *Judenfrage. Siedlung Ost* (Jewish Question. Settlement East) with his closest associates responsible for the resettlement policy in all of Europe.[70] Details are not known, but the discussion took place in the Führer's headquarters. On 17 September, it was certain that owing to the pressure by the *Gauleiters* and some mayors Hitler had authorized the deportation of several tens of thousands of German, Austrian, Czech, and Luxemburgian Jews even *during the war*. The trains were supposed to roll into the Lodz ghetto, that is, into Höppner's jurisdiction.

Eichmann had still not answered Höppner's query. On 29 September, Eichmann forwarded to him a copy of a letter whose original he had sent to the head of the main department for *Menscheneinsatz* (Employment of Human Resources) of the Reich Commissioner for the Strengthening of the German Nation: "Although the problems arising with respect to the settlement [of the ethnic Germans]" would not be "disregarded," Eichmann began, "at this time a recommencement of the evacuations cannot be expected." Moreover, to his own justification he added that his "efforts at finding a different territory as a temporary alternative for meeting the deportation quotas—the occupied Soviet areas had been considered"—had failed for the time being, "and that it was decided to await a better transportation situation."[71]

The letter makes clear the fact that in September 1941 the decision on the systematic extermination of all Jews in gas chambers had not yet been taken. The documents confirm what Martin Broszat formulated in 1977: "On the contrary, it seems to me that no comprehensive, general order for extermination existed at all. Rather, the 'program' for Jewish extermination evolved gradually out of individual actions in the framework of institutions and realities until the spring of 1942 and obtained its determining character after the establishment of the extermination camps in Poland (between December 1941 and 1942)."[72] In accordance with Broszat, I am assuming that to begin with—until April 1942—the practice of extermination was applied experimentally. This aspect reinforces the significance of the consensus attained by Heydrich at the Wannsee Conference, and leads to the question whether the machinery of extermination would not have been stopped or at least decelerated if during the first weeks and months serious resistance and problems of legitimacy had arisen. From this arise questions about the behavior, most of all of the Germans, which have to be posed to the same extent as the exculpating notion of a *"Führerbefehl"* (order from Hitler) is abandoned.[73]

Considering the documents in their entirety, Hitler's role cannot be viewed as that of an unrelenting commander but rather that of a politician who left his followers considerable room, encouraged them to let their imagination roam in order to make the impossible possible—and who backed them unconditionally. Those who had repeatedly postponed the deportation of the expropriated and ghettoized Jews openly discussed in the autumn of 1941, the possibility of a systematic, swift extermination. They conceived of mass murder as the easiest way to carry out the plans they had developed for years and had never been able to realize. The representatives of all the other institutions agreed to the new "path to a solution" because it would least affect their interests and because they had long since firmly included the prompt deportation of the Jews into their calculations—because they had expropriated them, herded them together, and treated them as if they did not even exist any longer.

On 16 December 1941, Hans Frank explained the impending murder of the Jews to the members of his government: "Therefore, with respect to the Jews, I will assume in principle that they have to disappear. They have to go." "But," Frank asked rhetorically "what shall happen to the Jews? Do you think they will be accommodated in village settlements in the eastern lands (*Ostland*). In Berlin they told us: Why do people give us this trouble; we have no use for them in the eastern lands [in the occupied Baltic states, G.A.] or in the Reich Commissariat [Ukraine, G.A.], liquidate them yourselves!" Perhaps Frank was reacting to an inquiring glance, but in any case, he added: "One cannot transfer preceding notions to such gigantic, unique events. However, we have to find a way that leads to success.... Where and when this will take place is a matter of the agencies we are implementing and creating here and whose legal effectiveness I will announce to you in due time."[74]

"I sat there behind my desk in Berlin," Eichmann later testified in Jerusalem, apparently confronted with the "fundamental commands given by Heyrdrich/Himmler" on the one hand, and on the other hand, faced the "reports of the people who now, owing to their experience, had to come up with proposals, so that different guidelines could be issued by the higher authorities." After all, according to Eichmann, "the entire complex" had been "in endless motion, in incessant fluctuation." What Eichmann offers with exonerating intent, reflects the extent of his freedom of action. He was positioned at an intersection between upper and lower spheres, between central instructions and actual possibilities. Part of his responsibility was to help structure this "incessant fluctuation" in a practical way. Just what this "fluctuation" looked like has become clear on the preceding pages. One other example may be added. On 7 October, Wilhelm Koppe, Himmler's regent in the Warthegau, gave the "binding order" for the rapid resettlement of several thousand ethnic Germans, who were becoming increasingly dissatisfied in the camps. Critical questions as to whether this "was still defendable" were simply dismissed by Koppe. Instead he gave those gathered some advice: The SS men of the Settlement Staffs had "to really stir things up continuously ... to maintain pressure on all official agencies involved in the settlement process" and "to be inventive with regard to the means that could be useful for the settlement."[75] Already among those means at this time was the murder of part of the Jews of the cities and rural districts set aside for settlement.

The "Final Solution" was not ordered, it was not drawn up by this "architect" or the other. What mattered was arriving at a consensus in the decisive situation. This corresponds to the more general insight into the polycratic structure of the National Socialist state which in view of the source evidence can no longer be doubted. However, it may not be—as happens sometimes—misunderstood as a conglomeration of vanities, petty jealousies, and intrigues of powerful Nazi figures. It also represented, at the least, real divergences of interests. Nevertheless, Franz Neumann was only conditionally correct when he observed as early as 1944 in Behemoth that "the decisions of the Führer are merely the result of the compromises achieved" between competing interests and leaderships.[76]

The term "compromise" requires some explanation. Even if the representatives of various institutions advocated contrary, mutually exclusive interests, collectively they were nevertheless willing to overcome, by means of robbery, slave labor, and extermination, the differences that their divergent conceptions, and particularly the intended speed of their implementation, would inevitably produce. From this derived the logic of the "special authorization by the Führer," desired and often enough anticipated by all the participants. They did not carefully weigh decisions for one variant over another; nor, as Neumann thought, did compromise characterize this logic until the autumn of 1941. Rather attempted to take into account diverging constellations of interests, plans, and "necessities" at the same time and to overcome the conflicts over objectives in terms of "finalized solutions" by using extreme measures. In other words: The more radical and far-reaching the various plans, resettlement projects, and war aims became, the greater—to express it in mathematical terms—the lowest common multiple had to become in which all of these schemes were contained.

In late summer and autumn of 1941, it became rapidly evident that the latest deportation project concerning the "Final Solution" would yet remain a scrap of paper. From this resulted the search for a perspective in which, possibly, all of the diverging interests could be realized simultaneously.

This multifaceted political process can and must be described and analyzed as accurately as possible—even if every dimension of the crime can no longer be uncovered. This leads to a historicization of the events, but it means just the opposite of denying the Holocaust; rather, what matters is to conceive comprehensively of the circumstances that finally led to its realization.

Notes

1. I find summarizing my own research on the murder of the European Jews dif-
    ficult. It necessarily leads to simplifications that are inadequate to the topic.
    Contrary to the framework of a lecture, they cannot be relativized in discus-
    sion. Yet I hope to stimulate interest in my own and others' studies, on which
    I have based my findings. Victor Klemperer, *Ich will Zeugnis ablegen bis zum
    letzten, Tagebücher 1933-1941*, 2 vols. (Berlin, 1995); Michael Wildt (ed.),
    Die Judenpolitik des SD 1935 bis 1938. Eine Dokumentation (Munich,
    1995); Susanne Heim, "'Deutschland muß ihnen ein Land ohne Zukunft sein'.
    Die Zwangsemigration der Juden 1933 bis 1938," in Götz Aly and Susanne
    Heim, *Vordenker der Vernichtung. Auschwitz und die deutschen Pläne für
    eine neue europäische Ordnung* (Frankfurt a.M., 1994); Götz Aly, *'Endlö-
    sung'. Völkerverschiebung und der Mord an den europäischen Juden* (Frank-
    furt a.M., 1996).

2. Exemplary for this is the opinion of Eberhard Jäckel, who maintains that "a
    collective discussion or decision-making," and consequently also a compara-
    tively prolonged decision-making process, can be "precluded": "In this state no
    important decision was made by an advisory body. On the highest level, Hitler
    made the decisions alone and proclaimed them." (Eberhard Jäckel, *Hitlers
    Herrschaft* (Stuttgart, 1986), p. 105.) The state of the research debate up to
    1985 concerning the controversy over the decision-making process is summa-
    rized in Eberhard Jäckel and Jürgen Rohwer (eds.), *Der Mord and den Juden
    im Zweiten Weltkrieg. Entschlußbildung und Verwirklichung* (Frankfurt a.M.,
    1987). For a more recent study on this, see Philippe Burrin, *Hitler und die
    Juden. Die Entscheidung für den Völkermord* (Frankfurt a.M., 1993).

3. *Schnellbrief* of Heydrich from 21 September 1939, addressed to the comman-
    ders of the *Einsatzgruppen* of the Security Police on the "Jewish question in the
    occupied territories," printed in Jüdisches Historisches Institut Warschau [Jew-
    ish Historical Institute in Warschau] (ed.), *Faschismus—Ghetto—Massenmord*
    (Berlin, 1962), p. 37ff.

4. "Berichte der SD Oberabschnitte zum Stand der Judenreferate auf der Schu-
    lungstagung in Bernau," 13–14 March 1936; Sonderarchiv Moskau,
    500/3/320; in Michael Wildt (ed.), *Die Judenpolitik des SD 1935-1938*
    (Munich, 1995), pp. 81-84; here 82.

5. Vermerk of February 20, 1937: An II 1, betr. Aufgaben für SS-Junker; ZASM,
    501/3/31, Bl. 182f.

6. "Memorandum des SD-Amtes IV/2 an Heydrich, 24. Mai 1934," Sonderarchiv
    Moskau 501/1/18; in Wildt, *Judenpolitik*, pp. 66-69 passim.

7. Klemperer, Vol. 1, p. 209.

8. "Lagebericht der Abteilung II 112 für die Zeit vom 1.1.–31.3.1937, 8. April
    1937"; Sonderarchiv Moskau, 500/3/316; in Wildt, *Judenpolitik*, p. 102.

9. "Richtlinien und Forderungen an die Oberabschnitte," drawn up by Wisliceny
    and Hagen, 21 April 1937, Bundesarchiv, R 58/544; in Wildt, *Judenpolitik*,
    p. 112.

10. Theodor Dannecker, "Das innerdeutsche Judentum: Organisation, sachliche
    und personelle Veränderungen, geistiges Leben und Methoden seiner Behand-
    lung"; Sonderarchiv Moskau, 500/3/322; in Wildt, *Judenpolitik*, p. 150.

11. Adolf Eichmann, "Das Weltjudentum: politische Aktivität und Auswirkung
    seiner Tätigkeit auf dir in Deutschland ansässigen Juden"; Sonderarchiv
    Moskau, 500/1/322; in Wildt, *Judenpolitik*, p. 139.

12. Wildt, *Judenpolitik*, p. 108.
13. Ibid., p. 166.
14. Klemperer, Vol. 1, p. 415.
15. Lagebericht der Abteilung II für das Jahr 1938; Sonderarchiv Moskau, 500/1/625; Wildt, *Judenpolitik*, p. 200.
16. Klemperer, Vol. 1, p. 398.
17. Susanne Heim and Götz Aly, "Staatliche Ordnung und 'organische Lösung.' Die Rede Hermann Görings 'Über die Judenfrage' vom 6. Dezember 1938," in Wolfgang Benz (ed.), *Jahrbuch für Antisemitismusforschung* 2 (1993): 378-404; here 385.
18. This number includes European Jews who lived west of the Soviet-German demarcation line. On the very top of materials in the preparation folder used by Heinrich Himmler for his "Vortrag über Siedlung" held on 10 December before a gathering of *Reichsleiter* and *Gauleiter* in Berlin, were three reports bearing Eichmann's sign; at the end, two sheets on "Die Judenfrage." The second point deals with "Die Endlösung der Judenfrage" (Materialsammlung Himmlers zum "Vortrag über Siedlung"; BA, NS19/3929.)
19. See the protocol of the Wannsee Conference, for instance in Kurt Pätzold and Erika Schwarz, *Tagesordnung Judenmord. Die Wannsee-Konferenz am 20. Januar 1942* (Berlin, 1992), pp. 102-112; see Aly, *Endlösung*, ch. 4, pp. 299ff.
20. Selected passages are contained in Aly, *Endlösung*, pp. 9f.
21. Ibid.
22. Diary entry on 27 March 1942; quoted from Ralf Georg Reuth (ed.), *Joseph Goebbels' Tagebücher 1924-1945*, 5 vols., Vol. 4: *1940-1942* (Munich, Zürich, 1992), pp. 1776f.
23. Hitler before the Reichstag on 6 October 1939; quoted from Max Domarus, *Hitler: Reden und Proklamationen 1932-1945*, 2 vols., Vol. 2: *Untergang (1939-1945)* (Neustadt, 1962f.), pp. 1383ff.
24. See detailed account in Aly, *Endlösung*, pp. 29-135; on the RKF still Robert L. Koehl's study, *RKFDV: German Resettlement and Population Policy 1939-1945* (Cambridge, 1957).
25. See for instance Dietrich A. Loeber (ed.), *Diktierte Optionen. Die Umsiedlung der Deutsch-Balten aus Estland und Lettland 1939-1941* (Neumünster, 1972); Dirk Jachomowski, *Die Umsiedlung der Bessarabien-, Bukowina- und Dobrudschadeutschen. Von der Volksgruppe in Rumänien zur Siedlungsbrücke an der Reichsgrenze (Buchreihe der Südostdeutschen Historischen Kommission*, Vol. 32) (Munich, 1984).
26. See on this principle, dubbed "Natural Restitution" by Himmler, the tables of the *"betreute Vermögenswerte"* of the German Resettlement and Trust Company Ltd. (*Deutsche Umsiedlungs-Treuhand-Gesellschaft m.b.H.*—DUT) and the "Zahlungen per 30. November 1940" of 7 Dec. 1940 (Signatures by Kulemann, Schmölder). BA, NS 19/3979, Bl. 12-14.
27. On Lodz see Florian Freund, Bertrand Perz, and Karl Stuhlpfarrer, "Das Ghetto in Litzmannstadt (Lodz)," in Hanno Loewy and Gerhard Schoenberner, *'Unser einziger Weg ist Arbeit.' Das Ghetto in Lodz, 1940-1944. Eine Ausstellung des jüdischen Museums Frankfurt am Main in Zusammenarbeit mit Yad Vashem* (Vienna, 1990), pp. 17-31.
28. How much Heydrich identified with these tasks assigned to Himmler's role as RKF is revealed by his secret speech held in Prague on 2 Oct. 1941; printed in Miroslav Kárn and Jaroslava Milotová (eds.), *Protektoráni politika Reinharda Heydricha* (Prague, 1991), pp. 98ff.

29. Report of the HSSPF (Higher SS and Police Leader) in the "Government General" (Poland), Krüger, about a conference in Berlin on 30 January 1940; in *Faschismus—Ghetto—Massenmord*, p. 50.

30. See Aly, *Endlösung*, p. 20.

31. Letter of the member of the Main Office for Resettlers in Lodz (UWZ/L), Kinna, dated 13 July 1943, to the Personnel Main Office of the SS; BDC, PA/Kinna. Kinna reported in this letter about his previous activities.

32. Quoted from Karl Stuhlpfarrer, *Umsiedlung Südtirol 1939-1940*, 2 vols, Vol. 1 (Vienna, Munich, 1985), p. 147.

33. On the following points see Aly, *Endlösung*, pp. 41-46.

34. See the diary entries in his "Official Diary" (*Diensttagebuch*), 8 November 1939, p. 61; 8 December 1939, p. 71 in Werner Präg and Wolfgang Jacobmeyer (eds.), *Das Diensttagebuch des deutschen Generalgourneurs in Polen, 1939-1945* (Stuttgart, 1975). Göring's decree was passed on on 8 April 1940; see Ulrich Herbert, "Arbeit und Vernichtung. Ökonomische Interessen und Primat der 'Weltanschauung im Nationalsozialismus'" in idem (ed.), *Europa und der 'Reichseinsatz': Ausländische Zivilarbeiter, Kriegsgefangene und KZ-Häftlinge in Deutschland 1938-1945* (Essen, 1991), pp. 384-426; here 392f.

35. Letter by Döring to Rapp of 9 January 1940. Archiv der Hauptkommission zur Untersuchung der hitlerischen Verbrechen, Warsaw (AGK), Umwandererzentralstelle/Posen (UWZ/P) 114, Bl. 12.

36. Teletyped message by Barth to Rapp of 7 March 1944; AGK, UWZ/P/129, Bl. 1.

37. See Aly, *Endlösung*, pp. 97f.

38. Thus retrospectively the *Regierungspräsident* of Lodz in the summer of 1941; quoted from *Dokumenty i Material do dziejów okupaji niemieckiej w Polsce (Getto lódzkie)*, Vol. 3 (Warsaw, Lodz, Cracow, 1987), pp. 177ff.

39. Goebbel's entry of 24 January 1940, in Elke Fröhlich (ed.), *Die Tagebücher von Joseph Goebbels. Sämtliche Fragmente. Teil 1: Aufzeichnungen 1924-1941*, 4 vols., Vol. 4: 1.1.1940–8.7.1941 (Munich et al., 1987), p. 21.

40. Frank on a conversation with Hitler on 4 Nov. 1940; in Präg and Jacobmeyer, *Diensttagebuch*, p. 302.

41. See "*Dienststelle Generalgouvernement*" of the *Reichskuratorium für Wirtschaftlichkeit* (RKW), founded in July 1940 and directed by Rudolf Gater; its report "Die wirtschaftlichen Grundlagen des Generalgouvernements" [The Economic Basis of the Government General] of Dec. 1940, written by Rudolf Gater; BA-MA, Rw 19 Anh. I/1349 and the report of the managing director of the *Sektion Wirtschaft am Institut für Deutsche Ostarbeit*, Helmuth Meinhold, "Die Industrialisierung des Generalgouvernements" [The Industrialization of the Government General], (*Manuskriptreihe des Instituts für Deutsche Ostarbeit. Nur für den Dienstgebrauch!*) Dec. 1941; BA, R 52 IV/ 144d as well as Werner Conze, "Die ländliche Überbevölkerung in Polen" [The Rural Overpopulation in Poland], in *Arbeiten des XIV. Internationalen Soziologen-Kongresses Bucaresti, Mitteilungen, Abteilung B—das Dorf*, Vol. 1 = D. Gusti (ed.), *Schriften zur Soziologie, Ethik und Politik. Studien und Forschung* (Bucarest, 1940), p. 40: "Rural overpopulation in large parts of east central Europe is one of the most serious societal and political questions altogether.... In Russia it has contributed decisively to the Bolshevik overthrow." Detailed account in Aly/Heim, *Vordenker der Vernichtung*, pp. 237ff. and Götz Aly, *Macht, Geist, Wahn. Kontinuitäten deutschen Denkens* (Berlin, 1997), pp. 153-183.

42. Reich Security Main Office (RSHA): "Madagaskar-Projekt," drafted in late July/early August 1940; PAA, lig/177, p. 201. See now Magnus Brechtken,

'*Madagaskar für die Juden*': *Antisemitische Idee und politische Praxis 1885-1945* (Munich, 1997).

43. This occurred in the period of 23 Jan. to 15 Feb. 1941. Letter of the Reich Finance Minister Schwerin von Krosigk of 11 Nov. 1940 to the Reich Minister of the Interior; BA, Reichsfinanzministerium, B 6158, Bl. 87f. In this letter, the Reich Finance Minister also expressed concern that the population of the ghetto would not "contribute to the public purse," i.e., pay taxes.

44. Niederschrift der Beauftragten des Rechnungshofs des Deutschen Reichs über die örtliche Prüfung der Ernährungs- und Wirtschaftsstelle Ghetto des Oberbürgermeisters der Stadt Litzmannstadt in Litzmannstadt, Hermann-Göring-Straße Nr. 21; ZstAp, Reichsfinanzministerium/B 6159, Bl. 84-103, here 98 (printed in *Beiträge zur nationalsozialistischen Gesundheits- und Sozialpolitik*, Vol. 9 (Berlin, 1991)). The remark obviously refers to Heydrich's intervention with Hitler aimed at conducting further evacuations into the Government General in 1941.

45. The directive for the assessment was issued by the director of the *Hauptabteilung Wirtschaft des Generalgouvernements*, Walter Emmerich. It took place as an immediate, critical reaction to the conceptual (and, in economic terms, optimistic) presentation of Waldemar Schön on the "formation of the Jewish residential sector in Warsaw." See note 61.

46. Reichskuratorium für Wirtschaftlichkeit, Dienststelle Generalgouvernement, *Die Wirtschaftsbilanz des jüdischen Wohnbezirks in Warschau* (Cracow, March 1941); Staatsarchiv Warschau, Der Kommissar für den jüdischen Wohnbezirk in Warschau / 125. The report contains 53 pages and 10 appendices; the author is Rudolf Gater (printed in *Beiträge zur nationalsozialistischen Gesundheits- und Sozialpolitik*, Vol. 9 (Berlin, 1991), pp. 85-138.)

47. Aktenvermerk des Leiters des SD-Abschnitts Posen, Höppner, betr. Überlegungen zu einer 'Lösung der Judenfrage' im Warthegau mit Anschreiben an Eichmann, 16.7.1941; quoted from Kurt Pätzold (ed.), *Verfolgung, Vernichtung, Vertreibung. Dokumente des faschistischen Antisemitismus 1933-1942* (Leipzig, 1987), p. 295.

48. On the figures see Aly, *Endlösung*, pp. 166-176.

49. This affected about 1,000 persons, who at this time occupied—in the view of the German administration, blocked—beds in Danzig and environs. Discussion on 29 Oct. 1939 between commissioner Ehlich of the EWZ/Gotenhafen, responsible for questions of health, Dr. Hanns Meixner, and Pg. Schram(m)el of the NSV about the "Versorgung der kranken und gebrechlichen Baltendeutschen" [Care of the sick and frail Baltic Germans], teletype by Meixner to Ehlich on the same day "Betr. Sicherstellung von Altersheimen" [Re. Seizure of Elderly Homes] for Baltic Germans in need of care; BA, R69/426.

50. Aktenvermerk der EWZ (Transport- und Unterkunftstelle) vom 4.11.1939 "Betr.: Transport von 700 geisteskranken Polen am 3.11.1939 und 700 gebrechlichen Baltendeutschen am 4.11.1939" [Re.: Transport of 700 mentally ill Poles on Nov. 3, 1939 and 700 frail Baltic Germans on 4 Nov. 1939], BA R69/426. The Polish patients were removed in eighteen freight cars, the frail Baltic Germans transported in third-class, some in second-class cars. "The Higher SS and Police Chief, *Gruppenführer* Hildebrandt" requested beforehand "exact information about the departure times." The institution at Schwetz was then officially redesignated as an elderly home and rebuilt at the considerable cost of 400,000 reichsmarks to be supplied by the RKF. See notes and letters of the RKF from 3, 21, and 22 November 1941; BA R49/2609.

51. On the "euthanasia" killing operation: Henry Friedlander, "Jüdische Anstalts-patienten in Deutschland," in Götz Aly (ed.), *Aktion T4 1939-1945. Die "Euthanasie"-Zentrale in der Tiergartenstraße 4* (Berlin, 1989), pp. 34-44.

52. A letter of the Higher SS and Police Leader Wilhelm Koppe, who was also a commissioner of the Reich Commissar for the Strengthening of the German Nation (RKF), to Jakob Schnorrenberg on 18 October 1941 reads in part: "The Sonderkommando 'Lange', put under my command for special missions" had been "assigned to Soldau in East Prussia and during this time evacuated 1,558 patients from the transit camp Soldau." On 22 February 1941 Koppe wrote to Karl Wolff: "In June 1940 I have taken over 1,558 cumbersome persons with a view to accommodating them otherwise." Quoted from: Vorun-tersuchungen gegen Wilhelm Koppe, LG Bonn, 13 UR 1/61 (Anlage zur Abschlußprüfung vom 30.9.1963); see Aly, *Endlösung*, pp. 188ff.

53. Aktenvermerk Höppners vom 24.6.1940; AGK, UWZ/P/252, Bl. 8. The passage is also contained in the two guidelines issued at the same time by Eich-mann on 23 Nov. 1940, "Richtlinien zur Durchführung der Evakuierungsak-tionen im Wartheland" [Guidelines for Evacuation Operations in the Warthe-gau] and "Richtlinien zur Durchführung der Evakuierungsaktionen im Kreis Saybusch" [Guidelines for Evacuation Operations in the district of Saybusch]; AGK, UWZ/L/1, Bl. 23ff.

54. Report of the SD Main Office Posen on the "Auswirkungen der Umsiedlung im Landkreise Posen" [Effects of the Resettlement in the District of Posen] from 19 Oct. 1940; AGK, UWZ/P/195, Bl. 4f. A similar Report dated 25 Oct. 1940 is contained in ibid./225, Bl. 5.

55. See Isaiah Trunk, *Lodzher geto* (New York, 1962), p. 251, and Frank Gol-czewski, "Polen," in Wolfgang Benz (ed.), *Dimension des Völkermords. Die Zahl der jüdischen Opfer des Nationalsozialismus* (Munich, 1991), p. 431.

56. Teletype of the *Gaustabsamtsleiter* of the *Gau* Office Mainfranken, Karl Hell-muth, on 24 September 1940 to the Ethnic German Liaison Office; BAK, R59/132; Bl. 279. The Werneck clinic was housed in the castle built by Balthasar Neumann, which was filmed for the propaganda movie of the "T4," "Dasein ohne Leben" [Existence without Life], as an example of the supposed excess care for the mentally ill. (See Karl Heinz Roth, "Filmpropaganda für die Vernichtung der Geisteskranken und Behinderten im Dritten Reich," in Götz Aly et al., *Reform und Gewissen. 'Euthanasie' im Dienst des Fortschritts* (*Beiträge zur nationalsozialistischen Gesundheits- und Sozialpolitik*, Vol. 2) (Berlin, 1985), pp. 125-193.

57. Letter from Ehlich on 4 February 1941 to the SS Standartenführer Max Soll-mann, who intended to turn the asylum into a *Lebensborn* center.; Berlin Document Centre (BDC), now BA, SS-Ordner (SS-HO) 5372. 70; quoted from Hans Georg Gebel, Heinrich Grießhammer, *Dokumentation zu den Krankenverlegungen aus den Neuen Dettelsauer Anstalten 1941, dem Verhal-ten von Innerer Mission und Kirche 1936-42 und der heutigen Reaktion von Kirche und Diakonie auf die Nachfrage nach den Ereignissen* (Berlin, 1977) (Private Printing).

58. See in general Hans Mommsen, "Umvolkungspläne des Nationalsozialismus und der Holocaust," in Klaus Bästlein, Helge Grabitz, and Johannes Tuschel (eds.), *Die Normalität des Verbrechens. Bilanz und Perspektiven der Forschung zu den nationalsozialistischen Gewaltverbrechen* (Berlin, 1994), pp. 68-84.

59. The term originated with Hitler himself. As a conversation between Canaris and Keitel on 12 September 1939 reveals, on 7 September Hitler had already

spoken to Brauchitsch of the need for a *"völkische Flurbereinigung"* in Poland. Aktenvermerk von Lahousen vom 14.9.1939 on the conversation in the Führer's railway car on 12 September 1939 in Illnau; quoted in Helmuth Groscurth, *Tagebücher eines Abwehroffiziers 1938-1940*, ed. Helmut Krausnick and Harold C. Deutsch (Stuttgart, 1970), pp. 357ff.

60. Lecture notes of Himmler for the "Vortrag vor den Reichs- und Gauleitern in Berlin am 10.12.1940"; BA, NS19/4007. As he specifically noted, Himmler appeared in "civilian clothes." (Terminkalender Himmler, Eintragung vom 10.12.1940; BA, NS19/3954.)

61. Bericht Schöns vom 20.1.1941 über die Bildung des Warschauer Ghettos; quoted from *Die faschistische Okkupationspolitik in Polen (1939-1945). Dokumentenauswahl und Einleitung von Werner Röhr u. a. (Europa unterm Hakenkreuz*, Vol. 3) (Berlin, 1989), p. 194. Because the total figure given by Heydrich for the first phase of the third *Nahplan* was 248,500 people, the deportees were apparently to be distributed evenly to the four districts of the Government General.

62. Franz Halder, Eintrag vom 25. März 1941 in his diary; quoted from Franz Halder, *Kriegstagebuch. Tägliche Aufzeichnungen des Chefs des Generalstabes des Heeres 1939-1942*, edited by Hans-Adolf Jacobsen, 3 vols., Vol. II (Stuttgart, 1962-1964), p. 328; see Helmut Krausnick, *Hitlers Einsatzgruppen. Die Truppen des Weltanschauungskrieges 1938-1942* (Frankfurt a.M., 1985), p. 116; Hans-Adolf Jacobsen, "Kommissarbefehl und Massenexekutionen sowjetischer Kriegsgefangener," in Martin Broszat, idem, Helmut Krausnick, *Konzentrationslager, Kommissarbefehl, Judenverfolgung (Anatomie des SS-Staates*, Vol. 2) (Olten, Freiburg, 1965), pp. 170ff.

63. Vermerk Heydrichs vom 26.3.1941 über den "heutigen Vormittag beim Reichsmarschall"; Zentrum zur Aufbewahrung historisch-dokumentarischer Sammlung (earlier Sonderarchiv) Moskau (ZASM), 500/6/795.

64. Brief Görings vom 31. Juli 1941 and Heydrich; quoted from Internationaler Militärgerichtshof (Nuremberg) (IMT) (ed.), *Der Prozeß gegen die Hauptkriegsverbrecher vor dem Internationalen Militärgerichtshof, Nürnberg, 14. November 1945–1. Oktober 1946*. [International Military Tribunal (ed.), *Trial of the Major War Criminals Before the International Military Tribunal, Nuremberg, 14 November 1945–1 October 1946*.], 42 vols., Vol. XXVI (Nuremberg, 1947f.), pp. 266f.

65. Officially he only attained this position with the decree signed by Hitler on 17 July 1941 on the "Verwaltung der neubesetzten Ostgebiete" [Administration of the Newly Occupied Eastern Territories]. Usually it is assumed that Rosenberg's appointment through Hitler took place on April 2, 1941. (See Alexander Dallin, *Deutsche Herrschaft in Rußland 1941-1945. Eine Studie über Besatzungspolitik*. Düsseldorf, 1958.). In fact, as Heydrich's note appears to suggest, this appointment took place earlier in spoken form.

66. See Aly, *Endlösung*, pp. 268ff. Clear echoes of this—older—concept appear in the Protocol of the Wannsee Conference.

67. While in custody in 1960, Eichmann also described under the heading "Meine Memoiren" [My Memoirs], among other things, his "problems" in the summer of 1941; quoted from Pätzold, Schwarz, *Tagesordnung*, pp. 160ff. (The comment of the two authors that this constituted "an invention" of Eichmann's is not correct.)

68. Vermerk Höppners vom 2.9.1941 für Eichmann und Ehlich mit Anschreiben vom 3.9.; BA, Zwischenarchiv Dahlwitz-Hoppegarten (BA-DH), ZR 890 A 2,

Bl. 222-238. Contained among the files of the UWZ-Lodz is a somewhat differently organized structure regarding the topic of this memorandum. The document is neither dated nor signed. (AGK, UWZ/L/3, Bl. 1.)

69. Thus Lösener about the conference in the Ministry of Propaganda, in which he participated as principal of the Ministry of the Interior, along with representatives of Goebbels, Speer, the RSHA, and others; in Bernhard Lösener, "Als Rassenreferent im Reichsministerium des Inneren," in VfZ 9 (1961): 303.

70. Thus the entry in Himmler's calendar; quoted from Peter Witte, "Zwei Entscheidungen in der 'Endlösung der Judenfrage': Deportation nach Lodz und Vernichtung in Chelmno," in Theresienstädter Studien und Dokumente (Prague, 1995), p. 51.

71. Schreiben Eichmanns an Fähndrich (sent as a copy by Eichmann to the UWZ-Posen) vom 19.9.1941; AGK, UWZ/L/1, Bl. 110.

72. Martin Broszat, "Hitler und die Genesis der 'Endlösung'. Aus Anlaß der Thesen von David Irving (1977)," in idem, Nach Hitler. Der schwierige Umgang mit unserer Geschichte (Munich, 1988), p. 63.

73. This is now confirmed on a very dense empirical basis by the recent studies of Dieter Pohl and Thomas Sandkühler. Dieter Pohl, Nationalsozialistische Judenverfolgung in Ostgalizien 1941-1944. Organisation und Durchführung eines staatlichen Massenverbrechens (Munich, 1996); Thomas Sandkühler, 'Endlösung' in Galizien. Der Judenmord in Ostpolen und die Rettungsinitiativen von Berthold Beitz, 1941-1944 (Bonn, 1996).

74. Hans Frank on 16 December 1941 before the cabinet members in Cracow; quoted from Präg and Jacobmeyer, Diensttagebuch, pp. 457ff.

75. Quoted from Aly, Endlösung, pp. 353f.

76. Franz Neumann, Behemoth. Struktur und Praxis des Nationalsozialismus 1933-1944 (Frankfurt a.M., 1984) [1st ed. 1944, 2nd ed. 1944; Behemoth. The Structure and Practice of National Socialism. Toronto, 1942.], pp. 542, 553ff.

– Chapter 3 –

THE MURDER OF JEWS IN THE GENERAL GOVERNMENT

Dieter Pohl

The worst mass murders of the entire "Final Solution of the Jewish Question" took place over the seven weeks from late July to mid-September 1942. Transports daily rolled through Poland from the ghettos to the Belzec and Treblinka extermination camps. We could choose any date, for example, 19 August 1942. From numerous publications we now know that on this day the 101st Police Reserve Battalion wiped out the Jewish community in the village of Lomazy near Lublin.[1] On the same 19 August, one deportation train left Lvov and another Jaslo in the Cracow District for the Belzec extermination camp; one train left Warsaw and another nearby Otwock for the Treblinka camp. In all these cases the victims were driven out of their houses and to assembly points where they were separated according to whether or not they had working papers. If not, German and Ukrainian police crammed them into freight trains which rolled in the broiling heat toward small locations near the villages of Belzec and Treblinka.

At the camps, under the blows of whips, totally exhausted people were pulled out of freight cars onto ramps, and a few of them were selected as workers. Finally camp guards drove the others in large groups through a double fence to another part of the grounds.

Notes for this section begin on page 100.

The Jewish men had to enter the building with the gas chambers first. After the air-tight doors were bolted shut, the victims were suffocated with exhaust fumes from a diesel motor. After some twenty minutes all were dead. The next group, which had waited near the ramps, took the same route. Thus, on this one day well over 25,000 people—the equivalent of a small city—met a gruesome death.[2] No less bestial was the Lomazy massacre, mentioned above, when Jews were shot by Order Police (*Ordnungspolizei*) at a large ditch. Thus, at this time mass murder on the scale of the Babi Yar shootings in Kiev was taking place daily. Nonetheless, for a long time researchers paid little attention to these events.

I

One of the central debates among researchers on the "Final Solution" concerns the question whether this development was prescribed from the outset or is primarily to be explained through the events of 1941/42. To answer that question, we must look backward at least to the Polish campaign in the fall of 1939. There is much evidence for the notion that it is only possible within certain limits to speak of an open situation after 1939; that is, a segment of Polish Jews were already condemned to death when the Wehrmacht marched in.

What does this mean? First we must point to the anti-Jewish acts of violence by the SS, but also by the Wehrmacht, in September 1939. These ranged from humiliations of allegedly typical Eastern Jews to mass shootings. It is conjectured that by the end of 1939 some 7,000 Polish Jews had been murdered. The wartime situation and the antisemitic mood here worked in concert. No concrete commands from Berlin to murder Jews have been produced for 1939.[3] Nevertheless, a threshold had already been crossed—and for good. From this point virtually every action against Poland's Jews was—directly or indirectly—connected with mass murder.

To be sure, the politics in Berlin were even more fatal than the acts of violence. Since November 1938 Jewish policy had fallen increasingly under the jurisdiction of the SS and Gestapo. Beginning in Austria what were known as total solutions of the "Jewish Question" appeared in the minds of policy planners. With the occupation of Poland, a multitude of agencies and institutions competed with one another to offer blueprints for the "reorganization" of Poland. One of these ideas was the plan for a "Jewish reservation" (*Judenreservat*). Developed in only a few weeks, this project was meant to provide a short-term "Final Solution" for most of Europe's Jews. Yet after beginnings that were as dilettantish as they were brutal, the entire project was dropped *ad acta* in the spring of 1940. It was, however, characteristic that this "Solution of the Jewish Question" —contrary to the previously pursued goal of Jewish emigration— already indirectly aimed at genocide, whether through starvation in barren regions or slave labor to the point of exhaustion.

Beginning in the spring of 1940 the General Government (*Generalgouvernement*) had established its administration to represent German sovereignty in central and southeastern Poland. In August 1941 east Galicia was added. In the interim, a stable civil administration had been created which assumed responsibility for nearly all aspects of the persecution of Jews and rejected the project of a "Jewish reservation" on its territory. Here we see the central characteristic of National Socialist rule, in particular in eastern Europe, namely, the disjunction between utopian projects and the reality of scarce resources and contested jurisdictions. With the French campaign, a new utopian total plan developed: the notion of deporting the Jews to the French colony of Madagascar.

At this time, the General Government became only a secondary focus of Berlin's planning. The persecution of Jews was largely steered locally. This was particularly evident in the construction of ghettos. Since all Jews were originally to be deported, the institution of fixed ghettos was at first not anticipated. Because the military and civil administrations had already partly expropriated the Jewish minority and thus pushed them to the margins of society, officials confronted a self-generated problem; they now had to use their own administration to provide for the Jews they themselves had pauperized.

As the deportation of all Jews was postponed indefinitely, regional administrations began to debate the total isolation of the Jews. Several *Landräte* had already established ghettos on their own initiative in late 1939. In 1940, ghettos were created in Warsaw, in particular, and then in Cracow. Here, too, local administrations provided critical motivation for isolating the Jews. Individual officials combined the creation of ghettos with the idea of a separate slave labor economy within a large city; others strove early on to use the predictably catastrophic living conditions to kill as many Jews as possible. Christopher R. Browning has demonstrated this to particular effect in regard to Warsaw.[4] While the ghetto operations never really became profitable, by the fall of 1941 these sections of cities became "death traps" (*Todeskisten*), as Goebbels once called them. Mortality rates in the Warsaw Ghetto reached levels that even the large concentration camps did not match. In Warsaw from June 1941 on, between 3,500 and 5,500 people died every month.[5]

It remains true that—contrary to popular belief—only part of the Jews in the General Government were confined behind ghetto walls before the beginning of 1941. Aside from Warsaw, this was the case above all in the Cracow and Radom districts. An important impetus in this regard was the Wehrmacht's deployment in Operation Barbarossa. After the spring of 1941 the German military began, on a grand scale, to confiscate Polish housing for its own uses. Poles were then housed in Jewish residences. Now homeless Jews were either expelled to central cities or locked up within ghetto walls. This was particularly the case in the Radom District and the city of Lublin in the spring of 1941. Elsewhere there were only a few stretches of barely enclosed "Jewish residential areas" (jüdische Wohnbezirke), in contemporary German officialese. At issue were, above all, shortages of guards and building materials, as well as the fear that population movement within the cities would spread disease, in particular due to the horrible living conditions in the ghettos. Extensive ghetto construction began with little notice during 1942 in an effort to make residents available for mass murder and to isolate Jewish skilled labor. Many ghettos were, to be sure, never as hermetically sealed off from the outside world as that of Warsaw.

In conjunction with preparations for the campaign against the Soviet Union, early in 1941 new plans arose in Berlin for the "Solution of the Jewish Question." For the first time, however, they now concerned more than the Jews in Germany or Poland. Under consideration were plans to expel all Jews from territories under German rule to the occupied Soviet Union, either to the Pripyat marshes in Belorussia or to the Arctic Sea. Accordingly, on 17 March 1941 Hitler remarked to Hans Frank that all Jews were to be expelled from the General Government eastward.[6] Thereafter the General Government administration halted until further notice all plans for Jewish policies. In particular, plans to construct more ghettos were put on hold.[7] The mass murder of Jews in the General Government, which began in October 1941,[8] can be divided into four phases.

1. The fundamental transition to direct mass murder was decided upon in the fall of 1941. Plans for large-scale transfers to the Soviet Union could no longer be realized because of the military situation. The attack on the Soviet Union itself brought a new stage in the persecution of Jews. At first particular groups of Jewish men in the newly occupied territories were murdered; after late July 1941 the elderly, women, and children also became victims of mass

murder. A parallel development took place in east Galicia, which the Soviets held until summer 1941. The German invasion was followed by brutal pogroms as well as mass murders of Jewish men. On the first of August, the region was annexed to the General Government. These crimes, as well as killings in territories further east, immediately became known throughout the General Government. During the fall of 1941, 100,000 Soviet prisoners of war were held captive under the most horrific conditions in General Government territory; most of them perished during the winter of 1941/42. In September 1941 the German police began to shoot those prisoners of war, including all Jews, who were categorized as "undesirable." Finally, all prisoners caught trying to escape were shot.[9] Since 1940 German authorities had been taking such measures against Jews who escaped from the Lodz ghetto. As epidemics threatened to spread from the prisoner-of-war camps to the cities and from there in particular to the weakened Jewish communities, the German administration used the occasion to impose death sentences on Jews who had fled the ghettos and—in Nazi jargon—were seen as "carriers of epidemics." The administration soon decided that a legal process was too cumbersome because the number of cases was so high. Thus the police undertook this task themselves, and in November 1941 decreed *ad hoc* a "Shooting Order" for all Jews captured outside the city. Thus already by the fall of 1941, a climate of mass murder was present in the General Government, even before the extermination camps were built.[10]

This was the overall situation. From September to October two particular regional developments began. Previously, in July, Himmler had assigned responsibility for the future settlement of Germans in the Lublin District and the occupied Soviet Union to Lublin SS and Police Leader (*SS- und Polizeiführer*) Odilo Globocnik. However, as it became clear in October 1941 that the Jews from this region would not be pushed eastward, Globocnik made a request to Himmler for "radical measures." On 13 October he negotiated in person with Himmler.[11] Around this time he was sent a group of "euthanasia" functionaries, who in November 1941 began laying out small extermination camps near Belzec and Sobibor on the edge of the district.[12]

The second regional development occurred in the Galicia District, where after June 1941 Jewish men from the so-called "intelligentsia" were murdered. After 6 October these crimes were then extended to women and children in southern Galicia. Two reasons were decisive. First, the civil administration urged the "resettlement" of east Galician Jews in ghettos, now that it had become clear that the deportation of Jews to the Soviet Union, which Hitler had announced, could no longer be counted upon, and the construction of Jewish ghettos was again being discussed. In order to make room in the Jewish quarter in Stanislau, part of the community was shot. The second cause was more general in nature: the overall radicalization of Jewish policy throughout eastern Europe. If a year earlier far-reaching plans had been worked out to organize deportations, the authorities now grasped at simpler measures. The Jews, for whom there was allegedly no room, no food, no work, no medicine, were now to be shot. Direct genocide against Jews in the General Government began no later than the widespread massacres of October. By year's end in east Galicia some 60,000 people had been murdered in mass shootings under horrible conditions.

2. The second stage of mass murder, the interim phase from March to May 1942, when the first deportations to extermination camps began, was probably seen as a sort of test phase for the entire General Government. For the foreseeable future, the killing facilities in the Belzec extermination camp were still much too small to kill all the General Government's Jews. Thus the police and civil administration established priorities. Those to be murdered were Jews considered "incapable of work," especially those from Lublin, Lvov, and cities in south Galicia. Jews continued to be deported from small cities in the Lublin District, to which a mixture of German, Austrian, Czech, and Slovakian Jews were simultaneously assigned. Only in May 1942 did it become clear that more than local mass killings were intended. With completion of the Sobibor camp, a more extensive killing began of all those in the Lublin District who were deemed unable to work.

3. The provisional regional developments ended with the third phase of genocide, which began around May or June 1942. Not until early May did concrete preparations begin in all five districts for a thoroughgoing "cleaning out" of the ghettos. In many places this included the temporary isolation of all Jews and their classification in three groups: "important to the war effort," "capable of work," and "incapable of work." This phase also included the civil administration's formal loss of jurisdiction over Jewish persecution. The Gestapo had previously had formal responsibility for the murder of Jews. Now their superiors, the SS, assumed primary control. Whereas the Security Police had a relatively small staff, the Order Police provided the SS and Security Police commanders enough troops in Poland to empty out ghettos and conduct mass shootings.

On the request of Globocnik, on 19 July 1942, Himmler, who was visiting in Lublin, gave the SS and police leaders official approval

to carry out the planned measures. At the same time the Reichsführer SS gave the order by year's end to kill all Jews in the General
Government who were "incapable of work." At the beginning of
this article I tried to sketch what followed. Destruction of the Warsaw Ghetto began on 22 July 1942. In addition, at Treblinka, in the
Warsaw district, an extermination camp much larger than the earlier ones at Belzec and Sobibor had been built. But in these two
places the old gas chambers were ripped out and replaced by larger
new ones.

The brutal reality of ghetto evacuations was obvious to everyone at the time, and news quickly leaked out about what was happening to the Jews who were transported. Ever more frequently the
police also pulled Jewish workers out of the factories, especially
when particular deportation quotas had to be met, whereas the SS
leadership wanted Jews to work only in armaments factories. Thus
in the fall of 1942 a debate developed with business concerns and
the Wehrmacht on one side and the SS on the other. As a consequence, in September 1942 even Hitler was willing to let at least
skilled workers temporarily live. However, they were to be quartered in closely guarded forced labor camps. Like the ghetto construction, these plans were only partially carried out; not only were
new camps built, the reduced ghettos were declared work ghettos.
Himmler's order to murder all Jews whom the Germans did not
consider capable of work could in any case not be fully carried out.
The Reich railroads did not have enough trains, organization at the
extermination camps often broke down, and police personnel
became ever scarcer because of harvesting duties and the beginning
of partisan fighting. Nonetheless, in all General Government districts except Galicia, the overwhelming majority of Jews were murdered by the end of 1942, in Lublin already by 9 November, the
Nazi holiday. According to German statistics, by year's end only
300,000 of the original two million Jews were still alive, most of
them slave laborers with families or in ghettos or camps.

The dissolution of ghettos continued in the spring of 1943.
Because the Belzec extermination camp had been closed, the police
in east Galicia began—as earlier in the fall of 1941—with mass
shootings. In Warsaw, however, the police encountered massive
resistance in January 1943. By April the Jews were engaging in
armed resistance, which in May was suppressed without mercy. On
18 June the police exterminated the last ghetto in east Galicia. Thus
Himmler's order was carried out within a year.

4. In the fourth and final phase of genocide, beginning in the
summer of 1943, Jews in the General Government—altogether per-

haps 130,000 persons—lived only in forced labor camps or illegally. The camps were divided into two large labor complexes: in
the Galicia and Lublin districts, Jews engaged above all in the man-
ufacture of textiles and wood products; in the Cracow and particularly in the Radom districts, they worked in armaments production.
In the Warsaw area, almost no Jewish slave laborers were left; the
Warsaw concentration camp held only some non-Polish Jews as
prisoners. In the eastern sector of the General Government, even the
slave laborers were soon killed. As early as the summer of 1943,
immediately after the ghettos were dissolved, the police killed nearly
everyone in the camps in east Galicia. When uprisings broke out in
the Treblinka and Sobibor extermination camps, Himmler ordered
the immediate killing of all Jews still living in the eastern part of the
General Government, particularly in the Lublin District, in "Operation Harvest Festival" (*Aktion Erntefest*) on 2-3 November 1943.
Only some of the Jewish workers in the armaments industry, mostly
in the Radom District, were able—despite the inhuman conditions
of labor and incarceration—to survive until 1944-1945, then to be
swept into the chaos of evacuations and death marches. Most of
them perished.

   Beyond German control, Jews who had gone underground hid
in the cities, using what were known as Aryan papers, or with
Poles, and in some cases with Ukrainians and Germans. Many of
them survived the war. In the forests, Jews who had gone underground joined together in partisan bands and conducted a war of
survival. Police patrols or German antipartisan units detected and
killed most of them.

   Altogether the number of surviving Polish Jews can be counted
in the tens of thousands, most of whom emigrated after the war.

II

When one examines the mass murders of the summer of 1942 in
greater detail, the question arises: how was an administrative apparatus able to organize such carnage? Historiography has long presented only a vague picture of ghetto clearings in the General
Government. Documents in eastern European archives and interrogation records in state attorneys' offices in the Federal Republic
now allow reconstruction of these events with relative precision.

   Closer examination of the perpetrator apparatus in the General
Government reveals structures that do not fit the picture of a perfectly functioning super-bureaucracy, in which every element need

only work like a cog in the larger machine. Rather one sees conditions reminiscent of a colonial administration that is as corrupt and criminal as it is dilettantish. In the General Government, and particularly in the Galicia District, which was established later, one finds a motley assemblage of career officials, individuals recruited for Emergency Service obligations (*Notdienstverpflichtete*), incompetent employees of the Reich administration, and, not infrequently, freelance soldiers of fortune. The cause was above all the notorious personnel shortage in the huge territory under occupation in the East.

Personnel recruitment was, however, only one side of the coin. The other, and ultimately more important factor was the reality of life as experienced by the rank and file of the occupiers. Götz Aly and Susanne Heim have characterized it as the "vitality of the master race" (*Lebensgefühl des Herrenmenschen*).[13] Fundamentally, there was enormous social mobility. Minor officials from municipal administrations in Germany sometimes ruled here alone over areas the size of a *Regierungsbezirk*. Particularly in the rural districts (*Kreisen*), independent action was not only required by circumstances but was demanded by officials in Cracow. A few personnel were expected to make maximum encroachments on Polish society: not only the isolation, exploitation, and murder of Jews, but also the elimination of any resistance, the plundering of the agrarian economy, and finally the recruitment of slave labor for the Reich.

Despite the various methods of personnel recruitment, the ideological conformity of the men and (occasionally) women in the occupation apparatus is amazing. Political examinations were carried out; and elements that appeared to be antagonistic to the Nazi viewpoint did not receive an administrative position. Antisemitism was altogether more widespread and massive than in the Reich. Communication within the caste of occupiers was critical. The Germans were constantly confronted with problems concerning the Jews, so there was constant talk about the so-called "Jewish problem." Indeed, hatred of Jews was a matter of course. The attitude toward Poles, or even more so toward the large number of Soviet prisoners of war interned in the General Government, was often not much different. The extent to which direct contact with Jews and their horrible living conditions affected the attitude and behavior of the occupation forces remains to be examined.

This altogether peculiar milieu differed in important ways from that in the Reich or occupied western Europe. Most members of the occupation apparatus were freed from their traditional social ties. A unique mixture of bureaucracy and de-bureaucratization pre-

vailed: the administrative apparatus had a critical practical importance for "Jewish policy," but efficient bureaucratic structure was
as rare as mandatory regulations or guidelines for decision-making.
Altogether there was an extreme ideological mentality among the
occupation personnel. The apparatuses were institutions of ideological warfare.

The civil administration, the General Government under Hans
Frank, with headquarters in Cracow, assumed central decision-
making authority, for instance over the persecution of Jews in the
summer of 1942.[14] A lot of information has since become known
regarding general policies, less about the apparatus itself, for example, the sections responsible for Jews, in particular those involved
with so-called population issues and welfare, which reached to the
Kreis level. In addition, the labor, food, and health offices had
authority over anti-Jewish measures, and the labor offices often
chose candidates for death.

Although relatively many contemporary documents are available, in the postwar period the highest General Government officials systematically obscured their participation in Nazi crimes.
Many of them rose to high positions in the Federal Republic, and
they not infrequently used their mutual connections to coordinate
testimonies. Nonetheless, there is no longer doubt that the civil
administration over a long period not only had ultimate jurisdiction over the persecution of Jews, but also systematically carried
out a radically anti-Jewish policy. In this regard the administrative
officials endeavored to solve such general problems as financial and
food shortages at the expense of the Jewish minority. Early on, the
death of many allegedly "dispensable" Jews entered into the calculation. At the latest, when it became clear that mass shootings of
Jews were already taking place in the regions to the east, the civil
administration switched over to a strategy of extermination, as formulated by General Governor Frank himself, in December 1941.[15]

The murder of Jews functioned increasingly as a reaction to
various problems—from the housing shortage to inadequate food
supplies and epidemics. To be sure, in individual branches of the
administration there was always a certain diversity of views, for
example in the regional Office for Labor and Agriculture. There is
little proof that the civil administration was a leading *instigator* of
the mass murders, such as took place in the Wartegau or the Reich
Commissariats in the East. To be sure, the administration had
always pushed for "removal" of the Jews and largely agreed to the
mass killings in the camps, indeed even applied pressure to expedite
the murder of Jews "incapable of work." At a minimum, district

administrations and *Kreise,* cooperated fully in organizing deportations into the summer of 1942.[16] Also, after the official loss of jurisdiction over this matter, the majority of chief local officials— *Kreishauptleute,* as the *Landräte* in the General Government were called—did not relinquish their involvement in these operations. What counted was not the formal jurisdictional boundaries and the permanent wrangling over power, but rather the common goal, the "removal" of Jews.

The Security Police, on the other hand, were ready for mass murder even earlier, as was illustrated not only by crimes against Jews and Poles in late 1939, but also by atrocities during the time of the established civil administration. In May 1940, the police shot thousands of Poles in the course of an "Extraordinary Pacification Operation" (*Außerordentliche Befriedigungsaktion*) and murdered invalids in Polish institutions. Some of the police personnel belonged to *Einsatzgruppe z.B.V.* in "Operation Barbarossa"; in July/August 1941, they shot ten thousand Jewish men in eastern Poland. Under the already mentioned order to shoot Jews who were apprehended outside cities, the numerically strong Order Police were increasingly deployed for mass shootings of Jews. After September 1941 they also participated in the killing of "undesirable" Soviet prisoners of war. Internal debates about these activities seem to have been limited to the Order Police, although documentary evidence is hard to find.

One can hardly say this of the Gestapo in Poland, the heart of the murder apparatus. In the districts and even more so on the *Kreis* level, Gestapo officers conducted few investigations. Rather they were regularly deployed, along with the Order Police, local auxiliaries, and often, as well, the Jewish Ghetto Police (*Ordnungsdienst*), in order to herd Jews to train stations or nearby execution sites. It is difficult to describe the brutality employed in the process, especially after the summer of 1942, when invalids and small children were systematically shot in their homes. Nearly every member of the Security Police/SD-*Außenstellen* (branch offices) in the General Government personally shot dozens or several hundred Jews. Relatively little is known about the internal functioning of these Gestapo offices,[17] especially compared to the many new publications on the Gestapo in the Reich. But as was the case with the Order Police, it seems that the personnel were by and large not selectively chosen, rather were often conscripted ethnic Germans or regular police who in 1937/38 were taken over by the Gestapo. The most important posts—that is, the chiefs of the branches (*Dienststellen-Leiter*), their deputies, and the so-called Jewish experts (*Judenreferenten*)—were, of course, occupied entirely by radical Nazis. For this reason it is necessary to examine more closely the interaction between the radical leadership group and ordinary police forces.

In the ghetto clearings, mass shootings, and deportation transports the division of responsibility was important only at the outset; on-site organization and implementation was carried out jointly, as preliminary discussions of the operations demonstrate. If personnel bottlenecks then appeared, the police went outside the bureaucracy and approached nearly all German institutions for office help, for example, customs officials, forest rangers, or railroad police, in one case even savings bank employees.[18] But because there was no legal basis for such a practice, it was left to the respective superior to decide whether to participate. In many cases they did so, but often they did not.[19]

What are the peculiarities of the development of the "Final Solution" in the General Government? Every third victim of the mass murder in Europe came from the General Government. Not just in terms of geography, the region occupies a middle position between the annexed eastern territories and the occupied Soviet territories. From west to east personal amenities and professional qualifications of German occupation personnel declined, and increasing independence and initiative was demanded of officials. While plans existed from the outset to "germanize" (*einzudeutschen*) the annexed eastern regions, plans for the future of the General Government remained unclear until late 1941. In the Soviet Union, as in Poland in 1939, mass shootings of particular populations began under cover of war. In Poland there was at least a momentary halt to further extension of the killing operations, prompted by protests from the Wehrmacht command as well as international public attention. There was no such opposition in the Soviet Union, where extermination policies were forced ever further. Between August and September 1941 the total destruction of Soviet Jews began, thereby reaching a point of no return and making "normal" occupation rule impossible.

The occupation authorities in Poland still intended to push the Jews "eastward," but already in the summer of 1941, they began to demand or encourage the killing of particular groups of Jews. The establishment of central camps for all European Jews in the Soviet Union was, to be sure, planned. But the fact that the war had not been won paved the way for so-called "territorial final solutions." The killing was to be organized and carried out on-site. This process was hastened by the fact that, after the fall of 1941, the General Government was pulled ever closer to the planning of settlements.

This was the hour of Odilo Globocnik, who would work not—as originally planned—in the Soviet Union, but rather in his own Lublin District.[20] Using the murder apparatus of the "Euthanasia Operation," Globocnik built the extermination machinery of "Operation Reinhard"—from the first small camps to the systematic mass murder of the summer of 1942. The civil administration largely went along on this path to mass murders, even though it had to relinquish ever more responsibilities within the General Government. It did retain extensive jurisdiction over the persecution of Jews in the Warthegau. In the occupied Soviet areas, as noted, the first wave of mass killings had already concluded before the establishment of the civil administration. Civilian occupation authorities did, however, participate fully in the second murder wave which began toward the end of 1941.

As in most other areas in the General Government, however, the persecution of Jews did not follow a straight path, rather it showed a more erratic evolution. Particularly in regions with a strong need for industrial workers, many Jews survived until 1944, although few of them made it through the atrocities of the final phase. The events from below—the building and clearing of ghettos, the mass shootings—occurred similarly in areas of Poland and the Soviet Union, although there was less Wehrmacht participation in the murder of Jews in Poland than in the Soviet Union. Native collaborators did not play an important role in Poland, with the exception of east Galicia, and notably at the SS Training Camp at Trawniki, near Lublin, which deployed ethnic German and Ukrainian auxiliary forces for ghetto clearings and extermination camps.[21]

In light of so much radicalism and activism the question arises whether the initiative for the "Final Solution" did not come from the periphery, in other words, the occupied areas. In fact, occupation authorities exerted constant pressure for removal of the Jews and made suggestions regarding mass murder. Yet in Berlin they met top leaders who themselves, based on "racial policy," pushed for "grand solutions." All settlement policy was centrally planned at the top (*am grünen Tisch*), as were strategic decisions, and this was not possible without Hitler. The indefatigable chief organizer of mass murder was, however, Himmler, who without pause received his satraps, made inspection tours, and drove forward the "Final Solution" with specific decisions. This was particularly apparent in Himmler's calendar, which recently turned up in Moscow. Documenting his activity on nearly every day of the year 1941/42,[22] it shows that Himmler intervened in the General Government—each time with Hitler's backing—at least eight times. Thus one must properly speak of a process of reciprocal communication between the center and the periphery, in which each side forced the radicalization process, while occasionally applying the brakes.

It is possible to simplify the process being described into seven factors:

1. The confrontation of German occupation authorities with Eastern Jews, who seemed to confirm all their prejudices,[23] in a Polish society that was largely paralyzed;
2. The war in 1939 and 1941, which created a situation of loosened inhibitions regarding mass murder, not only against Jews;
3. A new kind of administrative creation free of many formal restrictions, and a specific criminal milieu;
4. Large-scale projects that were envisaged in Berlin but which failed, and the corresponding home-made "unbearable conditions" on-site;
5. The myriad experiences with mass murder of members of the intellectual class in Poland and the Soviet Union, the killing of the disabled, as well as of Soviet prisoners of war;
6. Settlement plans that initially had indirect consequences in the annexed areas, then direct ones, above all in the eastern part of the General Government, especially up to July 1941[24] (further research on this connection is needed for the subsequent period); and finally,
7. Connected with this, the motivating and legitimizing function of the Nazi leadership, which cleared the path toward total extermination.

III

Why is it that until recently we have known so little about the "Final Solution" in the General Government? In the early sixties attempts were made in the Federal Republic to research this theme, although no books were written.[25] It was largely left to the Berlin historian Wolfgang Scheffler to provide reports on Nazi trials that reconstructed the criminal history of this mass murder before the courts. The history of Jews under German occupation has been written almost entirely by survivors such as Yitzhak Arad, Yisrael Gutman, and Shmuel Krakowski.

Until 1991, it was little known in the West that intensive research on the subject of the Nazi murder of Jews was also being conducted in Poland.[26] Polish publications have been particularly frequent up to the early sixties and since the eighties. Frank Golczewski deserves credit as the first Western historian to review this literature.[27] A more extensive exchange with contemporary Polish historiography is now desirable; unlike earlier, it need not take political concerns into consideration.

Research is needed to fill holes in many topics. In particular the role of the civil administration in the persecution of Jews, which it is now clear has been examined only from the periphery. The state of knowledge regarding the police apparatus is similarly inadequate. The history of the government in Cracow and of the SS and Gestapo Central Offices should be reconsidered.[28] The problems of sources are enormous because the central institutions apparently destroyed most of their records. Many of the more important documents survived rather in regional collections than in central ones.

Nonetheless, the history of most of the smaller Jewish communities and ghettos remains extraordinarily poorly researched.[29] One can compare, for example, the very numerous publications on Jewish communities in western Germany during the Third Reich with the few Polish-language articles on Jewish communities with memberships in the tens of thousands. Except for the large ghettos, relatively little is known about the history of Jews in the General Government, about their daily lives and deaths, the welfare organizations, and the political and social divisions.[30] Two controversial areas—the Jewish Council (*Judenrat*) and Jewish police—are in particular need of clarification.[31] A recent pioneering contribution is Thomas Sandkühler's study, which emphasizes the small cities of Boryslaw and Drohobycz, neither of which is, however, totally representative of the entire General Government. This points to the unevenness of regional research.

Without question, most publications deal with the Warsaw Ghetto. Several excellent comprehensive treatments concern the lives of Jews under German occupation.[32] The history of the perpetrators, in particular the Gestapo and the so-called Commissar for the Jewish Residential Area (*Kommissar für den jüdischen Wohnbezirk*), is far less well researched. Only in the case of the Warsaw Ghetto uprising in April/May 1943 have German actions, Jewish resistance, and the position of the Poles been clarified to some degree.[33] Beyond Warsaw, knowledge is scarce. Jews from the western communities were deported to the Warsaw Ghetto until 1941; there has been almost no research on the eastern part of the district.

The history of the Holocaust in the Lublin region was virtually unknown until 1978; however during the last decade many researchers have turned their attention to the Lublin District,[34] the site of Operation Aktion Reinhard and its leader Odilo Globocnik. Despite many research projects, a series of questions remain open. For example, research has only begun on the role of the civil administration in the persecution of Jews, particularly in rural areas, but also in the large slave labor projects. Still unclear is the fate of many Jews from Germany, Austria, and Czechoslovakia who in the spring of 1942 were transported to the Lublin area and nearly all killed.[35]

For the Cracow District, where a somewhat smaller Jewish community lived, the situation was similar to Warsaw's. We know relatively much about Cracow, but less about other cities in this region. So far, not even one useful article on this district has been published, although there are relatively good sources. German regional documents have often been worked through by Polish local historians. In the Federal Republic several Nazi trials have been based on crimes in the Cracow region.[36]

The same cannot be said for the Radom District, for which there are only a very few successful postwar reports from the Federal Republic. Thus one must depend on very useful Polish-language publications, particularly for the larger cities such as Kielce and Czestochowa, as well as for the many large slave labor camps.[37]

The Galicia District is so far the best researched, although more remains to be done. For example, the numerous KGB investigations against Ukrainians who collaborated in the killing of Jews need to be examined critically and in greater detail. Such work would show events on the micro-level, which the previously used sources cannot reveal.

The history of the four extermination camps in the General Government has been reconstructed in varying degrees of depth. Majdanek, a camp that was not originally planned for the murder of Jews, is an exception in that there has been significant Polish research,[38] which however has not yet used West German trial records. Reconstruction of the history of the Operation Reinhard camps—Belzec, Sobibor, and Treblinka—is considerably more difficult. These murder facilities were already razed in 1943, and nearly all documents destroyed. Despite important works by Adalbert Rückerl and Yitzhak Arad, more remains to be done, in particular establishing connections among regional histories of the "Final Solution."[39] The some 300 slave labor camps for Jews in the General Government are almost completely unknown in Western research,[40] although some, such as Cracow-Plaszow or Skarzysko-Kamienna, attained the size of the Dachau concentration camp.

The final large problem complex is the question of public awareness of mass murder and the reactions of non-Jewish society. Exploitation and mistreatment, as well as mass murder, were almost always public matters in occupied Poland.[41] This was unavoidable given the way in which all these crimes were carried out. But Poles and other non-Jews under German domination were also relentlessly oppressed by the occupation. Public opinion essentially played no role in German calculations.

Already in the summer and fall of 1941, even before the beginning of genocide in Poland, information about massacres in the regions further to the east trickled out to the west. The first large-scale mass shootings in east Galicia after October 1941 were, however, only known in limited circles, just as only a few officials were informed of the construction of the extermination camps. However, information about killings by means of poison gas after March 1942 spread very quickly in the region. Finally, by the summer of 1942 it was nearly impossible to hide information about genocide in the General Government from anyone. The ghetto clearings amounted to wild, day-long shooting sprees in particular sections of cities, at the end of which bodies were lying in the main streets leading to train stations. Using these empirical facts one can pursue the stream of information back to the Reich. By means of letters, and above all from frontline soldiers passing through on furlough, by the fall and winter of 1942 extensive knowledge had reached the Reich.[42] At the latest, by 1943 a part of the German public—its size not yet precisely quantified—knew about the mass atrocities in the East, and some knew about the poison-gas killings as well. We now know that there was also comparatively good knowledge among Allied governments and Jewish organizations abroad.[43]

Yet in Poland as abroad, organized reaction was very tentative, in particular on the part of the Polish underground movements and the churches. Opposition groups reacted to the persecution of Jews according to their respective political beliefs and general points of view. Help for Jews came above all from leftist Catholic and Communist groups, which themselves sometimes included Jews.[44] In the complexly-organized and dominant *Armia Krajowa*, the Home Army, the position on the persecution of Jews differed according to sub-unit. Antisemitism was widespread among right-radical Polish groups and the Ukrainian insurrectionary army; their actual behavior toward Jews is, however, controversial.[45] As for the churches, research has thus far been almost exclusively limited to individual rescue efforts.[46]

The position of Polish society on genocide was seen to be an issue in literature immediately after the war.[47] The subject was then politicized, and in Poland was for a long while viewed only positively. Thus it has long been acknowledged that not every Pole who helped Jews and was detected in the process was himself murdered. The taboo against acknowledging native antisemitism during the Second World War was only broken in 1987. Since then a public debate has taken place which has also included the prewar period.[48] However, empirical research on the behavior of Poles, as well as of Ukrainians in east Galicia, has not come very far. It is, nonetheless, necessary for a balanced picture of the history of Polish Jews in the Second World War. One point must, however, be emphasized. The Polish people had no possibility of halting the mass murder.

Notes

1. Adelbert Rückerl (ed.), *NS-Vernichtungslager im Spiegel deutscher Strafprozesse* (Munich, 1977), pp. 52-56; Christopher R. Browning, *Ordinary Men: Reserve Police Battalion 101 and the Final Solution in Poland* (New York, 1993), pp. 78-89; Daniel Jonah Goldhagen, *Hitler's Willing Executioners: Germans and the Holocaust* (New York, 1996), pp. 223-231.

2. According to contemporary estimates of the Polish underground movement, *Armia Krajowa*, in late summer 1942, 200,000 to 300,000 Jews were deported monthly to the extermination camps. Przeglad najważniejszych wydarzeń, no. 24, July 1943, Archiwum Akt Nowych, Department VI, Warsaw, 202/1, vol. 42, Bl. 51.

3. See Szymon Datner, *55 dni Wehrmachtu w Polsce. Zbrodnie dokonane na polskiej ludności cywilnej w okresie 1 IX-25 X 1939* (Warsaw, 1967); Hans Umbreit, *Deutsche Militärverwaltungen 1938/39* (Stuttgart, 1977); Christian Jansen and Arno Weckbecker, *Der "Volksdeutsche Selbstschutz" in Polen 1939/40* (Munich, 1992).

4. Chistopher R. Browning, "Nazi Ghettoization Policy in Poland, 1939-1941," *Central European History* 19 (1986): 343-368.

5. *Faschismus—Getto—Massenmord. Dokumentation über Ausrottung und Widerstand der Juden in Polen während des 2. Weltkrieges*, ed. Jüdisches Historisches Institut in Warschau (Berlin, 1961), p. 138.

6. Werner Präg and Wolfgang Jacobmeyer (eds.), *Das Diensttagebuch des deutschen Generalgouverneurs in Polen 1939-1945* (Stuttgart, 1975), p. 337.

7. Ibid., p. 386.

8. See Dieter Pohl, *Nationalsozialistische Judenverfolgung in Ostgalizien 1941-1944. Organisation und Durchführung eines staatlichen Massenverbrechens* (Munich, 1996), passim.

9. On Soviet prisoners of war interned in Poland, see Wiesław Marczyk, *Jency radzieccy w niewoli Wehrmachtu na ziemiach polskich w latach 1941-1945* (Opole, 1987), and the journal *Łambinowicki Rocznik Muzealny*.

10. All shootings reported by Polish authorities are listed in the collection *Rejestr miejsc i faktów zbrodni popełnionych przez okupanta hitlerowskiego na ziemiach polskich w latach 1939-1945*, with individual volumes for most *Woiwodships*. Unfortunately, it is available in almost no libraries in the West.

11. *Dienstkalender des Reichsführers-SS* (13 October 1941), Tsentr Khraneniya Istoriko-Dokumentalnykh kollektsii, Moscow, R-1372/5/23.

12. Dieter Pohl, *Von der "Judenpolitik" zum Judenmord. Der Distrikt Lublin des Generalgouvernements 1939-1944* (Frankfurt a.M., 1993), pp. 105f.

13. Götz Aly and Susanne Heim, *Vordenker der Vernichtung. Auschwitz und die deutschen Pläne für eine neue europäische Ordnung* (Hamburg, 1991), pp. 188ff.

14. See, for idiosyncratic interpretations, Aly and Heim, *Vordenker*, pp. 297ff.; also, Aly and Heim, "The Economics of the Final Solution: A Case Study from the General Government," in *Simon Wiesenthal Center Annual* 5 (1988): 3-48.

15. Präg and Jacobmeyer, *Diensttagebuch*, pp. 457f.

16. According to new research by Bogdan Musial (Hanover), there is evidence of General Government participation in the organization of Jewish murder at least until the end of 1942.

17. See Dieter Pohl, "Hans Krüger and the Murder of the Jews in the Stanislawow Region (Galicia)," in *Yad Vashem Studies* 26 (1997): 239-264 (Stanislau); Thomas Sandkühler, *"Endlösung" in Galizien. Der Judenmord in Ostpolen und die Rettungsaktionen von Berthold Beitz 1941-1944* (Bonn, 1996), pp. 310ff. (Drohobycz).

18. Pohl, *Judenpolitik*, p. 147.

19. Pohl, *Nationalsozialistische Judenverfolgung*, pp. 288f.

20. Wolfgang Scheffler, "Probleme der Holocaustforschung," in *Deutsche—Polen—Juden. Ihre Beziehungen von den Anfängen bis ins 20. Jahrhundert. Beiträge zu einer Tagung*, ed. Stefi Jersch-Wenzel (Berlin, 1987), pp. 259-281.

21. For a beginning, see Maria Wardzyńska, *Formacja Wachmannschaften der SS- und Polizeiführers im Distrikt Lublin* (Warsaw, 1992).

22. See n.11.

23. See John P. Fox, "Reichskristallnacht 9 November 1938 and the Ostjuden Perspective to the Nazi Search for a 'Solution' to the Jewish Question," in *Polin* 5 (1990), pp. 74-102.

24. See especially Götz Aly, *"Endlösung." Völkerverschiebung und der Mord an den europäischen Juden* (Frankfurt a.M., 1995).

25. These collections of materials by Thomas Harlan and Hanns von Krannhals, both of whom wanted to write comprehensive works, are available in Warsaw and Koblenz.

26. See the very critical Lucjan Dobroszycki, "Polska historiografia nad temat Zagłady: przegląd literatury i próba syntezy," *Holocaust z perspektywy półwiecza* (Warsaw, 1994), pp. 177-187. By far the most important journal in this field is *Biuletyn Żydowskiego Instytutu Historycznego*, published in Warsaw since 1950. Vol. 35 (1993) of *Biuletyn Głównej Komisji Badania Zbrodni przeciwko Narodowi Polskiemu* is almost entirely concerned with the murder of Jews in the GG.

27. Frank Golczewski, "Polen" in *Dimension des Völkermords*, ed. Wolfgang Benz (Munich, 1991), pp. 411-497; see Dieter Pohl, "Nationalsozialistischer Juden-

mord als Problem von osteuropäischer Geschichte und Osteuropa-Geschichtsschreibung," in *Jahrbücher für die Geschichte Osteuropas* 40 (1992): 96-119.

28. A pathbreaking disseration is Gerhard Eisenblätter, "Grundlinien der Politik des Reiches gegenüber dem Generalgouvernement 1939-1945" unpublished, (Frankfurt a.M., 1969).

29. See Christopher R. Browning, "Beyond Warsaw and Lodz: Perpetrating the Holocaust in Poland," in *Perspectives on the Holocaust: Essays in Honor of Raul Hilberg* (Boulder, 1995), ed. James S. Pacy and Alan P. Wertheimer, pp. 75-90. For encyclopedia articles on ghettos and Jewish communities, see Czesław Pilichowski (ed.), *Obozy hitlerowskie na ziemiach polskich 1939-1945. Informator encyklopedyczny* (Warsaw, 1979); Pinkas Hakehillot, *Encyclopedia of Jewish Communities* (Hebrew) (Jerusalem), Vol. 1, *The Community of Lodz and its Region* (1976); Vol. 2, *Eastern Galicia* (1980); Vol. 3, *Western Galicia and Silesia* (1984); Vol. 4, *Warsaw and its Region* (1989).

30. The first synthesis was Teresa Prekerowa, "Wojna i okupacja," in *Najnowsze dzieje Żydów w Polsce w zarysie (do1950 roku)*, ed. Jerzy Tomaszewski (Warsaw, 1993), pp. 273-384; see Frank Golczewski, "Zur Historiographie des Schicksals der polnischen Juden im Zweiten Weltkrieg," in *Verdrängung und Vernichtung der Juden unter dem Nationalsozialismus*, ed. Arno Herzig and Ina Lorenz (Hamburg, 1992), pp. 85-99.

31. Memoirs of a member of the Jewish ghetto police in Otwock in Calel Perchodnik, *Am I a Murderer* (Boulder, 1996).

32. Ruta Sakowska, *Ludzie w dzielnicy zamkniętej. Z dziejów Żydów w Warszawie w latach okupacji hitlerowskiej, październik 1939—marzec 1943* (Warsaw, 1993); see Charles G. Roland, *Courage Under Siege: Starvation, Disease, and Death in the Warsaw Ghetto* (New York, 1992); T. Bednarczyk, *Życie codzienne warszawskiego getta. Warszawskie getto i ludzie (1939-1945 i dalej)* (Warsaw, 1995).

33. See the bibliography in Teresa Sitkiewicz, "Materiały do bibliografii powstania w getcie, kwiecień—maj 1943 r.," in *Wojskowy Przegląd Historyczny* 38 (1993): 286-295.

34. See Pohl, "Judenpolitik," and, with additional material, his "Rola dystryktu lubelskiego w 'ostatecznym rozwiązaniu sprawa żydowskiego,'" in *Zeszyty Majdanka* 17 (1997): 7-24; Janina Kiełbon, *Migracje ludnosci w dystrykcie lubelskim w latach 1939-1944* (Lublin, 1995); Zygmunt Mańkowski, "Życie i zagłada Żydów w Lublinie," in *Biuletyn Głównej Komisji Badania Zbrodni przeciwko Narodowi Polskiemu* 38 (1995): 91-109.

35. See Peter Witte, "Letzte Nachrichten aus Siedliszcze," in *Theresienstädter Studien und Dokumente* (1996): 98-114.

36. Yael Peled, *Krakov ha-Yehudit, 1939-1943. "Amidah, mahteret, ma'avak,"* (Lohame ha-Geta'ot, Tel Aviv, 1993).

37. K. Urbański, *Zagłada ludnosci żydowskiej Kielc 1939-1945* (Kielce, 1994).

38. Tadeusz Mencel (ed.), *Majdanek 1941-1944* (Lublin, 1991) (Polish); Josef Marszałek, *Majdanek. Geschichte und Wirklichkeit eines Vernichtungslagers* (Reinbek, 1982), and numerous articles in *Zeszyty Majdanka*.

39. A recent beginning is the biography by Michael Tregenza, "Christian Wirth a pierwsza faza 'Akcji Reinhard,'" in *Zeszyty Majdanka* 14 (1992): 7-55, and "Christian Wirth: Inspekteur der Sonderkommandos 'Aktion Reinhard,'" in *Zeszyty Majdanka* 15 (1993): 7-55 (Polish).

40. See the camp encyclopedia by Pilichowski, *Obozy hitlerowskie na ziemiach polskich 1939-1945*. A comprehensive treatment of the slave labor camps in

the GG by Józef Marszałek is *Obozy pracy w Generalnym Gubernatorstwie w latach 1939-1945* (Lublin, 1998). See Dieter Pohl, "Die großen Zwangsarbeitslager der SS- und Polizeiführer für Juden im Generalgouvernement 1942-1945," in *Nationalsozialistische Konzentrationslager 1933-1945. Entwicklung und Struktur*, ed. Ulrich Herbert, Karin Orth, and Christoph Dieckmann (Göttingen, 1998), pp. 415-438.

41. See the outstanding publication on the reaction of the Polish underground press to the ghetto uprising in 1943 of Paweł Szapiro (ed.), *Wojna żydowsko-niemiecka. Polska prasa konspiracyjna 1943-1944 o powstaniu w getcie Warszawy* (London, 1992).

42. David Bankier, *The Germans and the Final Solution: Public Opinion Under Nazism* (Oxford and Cambridge, MA, 1992), pp. 101-115.

43. For a critical treatment of the Polish government-in-exile, see David Engel, *In the Shadow of Auschwitz: The Polish Government-in-Exile and the Jews, 1939-1942* (Chapel Hill and London, 1987), and *Facing a Holocaust: The Polish Government-in-Exile and the Jews, 1943-1945* (Chapel Hill, 1993). On the extermination camps, see Józef Marszałek, "Rozpoznanie obozów śmierci w Bełżcu, Sobiborze i Treblince przez wywiad Delegatury Rządu Rzeczypospolitej Polskiej na Kraj i Armii Krajowej," in *Zeszyty Majdanka* (1992): 39-59.

44. Most recently, Krzysztof Dunin-Wąsowicz, "Socjalisci polscy wobec walki i zagłady Żydów," in *Dzieje Najnowsze* 25 (1993): 41-60.

45. On these controversies, see John Lovell Armstrong, "The Polish Underground and the Jews: A Reassessment of Home Army Commander Tadeusz Bór-Komorowski's Order 116 Against Banditry," in *Slavonic and East European Review* 72 (1993): 259-276; for a polemical view of the UPA, Edward Prus, *Holocaust po banderowsku czy Żydzi byli w UPA?* (Wroclaw, 1995).

46. On the cloisters, see Ewa Kurek-Lesik, *Gdy klasztor znaczył życie. Udział zenskich zgromadzeń zakonnych w akcji ratowania dzieci żydowskich w Polsce w latach 1939-1945* (Warsaw, 1992); for a critical view, Franciszek Stopniak, "Duchowieństwo katolickie i Żydzi w Polsce w latach II wojny światowej," in *Studia nad faszyzmem i zbrodniami hitlerowskimi* 11 (1987): 196-217.

47. Michael M. Borwicz, *Organizowane wsciekłości* (Warsaw, 1947).

48. Anthony Polonsky (ed.), *"My Brother's Keeper?": Recent Polish Debates on the Holocaust* (London, 1990); Tomasz Szarota, "Zajścia antyżydowskie i pogromy w okupowanej Europie," in *Holocaust z perspektywy półwiecza*, pp. 153-175; on the prewar period, Jolanta Żyndul, *Zajścia antyżydowskie w Polsce w latach 1935-1937* (Warsaw, 1994); Ronald E. Modras, *The Catholic Church and Antisemitism: Poland 1933-1939* (Chur, 1994).

– Chapter 4 –

ANTI-JEWISH POLICY AND THE MURDER OF THE JEWS IN THE DISTRICT OF GALICIA, 1941/42

Thomas Sandkühler

It is an important objective of current Holocaust research to analyze the implementation of genocidal policy particularly in eastern and central eastern Europe. In this way, the possibility of an
order by the Führer (*Führerbefehl*), which has long distracted
researchers in the Federal Republic from an empirical treatment of
the Jewish Holocaust in the occupied territories, may be avoided.[1]
Researchers no longer debate the structures and processes of decision-making concerning the "Final Solution," the initiatives and
orders at the center of power in Berlin,[2] but rather focus on the
respective regional contexts with a view to potential impulses for
radicalization originating at the periphery.[3] In this respect, investi-
gators also identify, in some cases for the first time since the end of
the war, the perpetrators located at the mid-level of the Nazi power
structure. Researchers devote more attention to ideological factors,
without necessarily repudiating the interpretative model of a cumulative radicalization toward the "Final Solution."[4]

A peripheral region of the Third Reich that has long been
neglected in historiography was the district of Galicia, a region in

the southeastern part of Poland. After the beginning of the war against the Soviet Union, it was incorporated into the General Government under Hans Frank. The "Final Solution" in the district of Galicia claimed over half a million Jewish victims; beginning in October 1941, they were murdered in mass executions and subsequently above all in the gas chambers of the Belzec extermination camp.[5] Because the extermination of the Jews of Galicia began considerably earlier than in the rest of the General Government, the causes of the development from persecution of the Jews to mass murder have to be examined. On the other hand, the following discussion will also repeatedly pay attention to the peculiarities of the district and its significance for the totality of the "Final Solution"; dependent largely on the final objectives of anti-Jewish policy, these characteristics were thus subject to fluctuations. Three steps—from July to October 1941, from then to January 1942, and finally until May/July 1942—will be used to show that the district of Galicia was located at an intersection of differing paths to the "Final Solution," each of which by itself allowed for other alternatives, but in conjunction consequently resulted in genocide. First, though, the prehistory of the Jewish Holocaust in the district of Galicia needs to be addressed.

I

The region of eastern Galicia around the city of Lvov (Polish, Lwów; German, Lemberg) had belonged to Austria-Hungary from the Partitions of Poland to the end of the First World War and had subsequently been re-incorporated into the Polish Republic. By far the largest part of the rural population in the agricultural eastern Galicia was Ukrainian, followed by Poles and Jews who dominated commerce and the trades.[6] In the context of the increasingly severe Polish-Ukrainian conflict fought out since the 1920s, the Jews of eastern Galicia were also suffering; following the collapse of the Central Powers, they had repeatedly found themselves between the fronts. Added to this, the course of the following decade saw Polish antisemitism erupt in a number of instances as pogrom-like riots.[7]

However, for the German occupation force the Ukrainian national movement was much more important. After a political turn to the right at the beginning of the 1920s, Ukrainian nationalism became an integral ideology, characterized by anti-capitalist, anti-Bolshevik, and openly antisemitic elements. This made the Organization of Ukrainian Nationalists (OUN) a suitable alliance partner for Germany, which pursued a revision of its eastern borders and a weakening of Poland. Contacts between exiled conservative Ukrainian politicians and the *Reichswehr* had existed since the early years of the Weimar Republic. After the Nazis took power, these relations were intensified and the Ukrainian nationalists came increasingly under German control. It is a telling prelude to the first wave of killings in the district of Galicia that after the invasion of Poland the counter-intelligence department of the *Wehrmacht* under Admiral Canaris thought about instigating Ukrainian pogroms in eastern Galicia.[8]

In western and central Poland the German persecution of the Jews started during the first days of the war. Systematized since early 1940, it was significant for eastern Galicia simply because in the following year the "Jewish policy" of the General Government was extended to the new district.[9] In contrast to the German civilian administration, the Soviet occupational force did not pursue any antisemitic aims per se. On the contrary, initially Jews were given preference for certain job positions. This attitude, however, was short-lived because western Ukraine was practically annexed by the Soviet Union after the invasion of the Red Army in September 1939 and subjected to a severe Stalinist occupational policy. This regime suppressed the Jews politically and economically.[10] Nevertheless the OUN, which had moved its headquarters to the General Government, claimed that the terror of the Soviet Secret Service against the Polish and Ukrainian parts of the population was the work of the Jews.[11]

On one level there were vast displacements of populations that constituted a central element of German as well as Soviet occupation policy in Poland. For the most part, they occurred in an easterly direction. Polish and Jewish inhabitants fled by the hundreds of thousands from western and central Poland to eastern Galicia. From there, Ukrainians and even indigenous Jews fled from the Soviets to the General Government and into the areas annexed by the Reich. Poles, Jews, and Gypsies were deported from western Poland to the General Government under the direction of the Reich Security Main Office (RSHA) in order to make room for ethnic Germans; Himmler, in his role as Reich Commissar for the Strengthening of Germandom (RKF), had these people brought "Home into the Reich" from the Soviet occupied areas and interest spheres, including from eastern Galicia. Finally, in the course of 1940 the Soviet Secret Service (NKVD) deported to Siberian and other camps of the Gulag system tens of thousands of politically undesirable or otherwise "suspicious" inhabitants of eastern Galicia for forced labor. These deportations were also directed against the bulk of the Jews who had crossed the Soviet-German border during the previous year.[12] To this extent, the Soviet measures of persecution also encompassed the Jews as an entire ethnic group. Mass deportations as such were therefore by no means a uniquely German phenomenon, especially because in the conceptions of the relevant circles in Berlin the Jews were also to be resettled in Siberia. However, the NKVD deported Jews, but did not murder them. Without the Soviet deportations of 1940 far more Jews would have fallen into the hands of German units than those 530,000 who were murdered in the course of 1941 to 1943.[13]

Since the start of the war, particularly Himmler, Reinhard Heydrich and Adolf Eichmann had wanted to transport the German and Polish Jews as rapidly as possible and by force into certain areas, where they would be left to their own devices. However, these reservation-projects, ranging from the experiments at Nisko on the San River to the Madagascar plan, had barely evolved beyond an improvised stage. The refusal of the General Governor, Frank, to accept Jews from western Poland had contributed substantially to this outcome. Like that of other National Socialist rulers in the occupied areas, his special ambition was geared toward making the General Government a *"judenfreie"* (Jewish-free) zone as soon as possible.[14] In order to come closer to such projections Frank developed various schemes, according to which further areas were to be incorporated into the General Government, such as the Belorussian Pripya Marshes, to which the Jewish population would be deported. As early as March 1941, he was prepared to implement these plans. Hitler himself promised to make Frank's territory *"judenfrei"* immediately following the victory over the Soviet Union, raising the vague prospect of extending the General Government to the east. In Frank's opinion, however, the "eastern extension" had to be generous enough to accommodate all Jews from the General Government. As a precaution, therefore, he laid claim to parts of Belorussia including the Pripyat marshes, and subsequently also to eastern Galicia.[15]

It remains unclear whether the General Governor knew that the Pripya project was also seriously pursued by the Reich Security Main Office. Presumably, Heydrich assumed that the Jews deported "into the swamps" not only from Poland but from all of Europe would be used in massive improvement projects and at least some of them would perish through work and deliberate starvation.[16] There was no talk any more about an enlargement of the General Government. Rather, Heydrich's policy should be conducted de facto solely by the SS, but formally under the jurisdiction of the designated Reich Minister for the occupied eastern territories, Alfred Rosenberg. That eastern Galicia would be ceded to the General Government was no longer planned, because the region represented a central element of Rosenberg's Ukrainian policy. Before the war, Rosenberg and the counter-intelligence department of the OKW (Supreme Command of the German Armed Forces) had promised the Ukrainian nationalists to establish a pan-Ukrainian state extending from Lvov to Kiev.[17]

II

After the outbreak of the war against the Soviet Union, the *Einsatzgruppe* C of the Security Police and SD moved into eastern Galicia. It had received orders from Heydrich to establish order behind the front and to liquidate the ruling elite of Bolshevik Russia as in other occupied Soviet regions. Because in the minds of the Germans as well as the Ukrainian nationalists the Soviet state apparatus was dominated by Jews, this order applied above all to Jews. Therefore, the *Einsatzgruppen* had been instructed to stage as inconspicuously as possible pogroms by local antisemites.[18]

Even before the German invasion, the Ukrainian nationalists in Lvov had publicly vowed revenge on the Jews for their supposedly pro-Soviet stance.[19] However, no clear evidence exists for the supposition that anti-Jewish pogroms during the summer of 1941 were always initiated by the Germans. Rather, in this context other developments were also significant.

That is, immediately before the German invasion, the Soviet Secret Service in eastern Galicia had shot and sometimes tortured to death thousands of political prisoners, as well as a number of German prisoners of war. These murders now acted as a confirmation of the world-view of the German and Ukrainian antisemites; after all, both were certain that Jews dominated the Soviet Secret Service. In fact, the evidence shows that this was not the case; moreover, among the victims of the NKVD were numerous Jews. All the same, referring to the dead inmates found in the prisons, the Ukrainians began immediately their revenge against "Judeo-Bolshevism" after the German invasion. Parallel to this, SS detachments of *Einsatzgruppe* C under Otto Rasch, with active support of OUN militias, rounded up Jewish men old enough for military service and shot them publicly. The Wehrmacht also participated in these "acts of retribution." The High Command of the 17th Army explicitly approved of the pogroms; German soldiers accepted them passively or participated actively, for instance in Lvov and somewhat later in Tarnopol.[20]

Up to 10,000 Jews had already fallen victim to the pogroms and the shootings of the first half of July 1941.[21] Even after Einsatzgruppe C had left eastern Galicia and advanced into more eastward regions of the Soviet Union, the murdering was continued. Smaller SS commandos from the General Government, put together by the commander of the Security Police and the SD there in order to support the *Einsatzgruppe* in its rapid advance, began killing Jewish and parts of the Polish intelligentsia. These men later comprised the apparatus of Security Police and SD in the district of Galicia and carried out most of the killing operations after the summer of 1941.[22]

On 16 July 1941, Hitler gave orders to incorporate eastern Galicia into the General Government; however, this decision initially was not connected to the persecution of the Jews. Rather, it was an attempt to prevent the founding of a Ukrainian national state, which in reality was very disagreeable to the German leadership.[23] For Frank, though, the situation obviously appeared different. He now perceived the possibility—believing himself in agreement on this issue with Hitler—that the previous territory of the General Government would be included in the Germanization of the eastern areas and that the German settlement frontier would be moved forward. Frank interpreted the incorporation of eastern Galicia as a first step to the creation of a huge territory for deportation, where undesirable ethnic groups, above all Jews, could be taken. Encouraged by the Chief of the Reich Chancellery, Heinrich Lammers, Frank made further territorial demands. The area for deportations was yet to be substantially extended with a wide strip of territory from Bialystok in the north to Czernowitz in the south. The Pripya Marshes, too, should be included, and the Jews were meant to be chased there, as Frank wrote to Lammers.[24] In reality, however, the division of the newly occupied eastern territories was already completed, based primarily on strategic and pragmatic grounds. The General Government received no further "space for deportation" in the East. As a result of the incorporation of eastern Galicia, half a million more Jews lived under Frank's authority now than before the war against the Soviet Union. Therefore, on 1 August 1941 Frank was farther away from the objective of *"Entjudung"* of the General Government than ever before.[25]

What was to be done now completely eluded the responsible officials in the Cracow Government. At first, Frank banked on gaining time. He wished to avoid firm settlements and continued to work toward "acquiring" parts of the Reich Commissariat Ukraine in order to deport the Jews from the General Government there. To this end, for the time being he pursued a policy of planned tentativeness with the aim of keeping the eastern border of the General Government open and the option of a mass resettlement of the Jews on the agenda. For months, the district of Galicia was not integrated into the General Government but on the one hand plundered, on the other hand neglected.[26] Firm arrangements of any kind or medium-term measures were to be avoided in order to highlight the fact that the "Jewish question" in Poland was unsolved. The formation of ghettos in the new district was forbidden; the "Jewish decrees" effective in the original General Government did not come into force immediately—everything was done to keep the situation in balance.[27] The staff of the occupational force in the new territory, almost exclusively recruited from the old General Government, was small in number; and usually the ones sent there were administrators who had failed to prove themselves. The SD spoke candidly about a "counter-selection" (*Gegenauslese*). Factors like these accelerated the disintegration of administrative rationality and clear jurisdictions which had already progressed in the General Government. The neo-feudal conditions in the district of Galicia manifested themselves above all in rampant corruption.[28]

Thus in many cases the fate of the Jews lay in the hands of occupational functionaries who were badly qualified but almost always familiar with "Jewish policy" in the General Government due to their own experience. This applied not only to the civilian administration but also to the SD. With binding instructions from Cracow or Lvov still lacking, it was largely left to the judgement of the individual administrator how he would deal with "his" Jews.

While Frank therefore counted on winning time and portraying conditions concerning the Jews in the General Government, but particularly in Galicia, as "intolerable," there was clearly an interest in the lower echelons "to get rid of" the Jews in the individual districts as soon as possible. This constellation, which began to work well in the course of July to September, contributed decisively to the rapid radicalization of policy toward the Jews in Galicia that now set in. However, no uniform policy was pursued. Agreement on the objective by no means precluded conflicts about methods and scheduling.

Various district leaders and the *Stadthauptmann* of Lvov issued a large number of transit passes to Jews who wanted to leave eastern Galicia; for the most part, they ended up in the neighboring district of Cracow. Simultaneously, many Jews attempted to escape to the west and across the borders of Romania and Hungary. The occupation administration did not object to this, because the number of Jews in the district of Galicia was thus reduced. Yet this policy soon led to protests of the receiving areas who pressed for a stop to the influx of Jews.[29]

To concentrate the Jewish population in ghettos had been forbidden by Frank. Therefore, the concept of establishing forced-labor camps instead of ghettos, adopted from the original General Government, rapidly gained significance. Initially, the civilian administration was primarily interested in detaining in forced-labor camps Jews who had left their dwellings in the country without official permits.[30] The first camps, though, were under the command of the local SS and Police Leader, Friedrich Katzmann. He in turn acted on the instructions of the SS and Police Leader in Lublin, Odilo Globocnik, whom Himmler had authorized to prepare the settlement of the newly conquered "eastern territory" and to set up the first SS bases.[31] The civilian administration was quite agreeable to the establishment of such bases so that a network of such camps developed relatively quickly across Galicia.

In early September 1941, a large project began in the district, the construction of the so-called *Durchgangsstraße IV*. This road and railway connection was very important for German supplies on the Eastern Front; it ran via Lvov into southern Ukraine. Apparently, the Wehrmacht requested Jewish forced laborers first because not enough Ukrainian and Polish workers were available. On September 20, the Work Department of the district of Galicia officially proclaimed the Jewish obligation to work (*Arbeitszwang*).[32] This decree had an additional reason: Globocnik continued the expansion of his control to eastern Galicia and won Himmler's interest in the *Durchgangsstraße IV*. It seemed to be suitable as a settlement axis from central Poland to the Crimea and thus corresponded to an essential objective of the "General Plan for the East" (*Generalplan Ost*) commissioned by Himmler.[33] On the basis of these common interests, the SS, the civilian administration, and the military alike now supported the building of the road.

At this time, Frank still firmly expected to be able to deport the Jews of the General Government "to the East." The cause of such expectations was the capture of Kiev by the *Wehrmacht*. The assumption that the scenario of "eastern expansion" could eventually be realized in the form of the *Durchgangsstraße IV* was not simply a pipe dream of Frank's administration in Cracow; rather, it gave a concrete twist to the widespread conviction that the labor of the

Jews ought to be exploited and in the process their numbers reduced. Along these lines, the Chief of *Einsatzgruppe* C, Rasch, in a widely-quoted reflection on the economic effects of the mass shootings, cryptically recommended that in future the Ukrainian Jews be liquidated gradually, that is, through work.[34] Thus Rasch also expected a further expansion of the General Government to the east and at the same time alluded to the *Durchgangsstraße IV*, which was the only project in the region that required forced labor on this scale.

Assessing developments from July to October 1941, one can emphasize that the three processes portrayed here in sequence actually took place simultaneously and mutually influenced each other. First, there was Frank's desire to remove completely the Jews under his jurisdiction as soon as possible from the General Government to regions farther east and to avoid anything that might favor an extended stay of the Jews in those regions. The rapid pauperization of the Jews was an important political factor in this context.[35] Second, there was the construction project of the *Durchgangsstraße IV* and other similar schemes to combine the intended deportation of the Jews to the East with an exploitation of their labor. In the context of this plan, the notion of "natural decimation"—as Heydrich put it several months later at the Wannsee Conference—appears to have played a role very early on. The third element was the mass shootings, primarily of Jewish men, by the *Einsatzgruppen*, which began in Galicia, as in all regions of occupied Russia, after 21 June 1941. Until then such "operations" (*Aktionen*) against Jews had not yet taken place in the territory of the General Government. With the mass murders in Galicia, therefore, a new, far more radical variety of anti-Jewish policy had now been practiced in the General Government.

III

October of 1941 can be regarded as marking a caesura in the process described here, because in view of the military situation, the plan to conduct mass deportations to the Soviet Union had to be considered unfeasible for some time. As a result, those in charge in Poland slowly began to realize that they would have to "solve" the Jewish question in the General Government itself.

Conditions in the large ghettos—such as Warsaw, where famine and typhus were rampant and mortality had reached terrific levels—had by then become "intolerable" indeed as a consequence of Frank's dilatory policy. The civilian administration reacted increasingly more radically against these self-created problems. In order to prevent the spread of disease the Third Decree on Residence Restrictions (*3. Verordnung über Aufenthaltsbeschränkungen*) for the first time threatened the death penalty for Jews who left the ghetto. Jews arrested on rural roads were also to be executed immediately.[36] Thus a further step was made toward "solving problems through extermination of humans." Galicia now takes on the function of a hinge in the process of the persecution of the Jews between the summer of 1941 and the summer of 1942. In the area of the original General Government, the policy of Frank—geared completely toward deportation of the Jews—had lead to the described problems. The end of hope for a removal of all Jews now put Frank's administration under pressure to act. In the area of the former Soviet Union, however, the *Einsatzgruppen* had begun by June 1941 to shoot the majority of Jewish men. Since mid-August the mass shootings were also extended to women and children.[37]

In Galicia both developments converged. From the middle of October 1941, mass shootings set in, first in the southern part of the district, soon everywhere; however, in contrast to a few kilometers eastward around the same time, these were still justified in each case by various administrative measures or were at least connected to such measures. In Stanislav (Stanislau, Stanisławów), a border town in the south of eastern Galicia, the decision of the civilian authorities in early October 1941 to establish a ghetto was the beginning of a chain of orders. The ghetto as designed however was much too small from the outset to accommodate all the Jews of the city. This brought on hunger and disease. Added to this were a widespread famine due to flooding and the deportation to this area of Hungarian Jews, only part of whom had been deported to the Ukrainian city of Kamenetz-Podolsk (Kam'yanets' Podil's'kyy) and shot there. In order to adjust the number of Jews to the size of the town, the SS and Police Leader, Katzmann, and the Chief of the Security Police, Helmut Tanzmann, ordered the "superfluous" Jews of the city to be shot. Accordingly, on 12 October 1941, close to 10,000 Jews, males and females of all ages, were murdered by members of the Security Police–Stanislav Section, a company of the Reserve Police Battalion 133, and other units. This first and largest massacre in the district, the so-called "Bloody Sunday," was conducted virtually in public, in the Jewish cemetery of the city. It caused considerable agitation in the entire district.[38]

The prehistory of another large-scale mass shooting was similar; it took place in Lvov in the following month. Here the leadership of the German civilian administration was directly involved. The Governor of eastern Galicia, Karl Lasch, had urged for some time to have Lvov's Jews "disappear" from the face of his capital city; here too a ghetto was to be set up. During the first week of November, Lasch ordered the removal of about 120,000 Lvov Jews to a primitive "residential area" at the city's periphery that should not be fenced, in order to emphasize its transitional character. The German occupational forces deliberately calculated that many Jews would perish during such a resettlement in the middle of winter. Other factors also turned up, for instance the outbreak of a typhus epidemic caused by the mass deaths of Soviet prisoners of war and by the starvation policy of the German Department for Nutrition. The resettlement into the ghetto, therefore, led exactly to those conditions that provoked the demand for eliminating the Jews by radical measures. Starting in November 1941 SS and Police began to shoot in the nearby woods thousands of old and sick people, women and children, who had already been sorted out arbitrarily at the entrance of the new ghetto.[39]

During the fall and winter of 1941, at least 20,000 Jews were murdered in eastern Galicia. Besides Stanislav and Lvov, murder also took place in a number of cities and towns, centered mainly in the south of the district, which the fanatical *Hauptsturmführer* Krüger wanted to make *judenfrei* as soon as possible. Such *Aktionen*, however, were by no means conducted in all locations in the district in the period from October to December 1941. This fact indicates that besides the Security Police, other institutions were also influencing the persecution of the Jews, above all the local German administrative leaders, the *Kreishauptleute*. Various officials resisted the sensational shootings and urged their superior, the administrative superintendent (*Amtschef*) in Lvov, Ludwig Losacker, to intervene with the SS leadership. In fact, Losacker talked with Himmler at the turn of 1941/1942. However, the murder of the Jews was not the topic of his objections, but the fact that news of the massacres had reached the Reich. Most of all, though, the concern was that the mass shootings would "deprave" the units involved.[40] The form of the impending "Final Solution," its brutality and publicity had to be altered; after all, similar criticisms had also been voiced about the mass shootings in the Soviet Union.

Reacting to such reservations, Himmler had—presumably also in mid-October—commissioned the SS and Police Leader of the Lublin District, Globocnik, to explore new ways for decimating the Jewish population in Poland by other means. Accordingly, Globocnik began construction of the extermination camp Belzec in the Lublin District. Here the building of gas chambers had already started, but initially it progressed slowly and in a provisional man-

ner.[41] However, after the number of deaths due to typhus and starvation in the ghettos rose and the mass shootings had precipitated
criticism from various German authorities, Belzec gave a clue as to
how the German leadership would strive to escape this "dilemma."

At the same time Jewish forced labor increasingly became the
center of attention. Since the middle of October, Katzmann had been
erecting camps—apparently on Globocnik's orders—along the
Durchgangsstraße IV in which initially about 4,000 Jews were
imprisoned. Katzmann left no doubt about the intention to destroy
the Jews along the *Durchgangsstraße IV* through work. According
to him, they had started the war, therefore Galicia was enemy territory as well, and the Jews had to be fought like enemies in war. He
maintained that it was completely irrelevant how many forced laborers perished as long as the road was completed.[42] Soon a direct connection became evident between the construction of Belzec and the
building of forced labor camps. It established itself as the basis of the
National Socialist Jewish policy: Those who could work were used
in road construction, those who could not were murdered in Belzec.

The conditions along the *Durchgangsstraße IV* corresponded
to Katzmann's orders. Against a fee he leased out the Jewish forced
laborers to German and Austrian road construction companies.
Severe work without suitable tools, primitive quarters in the camps,
and the brutality of the guard commandos—among them Ukrainian policemen recruited from the former militias—resulted in a high
mortality rate. By mid-1943 at least 20,000 Jews had perished along
the *Durchgangsstraße IV*; up to 20,000 more inmates were shot in
the subsequent dissolution of the camps.[43]

However, considerable obscurity and contradictions existed in
the implementation of a policy vis-à-vis the Jews that was resolutely
geared toward their annihilation. In Galicia, particularly, the district
administration resisted Katzmann's methods for they interfered with
construction of the *Durchgangsstraße IV*. Instead, the manpower of
the Jewish slave laborers was supposed to be preserved and thus
made available in the long term. The civilian administration even
instructed the *Kreishauptleute* to send textiles, food, and consumer
goods to the slave labor camps in order to raise living conditions
there. The mentality that dominated the civilian administration,
however, becomes abundantly clear when one realizes that these
goods were those accumulated at the shootings of Jews in the context of so-called combat against illicit trade.[44]

Yet another dilemma of the German administration soon
emerged: The employment offices also made available forced laborers for other projects of the Wehrmacht and the SS—usually via the

Jewish Councils. On the other hand, German firms were in desperate need of Jewish skilled workers and tradesmen. From the perspective of the war economy, primarily represented by the armament commando (*Rüstungskommando*) in Lvov, it was essential to protect this source of labor from execution and deportation to the camps.

These contradictions openly surfaced for the first time at the massacre in Lvov in November/December 1941. In order to protect Jewish armaments workers, the district and city administration set up a special "quarter for skilled workers" for which special passes were distributed. Those who did not have a "skilled worker pass" were sent to the ghetto. Mostly the sick and—in German terms—those "unfit for work" fell victim to the *"Todesbrückenaktion"* mentioned above.[45]

This method became a model. The Employment Department of the district ordered a registration campaign. By now there was agreement between all the German agencies involved about the fate of Jews "unfit for work" and sometimes even of the unemployed. They would be murdered. Sometimes the employment offices handed the Jews over themselves for execution by the Security Police.[46]

Shortly before the original date for the Wannsee Conference in the second week of December 1941, high officials from the entire General Government gathered in Lvov for a larger discussion of ghetto questions; the meeting was convened by Governor Lasch. The main focus was the "emigration" of Jews from Cracow which was considered a model for similar measures in Lvov. On 16 December, Frank gave an address in which he announced to his subordinates the "liquidation" of the Jews in the General Government. About the means, however, by which this would happen Frank knew little.[47] At the turn of 1941/1942 instructions seemed to have come from Berlin to postpone the gassings in the General Government and thus also not to comply with similar requests from Lvov.[48] In any case, the mass extermination was delayed and at the same time centralized in the district of Lublin.[49]

The crucial contribution of the civilian administration lay in bureaucratizing the extermination of the Jews which became a characteristic of the process from then on. In the district of Galicia this took place primarily in terms of the work deployment (*Arbeitseinsatz*). Under the direction of the employment offices, the classification of Jews into three categories had been introduced as early as December 1941. On the highest level of the hierarchy were the tradesmen and skilled workers, followed by the forced laborers, and finally, those "unfit for work" or sick, who were murdered first.[50] However, it took several months until this regulation was enforced everywhere, as a result of which the relation between work and extermination continued to differ widely from one location to the other.

For the German authorities abstracting the murder of the Jews by means of this bureaucratic classification appeared an ideal option. For the protagonists could always refer to preparing subsequent mass deportations and to protecting "useful" Jewish laborers, even making them increasingly available to the war economy, such as became the case in the course of 1942. This very attempt at combining mass shootings with economic principles, however, contributed to the rapid development of a systematic program of extermination, because the employment offices established the previously missing link between the two strands of the "Final Solution" for the very first time. The tripartite division of the Jewish population was much less an expression of a reluctant concession to the war time economic situation than a necessary prerequisite for the transformation of mass murder into administrative conduct; and it was practiced in all its aspects in the district of Galicia *before* the "Final Solution" began in the entire General Government.

IV

For the district of Galicia the constellation of January 1942 was momentous. That all Jews would perish seemed to be definite by then. It was unclear, however, how and where this would be accomplished. Apparently, though, the new time plan was made known immediately, and by Himmler himself, who visited Lvov at that time. Losacker's protests against the mass shootings probably only confirmed the intention of the Reichsführer to include from the start eastern Galicia in addition to the district of Lublin in the mass deportations. Moreover, a change in jurisdiction took place, because Himmler probably instructed Katzmann to direct the "Final Solution" in the district of Galicia. The SS and Police Leader had aspired to this position for some time already.[51]

At the same time, the district administration paved the way for closer cooperation with the SS and police apparatus in order to emphasize its competency more than before. Spectacular was the replacement of the previous governor, Karl Lasch, who was arrested in the first week of January under allegations of corruption. Himmler had been trying for a long time to use the strong position of the SS in the district of Galicia for his struggle for extended police jurisdiction in the entire General Government. The arrest and subsequent execution of Lasch was mainly directed against Frank himself, who was pushed into the defensive by Himmler's "camarilla." On the other hand, it was no coincidence that Lasch's deputy, Losacker, was heading the district at exactly the phase when the details were set for the "Final Solution." In late January 1942, the Viennese SS General Otto Wächter took over the civilian administration of Lvov, subsequently cultivating a very close cooperation with Katzmann. This was also to Himmler's liking, who praised and confirmed this collaboration several times.[52]

In the first week of January 1942, the civilian administration undertook a number of steps toward the preparation of mass deportations. For example, the interior department ordered the *Kreishauptleute* to hand over to the Security Police all Jews who had moved to their districts without official permits since the beginning of the civilian administration. The Jews were to be used in a "lengthy, severe" work deployment. Thus, the rural districts were supposed to be "evacuated" retroactively. In future only closed ghettos were to be established; furthermore, from then on, the death penalty also applied in the district of Galicia for Jews who tried to escape from the ghetto.[53]

This directive marked a crucial point. So far, the protagonists planned to keep the ghetto in constant movement along *Durchgangsstraße IV*. Now the camp was still retained as a ghetto replacement, but the orientation "toward the east" fell by the wayside and thus also the previous objections against Katzmann's practice of exterminating the Jews through work.

Immediately thereafter, the senior officials of the district administration and the City of Lvov agreed on guidelines for the "resettlement of Jews from Lvov." They distinguished three groups according to the degree of ability to work and retained the already-existing division of the ghetto into an unproductive sector at the city periphery and a quarter for skilled workers. Tradesmen and specialists were to be moved to the latter together with their families. Unmarried Jews fit for work had to be divided according to gender and sent to the forced labor camp of the SS and Police Leader (presumably a camp at Janowska Street in Lvov), all others were "resettled." In the minutes, the euphemizing term "relocation" to the sparsely populated environs is mentioned. On the other hand, the participants in the discussion explicitly distinguished the terms "resettlement" (*Umsiedlung*) and "evacuation" (*Aussiedlung*), and the latter should by no means begin before spring of 1942—a clear indication regarding the Belzec extermination camp.[54]

In view of the described developments in Galicia, it becomes clear that Heydrich's remarks at the "Wannsee Conference" referred in part to the schemes initiated in Galicia. For there the Jews were indeed, as Heydrich formulated it, "led eastward building roads" (*straßenbauend in den Osten geführt*) and "the remainder treated appropriately" (*der Restbestand entsprechend behandelt*)—by mass shootings, and later with poison gas at Belzec. Very likely the formula of "*straßenbauend in den Osten*" was directly borrowed from the example of Galicia. With reference to the construction projects, the direction of Jewish policy proposed by Heydrich was certified and at the same time legitimized, i.e., gained the appearance of economic rationality.[55] However, everyone involved soon realized that the "Final Solution" would not take place at the Arctic Sea (*Eismeer*), as Heydrich had maintained as late as February 1942,[56] but in gas chambers in Poland.

The discussion at the Wannsee, however, had no noticeable impact on policy in the district of Galicia. Rather, the preparations continued in a "normal way." To achieve better coordination between civilian and police authorities than had been the case at the mass shootings, perhaps as early as February 1942, Katzmann announced to several of the *Kreishauptleute* in the presence of the new governor, Wächter, and the administrative chief, Losacker, the imminent deportation of the Jews. Immediately before the first extermination operation in the Lvov ghetto, Wächter made sure that Katzmann took over those Jews into his camps who had been given to him as forced laborers by the civilian administration. Afterwards, the governor ordered the distribution by 1 April 1942 of new work passes with the letter "A" for skilled workers and tradesmen. Through these steps the administrative basis was laid for the so-called ABC Registration which the Security Police and the employment offices carried out before and during the mass deportation. As shown, the criteria for this selection had been in place for some time. Some *Kreishauptleute* hastily erected tripartite ghettos in order to divide the Jewish population according to the "ABC Registration."[57]

The murder of the Jews in the General Government began in mid-March 1942 with the simultaneous evacuation of the ghettos of Lublin and Lvov. In particular, the "*Aktion*" in Lublin, commanded by Globocnik, became the model for all subsequent extermination transports; knowledge about the operation spread rapidly in the General Government and the Reich due to the brutality exhibited by the SS and police. From Lvov over 15,000 Jews were transported to Belzec and gassed there in the span of only two weeks, but because the civilian administration there had more influence on the "evacuation," it was not conducted with the same brutality as Globocnik's operation in Lublin.[58]

Outside of Lvov, the local detachments of the Security Police, Order Police, and local district administrations also carried out mass deportations; once again the operations centered on the south of the district which was supposed to be "evacuated" first, an extension of the earlier mass shootings. The relevant order by the district office to "clear" a wide strip of territory could also refer to the Hungarian border. Budapest had complained to the German Foreign Office about the return of Jews from eastern Galicia and requested it be stopped.[59] In some cases shootings also took place again in the course of the "ABC-Registration." The extermination of rural Jewry, though, was postponed to a later date. In April 1942 approximately 430,000 Jews remained in the district, only part of whom had been concentrated into ghettos by then.[60]

In Lvov itself, however, private firms and official agencies had raised an unexpectedly high demand for Jewish manpower; the Lvov Employment Office issued many more work passes to Jewish workers than previously thought.[61] This was primarily connected to the plan pursued since the beginning of the year by the Economics Department, the employment offices, and the Armaments Department in Lvov. It envisaged that the district be harnessed more than previously into the war economy, which in turn was linked to a more solid integration of the district into the General Government. The expectations of the Jewish population of the district, who had learned of the transports to Belzec, fit in with this plan. Because the transports from eastern Galicia had temporarily ended in April and were only resumed in late July 1942, hopes arose in the interval that the Germans might have returned to a more "reasonable" attitude and for this reason had stopped the exterminations.[62] At that time 86,000 Jews were still living in Lvov officially, of whom 40,000 men and 20,000 women received work passes.

In May 1942, however, the details were set definitively for the destruction of all Jews. For the General Government as a whole, this decision can be seen in the enlargement of the extermination apparatus in *"Aktion Reinhard."*[63] This development showed parallels in the district of Galicia. Since May, plans had been discussed in Lvov for a drastic reduction of the local ghetto that would go hand in hand with a simultaneous expansion of the Lvov-Janowska forced labor camp. In fact, during the following weeks, this camp was expanded to become a transit point for all transports from eastern Galicia to Belzec.[64] In this context, Katzmann demanded figures about Jewish employment from the *Kreishauptleute*, who took the opportunity to have part of the Jews deported to Lvov, where they were either used for the preparatory work in the Janowska camp or transported to camps along the *Durchgangsstraße IV* and murdered there.[65]

At the beginning of June 1942, Frank, having lost the power struggle with Himmler over jurisdiction regarding settlement and Jewish policy, handed over all police matters, including "Jewish affairs," to the Higher SS and Police Leader Friedrich Wilhelm Krüger. Only two weeks later, Krüger negotiated with the top district administrators about an expansion of the mass gassings to the entire General Government.[66]

With this, a phase lasting roughly one year was concluded in the district of Galicia, marking an end point in the initiation of the genocide. From this point on "extra-ideological" considerations did not play a role any more: The murder of the Jews no longer had to be justified with "danger of epidemics" or "illicit trade," nor did economic concerns have any influence. The freight cars rolling without interruption toward Belzec until the end of the year were loaded with men, women, and children using methods that even German propaganda agencies took offence to.

A considerable number of German functionaries were directly or indirectly involved in the Jewish extermination. In addition, the Ukrainian police and the Ukrainian municipal administration participated. If one considers moreover that there was hardly any secrecy about the "Final Solution" in Galicia, it is safe to assume that several thousand Germans and as many Ukrainians participated in the mass murder or were onlookers.[67] Without doubt, antisemitic motives played a great role in this participation, in the context of which the prejudices against the Eastern European Jews (*Ostjuden*) in the territory of the formerly "Imperial Austrian" Galicia had particular significance.[68] The perception of the Jewish extermination as a task and challenge for the administration, but also as a severe psychological strain that had to be endured for the fatherland was very widespread. The *Kreishauptmann* of Stryj (Stryi) lamented the economic effects of the *"Judenaktionen,"* only to close with the proud sentence that "the goal accomplished in all areas" was "to be appreciated all the more." Katzmann ended his final report with the observation that "only through the personal sense of duty of each leader and man" had it been possible "to get this *pestilence* under control in a very short time."[69]

However, to attribute the extermination of the Jews solely to hatred of the Jews or a specifically German "eliminationist anti-semitism," constitutes a considerable simplification,[70] for the simple reason that it obscures the functional spectrum of antisemitism. Ukrainian antisemitism, such as emerged particularly in the auxiliary police, was motivated by the fight against "Judeo-Bolshevism" as late as spring of 1942; later in the year, by contrast, the motive of greed for plunder came to the fore.[71] Katzmann, but also some officials on the level of the local districts were surely antisemitic fanatics. For other occupational functionaries, however, this does not apply to the same extent. Their motives must be sought in other areas.

In this context, the behavior of the civilian administration is of particular interest in the district of Galicia (but not only there); the functionaries fell back on feigned utilitarian considerations and specific official wording. The terminology of "work" played a very important role here, as is shown in the minutes of the Wannsee Conference and the "ABC Registration" with its preliminary stages. The logic of secondary rationalization worked particularly well in those instances, when the perpetrators could fool themselves and others into believing that such mass murders, especially under conditions of war, were a harsh necessity to be tolerated, if need be, in the interest of a greater goal. For this reason, the fateful mechanism of repeated states of emergency, supposedly necessitating extraordinary measures, remained in force until the end.

V

Anti-Jewish policy and the murder of the Jews in eastern Galicia were to a great extent a manifestation of its intermediate position in terms of occupation policies. Although the region was part of the General Government, it represented, de facto, a mixed type between the original General Government and the neighboring occupation zones to the east. This peculiarity was not least a result of Hitler's decree of July 1941 to incorporate eastern Galicia into the General Government, not the *Reichskommissariat* of the Ukraine.

The case of eastern Galicia confirms recent considerations that the impulses for radicalization came "from below," in this case from the periphery, to be bundled in Berlin and relayed back. The exact role of the central agencies in this process, however, is still unclear. For example, it remains undetermined whether they deliberately caused conditions such as those in eastern Galicia in order to gauge the acceptance of an extermination program in the contained space of a remote periphery.[72] Without doubt, however, the quasi-colonial structure of the district encouraged the policy of Jewish extermination. From the perspective of expectations existing in the Frank administration since March 1941, it was only logical and functional for the time being not to integrate the new district into the General Government. This opened up considerable freedom of action to both the SS and police apparatus and the civilian administration alike.

In the phase between the fall of 1941 and early 1942, the new district played a peculiar role in the entire process of the "Final Solution." This position rested primarily on the scheme to deport the Jews via the *Durchgangsstraße IV* to the Soviet Union. When, in the spring of 1942, its construction was pushed forward into eastern Ukraine, the original planning had already become obsolete. That it would constitute a transitional phenomenon, however, could not be foreseen in late autumn and early winter of 1941. Accordingly, the attempt of the civilian administration to reconcile work and extermination under the primacy of subsequent mass deportations contributed significantly to the rationalization and bureaucratization of the Jewish extermination.

Above all, the tripartite division of the Jewish population tied together two methods of Jewish extermination. Only in eastern Galicia did shootings occur on a scale corresponding to the "Final Solution" in the occupied territories of Soviet Union; and the mass extermination began significantly earlier in eastern Galicia than in the rest of the General Government, where Jews were for the most part gassed. Eastern Galicia represented a catalyst for the expansion of the murder of the Jews through *"Aktion Reinhard"* and finally to the million-fold gassings at Auschwitz-Birkenau. In this context, the initially predominant notion of killing only part of the Jews now in anticipation of a *later* "Final Solution" had important legitimizing effects. If Jews fit for work were to be led "to the East, building roads," then according to the logic of the perpetrators, a provisional killing facility was sufficient to murder Jews unfit for work on-site.

This constellation changed by January 1942 at the latest. The mass extermination would not take place farther to the east any more but in the General Government itself. As a consequence, the *Durchgangsstraße IV* lost its original importance. Even before the Wannsee Conference, the details were set in Lvov for the deportations to Belzec. Apart from Lublin, the district of Galicia was the scene of the first ghetto "evacuations," beginning in March of that year. The shift toward a greater exploitation of labor in eastern

Galicia was thwarted by the decision in May to murder *all* Jews. All utilitarian arguments now took a backseat—in any case, they were also not needed any longer.

Notes

1. See on this the contributions on various countries in Wolfgang Benz (ed.), *Dimension des Völkermords. Die Zahl der jüdischen Opfer des National-sozialismus* (Munich, 1996).
2. On this discussion see the summary in Eberhard Jäckel and Jürgen Rohwer (eds.), *Der Mord an den Juden im Zweiten Weltkrieg. Entschlußbildung und Verwirklichung* (Frankfurt a.M., 1987); also Ian Kershaw, *Der NS-Staat. Geschichtsinterpretationen und Kontroversen im Überblick* (Reinbek, 1988), pp. 165-208; [*The Nazi Dictatorship. Problems and Perspectives of Interpretation* (N.Y./London, 1993)].
3. Very stimulating in this respect is above all Christopher R. Browning, *Fateful Months. Essays on the Emergence of the Final Solution* (New York, 1985); idem, *The Path to Genocide. Essays on Launching the Final Solution* (Cambridge, 1992); see the research update of Dieter Pohl, "Nationalsozialistischer Judenmord als Problem von osteuropäischer Geschichte und Osteuropa-Geschichtsschreibung," in *Jahrbücher für die Geschichte Osteuropas* 60 (1992): 96-119.
4. Influential are the reflections of Martin Broszat, "Hitler und die Genesis der 'Endlösung': Aus Anlaß der Thesen von David Irving" (1977), in idem, *Nach Hitler. Der schwierige Umgang mit unserer Geschichte* (Munich, 1988), pp. 45-91; also Hans Mommsen, "Die Realisierung des Utopischen: Die 'Endlösung der Judenfrage' im 'Dritten Reich,'" in *Geschichte und Gesellschaft* 9 (1983): 381-420.
5. Thomas Sandkühler, *'Endlösung' in Galizien. Der Judenmord in Ostpolen und die Rettungsinitiativen von Berthold Beitz* (Bonn, 1996); Dieter Pohl, *National-sozialistische Judenverfolgung in Ostgalizien. Organisation und Durchführung eines staatlichen Massenverbrechens* (Munich, 1996), with some diverging assessments on the questions treated here.
6. See the overview in Paul-Robert Magosci, *Galicia: A Historical Survey and Bibliographic Guide* (Toronto/Buffalo/London, 1985).
7. Yisrael Gutman, "Polish Antisemitism between the Wars: An Overview," in idem et al. (eds.) *The Jews of Poland between the Two World Wars* (Hanover/London, 1989), pp. 97-108; Antony Polonsky, "A Failed Pogrom: The Demonstrations in Lvov, June 1929," ibid., pp. 109-125.
8. Notes of Lahousen, 14 September 1939, as cited in *Die faschistische Okkupationspolitik in Polen (1939-1944), Dokumentenauswahl und Einleitung von Werner Röhr* (Köln, 1989), p. 115.
9. See on this Dieter Pohl, *Von der 'Judenpolitik' zum Judenmord. Der Distrikt Lublin des Generalgouvernements 1939-1944* (Frankfurt a.M. et al., 1993).

10. Jan T. Gross, *Revolution from Abroad. The Soviet Conquest of Poland's Western Ukraine and Western Belorussia* (Princeton, 1988); Norman Davies and Antony Polonsky (eds.), *Jews in Eastern Poland and the USSR, 1939-46* (London, 1991).

11. See below note 19.

12. Frank Golczewski, "Polen," in Benz, *Dimension*, pp. 419-432; see on the "resettlements" in general Götz Aly, '*Endlösung.' Völkerverschiebung und der Mord an den europäischen Juden* (Frankfurt a.M., 1995).

13. Calculations are contained in Sandkühler, *Endlösung*, pp. 459-461.

14. Aly, *Endlösung*, pp. 111-114.

15. Sandkühler, *Endlösung*, pp. 49-53, 110f.

16. Aly, *Endlösung*, pp. 268ff.

17. Sandkühler, *Endlösung*, pp. 50-52.

18. Ralf Ogorreck, *Die Einsatzgruppen und die Genesis der 'Endlösung'* (Berlin, 1996), pp. 97-104; see also Peter Longerich, "Vom Massenmord zur 'Endlösung.' Die Erschießungen von jüdischen Zivilisten in den ersten Monaten des Ostfeldzugs im Kontext des nationalsozialistischen Judenmords," in Bernd Wegner (ed.), *Zwei Wege nach Moskau. Vom Hitler-Stalin-Pakt zum 'Unternehmen Barbarossa'* (Munich/ Zurich, 1991), pp. 251-290, here 256-260.

19. Leaflets of the OUN read: "You welcomed Stalin with flowers, we shall lay your heads at Hitler's feet as a greeting." Report of the *Lemberger Zeitung* Nr. 135 of 10 June 1942, p. 3.

20. See in detail Sandkühler, *Endlösung*, pp. 114-122.

21. Ibid., p. 461.

22. On the perpetrators see ibid., pp. 77-83, 426-458.

23. Minutes by Bormann on the meeting of 16 July 1941 (Nuremberg Document 221-L), in *Der Prozeß gegen die Hauptkriegsverbrecher vor dem Internationalen Militärgerichtshof [Trial of the Major War Criminals Before the International Military Tribunal]*, Vol. 38 (Nuremberg, 1949), p. 87, 89; Frank Golczewski, "Die Ukraine im Zweiten Weltkrieg," in idem (ed.), *Geschichte der Ukraine* (Göttingen, 1993), pp. 241-260, here 251f.

24. Werner Präg and Wolfgang Jacobmeyer (eds.), *Das Diensttagebuch des deutschen Generalgouverneurs in Polen, 1939-1945* (Stuttgart, 1975), p. 387 (entry on 18 July 1941); Frank to Lammers, 19 July 1941, Bundesarchiv Koblenz R 6/21, fol. 136f.

25. Sandkühler, *Endlösung*, pp. 63-67, 459.

26. Ibid., pp. 71-76.

27. Ibid., pp. 122f., 127.

28. Instructive in this respect is the so-called *Schenk-Bericht* on the "Verhalten der Reichsdeutschen in den besetzten Gebieten (Behavior of the Reich Germans in the Occupied territories)," Bundesarchiv Koblenz R 58/1002, which deals with numerous cases of corruption in the district of Galicia.

29. Sandkühler, *Endlösung*, p. 139.

30. Decree of the *Amtschef* Losacker regarding the restriction of residency in the district of Galicia, 1 September 1941, contained in a circular letter re. the approach to changes in residency of Jews thus far and the establishment of Jewish quarters, 7 January 1942, Lvov State Archive R 2042/1/155. fol. 3 Rs.

31. On Globocnik see Wolfgang Scheffler, "Probleme der Holocaustforschung," in Stefi Jersch-Wenzel (ed.), *Deutsche—Polen—Juden. Ihre Beziehungen von den Anfängen bis ins 20. Jahrhundert. Beiträge zu einer Tagung* (Berlin, 1987), pp. 259-281, here 271-274; Sandkühler, *Endlösung*, pp. 130-134.

32. Proclamation of the Labor Department, 20 September 1941, facsimile in Jewish Historical Institute (ed.), *Faschismus—Getto—Massenmord. Dokumentation über Ausrottung und Widerstand der Juden in Polen während des Zweiten Weltkrieges* (Berlin, 1960), p. 228.

33. See the overview by Czeslaw Madajczyk, "Vom 'Generalplan Ost' zum 'Generalsiedlungsplan'," in Mechthild Rössler and Sabine Schleiermacher (eds.), *Der 'Generalplan Ost'. Hauptlinien der nationalsozialistischen Planungs- und Vernichtungspolitik* (Berlin, 1993), pp. 12-19.

34. Ereignismeldung UdSSR, Nr. 86, 17 September 1941, on this see Longerich, "Massenmord," p. 266.

35. Ulrich Herbert, "Arbeit und Vernichtung. Ökonomisches Interesse und Primat der 'Weltanschauung' im Nationalsozialismus," in Dan Diner (ed.), *Ist der Nationalsozialismus Geschichte? Zu Historisierung und Historikerstreit* (Frankfurt a.M., 1987), pp. 198-236, here 209f.

36. Pohl, *Judenpolitik*, pp. 92-94.

37. On this topic, see the contribution by Christoph Dieckmann in this edition.

38. Elisabeth Freundlich, *Die Ermordung einer Stadt namens Stanislau. NS-Vernichtungspolitik in Polen* (Vienna, 1986), pp. 154-164; Sandkühler, *Endlösung*, pp. 149-152.

39. Ibid., pp. 155-159.

40. Ibid., p. 162, 140.

41. Pohl, *Judenpolitik*, p. 101, 105f.

42. Sandkühler, *Endlösung*, pp. 142f.

43. See Katzmann's final report "Lösung der Judenfrage im Distrikt Galizien," 30 June 1943, Nuremberg Document L-018, partially edited in *Der Prozeß gegen die Hauptkriegsverbrecher [Trial of the Major War Criminals]*, Vol. 37, pp. 391-431, here 392f, 401.

44. Sandkühler, *Endlösung*, p. 146.

45. Philip Friedman, "The Destruction of the Jews of Lvov, 1941-1944 [1956]," in idem, *Roads to Extinction. Essays on the Holocaust*, ed. Ada J. Friedman (New York, 1980), pp. 244-321, here 262; Sandkühler, *Endlösung*, pp. 155-159.

46. Ibid., pp. 316-318.

47. Präg and Jacobmeyer, *Diensttagebuch*, pp. 457f. (entry of 16 December 1941).

48. Between mid-November and Christmas of 1941 the district physician, Dr. Dopheide, had negotiated with the *Euthanasie-Zentrale* in Berlin in order to be able to conduct a supposed "*Aktion der Geisteskranken*" (operation of mental patients) (Lvov State Archive R 35/13/58, fol. 1-3). Presumably, in this manner gassings of Jews were meant to be prepared.

49. Wolfgang Scheffler, "Chelmno, Sobibór, Belzec und Majdanek," in Jäckel and Rohwer, *Mord*, pp. 145-151, here 149f.

50. Sandkühler, *Endlösung*, pp. 146f., 317f.

51. See Bundesarchiv Berlin, SS-Offiziersakte Friedrich Katzmann, as well as the Katzmann-Bericht (note 43).

52. Bundesarchiv Berlin, SS-Offiziersakte Otto Wächter.

53. Circular letter of 7 January 1942 (note 30).

54. Note on the conference of 9 January 1942 regarding the transfer (*Aussiedlung*) of Jews from Lvov, 10 January 1942, Lvov State Archive R 37/4/140, fol. 61-63.

55. So-called Wannsee-Protokoll, 20 January 1942, here according to *Faschismus—Getto—Massenmord*, pp. 263-268, quoted from pp. 266f. The aspect of legitimation is also emphasized in Herbert, *Arbeit und Vernichtung*, here p. 216.

56. Aly, *Endlösung*, p. 274.
57. Sandkühler, *Endlösung*, pp. 173f., 242f.
58. This is particularly evident in a comparison with the second reduction of the Lvov ghetto in August 1942; ibid., pp. 208ff., 219ff.; on Lublin see Pohl, *Judenpolitik*, pp. 113-117. Katzmann dated the beginning of the "Final Solution" in the district of Galicia to April 1942: Katzmann-Bericht, p. 398.
59. Circular letter to the *Kreishauptleute* in Drohobycz, Stanislau and Kolomea, 19 March 1942, Lviv State Archive R 2042/1/84, fol. 86.
60. Sandkühler, *Endlösung*, p. 181. As late as November of that year the Higher SS and Police Leader Krüger identified considerably more Jewish "residential areas" than in other parts of the General Government; *Faschismus—Getto—Massenmord*, p. 345.
61. Sandkühler, *Endlösung*, pp. 212f.
62. Ibid., pp. 213-216, 325-334.
63. Pohl, *Judenpolitik*, pp. 129-131.
64. See Thomas Sandkühler, "Das Zwangsarbeitslager Lemberg-Janowska, 1941-1944," in Ulrich Herbert, Karin Orth, and Christoph Dieckmann (eds.), *Die nationalsozialistischen Konzentrationslager. Entwicklung und Struktur* (Göttingen, 1998), pp. 606-635.
65. Sandkühler, *Endlösung*, pp. 229f.
66. Präg and Jacobmeyer, *Diensttagebuch*, pp. 510f. (entry of 18 June 1942).
67. In September 1942 the district of Galicia numbered 14,366 Reich Germans (including SS, Police, and family members), that is, 0.3 percent of the population. Of these approximately 2,000 persons participated in the Jewish extermination as direct perpetrators (Security and Order Police as well as direct subordinates of the SS and Police Leader) or in the administration. On the non-German side, there were additionally the Ukrainian police with about 3,000, in the end, 4,000 men. The number of onlookers was obviously much higher than that of the 6,000 directly or indirectly involved persons. See on the categories still Herbert Jäger, *Verbrechen unter totalitärer Herrschaft. Studien zur nationalsozialistischen Gewaltkriminalität* (Olten/Freiburg, 1967).
68. Thus Frank publicly got his enthusiastic audience in the mood for the impending murder of tens of thousands of Lvov Jews, whom he derided as "*Plattfußindianer*." Präg and Jacobmeyer, *Diensttagebuch*, pp. 532-535 (entry of 1 August 1942).
69. Sandkühler, *Endlösung*, p. 385; Katzmann-Bericht, p. 410.
70. Daniel J. Goldhagen, *Hitlers willige Vollstrecker. Ganz gewöhnliche Deutsche und der Holocaust* (Berlin, 1996) [*Hitler's Willing Executioners. Ordinary Germans and the Holocaust* (New York, 1996]; among the criticisms see most recently and comprehensively Dieter Pohl, "Die Holocaust-Forschung und Goldhagens Thesen," in *Vierteljahrshefte für Zeitgeschichte* 45 (1997): 1-48; Ruth-Bettina Birn, "Revising the Holocaust," in *Historical Journal* 40 (1997): 195-215.
71. Sandkühler, *Endlösung*, p. 212, 349f.
72. Thus the interpretation of Aly, *Endlösung*, pp. 384-386, 399f.

– Chapter 5 –

THE GERMAN MILITARY COMMAND IN PARIS AND THE DEPORTATION OF THE FRENCH JEWS

Ulrich Herbert

The availability of new source material following the opening of archives in the former East Bloc, especially in the Soviet Union, has caused both scholarly and public debate over how the "Final Solution to the Jewish problem" came to be implemented to focus more sharply on the role of the Wehrmacht and the individual German occupation authorities. Recent studies have shown that, especially in the early phase of the Nazi regime's deportation and extermination policy, the importance of regional initiatives, some of which were not approved by the central authority in Berlin until after the fact, was greater than hitherto surmised, and that even Wehrmacht authorities played a decisive role.[1] Hence the time-honored distinction among SS, party, and RSHA (*Reichssicherheitshauptamt*) on the one hand and the Wehrmacht and civilian occupation authorities on the other has become increasingly dubious. Finally, it is becoming increasingly apparent that, up until the end of 1941, not all—probably not even most—initiatives undertaken by regional authorities were meant from the outset to result in the murder of *all* European Jews. Hence the original function of the central authorities in Berlin—especially the RSHA, Himmler, and above all Hitler himself—should be regarded as one of coordinating, generalizing, and standardizing local initiatives rather than as a command-like initiation and direction of the process.[2]

Of course, most recent research deals with eastern and southeastern Europe, regions in which, from the very outset, German occupation authorities acted with extraordinary brutality, motivated and provided as they were with a cloak of legitimacy by Hitler's orders and programmatic pronouncements. But what was the situation in the occupied countries of western Europe? To what extent did the civilian and military authorities initiate or pave the way for the deportation of Jews "to the East"? Or was RSHA policy the sole determining factor in those countries? In this regard, France is an especially important example, not only because France was by far the most important western country under German occupation, but also because France was the scene of especially sharp conflicts between the occupation authorities and the central authorities in Berlin. Disagreements between the German military command in Paris and the German central authorities, especially Hitler and Keitel, over the suppression of French resistance or the confiscation of French art treasures previously owned by Jews had led to serious confrontations early on. These conflicts reached critical proportions with the resignation of the military commander Otto von Stülpnagel at the beginning of 1942, and culminated on 20 July 1944, when Paris, next to Berlin, became a center for the attempted coup, in which numerous senior military officers of the German occupation were directly or indirectly involved, among them the military commander, Karl-Heinrich von Stülpnagel.[3]

The role of the military in initiating the deportation of French Jews in late 1941 and early 1942, however, is still as unclear as ever, not least of all because the various aspects of occupation policy are generally studied in isolation. Thus, issues such as how disputes over the "hostage question" might have been connected to the onset of the deportation of French Jews are not stressed. The following is an attempt to examine such connections more closely and especially to draw distinctions among individual groupings within the German occupation force in Paris regarding their various understandings of policy, political aims, and values. Insights derived from recent studies of occupied territories in eastern Europe require us to investigate the (possibly different) motivations of the various power centers in Paris, as well as the political contexts in which measures first leading to the deportation of French Jews were undertaken.

I

What form German occupation assumed in the defeated and conquered countries of Europe at any given time derived from a multiplicity of factors and was, in any event, not centrally coordinated. It was obvious on compelling material grounds that defeated France could not be governed or administered by the German authorities themselves, as was the case in the Government General in the eastern part of the former Poland. The Reich lacked both the personnel and financial resources that such an undertaking would have required. While the role that France might eventually play in a postwar, German-dominated Europe was still altogether unclear, Nazi Germany's short- and intermediate-range interests lay in making sure that peace and security reigned in France and that maximum industrial and agricultural deliveries to the Reich were achieved with a minimum of military, financial, and administrative investment on the part of German authorities.[4]

To that end, France was divided into three occupation zones, and the Petain government was installed in Vichy, suspended in a curious no-man's-land between dependence and independence. But Germany's interest in achieving in France the greatest effect at the least expense found its clearest expressions in the post of the Military High Command.

The idea underlying this form of occupation was that the French bureaucracy would continue to function fully and without interruption while being monitored occasionally by officers of the German occupation forces. Of course, this arrangement assumed a readiness on the part of the French government, the bureaucracy, and not least of all the general population to cooperate thoroughly, albeit involuntarily. Such readiness, following France's complete and demoralizing military defeat, enabled the Germans to establish a form of occupation that made do with around 200 officers and officials at central headquarters in Paris and less than 1,000 in the entire occupied zone while still managing to govern occupied France according to German wishes, without major friction.

At the head of the military administration stood the Militärbefehlshaber (military commander), a general who had few troops at his disposal and functioned rather like a governor. Chief of Staff Hans Speidel clearly stood out among the leading figures of the German military bureaucracy as a conservative non-Nazi of great talent who saw to it that the staffs of the military commander consisted primarily of professionals of a national conservative stripe, men in their middle and later years who already knew each other and hired themselves one to each other. Consequently, the staff officers formed a relatively homogenous group of conservative elitists who, out of intellectual contempt, social arrogance, and political enmity maintained a distance from Hitler and the "party people." The group was characterized by German-nationalist patriotism and was rarely disturbed by outsiders. Beginning in October 1940, the military commander in France was General Otto von Stülpnagel. "Humorless, stiff, something of a tin soldier," and yet characterized by "correctness to the point of rigidity and a sense of historical mission. No follower of Hitler, but a rock-ribbed conservative," in the assessment of Walter Bargatzky, who was, from 1940 to 1944, administrative advisor in the judicial division and one of the most perceptive observers of events in Paris during that period.[5]

The military command itself consisted of a command staff, which had authority over the occupation troops, and an administrative staff, which monitored the French bureaucracy. The latter was subdivided into two sections. One was responsible for economic issues; the other supervised the entire French bureaucracy and contained in its police, justice, and finance divisions departments crucial to the success of the German military bureaucracy. The subordinate offices in the districts and prefectures were organized along the same lines as the Paris headquarters and were charged with overseeing the regional and local administrative authorities. Since the Vichy government held to the principle of a unified administration for the entire country and applied laws and regulations promulgated in occupied France to the unoccupied region, the influence of the Paris military command extended in practice into the southern part of the country even before the south was occupied by German troops in 1942.[6]

The director of this administrative section thus functioned as something of a supervising minister of the interior for France and was doubtlessly a key figure in the collaboration, because the military administration had no choice but to rely on the French bureaucracy for efficient and trouble-free execution of directives, and, especially given the lack of German personnel for enforcement, on the dedication of the French police. In SS-Brigadeführer Dr. Werner Best, the position had a prominent if unusual occupant. Until the early summer of 1940, Best had served in the RSHA as its director and as Heydrich's representative. At Gestapo headquarters in Berlin, he had functioned simultaneously as head of personnel and organization as well as legal advisor and chief ideologist; there he was considered both a competent administrator and an ideologically radical SS leader. Regarding the Jews, he had early taken a hard-line position in favor of rigorously executed expulsions, and shortly before his appointment to the Paris office, he had published a plan to establish a German-dominated Europe in which ethnic groups that offered resistance would be expelled and, if necessary, exterminated. On the other hand, as part of that scheme, he supported a rational, long-term occupation policy of weighing expenditures against returns and making allowances for the political and "racial" realities in each of the occupied countries. Best was initially regarded as something of an alien being by the German nationalist officers of the military command, but it soon turned out that he worked excellently with them because he did not play the role of the "ferocious Nazi" but, on the contrary, behaved modestly, cooperatively, and "reasonably," although he made no secret of his political convictions, nor of his intention to apply them to the Paris operation.[7]

The staff of the military commander was the most important power center of the German occupation in France, but not the only one. Officials from the Foreign Office and the RSHA were also present in Paris, along with a number of representatives, liaison units, and special staffs with their own special interests and methods of influencing policy.

The German Embassy in Paris, under Ribbentrop's confidant Otto Abetz, had a somewhat ill-defined jurisdiction over all political matters in both occupied and unoccupied France. It differed from the staff of the military commander not so much over current methods of implementing occupation policy but rather in its pursuit of goals that were more overtly political.

The position of Commander of the Security Police and the SD (Beauftragter der Sicherheitspolizei und des SD; BdS) had been established to represent Heydrich in Paris. Following fierce disputes over the role of the *Einsatzgruppen* in Poland, the leadership of the Wehrmacht had succeeded in France in vesting the sole executive authority in the military commander and in preventing RSHA *Einsatzgruppen* from being formed there. Thus, the position of the BdS in France was at first relatively weak, despite the fact that Heydrich had entrusted the BdS with responsibility for waging the "ideological struggle." Helmut Knochen, who held a doctorate in English, directed the office. He had joined the SD in 1936, where he had managed, first, Section II.11 (Ideological Opposition) and then Section II.12 (Political Opposition). His closest colleagues were: Kurt Lischka, Knochen's personal representative and director of the Security Police (Sicherheitspolizei; Sipo) and SD in the Paris area, who had earlier directed the Berlin headquarters for Jewish

emigration and the office of state police in Cologne; Theo Dannecker, who came from Eichmann's SD Section II.112 for Jewish
matters and became France's resident expert on Jewish matters;
and Herbert Hagen, former director of the same Section II.112 and
commander of the Security Police and SD in Bordeaux. Of the three
power centers in Paris, the Security Police had the youngest personnel: Knochen had just turned thirty, Lischka was thirty-one, and
Hagen was twenty-seven.[8]

In addition to the military commander, the embassy, and the
Security Police, the office of the Wiesbaden Armistice Commission
and representatives of the Board for the Four Year Plan were also
important players on the Paris scene. But the center of conflicts and
internal struggles that eventually arose among the multiple players
and competing interests was the headquarters of the military commander. That the military command had established its headquarters
in the Paris luxury hotel Majestic—the "original face of the international world," as Bargatzsky puts it—was not lacking in symbolism.[9]
One of the glittering centers of an elegant metropolis, the hotel had
nothing military or bureaucratic about it, but constantly confronted
the German officers residing in its rooms and suites with the French
lifestyle that they both admired and envied, thus conveying an altogether civil and "peaceful" atmosphere that contrasted markedly
with the announcements and directives arriving daily from Berlin
and the fronts.

II

The French government in Vichy had already signaled to the German occupation force its readiness to accommodate developments
in Germany by adopting a sharply antisemitic stance. As early as 22
July 1940, a commission had been established to examine and
revoke the citizenship of Jews who had been naturalized in recent
years. At the end of August, the ban on antisemitic propaganda was
lifted. On 3 October the "Jewish Statute" was proclaimed: For the
first time, Jewry was referred to as a "race" rather than as a religious community, as had hitherto been the case, and Jews were
denied access to public employment and the free professions. On 4
October, the Laval government decreed that foreign Jews currently
residing in the unoccupied zone would be interned in special camps
for Jews under the authority of the prefects.[10]

On the German side, however, it was not the BdS, which at first
operated without noticeable influence, that took the lead in Jewish

policy, but rather the embassy and the military administrative staff. As early as 17 August, the result of a discussion between Abetz and Best was transmitted in the form of a "recommendation" (*Anregung*) from the embassy to the military command: The latter should consider (a) arranging, effectively immediately, for no more Jews to enter the occupied territory; (b) preparing for the expulsion of all Jews from the occupied territory; (c) examining the possibility of seizing Jewish property in the occupied territory.[11]

These quite far-reaching guidelines made clear very early the administrative staff's policy aims relating to Jews. This must be seen against the background of the Madagascar plan, which was being discussed at that time although it was then no more than an idea.[12] Abetz then approached the Foreign Office with a "Request for Approval of Immediate Antisemitic Measures," whereupon Hitler's approval in principle of the catalog of measures was obtained on 26 August.[13]

The "recommendation" that Best had worked out with the embassy was then submitted to the individual subsections of the administrative staff for their reactions. The responses, though critical of individual points, were basically positive. Military administrative adviser Mahnke cautioned that "opening up the race question" might be seen as implying an intent to annex territory, thus conflicting with the operational guidelines of the military command; such concerns might be allayed, however, if the measures were promulgated piecemeal and justified by the need to protect Wehrmacht interests against the Jews. Mahnke went on to point out that one might point specifically to Jewish hostility toward Germany, to acts of espionage, and to the danger inherent in a situation in which French companies essential to the war effort were owned by Jews.[14] Mahnke's colleague Storz also responded positively. "Naturally, the military command cannot continue to remain passive in its attitude concerning the Jewish question. On the contrary, the time has come to create in occupied France the preconditions necessary to attain German long-range political objectives in this area. Those goals clearly include the radical eradication of Jewish influence in all areas of life, including the economic sphere."[15] Walter Bargatzky spoke for the legal section in saying that the proposed measures were acceptable if they could be justified based on the security concerns of the occupation forces. That was certainly the case as far as expulsions and a ban on return were concerned, while the planned aryanizations would have to "publicly take the form of private transfers of property."[16]

Thus, as long as certain legal and political niceties were observed, the military commander's administrative staff was signaling its willingness to effect harsh anti-Jewish measures at a point when neither the BdS in Paris nor the RSHA had attempted to intervene to that end. When asked, Heydrich had merely expressed his approval of Abetz and Best's proposals and asked that the Security Police, "which has personnel experienced in Jewish matters," be involved in the formulation of measures in the future.[17]

After the High Commander of the Army, von Brauchitsch, had given the green light in mid-September and the military administration staff had begun urging that the measures planned against the Jews, especially in the economic realm, be implemented without delay, the administrative staff issued on 27 September the "First Directive Regarding Jews," which corresponded closely to the agreements reached with Best.[18] Jews were denied entrance into occupied France. That had the effect of preventing the return of Jews who had fled to unoccupied France to escape the Germans and increasing the number of Jews who had to eke out an existence characterized by privation and fear in the internment camps that the Vichy government had begun establishing in the unoccupied territory on 4 October. Second, the French prefects were ordered to compile and maintain a comprehensive list of resident Jews in preparation for "the removal of all Jews from the occupied territory," as it had been phrased on 17 August. And third, the identification of all Jewish businesses and the registration of all Jewish property was ordered as a first step toward the agreed-upon aryanization.

This directive of 27 September 1940 had considerable significance beyond the borders of France. It was the first of its kind in the German-occupied countries of western and northern Europe that foresaw such radical measures, and it was taken by the other German occupational authorities as the occasion and model for similar measures.[19]

Two weeks later came the Second Directive, which introduced compulsory registration for all Jewish business enterprises as a preliminary step toward the dispossession of the Jews and the aryanization of their property.[20] Von Brauchitsch especially urged the military administration to expedite aryanization because, since the end of the war was clearly imminent, it was anything but certain how long it would be possible for the Reich to effect events in France. By early December, the military administration was able to announce initial "successes," and in the following months the economic dispossession of the Jews in the occupied territory was rapidly accelerated.[21]

Thus, within a few months of the establishment of German occupation in France, the campaign to deprive French Jews of their legal rights had reached a point comparable to the situation in Ger-

many in the summer of 1938. Without having been subjected to
any detectable pressure, the military administration had not so
much acquiesced in the process as initiated and expedited it. The
administrative staff in overall charge of the process found willing
supporters both in the economic staff and even in the command
staff under Speidel—and in Stülpnagel and von Brauchitsch as well.
The antisemitism of the conservatives, which varied from individual to individual from sometimes pronounced to mostly disinter-
estedly traditional, now came to complement the radically *völkisch*
views typical of the personnel of the BdS, and even of Best, because
the planned measures against the Jews was supported by an underlying conviction that German occupation would meet its staunchest
opponents among the Jews. In this way, "security aspects" seemed
to be the primary concern. At the same time, of course, the anti-
Jewish measures now adopted rested on a "legal" basis, while "illegal excesses" would presumably have met with indignant opposition
among the colleagues of the military commander. Thus, for the
conservative military officers, the "Jewish Question" was rather a
sideshow to the war that all in all aroused little interest and clearly
took second place to the battles, regarded as honorable, that they
waged against the Berlin centers of party and government, e.g., those
disputes that had erupted over the theft of "abandoned" (read:
"Jewish-owned") objects of art by Göring, Rosenberg, and others.[22]

III

The initial phase of the German occupation of France, up until the
early summer of 1941, had for the most part proceeded quietly
and, from the point of view of the military administration in Paris,
successfully; even cooperation with the Berlin regime had proven
cordial and trouble-free. Of course, the conflicts that had arisen
over the issues of "art-theft" and the expulsion of the French population of Alsace-Lorraine had revealed divergent views on important issues, but in view of the foreign policy and military successes
of the Reich government, these had not proven crucial. In this
period, the relations of the Paris military administration with the
Berlin government were characterized by conflicts over secondary
issues but agreement on principles.

In the second phase of the occupation, which extended to the
spring of 1942, the situation reversed. Conflicts between Paris and
Berlin now involved fundamental issues of occupation policy; they
shattered the loyalty of the military commander's staff to the Reich

government, especially to Hitler and Keitel, and marked the point at which the command and administrative staff officers were alienated by Hitler's policy—a process that ultimately led many of them to join the conspiratorial circles of 20 July, or to side with them.[23] This second phase of the German occupation of France was characterized by two developments that require rather detailed examination: the mass shootings of hostages as a "reprisal" (*Sühnemaßnahme*) following attempted assassinations and the escalation of German policy toward the Jews from discrimination to deportation. Those events were linked in a characteristic manner.

In the early morning of 21 August 1941, the German *Marinehilfsassistent* Moser was shot and killed on the way to the Metro station Barbes-Rochechouart in Paris by two unidentified young men. A few hours later, at the Metro station Bastille, a German *Unteroffizier* named Schölz was badly wounded. German authorities immediately assumed the perpetrators to have been members of a Communist youth organization, which was indeed confirmed in subsequent investigations and criminal proceedings.

At military headquarters in Paris, these attacks were regarded as the opening round of an active armed struggle by French Communists against German occupation forces in response to Germany's invasion of the Soviet Union; more attacks were anticipated. This assumption was also confirmed by future events. The time of peaceful and, for German occupation personnel, thoroughly pleasant duty in Paris was past; once more the war had reached Paris.[24]

The German leadership in France thus found itself facing a fundamental dilemma that was to define its situation and dictate its actions in the following months, and from which it would not manage to extricate itself. If it reacted to the attacks with the degree of restraint consistent with its policy of supervisory management and collaboration, thus limiting itself to police investigations and preventive measures, it would have to expect sharp protests both from active Wehrmacht units, which judged such cases according to military law, as well as from the OKW (High Command of the Armed Forces) and Hitler. If, on the other hand, it reacted with the same harshness and brutality as the German occupation authorities in the East, then it could expect an end to the cooperation of the French government and bureaucracy as well as the disaffection of the French population.

Until the summer of 1941, the political situation in occupied France had always been described as very quiet—the primary reason for which was without doubt the "Reich's" quite irresistible military might, which made any resistance appear hopeless from the outset. Moreover, French leftists, especially the Communist Party, had been politically paralyzed by the German-Soviet Pact and were even considered especially willing collaborators.

Up to this point, therefore, even the security policy of the German authorities had been relatively restrained. True, in September 1940, guidelines for discouraging sabotage had been promulgated that envisioned the taking of hostages by the occupying power.[25] But given the peaceful situation in occupied France, such collective measures were neither necessary nor prudent. Instead, whenever the decrees of the occupation forces were violated, the French police swung into action, and both German and French courts passed severe sentences. By May 1941, ninety-three death sentences had been pronounced by German courts alone in France, a third of which were carried out.[26]

In a summary decree of May 1941, the administrative section of the military command went so far as to question the effectiveness of hostage-taking in preventing hostile actions "unless by chance there exist exceptionally strong bonds of sympathy (*Solidarität*) between perpetrators and hostages. Fanatics and criminals show no consideration for the lives of hostages. Hostages should, therefore, be seized only if serious acts of violence are expected *and* other appropriate means are not available." And in May the administrative staff was even considering whether the seizing of hostages in occupied France should not be proscribed altogether.[27]

The German authorities' relatively restrained security policy underwent a change during preparations for war against the Soviet Union, and that shift became more pronounced after the outbreak of hostilities. As early as 23 May construction of internment camps for Communists was authorized in occupied France.[28]

The basis of this change was the decrees that had been issued in the fall to security and police forces in anticipation of increased attacks on German occupation forces by the Communist Party of France. And in fact, following the German attack on the USSR, demonstrations occurred in Paris and reported acts of sabotage increased. Consequently, by the end of July 1941, the army was demanding that the military command in Paris "act drastically and ruthlessly" and promulgate guidelines for the shooting of hostages as "reprisals" aimed at preventing further attacks on occupation forces.[29] Accordingly, on 4 August Stülpnagel ordered the death penalty for "Communist subversion" and responded to mass anti-German demonstrations by ordering the French police to conduct mass arrests, in the course of which more than 4,000 people—all Jews—were arrested and taken to Camp Drancy.

After the murders of 21 August, even harsher responses could be expected on the part of the military commander. Even the military's initial reaction was far-reaching and preordained further escalation. On 22 August, all French citizens currently detained by or for German authorities in occupied France were collectively declared hostages, of whom "at each further incident a number reflecting the seriousness of the crime shall be shot."[30] In addition, the German leadership in Paris exerted strong pressure on the French government to take harsh measures of its own, and the administrative staff ultimately announced its approval of the Vichy government's recommendation that the most prominent Communist leaders being detained in French jails should be sentenced to death by a French court. Seven people were subsequently condemned in show trials and executed.[31] Given these initial events, a rapid worsening of the conflict could hardly have been prevented. When a further assassination took place on 3 September, the military commandant had three hostages—again Communists in detention—shot "merely for reasons of prestige."[32]

At that point, Keitel and Hitler became involved. Keitel passed along to the commander a "Führer comment to be noted": Hitler viewed the reaction of the Paris military administration to the assassinations as most inadequate. "The acts of reprisal taken against the three hostages is far too mild! The Führer considers one German soldier to be worth much more than three French Communists. The Führer expects such instances to be responded to with the harshest reprisals … At the next assassination at least 100 shootings for each German [killed] are to take place without delay. Without such draconian retribution, matters cannot be controlled."[33]

This policy was clearly at odds with views held almost unanimously in Paris. Stülpnagel enumerated countervailing arguments in his response: One needs to be flexible rather than mechanical in one's response to attacks, thus leaving open the option of gradually increasing the number of shootings. Mass shootings would risk losing the loyalty of the French population, render more difficult future cooperation between Germany and France, and compromise the French government.[34] Stülpnagel's arguments reflected the view that it was necessary to maintain in principle the policy of administrative supervision, and that the assassinations should be regarded as an attempt by French Communists to provoke the occupation forces into abandoning their velvet-glove approach and thus to end the policy of collaboration, which was compromising the French people. At Hitler's headquarters, however, the attacks in Paris were viewed in conjunction with the struggle with partisans in the Soviet

Union and Yugoslavia. As Keitel stressed on 16 September, what was involved was basically a "centrally coordinated mass movement," specifically a Communist rebellion in all countries under German occupation. The situation was not to be judged according to conditions within France but rather as part of the struggle against international Communism. Thus, the Führer had issued essentially the same orders in both the East and the West, and those orders were to intervene "with the harshest means" in order to defeat the movement as quickly as possible. "Only in this manner, which throughout the history of the expansion of great peoples [*Völker*] has always met with success, can peace be restored.... The political relations between Germany and the specific country in question are not the primary factor in determining the conduct of the military occupation authorities."[35]

This last sentence went to the heart of the dispute. For it was precisely the political relations with the individual countries—more precisely, one own political and cultural evaluation of those countries—that guided the conduct of military authorities in the occupied areas. While the German military authorities in, say, Serbia executed more than 20,000 people in reprisals without much discussion, and while the numbers in the same period in the Soviet Union were running even a good deal higher,[36] orders to carry out incomparably fewer shootings of hostages in France met with the vigorous protest of the German military authorities in Paris, which finally escalated to the point that the commander resigned.

The future course of the hostage issue in France was determined by these contradictions. The administrative and command staffs first worked up a procedural directive for taking hostages and carrying out reprisals, which was published on 28 September; it represents an attempt to codify the procedure for mass shootings.[37] But when, on 20 October, the Field Commander in Nantes was shot and, one day later, a military advisor at Bordeaux, even these legal restraints gave way. Under massive pressure from Hitler's headquarters, the military commander was forced to announce that 100 hostages would be shot for each assassination. After the French government intervened along with Stülpnagel, who warned repeatedly against "the application of Polish methods to France," Hitler finally ordered that 50 hostages be shot at once and the other 100 two days later if the perpetrators had not been captured. On 22 and 24 October, ninety-eight hostages were in fact executed—a move that provoked disgust and great outcry both in France and abroad.[38]

These events marked the collapse of the military's delaying tactics. "The mood in the Majestic is primarily one of rage," according to Walter Bargatzky's description of the reaction of the occupation authorities, "rage over the murders, over the disproportion of the reprisals ordered. One senses that the first, lenient phase of the armistice is over. The reputation of the 'Majestic' is about to change drastically [*nähert sich der Peripetie*]."[39]

Opposition to the shooting of hostages was especially firm in the administrative staff, which thus proceeded to develop for Stülpnagel a series arguments he might use in countering future demands by Hitler and Keitel for harsher reprisals: "(1) the enemy's objective is not a military weakening of the German Wehrmacht but rather the political consequences of German reprisals; (2) the consequences of the policy will make administering the country increasingly difficult and jeopardize the occupation and its goals; (3) progressive reprisals—30, then 50, then 80, and so on—hostages shot for each murder will soon lead of necessity to a quantitative absurdity and thus be abandoned. At that point, this tactic will have been squandered after harming more than it will have helped, and the loss of prestige resulting from calling a halt will be worse than if it had never been employed; (4) in summary, by employing these reprisals we are playing precisely the enemy's game."[40]

And yet, since Hitler's hard line was known, the administrative staff, which was, after all, in charge of the internment and police camps in occupied France and thus responsible for selecting hostages to be shot from among the camp inmates, searched for other methods of reprisal and repression that might have a chilling and preventive effect on the assassins without stoking up anti-German sentiment in the country and torpedoing the policy of collaboration in the long term.[41] Two methods were given serious consideration: the imposition of collective fines and the deportation of a large number of people "to forced labor in the East." Both measures were to be directed, apart from Communists, above all against the Jews, who, thanks to the not inconsiderable antisemitism in France, especially against foreign Jews who had immigrated into France from eastern Europe after the First World War, could presumably expect little sympathy from the French population as long as there were no public shootings. Since Jewish resistance fighters were also to be found among the assassins who had been arrested, repressive measures based on political and ideological motives could be joined. An additional motive, which would be important later, was that one could largely relieve overcrowding in the camps in Drancy, Compiègne, and other locations by turning responsibility for the prisoners over to others without having to worry about their fate.

When news of the next assassination, which claimed three German soldiers, came on 28 November, the military command for the first time attempted to apply this new concept. Instead of shooting 300 hostages, as Hitler demanded, Stülpnagel proposed to the OKH (Army High Command) the shooting "50 Jews and Communists" followed by "imposing a damages payment of one billion francs on the Jews of Paris" and interning Jews with records of criminal or anti-German activities for deportation to the East. The last item, it was thought, would affect as many as 1,000 Jews.[42]

More assassinations a few days later resulted in the commander proposing to increase the number of shootings by 50 and deportations of an additional 500 Communists—a macabre haggling over human lives. At last, after Hitler agreed, 95 people were executed, 58 of them Jews.[43] To "compensate" for the fact that the original quota of shootings had not been achieved, an additional 1,000 Jews along with 500 inmates of internment and police camps designated as Communists were earmarked for transport "to the East," but were temporarily kept in the camps in France because of "transport problems."

But even that did not resolve the matter, for further cycles of assassinations followed by shootings and deportations were already underway. The number of hostages actually killed rose to 264 by mid-January. The administrative staff now proposed other measures by which hostage shootings might be avoided or called something else: French courts should respond to assassinations by passing death sentences for giving aid and comfort to the enemy even in cases involving trivial Communist activity; death sentences already pronounced should be stayed and then carried out only if more attacks occurred; French officers who had been released should be re-imprisoned following assassinations. All of these initiatives proved unfeasible for legal or practical reasons.[44]

Finally, on 15 January, Stülpnagel made a final attempt to convince Hitler and Keitel to desist: "Knowing as I do the general situation and the effects of such harsh measures on the whole population and on our relations with France, I can ... no longer reconcile mass shootings with my conscience, nor answer for them before the bar of history." He went on to point out that further arrests of Jews and Communists were impossible in any case, because roughly 10,000 Jews and 3,500 Communists had been arrested in the occupied zone alone and there was no room in existing camps for any more prisoners. Thus, Stülpnagel argued, there remained only one conceivably effective method of reprisal—"the incident-by-incident transporting to Germany or the East of a certain number of Communists or Jews who are *already* interned ... assuming that the transportation system is up to the task and security is not jeopardized. Such a measure is certain to unleash a strong public reaction."[45]

Hitler and Keitel, however, stuck to their position, although they did endorse Stülpnagel's proposal for mass deportations—not as a substitute for shooting hostages but as a supplementary measure. Keitel informed the commander that his ideas concerning the measures called for "do not take into account the Führer's basic position." At that point, Stülpnagel stepped down.[46]

Two aspects of this controversy over the hostage issue and Stülpnagel's ultimate resignation need to be stressed. First, we should note the shrillness with which the dispute was waged and the unanimity with which the commander's staff rejected Hitler's and Keitel's demands. This posture arose from a variety of motives involving the military code of conduct, legal misgivings, and moral scruples, combined with ideological concerns for the future of Europe, the cultural or "racial" level of the French people, or the future course of German-French relations. In each instance, there was general agreement that the German treatment of the French needed to differ markedly from the way in which one might deal with Serbs, Russians, or, of course, Jews.

Second, it can not be overlooked that the military's attempt to prevent, or call a halt to, the mass shooting of hostages evolved into the proposal to substitute mass deportations of French Jews and Communists "to the East," as Stülpnagel once more stressed in his private letter of resignation to Keitel: "I believed that I could accomplish the clearly necessary reprisals for assassinations of Wehrmacht personnel by other means, i.e., through limited executions, but primarily through transporting massive numbers of Jews and Communists to the East, which, in my informed opinion, has a far more chilling effect on the French population than these mass shootings, which the French do not understand."[47] Stülpnagel's proposal soon became common practice. In April it was formalized in a Führer decree which stipulated "that for each future assassination, apart from the execution by firing squad of a number of appropriate persons, 500 Communists and Jews are to be turned over to the RFSS and the German Chief of Police for deportation to the East."[48]

From that point on, shooting hostages and issuing deportation orders became automated: 18 April—24 executions, 1,000 deportations; 24 April—10 executions, 500 deportations; 28 April—1 execution, 500 deportations; 5 May—28 executions, 500 deportations; 7 May—20 executions, 500 deportations. By 31 May, 993 executions had been ordered and 471 actually carried out; the number of deportations of "Jews and Communists" ordered as "reprisals" for the same period was roughly 6,000.[49]

On 23 March 1942, the first transport left Compiègne for Auschwitz. This marked the beginning of the mass deportation of French Jews to the extermination camps in the East. The political efforts of the Paris military command to end the shooting of hostages, which had been a matter of central concern for months for both the German authorities in France and the French public—the decent motives behind which were universally recognized after the war—were thus directly connected to the beginning of the "Final Solution of the Jewish question" in France.[50]

IV

By the end of 1940, legally depriving French Jews of their rights and property, as agreed to in principle by the embassy and administrative staff on 17 August, had already become a large-scale operation and had progressed further than in all the other northern and western European countries under German occupation. Due to parallel operations by the Vichy government, the same was also true for the unoccupied zone, and following the internment of Jews of non-French nationality, the Jews' predicament in southern France was in some respects even worse than in the occupied north.

While the prevention of Jewish immigration into occupied France and the seizure of Jewish property, to which Abetz and Best had agreed, was largely accomplished by the end of 1940, the third point—preparing for the "removal" of Jews from the occupied area—had become bogged down because it was still not clear where the Jews of France were to be taken, especially since the so-called Madagascar project had met with far stiffer opposition than had originally been anticipated.

In January 1941, Knochen, the BdS in Paris, and his Jewish expert, Dannecker, seized the initiative by demanding that the military administrative staff quicken the pace of anti-Jewish policy. Preparations for the "total expulsion of the Jews," which had already been foreseen in the agreement of August 1940, should in their view be managed not from the German side but by a "Central Office for Jewish Affairs" under French direction supervised by the BdS. Anti-Jewish policy was to be organized and coordinated in that office.[51] Knochen went on to say that measures should be aimed initially at Jews of non-French nationality, who should be put in concentration camps, as was already occurring under French authority in unoccupied France. French antisemitism, he pointed out, was aimed primarily at resident foreign Jews and not at the established Jews of France; "nurturing opposition to the Jews on idealistic grounds" was therefore hardly possible. Hence, one must appeal to the material self-interest of the French people. The imprisonment of the roughly 100,000 foreign Jews living in Paris might enable many French to move into their professional positions and rise socially so that "approval of the anti-Jewish struggle will be more likely to come about because of the arising financial advantages."[52]

Interest in the Jewish question on the part of the military command was, as always, not great; it was regarded as an unpleasant, albeit unavoidable, peripheral problem that one would very much like to leave to Heydrich's people in the Avenue Foch. But that would have meant giving up turf in police matters to the BdS, thus considerably undermining the position of the military commander as the sole wielder of executive authority in occupied France. The continuation and intensification of anti-Jewish policy therefore needed to be carried out within the military command structure itself in the already developed form of "administrative supervision." That was the province of the administrative staff, which hence, beginning in early 1941, concentrated increasingly on Jewish policy.

Regarding the goals and requisite acceleration of anti-Jewish measures, there was complete agreement with the BdS. Thus it came as no surprise that the administrative and command staffs, in a joint meeting held a few days after Knochen's memorandum, were able to reach prompt and joint agreement on how to proceed further on the "Jewish question." The proposed "Central Jewish Office" was to be established, but in order—in Lischka's words—"to eliminate the negative reaction of the French people against anything coming from the Germans," the office was to be directed by the French. Laws promulgated by the French would also require the usual approval of the German supervisory authorities. It was at this point, it was stressed, that the military command, in cooperation with the BdS and the embassy, could effectively exert its influence. In this way, the representatives of Speidel's command staff concluded, it might be possible in specific cases to regain direct German participation in the campaign against Jews.

Thus, at the conference of 30 January 1941, there was broad agreement among the German sections in Paris on the goals of Jewish policy and on the need to accelerate its implementation. By contrast, the matter of which German agency would supervise the

Jewish office was at that point a secondary concern, and was shelved for future discussion.[53] The strategy preferred and adopted by the military of adhering to the method of "administrative supervision" even with regard to Jewish policy, proved its worth. Within days, the Vichy government agreed to establish a "Central Jewish Office," and on 8 March Xavier Vallat, a well-known antisemitic activist, was named General Commissioner for Jewish Affairs with the rank of undersecretary.[54]

The establishment of the Central Jewish Office raised several expectations among the officers on the command staff. They hoped to leave Jewish policy, and especially the interning of Jews, to this agency, because it was perceived as threatening to the smooth functioning of the collaboration policy. But they were deceiving themselves.

One day before Vallat introduced himself to the officers at the Hotel Majestic, Best outlined the goals of Jewish policy with a degree of clarity that must be regarded as unusual for March 1941 and which indicates that he was especially well-informed due to his earlier activities in the RSHA. "Germany's interest lies in progressively relieving all European countries from Jewry with the goal of a completely Jew-free Europe [Entjudung]." To that end, one should strive first to expel Jews of non-French nationality, and then, as a second step, to intern 35,000 Jews of *any* nationality (thus including French Jews), who were seen as "dangerous and undesirable," while promoting a more anti-Jewish French legal code. Finally, Best envisioned the Central Jewish Office preparing for a later "emigration" of all Jews of French nationality.[55] But when Stülpnagel and Best met with Vallat, it turned out that Pètain had given Vallat a much narrower brief, basically limited to a more rigorous "aryanization." Vallat emphasized the need for a Jewish policy that "takes into account circumstances particular to France and the mood of the people," especially since "serious antisemitism has hitherto existed in France only in small measure." Expelling and interning Jews, Vallat explained, was a matter for the French bureaucracy and police officials; that was not his job.[56] The hopes of German officials that Jewish policy would be managed in the future by Vallat's new agency were consequently dashed. The military leaders noted with disappointment that they would "still be stuck with the unpleasant part, namely with carrying out expulsions and internments."[57]

With Vallat's demur, the problem of the division of responsibility for Jewish policy assumed new urgency, and the BdS pressed hard for a free hand. Already by the end of February, Abetz,

Zeitschel, and Achenbach from the embassy had agreed with Dannecker to try to persuade the military commander "to give the SD full authority to detain all Jews."[58] But that proposal met with Stülpnagel's energetic resistance—not because he was opposed to the goals of Jewish policy as formulated, but because he detected in the move an attack on his own authority. The result was that now the administrative section was pressured by the commander to pick up the pace in implementing the Jewish policy so as to leave no opening for the BdS to pursue its ambitions. In this way, an acceleration factor was created that made the "Jewish Question" suddenly appear urgent, which had not been the case for the military command beforehand.

And yet, at the same time, concerns about German-French relations after the war ended, which was regarded as imminent, dictated adherence to the principle of collaboration and restraint on the part of German authorities. The dilemma that had now arisen was obvious: the military administration was supposed to pursue a policy against French Jews that was, on the one hand, accelerated and, where possible, radical, but on the other hand, was consistent with the method of "administrative supervision," thus maintaining the competence of the military administration without jeopardizing the army's close cooperation with the BdS.

The first step on this path was the internment of foreign Jews. The initial preparations were commenced already in March after the consent of the Vichy regime to this course of action had been secured.[59]

On 14 May 1941 the first blow fell: 3,733 foreign Jews were arrested by French police at the behest of the administrative staff and consigned to the internment camps at Pithviers and Beaune-de-Roland.[60]

All of the Jews arrested in May 1941 were Polish, Czech, or Austrian citizens. Of the roughly 150,000 Jews listed in the files of the Prefect of the Paris police, only about half were French citizens. While the Vichy government and its representatives in Paris bowed to the wishes of the German army regarding measures aimed at foreign Jews, they opposed the interning of French Jews merely because they were Jews. In order to proceed against French Jews, German authorities needed to justify their actions on different grounds—and it was at that point that Jewish policy became linked to the hostage issue.

The beginning of the war against the Soviet Union had, as we saw earlier, caused a sharp increase in anti-German activity in France, above all by French Communists, leading to several demonstrations in Paris beginning at the end of June 1941. But before the first assassinations rendered the issue of "reprisals" acute, preparations had already been made at the Commander-in-Chief's office to respond to especially the army's demand for "more vigorous action against the opposition, particularly the Communists." Here was the pretext that had been sought since the spring for proceeding against Jews with French citizenship. Claiming that the demonstrations had been arranged by Jewish Communists, the military had the French police schedule raids for 20 August directed exclusively against Jews, including many with French citizenship. In order to prevent protests from the Petain government, the French delegation was not officially briefed. True, the military consulted the French minister of the interior, but the operation itself was carried out on direct orders of the military by more than 2,000 French police under German officers and NCOs without the involvement of the Vichy government.[61]

After the assassinations of 21 August, the military ordered a second wave of sweeps in which a total of 4,323 people were arrested and taken to the camp at Drancy—all of them Jews. But in the wake of the debates over German reprisals and the uproar over the first hostage shootings, this operation was largely ignored and played only a secondary role both publicly and in negotiations between German and French officials. Indeed, given the instructions issuing from Berlin that assassinations be answered with mass executions of hostages, the arrests and mass internment of Jews almost came to be viewed as mild measures, especially by the responsible military officers. For Stülpnagel's staff, which considered mass arrests of Jews less likely to provoke outrage in the French population than the arrests of non-Jewish French citizens, the mass arrests of Jews offered a kind of fall-back position to which the army could retreat whenever it wanted to demonstrate harshness while avoiding shooting hostages.

For the German authorities dealing directly with Jewish policy, the mass arrests between 20 and 23 August marked an important step in that the Vichy government's resistance to imprisoning Jews with French citizenship had been broken. And yet, the continuation and extension of such measures was now prevented by the lack of suitable internment camps and the impossibility of building additional camps in the immediate future.[62] Zeitschel, who was responsible for Jewish policy in the German embassy, pointed this problem out to Ambassador Abetz. On the day after the first assassination, he complained that in France, "where we are working with the greatest possible intensity toward a quick solution to the

Jewish problem, its implementation is most severely hampered by an insufficiency of camps in which to detain Jews." This situation made it necessary to transport the Jews to the East. Since the Madagascar plan was clearly impractical, Zeitschel considered it absolutely essential to transfer all the Jews of Europe to a "special territory" in the East.[63]

It is most revealing that the lack of accommodation in camps located on French soil served as a justification for urging a further intensification of the Jewish policy. This "calculated dilemma" (*Kalkül des Sachzwangs*) had already been a prominent feature of the far-reaching decisions of September 1939, when the issue confronting the RSHA was the mass deportation of Jews and Poles from territories in western Poland. The same arguments were made simultaneously, for example, by General Governor Frank in Poland and Gauleiter Greisler in the "Warthegau": "Intolerable conditions" in the camps and ghettos made a mass deportation of the Jews "to the East" unavoidable. It lay clearly in the interest of the individual German rulers in areas under German occupation to keep the number and capacity of camps and ghettos as low as possible in order to document that the continued detainment and protracted stay of interned Jews in their territories was not possible.[64]

Their refusal to build more camps thus produced an artificial dilemma and consequent pressure to transport the interned Jews out of France. This aim was also promoted by a contrived worsening of living conditions in places like the camp at Drancy, where as early as a few weeks after the arrival of those Jews arrested in August, overcrowding and insufficient food had resulted in famine, edemas, and malnutrition in more than 800 inmates.[65] Claiming that a lack of capacity was preventing continued implementation of the Jewish policy in France, Abetz was still appealing to Himmler in September 1941 to move 10,000 Jews from French camps to the East in order to create the space needed to intern still more Jews. The Reichsführer SS granted this request at once. As soon as transport was available, the shifting of French Jews to the east was to begin.[66]

In view of the hectic events attendant upon the assassinations and hostage shootings, Jewish policy still represented only a secondary problem for the military, which viewed Jewish policy as an instrument rather than as an independent aim of occupation policy. Knochen and Dannecker, by contrast, now tried to move the "Jewish question" to the top of the agenda by taking spectacular action in hopes of gaining the sole control of anti-Jewish measures for which the BdS had long been striving. On 3 October, Knochen, in cooperation with the French antisemitic group of Deloncle, organized a series of bombings of Paris synagogues modeled on the events of November 1938 in Germany, which were designed to create the impression that there was something like a pogrom sentiment in the French population.[67] But when it became clear after a few days that the attacks had been organized by the BdS, a rupture developed between the military and the BdS, and Stülpnagel demanded categorically that Knochen be removed.[68] When Heydrich as categorically refused, took personal responsibility for the attacks, and expressly remarked that, "based on our past experience in working with the military commander, he cannot be counted on to grasp the need to carry out these measures in the struggle with our ideological opponents "[69]— a regular turf-battle was ignited. The military administration now had to defend itself against Hitler and Keitel on the hostage issue, and against Himmler and Heydrich over responsibility in police matters. There was now no doubt that the military would lose.

Shortly after the BdS's synagogue attacks, the military proposed responding to future assassinations not with more hostage shootings but with mass deportations of French Jews, which were first announced in a communication from Stülpnagel to the OKH following the assassinations of 28 November.[70] This unleashed that operation of 12 December in which the military administration, in a departure from earlier practice, authorized German executive forces to arrest 743 mostly wealthy Jewish men, mostly of them French citizens, and take them to the German-run camp at Compiègne, whence they were to be transported to the East. In order to reached the figure of 1,000, 300 prisoners were transferred from the Drancy camp.[71] The military commander announced shortly thereafter that "a large number of criminal Jewish-Bolshevist elements" were being "deported to take up forced labor in the East" in retribution for attacks on German soldiers. Further attacks would result in further and even larger deportations.[72]

In the meantime, the RSHA had decided to deport all European Jews to the East and made the necessary arrangements for France as well. At a meeting of Judenreferenten on 4 May in Berlin chaired by Eichmann, the request of the Paris military command that the first 1,000 Jews be transported from the camp at Compiègne to Auschwitz was finally granted. Transport was scheduled for 24 March, and a further deportation of 5,000 French Jews was projected for 1942. At the same time, Heydrich had announced more and larger transportations in the future. On 24 March, after a delay of three months, the first transport of 1,112 Jews left France for Auschwitz—among them those arrested in the sweep of 12 December.[73]

The process had thereby come full circle. The military administration itself had authorized and arranged not only the detention
first of foreign, then, in August 1941, of French, Jews, but also the
first mass deportations "to the East." It was the military officers of
the commander-in-chief's administrative staff who had first proposed this operation to Stülpnagel. They had selected those to be
deported. They had a special section—the "Jewish Camp"—established at Compiègne, in which people designated for deportation
were housed. They had repeatedly urged the RSHA in Berlin to
agree to the deportation of Jews; even the bill for the first railway
transport to Auschwitz was footed by the military administration.[74]

Focused on their dispute with Hitler and Keitel over the shooting of hostages, the military officers at the Hotel Majestic perceived
the mass deportation of Jews as an avenue of escape from the
dilemma in which they had landed. First, they believed that they
would be able in this way to react harshly to assassinations without striking directly at the French. Second, they hoped that they
might thereby yield to growing pressure from Hitler's headquarters
and the demand for "harsh" reaction to attacks by the resistance
without jeopardizing the entire collaboration policy in France. At
this point the interests of the military coincided with the simultaneously crystallizing plan of the regime's leadership in Berlin to
deport the Jews from France, as well as from all other European
countries under German occupation, "to the East"—and there to
murder them.

Walter Bargatzky speculated in his notes about why the same
officers and officials who had taken such a hard line against orders
to shoot hostages acted with such complete indifference to the fate of
the Jews. Using Stülpnagel as an example, he traced this posture to
the fact that Stülpnagel probably considered it hopeless "to take up
the struggle against the internment of the Jews while opposing the
theft of art and the shooting of hostages."[75] This sounds convincing.
But the surviving records make it clear that opposing the internment
of the Jews was never considered; on the contrary, every effort was
made to promote their internment and eventual deportation. For the
conservative military officers, the Jews, like criminals and Communists, were not recognized as honorable opponents. Opposing the
illegal removal of art treasures was honorable; opposing the removal
of their owners was not. And yet, by the fall of 1941 at the latest, the
military command had few illusions about the fate of the Jews "in
the East." Bälz, who headed the justice division, had received
detailed information about the mass murder at Babi Yar from an
officer who had been transferred to Paris from the Eastern Front,

and Bälz had seen to it that the information became general knowledge within the military administration. "From now on," wrote Bargatzsky, "there is no more not-knowing in the 'Majestic'."[76]

The resignation of General Otto von Stülpnagel on 15 February 1942 marked a break in the history of the German occupation force in France, and Berlin exploited the opportunity to effect a thorough overhaul of the Paris military administration.[77] For one thing, the appointment of Karl Oberg as Higher SS and Police Leader was intended to put an end to the escalating conflicts between the leaders of the Reich and the commander-in-chief over the issue of "reprisals," and bind policy in France to directives from Berlin. Additionally, Himmler and Heydrich succeeded in face of the military's opposition in taking over police matters through the RSHA. The HSSPF would henceforth—and this was especially stressed—be responsible for carrying out "reprisals against criminals, Jews, and Communists."[78] That this meant more than a mere reorganization and reassignment of responsibility for the hostage question was immediately clear to those in the know in Paris. Zeitschel, the "Jewish expert" in the Paris embassy, went so far as to stress triumphantly in an internal memorandum, "The new arrangement will have very favorable implications for the Final Solution to the Jewish question."[79]

On 6 May, Heydrich came to Paris for Oberg's installation. On this occasion, as had been announced, he laid out general guidelines for future political and police activities in France to the assembled higher ranks of German officers in Paris. To a somewhat smaller circle, he then gave a detailed report on the status and future plans regarding what was by then generally being referred to as "the Final Solution to the Jewish question." In this session, as Bälz again reported, Heydrich provided information, complete with detailed explanations, about decisions formulated by the participating government agencies at the Wannsee Conference: "Busses detailed to transport Jews, from depot to camp, from camp to work place, into which deadly gas is pumped en route. An attempt that fails, to Heydrich's dismay, due to ineffective technology. The busses are too small, the mortality rates too low, along with still other annoying shortcomings. For which reason he finally announces larger-scale, more sophisticated solutions providing a higher yield.... Just as with the Russian Jews in Kiev, the death sentence has been pronounced on all the Jews of Europe. Even of the Jews of France, whose deportations begin in these very weeks."[80]

Given the historical prelude described above, it was not surprising that the conservative nationalists in the military administration voiced no protest against, and mounted no resistance to, the deportations that they themselves had set in motion—even though most of them had never intended, and perhaps did not condone, the policy of the "Final Solution" now being implemented in France.

V

Returning to the questions posed at the outset, our investigation makes it possible to draw certain conclusions regarding how the "Final Solution to the Jewish question" came about in general, and what role the Wehrmacht and the RSHA played in particular.

1. It becomes clear that any investigation of the process setting the "Final Solution" in motion that limits itself to countries and territories under German occupation in eastern Europe, especially Poland and the Soviet Union, is necessarily insufficient. It turns out that the radicalization of anti-Jewish policy in France had already begun gathering momentum by the fall of 1940 and passed from persecution to deportation "to the East" between the summer of 1941 and the spring of 1942. An explanation of that process that extrapolates solely from the political motivations of the German masters in the East relating to population resettlement would either ignore the parallel processes at work in the West or reduce them to subsequent decisions of lesser importance.

2. France, perhaps even more than other regions, makes it obvious that the acceleration of the anti-Jewish policy was influenced primarily by two factors: First, Heydrich's agents in Paris were a force representing the increasing influence of the RSHA in Berlin, which was constantly urging a harsher policy toward the Jews, and to that end exploited every opportunity that day to day politics presented. It would, therefore, be problematic to equate the constantly shifting arguments in support of such demands with the actual motivations of the BdS representatives. On the contrary, one must assume an ideological, radical anti-Jewish orientation that early on had already set its sights on the complete "removal" of Jews from Europe.

Second, for the leading officers and officials of the Wehrmacht, by contrast, the issues of the hostages and the Jews were not originally directly connected. Their anti-Jewish politics were doubtlessly based on a pronounced antisemitism, but one that clearly did not occupy as central a position in their world-view as was the case with the higher officials of the Security Police and the SD. After the summer of 1940, discrimination against and persecution of the Jews

in France quickly reached the level in Germany after November
1938. But the antisemitism of the administrative officers was not
sufficient in itself to link the Jewish question with the hostage issue
and thereby set the deportations in motion. Other factors came into
play. There was the massive pressure to which the administrative
staff was subjected due to its efforts to maintain the collaboration
policy of "administrative supervision" in spite of the assassinations.
The officers were prepared to make concessions on secondary issues
in order to win the main point. In the eyes of the protagonists, the
treatment of the French Jews was just such a secondary issue. If one
absolutely had to demonstrate "hardness," then it was best demonstrated against a group of people who did not count as French, who
already suffered from widespread discrimination, who were without
powerful allies, and who were suspected of harboring among their
number the organizers of the assassinations, if not the core of the
anti-German opposition in general. This last attitude was clearly
decisive, for it freed the deportation of Jews from its ideological
context and gave it an objective, rational justification.
    3. This example demonstrates how methodologically dubious
it is to presume that the individual protagonists were exclusively concentrated on their own sphere of control. Clearly the uncommonly
well-informed upper echelons of the Wehrmacht and the Security
Police had far greater and far more detailed knowledge of what was
happening both at the fronts and in other occupied areas than is generally assumed. Especially reports of mass shootings, such as had
taken place in Babi Yar, provided not least of all by men who were on
leave or had been transferred, spread like wildfire. One must assume,
therefore, that the deportations were set in motion in Paris in full
knowledge of the reported mass killings by the *Einsatzgruppen* in the
East and thus cannot be construed as merely emergency responses to
an ostensibly difficult situation. Analogously, the regional bosses and
their staffs in other regions attempted to represent their actions
against the Jews as necessitated by situational dilemmas and "untenable conditions"—as the results of objective decisions by which the
fundamental political and ideological assumptions of National
Socialism happened to be empirically confirmed yet again. But in
point of fact, they were well informed about developments in other
regions, and they knew that, in context, their recommendations or
decisions meant more than what they appeared to mean.
    Finally, the case of France discussed here shows that the notion
of an early, all-encompassing *Führerbefehl* has little to recommend
it. Without exception, the initiatives leading to the deportation of
the Jews came from below—in this case from the military com-

mander-in-chief—and were generalized, coordinated, and organized by the central authority in Berlin. Only from this perspective does it become apparent that the multiplicity of regional initiatives flowed together into a uniform procedure—which was then called the "Final Solution." And yet, it cannot be denied that there were people in the Jewish Section of the RSHA who were ready to exploit such initiatives. In this regard, investigating the predicaments and initiatives of the local authorities has the effect of focusing attention once more on how the dictator himself reacted to the many such recommendations that arrived in Berlin in the winter of 1941/42.

Notes

1. See Walter Manoschek, *"Serbien ist judenfrei!" Militärische Besatzungspolitik und Judenvernichtung in Serbien 1941/42* (Munich, 1993); Klaus Naumann (ed.), *Vernichtungskrieg. Verbrechen der Wehrmacht 1941-1944* (Hamburg, 1995); Omer Bartov, *Hitler's Army* (Oxford, 1995); Jörg Friedrich, *Das Gesetz des Krieges* (Munich, 1994).

2. Götz Aly, *"Endlösung". Völkersverschiebung und der Mord an den europäischen Juden* (Frankfurt a.M., 1995). For a similar treatment with impressive documentation, see Christopher R. Browning, *The Path to Genocide. Essays on Launching the Final Solution* (Cambridge, 1992). Recent publications include: Thomas Sandkühler, *"Endlösung" in Galizien. Der Judenmord in Ostpolen und die Rettungsinitiativen von Berthold Beitz* (Bonn, 1996); Dieter Pohl, *Nationalsozialistische Judenverfolgung in Ostgalizien. Organisation und Durchführung eines staatlichen Massenverbrechens* (Munich, 1996). See also Hans Safrian, *Die Eichmann-Männer* (Cologne, 1993); Andrej Angrick et al., "'Da hatte man schon ein Tagebuch führen müssen.' Das Polizeibataillon 322 und die Judenmorde im Bereich der Heeresgruppe Mitte während des Sommer und Herbstes 1941," in Helge Grabitz, et al. (eds.), *Die Normalität des Verbrechens* (Berlin, 1994), pp. 325-385; summary evaluation in Hans Mommsen, "Umvolkungspläne des Nationalsozialismus und der Holocaust," in *Ibid.*, pp. 68-84; see also the discussion in the introductory article in this volume.

3. See Wilhelm von Schramm, *Aufstand der Generale. Der 20. Juli in Paris* (Munich, 1964); Walter Bargatzky, "Die letzte Runde in Paris," in Erich Zimmermann, and Hans-Adolf Jacobsen (eds.), *Der 20. Juli 1944* (Bonn, 1960).

4. For the following, see Eberhard Jäckel, *Frankreich in Hitlers Europa. Die deutsche Frankreichpolitik im Zweiten Weltkrieg* (Stuttgart, 1966); Hans Umbreit, *Der Militärbefehlshaber in Frankreich 1940-1944* (Boppard, 1968); idem, "Der Kampf um die Vormachtstellung in Westeuropa," in *Das Deutsche Reich und der Zweite Weltkrieg*, published by Militärgeschichtliches Forschungsamt, Vol. 2 (Stuttgart, 1979), pp. 235-327; idem, "Auf dem Weg zur Kontinentalherrschaft," in *Das Deutsche Reich und der Zweite Weltkrieg*,

Vol. 5 (Stuttgart, 1988), pp. 3-334; Robert O. Paxton, *Vichy France—Old Guard and New Order 1940-1945* (New York, 1972); Lucient Steinberg, *Les Allemands en France, 1940-1944* (Paris, 1980); Henri Michel, *Paris allemand* (Paris, 1981); David Pryce-Jones, *Paris in the Third Reich. A History of the German Occupation 1940-1944* (New York, 1981); *La France et l'Allemagne en guerre, septembre 1939-novembre 1942* (Paris, 1990); Bernd Kasten, *"Gute Franzosen". Die französische Polizei und die deutsche Besatzungsmacht im besetzten Frankreich 1940-1944* (Sigmaringen, 1993); Ahlrich Meyer, "Großraumpolitik und Kollaboration im Westen," in *Modelle für ein deutsches Europa—Ökonomie und Herrschaft im Großwirtschaftsraum*, Vol. 10 of *Beiträge zur nationalsozialistischen Sozialpolitik* (Berlin, 1992), pp. 29-76; also articles in Gerhard Hirschfeld and Patrick Marsh (eds.), *Kollaboration in Frankreich. Politik, Wirtschaft und Kultur während der nationalsozialistischen Besatzung 1940-1944* (Frankfurt a.M., 1991).

5. There arose "the feeling of belonging to a team, to a circle that was aware that it formed a community similar to a religious order. In time, mutual confidence comes to be so great that one can often express one's opinion openly about those who are known to be convinced Nazis ... Usually, thanks to our group cohesiveness, we are able to draw those who have other views into our group. When that proves impossible, they are isolated"; Walter Bargatzky, *Hotel Majestic. Ein Deutscher im besetzten Frankreich* (Freiburg, 1987), pp. 50ff. Of the numerous written reminiscences of the men involved, Bargatzky's thin volume offers by far the most impressive and detailed, as well as the most critical, description of the course of events at the military administration in Paris. Also informative, though highly ideological, are the unpublished memoirs of Werner Best: *Erinnerungen aus dem besetzten Frankreich* (Spring 1951), Ms., BA, NL 23. Speidel's memoirs (Hans Speidel, *Aus unserer Zeit: Erinnerungen*, Berlin, 1977) treat the period only superficially; the reminiscences of most of the participants are highly self-exculpatory, above all Otto Abetz, *Das offene Problem. Ein Rückblick auf zwei Jahrzehnte deutscher Frankreich-Politik* (Cologne, 1951); Friedrich Grimm, *Frankreich-Berichte* (Bodenau, 1972); Rudolf Rahn, *Ruheloses Leben: Aufzeichnungen und Erinnerungen* (Düsseldorf, 1949).

6. For insights on the German occupation policy from the viewpoint of the German occupation staffs, see the voluminous activity reports that are recorded in Bundesarchiv/Militärarchiv in Freiburg under RW 35/243-247.

7. See Herbert, *Best. Biographische Studien über Radikalismus, Weltanschauung und Vernunft 1903-1989*, (Bonn, 1996).

8. Michael Wildt (ed.), *Die Judenpolitik des SD, 1935 bis 1938* (Munich, 1995).

9. Bargatzky, *Hotel Majestic*, p. 40.

10. Michael Marrus and Robert Paxton, *Vichy France and the Jews* (NewYork, 1981), pp. 3-21; Serge Klarsfeld, *Vichy—Auschwitz. Die Zusammenarbeit der deutschen und französischen Behörden bei der "Endlösung der Judenfrage" in Frankreich* (Nördlingen, 1989), pp. 20ff. For the following, see also Jäckel, Umbreit, and Meyer, *Großraumpolitik*, and idem, "'Fremde Elemente.' Die osteuropäisch-jüdische Immigration, die 'Endlösung der Judenfrage' und die Anfänge der Widerstandsbewegung in Frankreich," in *Arbeitsmigration und Flucht. Vertreibung und Arbeitskräfteregulierung im Zwischenkriegseuropa*, Vol. 2 of *Beiträge zur nationalsozialistischen Gesundheits- und Sozialpolitik* (Berlin, 1983), pp. 82-129; Raul Hilberg, *The Destruction of the European Jews* (New York, 1985), pp. 641-701; Juliane Wetzel, "Frankreich und Belgien" in Wolfang Benz (ed.), *Die Dimension des Völkermords. Die Zahl der*

jüdischen Opfers des Nationalsozialismus (Munich, 1992), pp. 105-135; Serge Klarsfeld (ed.), *Die Endlösung der Judenfrage in Frankreich. Deutsche Dokumente 1941-1944* (Paris, 1977); Joseph Billig, *Die Endlösung der Judenfrage. Studie über ihre Grundsätze im 3. Reich und in Frankreich während der Besatzung* (Frankfurt, 1979); Billig, *Le commissariat général aux questions juives, 1941-1944*, 3 vols. (Paris, 1955-1960); Kasten, *Gute Franzosen*, pp. 95ff.; also "Ermittlungsvermerk der Zentralen Stelle der Landesjustizverwaltungen betr. Endlösung der Judenfrage in Frankreich" (preliminary investigations of Best, et al.), ZStl., 1104, AR-Z, 1670, Vols. 4 and 5.

11. Memorandum of MBF /Verw.St., Abt. Verw [Military Occupation Command/Administrative Staff /Administrative Section] (Best), 19 August 1940, cited in Klarsfeld, *Vichy*, p. 356.

12. According to Abetz, Hitler had informed him on 3 August of plans to remove the Jews from Europe (IMT, Dok. NG-1893). The plans of Rademacher, the responsible consultant in Section Germany of the Foreign Office, relative to the Madagascar project date from 3 July 1940 (IMT, Dok. NG-2586-B), 5 August (Dok. NG-5764), and 12 August 1940 (Dok. NG-2596-B); Magnus Brechtken, *"Madagaskar für die Juden". Antisemitische Idee und politische Praxis 1885-1945* (Munich, 1997).

13. Abetz to the Foreign Office, 20 August 1940, ADAP, D 10/368. Sonnleithner reported on 21 August that the reaction of the Foreign Office was essentially positive, but stated that the issue would be decided "at a higher level"; on 26 August 1940, Hitler gave his approval; Franz Halder, *Kriegstagebuch. Tägliche Aufzeichnungen des Chefs des Generalstabes des Heeres 1939-1942*, Hans Adolf Jacobsen (ed.), 3 vols. (Stuttgart, 1962-1964), here Vol. 2, p. 77; see also Best's communication of 30 August 1940, HStAD, Rep 242/Plc(40).

14. Memorandum by Mahnke, Verw.Stb./Abt. Verw (Gruppe I) [Administrative Staff/Administrative Section], 22 August 1940, cited in Klarsfeld, *Vichy*, pp. 356f.

15. Memorandum by Storz, no date (in the last week of August 1940), cited in Klarsfeld, *Vichy*, 358. This note is falsely signed "Abetz"; see Umbreit, *Militärbefehlshaber*, p. 262.

16. Memorandum by Bargatzky, 26 August 1940, cited in Umbreit, *Militärbefehlshaber*, pp. 262.

17. Heydrich to the Foreign Office (Luther), 20 September 1940, PA/AA, Inl. II geh. 189, 83. The OKW acceded to Heydrich's request to grant the BdS in Paris authority over Jewish matters on 4 October 1940; that, however, related to responsibility in political matters, not for the exercise of executive authority; see Klarsfeld, *Vichy*, p. 21.

18. VO betr. Maßnahmen gegen Juden [Directive Relating to Measures Against Jews], 27 September 1940, in VOBl.MBF [Decree of the Military Occupation Command] of 30 September 1940; Durchf. VO:RdSchr. d. Ch. d. MVerw, Verw.St/Abt. Verw., betr. Maßnahmen gegen Juden [Memorandum of the Head of the Administrative Staff/Administrative Section concerning Executing the Directive regarding Measures Against Jews, BA/MA, RW 35/772.

19. See note by Luther (Foreign Office) of 21 August 1942 regarding Jewish policy since 1939; ADAP, E X/209; Umbreit, *Weg*, p. 294.

20. 2. VO über Maßnahmen gegen Juden [Second Directive Relating to Measures Against Jews], 16 October 1940, VOBl. MBF [Military Occupation Command], 18 October 1940, disseminated by the Economics Division of the

Administrative Staff; see the communication of 14 October 1940, BA/MA, RW 35/772.

21. Von Brauchitsch had already requested on 16 October 1940 an "acceleration of measures"; memorandum on discussion at von Brauchitsch's headquarters in Paris on 16 October 1940, BA/MA, RW 35/772; also [von Brauchitsch's] recommendation to Stülpnagel on 12 November 1940 ("... that swift action be given high priority"), BA/MA, RW 35/255. Stülpnagel issued orders on that same day to begin the aryanization of Jewish property in France; see Umbreit, *Militärbefehlshaber*, p. 262, note 11. Regarding the further course and results of aryanization, see the summary report of the Economic Section [Abt. Wirtschaft/Wi I1], no date (end of 1944): Die Entjudung der französischen Wirtschaft [Removal of Jewish Interests from the French Economy], BA/MA RW 35/255; also Hilberg, *Vernichtung*, pp. 649ff.

22. The issue of the "protection of art" in France has often been described and has been thoroughly researched; the great interest in this question reflects the importance attached to it at the level of the military commander and contrasts markedly with the inadequate research done in other areas that appear from today's perspective to have been much more important, such as the persecution of political enemies and Jews in France, or even the economic exploitation of the country through the German occupation forces; see Umbreit, *Militärverwaltung*, pp. 184-195; idem, *Auf dem Weg zur Kontinentalherrschaft*, pp. 316ff.; Jäckel, *Frankreich*, pp. 307ff. The most important source has been edited: Walter Bargatzky, *Bericht über die Wegnahme französischer Kunstschätze durch die deutsche Botschaft und den Einsatzstab Rosenberg*, Wilhelm Treue (ed.), *Vierteljahrshefte für Zeitgeschichte* 13 (1965): 285, 337. See Bargatzky, *Hotel Majestic*, p. 64, 81.

23. See note 3 as well as Bargatzky, *Hotel Majestic*, pp. 118ff.; Jäckel, *Frankreich*, pp. 331ff. No more recent study of the 20 July plot in Paris exists.

24. For the following, see the reports of the members of the administrative staff: "Das Geiselverfahren im Bereich des Militärbefehlshabers in Frankreich vom August 1941 bis Mai 1942" [The Hostage Operation in the Area of the Military Commander in France from August 1941 to May 1942]; BA/MA/RW 35/524; and "Vorbeugungs- und Sühnemaßnahmen des Militärbefehlshabers in Frankreich zur Bekämpfung der Sabotage in Frankreich" [Prevention and Reprisal Measures taken by the Military Commander in France for the Suppression of Sabotage in France], no date, BA/MA, RW 35/308, Bl. 109ff. Concerning the author (George) and history of the report, see Bargatzky, *Hotel Majestic*, pp. 82f.; see also Hans Luther, *Der französische Widerstand gegen die deutsche Besatzungsmacht und seine Bekämpfung* (Tübingen, 1957), pp. 160ff.; Jäckel, *Frankreich*, 180ff; Umbreit, *Militärbefehlshaber*, pp. 124ff.; idem, *Weg*, pp. 196ff.; Kasten, *Gute Franzosen*, pp. 55ff., 67ff., Best, *Erinnerungen Frankreich*, p. 22; Memorandum of the Zstl. concerning implementation of reprisals by mobile units in France, 104 AR-Z. 1670/61. Bd. 10, Bl. 2035-2040.

25. *Richtlinien d. Verw.St. (Justiz)* [Guidelines of the Justice Division of the Administrative Staff), 12 September 1940; Luther, *Widerstand*, pp. 163f.; Umbreit, *Militärbefehlshaber*, p. 124.

26. Jäckel, *Frankreich*, p. 186.

27. Erl. d. MBF/Verw.St. [Decree of Military Occupation Command/Administrative Staff], 26 March 1941, BA/MA, RW 35 /548, 16ff., emphasis in original; MBF/Verw.St., 7 May 1941, BA/MA, RW 35 /308, 1.

28. Erl. d. MBF/Verw.St., 23 May 1941 and 26 June 1941, *HStAD*, Rep. 242/Plc (41).
29. Luther, *Widerstand*, p. 173.
30. Bekanntmachung d. MBF [Proclamation of the Military Occupation Command], 22 August 1941, Dok. PS-1588, IMT, Bd. 27, p. 365.
31. Luther, *Widerstand*, p. 174; Jäckel, *Frankreich*, p. 188.
32. "Das Geiselverfahren" (see note 24), p. 41; Umbreit, *Militärbefehlshaber*, p. 126.
33. OKH (Wagner) to MBF, 7 September 1941, BA/MA, RW 35/ 543, 18.
34. MBF to OKH, 11 September 1941, BA/MA, RW 35/ 543, 23f.
35. Chef OKW [Head of the High Command of the Armed Forces], 16 September 1941, BA/MA, RW 35/543, 19ff.
36. Christopher R. Browning, "Wehrmacht Reprisal Policy and the Mass Murders of Jews in Serbia," in *MGM* 31 (1993): 31-47; Manoschek, *Serbien*; Umbreit, *Weg*, pp. 198ff.; see Manoschek's article in this volume.
37. MBF/Verw. u. Kdo.Stab [Military Occupation Command/Administrative and Command Staff], 28 September 1941, BA/MA, RW 35 /548, 35-42. This so-called "Hostage Code" play a significant role in the trial of the chief war criminals at Nuremberg. A comparative analysis of repressive measures and executions of hostages by the German military commands during the Second World War and the judicial and political disputes arising from them is seriously needed and might produce important discoveries regarding the process of cumulative radicalization.
38. MBF to OKH, 24 October 1941 in Luther, *Widerstand*, pp. 206f.; Stülpnagel's diary notations from 20 to 26 October 1941 are reproduced in Umbreit, *Militärbefehlshaber*, pp. 128-132; they give an vivid impression of how hectic those days were.
39. Bargatzky, *Hotel Majestic*, p. 87.
40. The passage quoted here appears in Best, *Erinnerungen*, p. 261. The originals are not extant; Best's postwar notes are, however, confirmed by the exchange of communications in the following weeks.
41. Memorandum of the Administrative Staff (Best), 31 October 1941 (Preventive Detention and Selection of Hostages), HStAD, Rep. 242/Plc (41); also Best's memorandum (Selection of Hostages for Execution), 24 November 1941, BA/MA, RW 35/548, 63f.
42. MBF to OKH, 1 November 1941, *Das Geiselverfahren* (note 24), p. 77.
43. Luther, *Widerstand*, p. 184; *Das Geiselverfahren* (note 24), p. 81; Jäckel, *Frankreich*, pp. 193f.
44. Notation of the Administrative Staff to Best's report of 6 January 1942, HStAD, Rep. 242/312; Best to the Administrative Staff (Gr. 8, 7.1.1942, BA/MA/RW 35/308, 47 and 52f.; Administrative Staff (Justice Section) to Best, 8 January 1942, BA/MA/RW 35/308, 48f.
45. MBF to OKH, 15 January 1942, BA/MA/RW 35/543, 51ff.; Luther, *Widerstand*, p. 211.
46. OKH to MBF, 3 February 1942, BA/MA/RW 35/543, 58. MBF to OKH, 15 February 1942, see Umbreit, *Militärbefehlshaber*, pp. 138f. Regarding Stülpnagel's role in this affair, see Ernst Jünger, *Strahlungen*, pp. 98ff.: "Given the superior position of his opponent, withdrawing to a tactical argument probably seemed the only possible course of action to him. Thus he tried to stress above all that taking mass actions would be doing the resistance movement in France a great favor... In such figures [as Stülpnagel], the general weakness of the bourgeoisie and the aristocracy becomes apparent. They see clearly enough

to perceive the course of events, but they lack strength and tactical skills when confronted with minds who recognize no reasons other than violence." Jünger had been assigned by Speidel to prepare notes on conflicts between the military occupation authority and the Führer's headquarters over the hostage issue. See Speidel, p. 110; Umbreit, *Militärbefehlshaber*, pp. 13, 22.

47. Stülpnagel to Keitel, 15 February 1942; see Umbreit, *Militärbefehlshaber*, p. 139.

48. Erl. D. MBF [Decree of the Military Occupation Command], 10 April 1942, IMT, Dok. RF-1241. Also Schleier (Paris Embassy) to the Foreign Office, 11 April 1942, ADAP, E. 11, 128. The basis for the deportation of French citizens whose conviction and imprisonment in France was neither expected or desired was Keitel's "Night and Fog" decree of 7 December 1941 (IMT, Dok. NG-3571.) The number of French citizens brought to German concentration camps on the basis of the "Night and Fog" decree reached a total of about 5,000 by the end of the war; Umbreit, *Militärbefehlshaber*, p. 145.

49. *Das Geiselverfahren* (note 24), pp. 40ff.; Luther, *Widerstand*, p. 186.

50. This connection is treated in detail in Klarsfeld, *Vichy*, pp. 28ff.; for a different view, see Umbreit, *Militärbefehlshaber*, p. 139 and 263, and Jäckel, *Frankreich*, p. 227.

51. Dannecker's notes of 21 January 1941, Klarsfeld, *Vichy*, pp. 361ff.

52. BdS to Verw.stab /Abt. Verw., 28 January 1941, pp. 363f. The document's reference makes it clear that this document was also the work of Dannecker. On the subjects of how French antisemitism was concentrated on foreign Jews and of how many of the Jews who had emigrated to France after the First World War participated in the resistance, see Meyer, *Fremde Elemente*.

53. Memorandum on the results of the discussion of 30 January 1941 on the future treatment of the Jewish question in France, 3 February 1941, Klarsfeld, *Vichy*, p. 364.

54. Marrus and Paxton, *Vichy France*, pp. 73ff.

55. Best's talking paper for Stülpnagel, 4 April 1941, Klarsfeld, *Vichy*, pp. 366ff.

56. Best's memorandum concerning meeting with Vallat, 5 April 1941, BA, R 709 (Frankreich), 23.

57. Memorandum by Zeitschel concerning conversation with Best of 5 April 1941, ibid., Vallat was relieved his duties at the urging of Best and Achenbach in March 1942. Best complained to Ambassador de Brinon that Vallat viewed his task as being "apparently protecting Jews rather than carrying out measures directed against them"; conversation of 19 February 1942, HStAD, Rep. 242/Dok. O 29. On Achenbach's recommendation, Darquier de Pellepoix became the new Commissar of Jewish Affairs.

58. Note on a conversation involving Abetz, Dannecker, Achenbach, and Zeitschel on 28 February 1941, Klarsfeld, *Vichy*, p. 365.

59. Verw.stab/Abt. Verw. (Best) to the district military commanders, 27 March 1941, HstAD, Rep. 242/Plc (41). The agreement of Ingrand, the responsible French liaison official, had already been obtained on 26 March 1941; see Klarsfeld, *Vichy*, p. 24.

60. Marrus and Paxton, *Vichy France*, p. 223; Klarsfeld, *Vichy*, p. 25.

61. Ingrand, the representative of the French Minister of the Interior Pucheu, lodged a complaint about this action with the Germans, stressing that the Germans had for the first time ordered the mass arrest of Jews of French nationality and that "these anti-Jewish measures had been ordered by General Stülpnagel and carried out by the commander in Paris with the aid of the Pre-

fect of Police"; thus it was not, as has been assumed, Dannecker who ordered the arrests; Prefect of Police to the representative of the French Interior Minister (Ingrand), 21 August 1941; Ingrand's communication to Interior Minister Pucheu on 21 August 1941, Klarsfeld, *Vichy*, pp. 29f.; Best calendar notation of 19 and 20 August 1941; Luther, *Widerstand*, p. 173; Billig, *Commissariat*, Bd. 2, pp. 17f.; Marrus and Paxton, *Vichy France*, p. 223.

62. Zeitschel to Abetz on 22 August 1941, Klarsfeld, *Vichy*, p. 367.

63. Ibid.

64. See Ulrich Herbert, "Arbeit und Vernichtung. Ökonomisches Interesse und Primat der 'Weltanschauung' im Nationalsozialismus," in Ulrich Herbert (ed.), *Europa und der "Reichseinsatz"*, pp. 384-426; Aly, *Endlösung*, pp. 163ff., 317ff.

65. Marrus and Paxton, *Vichy France*, pp. 252ff.

66. Zeitschel's notes for Abetz, 10 September 1941; Zeitschel to Dannecker 8 October 1941, cited in Klarsfeld, *Vichy*, pp. 109ff.

67. Written exchange between the BdS (Knochen) and MBF from 3 to 6 October 1941: IfZ, MA 280; interview of Speidel in Price-Jones, *Paris*, p. 236; Bargatzky, *Hotel Majestic*, pp. 104f.; Umbreit, *Militärbefehlshaber*, pp. 109ff.

68. MBF to OKW, 8 October 1941, IfZ, MA 280.

69. CdS [Head of Security Police] to OKH, 6 November 1941, in Klarsfeld, *Vichy*, p. 369. Following this exchange, Stülpnagel reiterated his demand that Knochen be removed; he was supported by the OKH; MBF to OKH, 8 November 1941; OKH to CdS, 2 December 1941; both in IfZ, MA 280.

70. MBF to OKH, 1 December 1941, in *Geiselverfahren* (note 24), p. 77.

71. On 5 December 1941, Best had given instructions concerning what persons were to be marked for deportation and had instructed the commander of Greater Paris to arrest 1,000 Jews for that purpose; mentioned in an Administrative Staff notation (Bälz) of 16 December 1941, in ZStL, 104 ARZ 1670/61, Bd. 10, p. 34; communiqué of the MBF of 14 December 1941, Klarsfeld, *Vichy*, p. 34.

72. Communiqué of the MBF, 14 December 1941, cited in *Die faschistische Okkupation in Frankreich (1940-1944)* (Berlin, 1990), p. 192.

73. Danneckers's entry concerning the discussion of the Jewish experts, 4 February 1942 in Berlin, Klarsfeld, *Vichy*, p. 374; Dannecker's communication to Knochen and Lischka of 10 March 1942, Klarsfeld, *Endlösung*, document number 28; Zeitschel's note of 11 March 1942, BA, R 70 (Frankreich); Foreign Office to the embassy in Paris, 13 March 1942, PA/AA/Inl. II geh./189, 149. Dannecker to the MBF, Kdo.Stab [Military Occupation Command/Command Staff] (Speidel), 14 March 1942, Klarsfeld, *Endlösung*, document number 31; Rademacher (Foreign Office) to RSHA, 20 March 1942, ADAP, E II, 56.

74. MBF/Verw. (Best) to BdS, 2 January 1942 (Postponement of Transport), BA, R 70 (Frankreich)/23, Bl. 8f.; MBF/Verw. (Best) to BdS, 4 February 1942 (Action Against Jews in Rouen), HStAD, Rep. 242/Plc (42); Dannecker's entry of 20 February 1942 (Section "Jewish Camp" in Compiègne), ZStl. 104, ARZ 1670/61, Bd. 1, p. 10; Dannecker's entry of 28 February 1942 ("Transfer of Jews Designated for Deportation from Compiègne to Drancy"), ibid. On the later history of the deportation of Jews in France, see Marrus and Paxton, *Vichy France*, pp. 215ff.; Klarsfeld, *Vichy*, p. 44.

75. Bargartzky, *Hotel Majestic*, p. 99.

76. Ibid., p. 103.

77. Umbreit, *Militärbefehlshaber*, pp. 141f.; 107ff.; Jäckel, *Frankreich*, pp. 194ff.; for information on Carl-Heinrich von Stülpnagel, see the biography by Hein-

rich Bücheler: *Carl-Heinrich von Stülpnagel. Soldat, Philosoph, Verschwörer* (Berlin/Frankfurt a.M., 1989), which is not, however, well-grounded in the politics of the period.

78. "Führerbefehl" of 9 March 1942, BA, R 70 (Frankreich)/13; see Ruth Bettina Birn, *Die Höheren SS- und Polizeiführer. Himmlers Vertreter im Reich und in den besetzten Gebieten* (Düsseldorf, 1986), p. 253.

79. Zeitschel's note for Schleier and Achenbach, 18 March 1942, Klarsfeld, *Endlösung*, document number 32.

80. Bargatzky, *Hotel Majestic*, pp. 103f.; Pryce-Jones, *Paris*, p. 127.

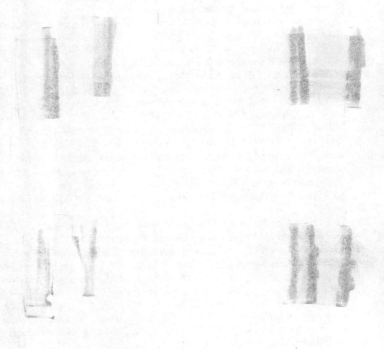

– Chapter 6 –

THE EXTERMINATION OF THE
JEWS IN SERBIA

Walter Manoschek

When German troops invaded Yugoslavia without a declaration of war on 6 April 1941, approximately 80,000 Jews lived in that country. About 55,000 to 60,000 Yugoslavian Jews and another 4,000 or so foreign Jewish refugees ended up falling victim to the Holocaust.[1] As a result, Jews in Yugoslavia suffered one of the proportionately highest death rates of all European Jewish populations.

After Yugoslavia's military capitulation in mid-April 1941, the Yugoslavian state was shattered and divided up among the Axis powers. The process of exterminating Yugoslavia's Jews varied along regional lines. Depending on whether they lived under Bulgarian, Hungarian, Italian, or German occupation, or in the territories of the Croatian Ustasha state, they fell into the clutches of the extermination apparatus at varying times and under differing circumstances. Thus, the majority of Jews living in Croatia were murdered in the numerous camps of the Croatian Ustasha (such as Jasenovac or Stara Gradiška, to give only two of the most notorious examples), and a relatively small minority were deported to Auschwitz since 1943 in the course of the "Final Solution." Whereas about 16,000 Jews living in the regions annexed by Hungary, such as the South Baranya and Bacska, managed to avoid mass extermi-

nation until German troops marched into Hungary in March 1944.
In Serbia the head of the Security Police (Sicherheitspolizei or Sipo)
and SD, Emanuel Schäfer, was already able to report in June 1942:
"Serbia is free of Jews."[2] In little more than one year of military
occupation, the Wehrmacht and Security Police murdered the entire
population of 17,000 Jews living in Serbian territory.[3]

I

The attack on the Balkan states in April 1941 was not planned as
an ideologically-motivated war of racial extermination. The destruction and partition of the Yugoslavian state, coupled with the Axis
occupation of Greece, was primarily intended to secure the Reich's
southeastern flank, with the smallest possible number of troops, for
the war against the Soviet Union, while the region's resources were
to be plundered for the German war economy. After the rapid
capitulation of the Yugoslavian and Greek armies, the Wehrmacht
continued to occupy only Serbia in its pre-1912 borders and a relatively small part of Greece.

Following the withdrawal of German combat forces from the
Yugoslavian theater, four specially-created occupation divisions
were dispatched to Serbia and Croatia. Two of these, the 717th and
718th Infantry Division (ID), were established in the Ostmark
(Austria's provincial designation after the Anschluss in March
1938). The composition of the units bespoke their geographic origins: in both divisions, Austrians made up a majority of officers and
enlisted men. The occupation divisions were supplemented by six
Landesschützenbataillone (Home Guard Battalions), of which four
also stemmed from the Ostmark. Thus, foot soldiers from the Ostmark constituted the core of the military occupation apparatus
after the spring of 1941.[4] The disproportionately strong represen-
tation of Austrians was by no means a coincidence. In fact, where
Serbia was concerned, Hitler had, according to Franz Neuhausen,
the general plenipotentiary for the Serbian economy, "assumed the
same standpoint that the Austrians had taken in 1914. As an Austrian, he never wavered from that standpoint, in accordance with
which he ordered strict measures against the Serbs. Furthermore, he
believed that only the Austrians knew the Serbs and that they were
the only ones competent to assess the political, economic, and other
questions in Serbia."[5]

The traditional hostile image of Serbia from 1914—the Austrians held the Serbs responsible for the war which cost them their

empire—formed a solid foundation upon which the racial-ideolog-
ical objectives of National Socialism could be built in 1941. In early
1941, the Wehrmacht leadership had been committed to participating in a "crusade against Jewish Bolshevism" (according to the
Chief of the Wehrmacht Supreme Command, Field Marshal Wilhelm Keitel) and the institutional cooperation between the army, on
the one hand, and Himmler's "special political police units," (the
Security Police, the SD, and the SS) on the other hand, had been
formalized.[6] In the Balkan lands, Himmler's "special units" were
empowered to act not only against "emigrants, saboteurs, terror-
ists, etc.," but also against "Jews and Communists."[7]

The first steps in the process of exterminating the Jews immediately followed the establishment of the occupation regime. They
occurred in the same sequence previously employed in other occupied countries: registration, marking, deprivation, social exclusion.
Two days before the Yugoslavian army capitulated, the chief of the
Einsatzgruppen (Action Squads) in Belgrade, Wilhelm Fuchs, had
ordered all of the city's Jews to report for registration. "Jews who
fail to obey this order will be shot dead,"[8] decreed posters pasted
on the walls.

From the beginning, military agencies were also active in persecuting the Jews. Already in April 1941, for example, in the Banat
city of Großbetschkerek (Zrenjanin), the local commandant mandated that Jews wear the Star of David and arranged for the approximately 2,000-member Jewish community to be committed to a
ghetto of the city.[9] In Belgrade, the field commander, Colonel von
Kaisenberg, decreed limitations on Jews' freedom of movement and
on the hours that they could shop.[10]

Wehrmacht organizations were also involved in robbing Jews of
their property. The military police confiscated Jewish apartments and
businesses, as well as their inventories. Moveable goods were
deposited in warehouses, from which members of the occupation
forces could purchase them at affordable prices, with appropriate cer-
tification issued by the field command's administrative organization.[11]

The effect of the material deprivation of the Jews on the consciousness of Wehrmacht members should not be underestimated. A
staff officer stationed in the Banat described the practical advantages
of persecuting the Jews in a field mail letter: "Just a few weeks ago
the war still raged here. Now, there are no traces to be found, since
the enemy only turned and ran, and our tanks followed him. But
there are traces, however, insofar as the Jews have been chased out,
shot, and incarcerated. Entire palaces, mansions in all their pomp

stand empty. Our infantrymen, noncommissioned officers, etc., feel very much at home in them. They are living like kings in there."[12]

Wehrmacht propaganda, too, fostered the image of the "Jew as enemy." Thus, Jews were held responsible for the anti-German sentiment in Serbia. In their reports on the public mood, the propaganda department determined "that the negative attitude of the intellectual circles has in no way changed. Here, the Jews play an important role." In May 1941, the "start of a large-scale anti-Jewish propaganda effort was made." "Presentations on the Jewish question" were prepared for radio broadcasts , while "up-to-the-moment information to counter Communist propaganda, as well as on the activities of Jewry in the Balkans, was made available" for the Serbian press.[13]

If the first measures of Jewish persecution took place in an unsystematic and uncoordinated fashion, then the following stages of oppression were coordinated between the highest military authorities and the remaining occupation agencies. Six weeks after the occupation began, the Wehrmacht commander in Serbia, General Ludwig von Schröder, decreed the identification, registration, and marking of Jews and Gypsies with yellow armbands; their dismissal from all public offices and private operations; the "aryanization" of their property and assets; and the introduction of forced labor.[14] Thereby, the measures of racist persecution attained a level of uniformity, with a common denominator for the entire Serbian area of occupation.[15] In other words, the three first steps of the extermination process were set in motion in a single day. Concurrently, German authorities considered establishing a Jewish ghetto in the Serbian town of Majdanpek.[16] That plan, however, did not come to fruition. In response to the dynamics of unfolding events, the phase of ghettoization, as previously implemented in Poland, was "leapfrogged" in Serbia, where a locally-developed variant of the "solution to the Jewish question" emerged.

In coordination with the civilian and police agencies, the military commander enacted measures against Jews and Gypsies from the very beginning. As far as can be determined from the sources, cooperation on Jewish and Gypsy policies functioned without a hitch. In the first phase, until the invasion of the Soviet Union, the racist norms that already obtained in other occupied regions were adopted and adjusted to the conditions in Serbia. Wehrmacht agencies were tied into this process at every level of racist persecution and shared responsibility for it. Military pretexts or special justifications were not required. The process of registration, marking, deprivation, and social exclusion already constituted an integral component of National Socialist Jewish policies and the

Wehrmacht, in addition to the police and security forces, shared responsibility for making it such.

With the attack on the Soviet Union in June 1941, the situation for the German occupiers of Serbia changed radically. As the German Ostheer (Army of the East) marched into the Soviet Union on 22 June 1941, with 136 divisions and over three million men, only four occupation divisions with a total of approximately 25,000 men, augmented by three police companies and their own Home Guard regiments, remained in Serbia. The average age of the soldiers was thirty years, considerably higher for the men of the Home Guard units. These men had no combat experience and their military education was limited to a training course lasting only a few weeks, which consisted of little more than repeated trips to the firing range. With the exception of a handful of noncommissioned officers, none of these men had any active service and even the officer corps consisted exclusively of reservists.[17] This was an occupation mechanism designed for "quiet times." But the quiet times in Serbia came to an abrupt end in the early summer of 1941, when the partisans under Tito's leadership took up their armed struggle. The occupying forces were now confronted with a well-organized guerrilla movement, for which they were prepared neither tactically nor by their training experience.

At first, the new military commander, General Heinrich Danckelmann, assigned the *Einsatzgruppe* of the Security Police and the Security Service (SD), the Secret Military Police, a police battalion, and the regular military police to combat the partisans.[18] The so-called "police struggle against the partisans" meant, in plain language, shooting and hanging civilians "suspected of being partisans." As a precautionary measure, a "hostage reservoir" had already been accumulated by the time of the Soviet invasion. It consisted of those groups that had been identified as targets for extermination in the eastern campaign: Jews and Communists.[19] By the summer of 1941, the murder of hostages had already become an everyday occurrence in the occupation.

Lieutenant Peter G. reported on this "anti-partisan struggle" at regular intervals in his letters:

> 26 July 1941: Entire hordes of Communists are now shot and hanged almost daily. Otherwise, the situation is relatively calm.

> 29 July 1941: Do you receive Belgrade with your radio, which also gives German news evenings at 8 p.m. and 10 p.m.? Maybe you'll have the chance some time to listen? Don't get scared, though, if they happen to announce the totals of executed Communists and Jews, which they give at the end of the news broadcast. Today there was a

record! This morning in Belgrade, we shot 122 Communists and
Jews. You can even hear my town ... from time to time. It is often
mentioned ... yesterday, over 30 people were shot.[20]

With complete openness, Lieutenant G. tells of attacks by the
Communists and of the occupiers' reaction: the shooting of Communists *and* Jews. These actions were announced on public broadcasts
and proudly described in letters destined for home. Within a few
weeks, the fight against "Jewish Bolshevism" turned into an everyday
norm in the microcosm of Serbia, as it did elsewhere. The crimes
occurred with the knowledge, and in accordance with the orders of,
the military commander and in front of the troops' own eyes. Against
the backdrop of increasing partisan activity, the Wehrmacht leadership, but also the troop units, had quickly adjusted to the new norms
and values of *Gegnerbekämpfung* (the fight against opponents) and
internalized them, although the core of the troop units had not yet
acquired first-hand experience of these brutal repression policies.
Because of the small size of the German occupation administration in
Serbia, and in the face of a threatening situation, there developed very
rapidly, across all organizational boundaries, clear indications of a
sense of community, characterized by a circle-the-wagons mentality
and bound by a code of loyalty customary in such situations.

Despite a balance of over 1,000 shot or hanged Jews and Communists in July and August 1941, the activities of the partisans
spread ever more rapidly. In August 1941, Hitler assigned the
Wehrmacht the task of combating partisans in Serbia: "On account
of the rise in disturbances and acts of sabotage, the Führer expects
the army to take immediate action to restore law and order through
swift and severe intervention."[21] With that, the members of the SD,
police, and Wehrmacht closed ranks in a mutual struggle against
their opponents. Each battalion established mobile pursuit teams
(*Jagdkommandos*), consisting of soldiers, policemen, and SD members. These mixed pursuit teams represented a transition in the
anti-partisan struggle from a policy of divided labor to direct cooperation between the army and the police apparatus. Through the
subsequent commingling of personnel, the soldiers absorbed the
combat methods and specialized forms of *Gegnerbekämpfung*
favored by the police forces and SD.

Neither the methods of conducting this combat nor the definition of the enemy groups changed with the Wehrmacht's assumption of the anti-partisan struggle. Since fighting the partisans with
available forces proved to be militarily hopeless, the policy of mur-

dering hostages (*Geiselmordpolitik*) remained the centerpiece of the campaign. Jews and Communists were the primary victims.

The German failure to militarily subdue the partisans eventuated in uncoordinated acts of revenge against the Serbian civilian population. The murder of innocent civilians at the hands of soldiers did not result in a single prosecution by the military courts. To the contrary, commanders took an understanding approach to these breaches of military discipline, though they also acknowledged negative consequences: "It is understandable that soldiers who are ambushed by Communist bands should cry out for revenge. In the course of such operations, people who happen to be out in the fields are frequently arrested and executed. In most cases, however, one will not capture the guilty parties, who have long since disappeared, but instead innocent people, and thereby create a situation where the previously loyal population goes over to the partisans, out of fear or embitterment .... That German soldiers may under no circumstances execute women without judicial process, except when these attack the soldiers with weapon in hand, goes without saying" read one directive that was circulated to all companies.[22]

That directive makes clear how far the Wehrmacht had distanced itself from the legal norms of warfare. Partisans, or persons suspected of being partisans, with the exception of women, were allowed to be executed without any sort of judicial proceedings. For murdering innocent civilians, soldiers were not prosecuted by the military courts. Their murderous actions mainly met with the approval of their superiors and were rejected only for political or tactical reasons, not because they violated legal principles of war.

The army's murderous activities in the summer of 1941 had the characteristics of spontaneous acts of revenge, set off by frustration over the failures in the anti-partisan campaign. These acts of excess did not result in military prosecutions but nevertheless proved to be counterproductive in the end. Not only were they impotent to check the spread of partisan activity, but they also endangered the internal discipline of the troop units. In place of such spontaneous excesses, therefore, a policy of systematic repression was introduced.

For that, the Wehrmacht leadership in Berlin sought a suitable candidate, a man who was prepared to execute Hitler's directive "to restore order with the severest means."[23] The task fell to Franz Böhme, a general of Austrian parentage. Recommended by his superior, General Field Marshal List, as a "first-rate expert on the Balkan situation,"[24] Böhme was appointed by Hitler in September 1941 as plenipotentiary commanding general in Serbia and all military and civilian agencies there were placed under his command.

The former director of the Austrian military intelligence service had long enjoyed Hitler's trust. In February 1938, during a meeting with the Austrian Chancellor Schuschnigg at the Obersalzberg, the Führer had demanded that Böhme be appointed chief of the Austrian general staff. After the war in Poland and France, Böhme had participated in the invasion of Greece as commanding general of the XVIII Army Corps.

By the time General Böhme arrived in Belgrade in mid-September, Serbia, with the exception of only the largest cities, had fallen under the control of the partisans and the nationalist Chetnik bands. Böhme recognized that his forces were too weak to bring the country back under the control of the occupiers by military means, despite the recent arrival of reinforcements. Instead, he withdrew the fragmented units that had been scattered all across Serbia—and thus presented an ideal target for partisan attacks—to strategically important areas. Thereby, he hoped to reduce losses and reverse the trend toward demoralization among the troops. Concurrently, Böhme set the ideological, disciplinary, and organizational course for systematizing what had previously been uncoordinated measures of repression.

The conviction that Bolshevism and Judaism shared a structural identity—a conviction that extended far beyond the ranks of professed National Socialists—served to legitimize that summer's police and SD killings of Communists and Jews, which were labeled "measures of atonement." Whereas in the war against the Soviet Union, the racist mantra of "subhuman Slavs" helped destroy moral inhibitions over exterminating entire populations, in Serbia the Austrian Böhme resorted to an ancient Austrian image of the Serb as enemy. Fully aware that the overwhelming majority of his soldiers were Austrians, he invoked the historical dimension of their mission: "Your objective is to be achieved in a land where, in 1914, streams of German blood flowed because of the treachery of the Serbs, men and women. You are the avengers of those dead. A deterring example must be established for all of Serbia, one that will have the heaviest impact on the entire population. Anyone who carries out his duty in a lenient manner will be called to account, regardless of rank or position, and tried by a military court."[25]

The war against the civilian population thereby acquired a new legitimacy. No longer did the killing of civilians at the hands of the Wehrmacht constitute an "understandable," if unsoldierly "violation," an officially unsanctioned breach of military discipline. Instead, it became a legalized and integral component of German military occupation policy. By invoking memories of the First World War, the army attempted to establish a historical justification as it accommodated its code of military justice to the National Socialist values system.

So that any potentially diverging subjective sense of moral right on the part of the soldiers would be brought in line with the National Socialist legal outlook, Böhme redefined the norms of appropriate behavior. "Leniency" toward the civilian population now counted as "a sin against the lives of comrades"; whoever was unwilling to accept these rules and act in accordance with them would be threatened with military legal proceedings, "regardless of rank or position." This directive of Böhme's, which was to be destroyed once disseminated, was intended to instill in the troops a sense of their ideological and historic mission, and to accustom them to the collective punishment of the Serbian civilian population. The disciplinary pressure from above, coupled with the opportunity for soldiers to take out on the civilian population their fears, frustrations, and aggressions that had accumulated in the course of the unsuccessful anti-partisan operations, created the psychological preconditions for the planned mass murder.

Böhme's order established new foundations for the occupation policy in Serbia, which Omer Bartov also identifies as the symptomatic characteristics of the military occupation in the East. The army, according to Bartov, "reverted to the most primitive moral rules of war, in accordance with which everything that secured one's own survival was permitted (and therefore considered moral) and everything that could threaten it in even the remotest sense (and was by definition immoral) must be destroyed."[26]

General Böhme had received the directive from Hitler "to restore order with the severest measures." This was one of Hitler's characteristically vague orders; it did not specify the measures to be taken to restore "law and order" in Serbia and left much room for individual decision-making. Execution depended upon the decoding abilities of each military commander ("What does the Führer expect?") and on their respective readiness to throw overboard the legal conventions of war and human rights, as well as to accommodate their views of military justice to the new values system.

A directive from OKW Chief Keitel, issued on the day that Böhme took up his post in Serbia, served as an indicator of the way the new commander would proceed. For the fight against "the movement of Communist uprisings in the occupied territories," Keitel established a guideline for all of German-occupied Europe: "As penance for the life of one German soldier, the death penalty for 50-100 Communists must be considered appropriate in these cases. The method of execution must serve to raise the deterrent effect."[27]

II

When General Böhme assumed his post in Serbia in mid-September 1941, the geographic concentration of Jews was already underway. In August, the Jews were deported from the Banat to Belgrade, and from the beginning of September the male Jews and Gypsies of the capital were also interned.[28]

Since the middle of August, the German envoy in Serbia, Felix Benzler, and the "Jewish expert" sent by the Foreign Office to assist him, Edmund Veesenmayer, had become active in shaping Jewish policy. In numerous telegrams to the Foreign Office in Berlin, they emphatically demanded the deportation of at least 8,000 male Jews from Serbia, since the "speedy and draconian solution to the Serbian Jewish question was the most urgent and expedient necessity."[29] They justified their demands with arguments couched in the language of security policy: Jews had emerged as culprits in numerous disturbances and cases of sabotage; concentrations of Jews detained and endangered the troops; Jews were demonstrably making decisive contributions to the unrest in the country; the initial deportation of male Jews was the necessary prerequisite for restoring orderly conditions—so read several of the justifications formulated by the German envoy.[30] After Adolf Eichmann, in response to a query from the Foreign Office, had declared the transfer of Jews from Serbia to occupied Poland or the Soviet Union to be impossible, State Secretary Martin Luther recommended to his envoy in Belgrad "a hard and inflexible proceeding" against the Jews, so as to "deprive them of their appetite for spreading unrest in the country. The Jews that have been collected in camps will just have to serve as hostages to guarantee the good conduct of their comrades-in-race (*Rassegenossen*)."[31]

This "security policy" argument for the ideology of racial extermination went hand in hand with General Böhme's military "pacification concept." At first, Böhme, together with Minister Benzler, pushed Reich Foreign Minister Ribbentrop to authorize the deportation of the Jews that were already interned in camps, so that enough space might be cleared for the planned incarceration of tens of thousands of Serbian civilians. Only a few days later, however, Böhme recognized the possibilities that the already-accomplished imprisonment of the male Jews presented: Jews and Gypsies stood available as "hostages on call" for executions.

After a fire-fight with partisans, which cost twenty-one Wehrmacht members their lives, General Böhme for the first time resorted to shooting Jews in retaliation. Böhme established the organizational blueprint for the course the mass executions would take and determined the selection of victims: "As reprisal and atonement, 100 Serbian prisoners will be shot immediately for every murdered German soldier. The chief of the military administration is requested to select 2,100 prisoners from the concentration camps Šabac and Belgrade (predominantly Jews and Communists) and to establish place, time, and burial sites. The execution details shall be formed by the 342nd Division (for the Šabac camp) and Corps Intelligence Detachment 449 (for the Belgrade camp)."[32]

With this order, General Böhme inaugurated a new phase in the persecution of the Jews. The existing practice of murdering Jews and Communists through *Einsatzgruppen* was now systematized, militarily decreed, and carried out by the soldiers themselves. It in the summer it had been the SD and the police who executed Jews and Communists, from now on the task would be carried out by the army. The Security Police would be called upon to assist only by delivering a specific number of execution victims upon demand.

Even as the first mass executions of Jews and Communists at the hands of the Wehrmacht were underway, General Böhme identified who the victims of future shootings would be: "All Communists, male residents suspected of being Communists, all Jews, a certain number of nationalist and democratically-minded residents"[33]—with the exception of collaborators, virtually the entire population was potentially affected.

Shifting "hostage shootings" from Himmler's special units to Wehrmacht soldiers presupposed that the soldiers' sense of moral right was already so distorted that they would be prepared to carry out these murderous actions. The troop commanders—General Böhme in the lead—now attempted to prepare the soldiers psychologically and mentally for their role in the bloody program of suppression. That occurred in a wide range of ways. Above all, the troops were inculcated with reminders of their "historic mission." "The streams of German blood that in 1914 flowed because of the treachery of Serbs, men and women," according to General Böhme, were to be avenged in 1941. The soldiers' senses of honor and comradeship were instrumentalized: General Böhme ordered that, "whenever possible," the "troop unit that suffered the loss be tasked with the execution." The pressure of disciplinary measures was increased; in the event of "cowardice in the face of the enemy," soldiers were threatened with military legal proceedings. Male fears were stirred up; although the commanders possessed evidence to the contrary, the chain of command pointedly spread the rumor that soldiers would suffer genital mutilation in the event of capture by the partisans.

This agglomeration of historical animosities, propaganda scare stories, perverted conceptions of discipline and comradeship, and the associated summons to officially-sanctioned mass murder would prove to be an effective, goal-oriented method by which the Germans' wounded sense of superiority and racist animosities could be channeled, militarily legitimized, and converted into mass murder. The orders from above, and the growing readiness below to carry out those orders, unleashed a dynamic of mass murder in the fall of 1941.

In the process, the logic of racist extermination was closely bound to the practical rationale of occupation rule: the overwhelming portion of approximately 8,000 adult male Jews, the unsettled Gypsies, and "suspicious Communists" were already interned in camps and stood "on call" at all times for executions. Now, the victims were selected in accordance with the National Socialist racial hierarchy: first, all Jews and Gypsies; then, those persons suspected of being Communists; and finally, the remaining populace, whereby assignment to either of the latter two groups was in practice rather arbitrary. Accordingly, the Jews and Gypsies were the first to be murdered. After suffering losses in the anti-partisan struggle, units requested from the appropriate staff agency that a contingent of hostages (in the ratio of 1:100 for each killed soldier, 1:50 for each wounded soldier, respectively) be made available to them. The administration chief, Dr. Harald Turner, conducted the selection of hostages and determined the time and place of the executions. A volunteer firing squad from the unit in question drove a truck to the camp, picked up the victims, and transported them to the execution site. The site would be cordoned off at a considerable distance and the victims dug their own graves before they were shot. The executions were filmed by the propaganda company and photographed. After the completion of the operation, the presiding officer prepared a detailed report on the "shooting of Jews and Gypsies," which was forwarded to higher military headquarters in Serbia, as well as to the 12th Superior Army Command in Salonika, Greece, the highest Wehrmacht headquarters in the Balkan region. Larger shootings lasted from early morning until evening, and often required several days to complete.

In one execution report from 1 November 1941, the officer in charge discussed advantages and disadvantages of this process:

In coordination with the SS office, I picked up the selected Jews and Gypsies from the Belgrade prison camp. The trucks of Field Command 599 that were made available to me for this purpose proved to be unsuitable for two reasons:

(1). They are driven by civilians. Maintaining secrecy can therefore not be guaranteed.

(2). They were all without a cover or a canvas, so that city's residents saw who we had on the vehicles and to where we then drove. In front of the camp, the Jews' women had gathered, screaming and crying as we drove away.

The place where the execution was carried out is very propitious. It lies north of Pančevo, directly on the road from Pančevo to Jabuka, which is bordered by an embankment that is so high, a man could climb up it only with difficulty. Across from this embankment is swampy terrain, behind that a river. During flood conditions (as on 29 October), the water reaches almost to the embankment. Any escape attempt by prisoners can therefore be prevented with a handful of men. Also advantageous is the sandy soil there, which makes digging the pits easier and therefore also shortens the work time.

After arriving approximately 1.5 to 2 km before the selected site, the prisoners disembarked, marched to the spot on foot, while the trucks with their civilian drivers were immediately sent back, in order to provide as few clues as possible for them to develop any suspicions. Then I had the road blocked off for reasons of safety and secrecy.

The execution site was secured by 3 l. M.G. [light machine guns— W.M.] and 12 riflemen:

(1). Against escape attempts by the prisoners

(2). For self defense against eventual attacks by Serbian bands.

Digging the pits takes up the largest portion of the time, while the shooting itself goes very quickly (100 men, 40 minutes).

Baggage and valuables were collected beforehand and transported in my truck, to turn them over to the National Socialist People's Welfare Organization (*Nationalsozialistischen Volkswohlfahrt* or NSV).

Shooting the Jews is easier than shooting the Gypsies. One has to admit that the Jews go to their deaths in a very composed manner— they remain very calm—while the Gypsies sob, scream, and continue to move around, even when they are already standing on the spot of their execution. Several even jumped into the pit before the firing volley and pretended to be dead.

Initially, my soldiers were not affected. On the second day, though, one noticed that this one or that one doesn't have the nerves required to carry out an execution over a longer period of time. My personal impression is that one doesn't experience any mental reservations during the execution itself. However, these begin to set in when after a few days one thinks about the events in the quiet of the evening.[34]

A first lieutenant reported with regret that the detail under his command had to be relieved during an execution: "All in all, 449 men were shot dead on 9 and 11 October 1941 by the mentioned units. Unfortunately, because of operational reasons (*Einsatzgründen*), a further execution by the mentioned units had to be discontinued and responsibility for the assignment transferred to Major Pongruber's unit."[35]

While some carried out their duties with enthusiasm, in other executions "human weakness" and "mental reservations" came to light. It is important to hold on to the fact that soldiers were not forced to take part in the shootings. Whoever proved to have nerves that were "too weak" or was unable to overcome possible moral inhibitions could get out of such assignments. Nevertheless, the mass executions performed by the Wehrmacht came off smoothly. In their execution, no notable delays or impediments occurred. Alone in the two shooting actions described above, a total of 4,400 Jews and Gypsies were murdered. There are no indications of any negative effects on the internal discipline of the troops.

Where Jews and Gypsies did not exist in sufficient numbers for mass executions, other Serbian civilians filled out the pool of victims, for example in the cities of Kraljevo and Kragujevac, where among others, units of the 717th Infantry Division shot over 4,000 residents in the span of a few days. The manner in which these massacres were carried out characterizes the army's coordination system. In Kraljevo, 300 "Communists, nationalists, democrats, and Jews" were first murdered, before 1,400 randomly accumulated men fell victim to the execution squads on the following day.[36]

In Kragujevac, a similar "selection process" occurred. First, Jews, Communists, and prisoners from the local jail were shot; the troops liquidated the rest of the civilians only the next day—a total of 2,300 people.[37]

By the fall of 1941, massacres of Jews, Gypsies, and other Serbian civilians belonged to the established everyday routine of the Wehrmacht occupation. During these unrestrained mass murders, oversight over the victims was lost—even collaborators were caught up in the liquidation machinery. The head of the military administration, Turner, called upon the district and field commanders to be more selective in choosing their hostage victims, although he was fully aware of the Germans' self-made problem: at a ratio of 1:100, adequate numbers of victims "can no longer be produced, if at least a minimal degree of guilt, even based solely on the general attitude of those to be arrested, is still to be taken into account."[38]

In the case of Jews and Gypsies, however, such diluted selection criteria did not need to be taken into consideration: Turner emphasized that "in all cases, all Jewish men and all male Gypsies (would continue to) be held available for the troops."[39]

In relation to the high demand for shooting victims, the number of available Jews and Gypsies was relatively low. Although this "hostage reservoir" had been enlarged by the 400 or so male, mostly Austrian captured Jewish refugees from the "Kladovo transport,"[40] it was nonetheless exhausted after only a few weeks. Already in early November 1941, Legation Counsel Rademacher, the Foreign Office official entrusted with the "solution to the Jewish problem," reported: "The male Jews will all be shot by the end of this week, thereby the problem addressed in the mission report will be resolved."[41]

In their correspondence, the occupation agencies attempted to legitimize the extermination of the Jews and Gypsies through military euphemisms and pseudo-argumentation. Thus, the head of the military administration, Turner, justified the extermination policies to military agencies by observing "that the Jewish element is considerably involved in leading the bands [of partisans] and especially Gypsies are responsible for exceptional atrocities and intelligence gathering."[42]

Among friends, Turner did not need to fall back on such justification techniques. In a private letter to SS-Gruppenführer Richard Hildebrandt, Turner quite openly laid out the actual motivations for the killings: "In the last 8 days, I have had 2,000 Jews and 200 Gypsies shot dead, following the quota of 1:100 for brutally murdered German soldiers, and a further 2,200, also nearly all Jews, will be shot in the next 8 days. That is not pleasant work! But it must be done, in order to make it clear to people what it means just to attack a German soldier, while at the same time, the Jewish question solves itself most quickly in this way. Actually, it is wrong, if taken literally, that for murdered Germans, for whom the ratio of 1:100 should come at the expense of the Serbs, 100 Jews will now be shot, but they are the ones we happened to have in the camp—besides, they are also Serbian citizens and they, too, have to disappear."[43]

The soldiers who participated in the executions were also fully aware that the logic of the Jewish executions was skewed. In an interview, a soldier who took part in shootings of Jews admitted it was obvious to all involved "that the shooting of Jews bore no relation to partisan attacks, which were used only as an alibi for the extermination of the Jews.... Most of the members of the firing squad never fired a shot in anger, neither before nor after (the executions)."[44]

Pushing the war beyond the boundaries of all existing norms of warfare was the shared undertaking of all occupation authorities. The genocide of the Jews and of portions of the Gypsy population was a collective endeavor of all occupation agencies, as were the massive repressions against the remaining civilian population of Serbia. In the process, the Wehrmacht, as the reigning authority on the scene, had seized the initiative to issue the orders during the decisive phase in the fall of 1941. The soldiers, in turn, translated these orders into deeds.

The balance that General Böhme left behind in December 1941, after only two months as plenipotentiary commander in Serbia: 160 killed and 278 wounded Wehrmacht members were offset by an official total of 3,562 partisans killed in action,[45] and between 20,000 and 30,000 executed civilians—including all adult male Jews and Gypsies.[46]

III

Even as the murder of male Jews was underway in the fall of 1941, the military administration chief, SS-Gruppenführer Harald Turner, enacted the first measures for interning Jewish women and children in the Sajmište concentration camp near Belgrade: "Preliminary work for Jewish ghetto in Belgrade completed. Following the liquidation of the remaining male Jews, already ordered by the commander in Serbia, the ghetto will contain approximately 10,000 Jewish women and children."[47]

With that, the initiative in the extermination of the Jews passed back again from the Wehrmacht to the police and SS organizations, enabling the Wehrmacht to legitimize the incarceration even of women and children with absurd military pretexts. To justify the abduction of women and children to the Sajmište concentration camp—a former fairgrounds near Belgrade—the counter-intelligence unit Ic/AO in Salonika (to which Kurt Waldheim would belong a few months later) insisted: "All of the Jews and Gypsies are being transferred to a concentration camp in Semlin (Sajmište) .... They were proven to be pillars of the intelligence service of the insurgents."[48]

Around the turn of the year 1941-1942, approximately 7,000 Jewish women, children, and old men, as well as 500 Jewish men— they had been spared from earlier executions in order to serve on the camp security force (*Ordnungsdienst*)—and 292 Romany women and children were committed to the Sajmište concentration camp.

At the time of their incarceration—in other words, prior to the Wannsee Conference in January 1942—their fate was already determined. Late in 1941, the military administration chief, Turner, with the assistance of the SD office in Belgrade, requested from Berlin the latest technological innovation for exterminating Jews: a gas van.[49]

The Sajmište concentration camp was situated within view of Belgrade on the other side of the Sava River. With binoculars, it was possible to recognize the camp's inmates from the Belgrade fortress, the Taš Majdan. The former fairground structures had been only inadequately converted to housing for 7,000 people. Women and children were quartered in makeshift barracks that could barely be heated. As a consequence, the mortality rate, especially among children, was very high during the ice-cold winter of 1941-1942.[50]

The concentration camp's administration was relatively simple. The approximately 500 Jewish men who had been exempted from that fall's shootings administered the camp in so-called "self-administration." They were responsible for distributing food, dividing up labor, and organizing a Jewish guard force, which patrolled along the camp's barbed wire fence.[51] The camp's exterior was guarded on a rotation basis by 25 members of Reserve Police Battalion 64.[52]

The camp commandant since January 1942 was the native Austrian SS-Untersturmführer Herbert Andorfer. At the beginning of March 1942, Andorfer received the word from the BdS office (Befehlshaber der Sicherheitspolizei-SD/Commander of the Security Police-SD) in Belgrade that a special van had been sent from Berlin, which would make it possible to gas the Jewish camp inmates. Immediately thereafter, the Romany women and children were released from the camp.

In order to ensure that the gassings would proceed smoothly, Andorfer put out announcements to delude the prisoners into believing they would soon be transferred to another, better-equipped facility. Andorfer even posted fictitious camp regulations and announced that prisoners would be allowed to take their baggage with them.

Prisoners registered in droves for the alleged transfer, hoping to escape the gruesome conditions of the Sajmište camp. In the time between early March and early May 1942, trucks drove every morning, with the exception of Sundays, from Belgrade to the Sajmište camp. Once there, 50 to 80 women and children stowed their baggage and boarded another, grey-painted Saurer truck, where they took their places on ten benches that had been set up in the interior. Then, both vehicles drove off in the direction of Belgrade. After crossing the bridge over the Sava that led to Belgrade, the baggage truck branched off and delivered the victims' belongings to the Belgrade depot of the National Socialist Volksfürsorge (Peoples Welfare).

The gas van stopped briefly. One of the two drivers, Wilhelm Götz or Erwin Meyer, got out and turned a lever on the van's exterior, causing the exhaust fumes to be channeled into the van's interior. During the subsequent drive straight through Belgrade toward the destination, Avala (about 15 km southeast of the capital), the Jews in the back of the van were gassed. Once arrived at the Avala shooting range, a detail of prisoners from the Belgrade prison unloaded the dead, supervised by members of Reserve Police Battalion 64, and buried them in previously dug pits.

Until the beginning of May 1942, during a span of only two months, the approximately 7,500 Jewish camp inmates were murdered in this fashion. After the completion of this murderous mission, the gas van was returned to Berlin. There, it received a technical upgrade and was sent on to Belorussia, where it was used to gas Jews in Minsk.

The gassing sequence transpired in an efficient manner, according to the logic of the perpetrators. The transport of the victims from the concentration camp in the gas van ran very smoothly. The killing required only limited personnel: both gas van drivers; seven prisoners for unloading the dead, and digging and filling in the graves—after the last gas transport, they, too, were shot—and four police officers to guard the prisoners.

Despite the small numbers of people involved in the killings, word quickly spread of the mass murders. Within the SD it was, according to the camp commandant's adjutant, Edgar Enge, an "open secret that the Jews were gassed with this van."[53] In Reserve Police Battalion 64, too, one knew what was going on. Accordingly, a policeman involved in the gassing operations said in an official statement that their activities, "in spite of all security measures, were gradually leaking through to the company, particularly since a guard detachment from our company was also posted at the gas van's parking site and had numerous opportunities to see the gas van."[54] In a postwar witness statement, a department head in Turner's administration once again remembered hearing "from ethnic German circles in early 1942 that the Jewish prisoners of the camp were gassed to death."[55]

The staff of the military commander also was informed about the gradual decimation of the Sajmište camp's inmates. The staff section's ten-day reports duly recorded the systematic decline in the number of the camp's prisoners.

The Wehrmacht's soldiers also had at least a partial view into the proceedings. The victims' bodies were buried at the Avala shooting range, where German soldiers regularly held firing exercises. A truck driver of the Belgrade field command recalled how he discovered pits containing the bodies of gassed Jews while setting up firing targets for his unit's marksmanship training at the end of the range. To the left and right of the road, he noticed the contours of numerous four-sided mounds, which emitted the sweetish smell of decomposing flesh. He saw that women's clothing stuck out from crevices in the mounds and deduced that they must contain the mass graves of women.[56]

In the early part of 1942, the murderers were not so particular in their efforts at secrecy. Only later, as the German defeat began to seem like a distinct possibility, did they frantically attempt to wipe away the traces of their mass murders. In November 1943, the "special commando 1005" of *Einsatzgruppe* leader Paul Blobel arrived in Belgrade. For four months, the corpses of those who had been shot in the fall of 1941 and gassed in early 1942 were dug up, stacked on massive pyres, and incinerated.[57]

When General Löhr returned to the Balkans as Wehrmacht Commander Southeast in August 1942, the head of the military administration in Serbia, Harald Turner, proudly reported: "Jewish question, just like Gypsy question, completely liquidated: Serbia the only country in which the Jewish question and Gypsy question solved."[58] After Estonia, Serbia became the second land in the National Socialist empire that was made "free of Jews."

IV

The process of extermination in Serbia occurred in four uninterrupted sequential phases: (1) the identification of the victims, their loss of legal rights, their social exclusion, and confiscation of their possessions in the first half of 1941 was followed, with the beginning of the partisan struggle that summer, by (2) the murder of some male Jews by police and members of the SD. When the Wehrmacht assumed responsibility for the anti-partisan fight, and with the arrival of General Böhme, the army (3) extended the extermination program to all male Jews. While the men were still being murdered, (4) the women and children were interned in the Sajmište concentration camp and gassed in early 1942.

The extermination of the Gypsies occurred only partly parallel to the extermination of the Jews. The anti-Jewish directives of early 1941 counted only briefly for all Gypsies. After a few weeks, the occupiers differentiated between Gypsies with and without domicile: Serbian citizens of Gypsy descent who held respectable jobs, led an orderly lifestyle, and whose ancestors could be proven to have been settled since at least 1850, were exempted from anti-Jewish directives after July 1941. It is not possible to determine exactly how many Gypsies fell victim to the Wehrmacht's mass shootings in the fall of 1941. If one examines the ratio of Jewish and Gypsy women and children interned in the Sajmište camp (7,000 to barely 300), then their total may have been relatively low. The Romany women and children were released from the Sajmište camp shortly before the start of the gassings of Jews.

The first phase of the extermination program depended on neither the existence of a comprehensive order for Jewish extermination nor on Hitler's approval of the systematic murder of the Jews. In Serbia, the German occupation authorities determined independently to begin the "Final Solution of the Jewish question" in their sphere of responsibility.

The institutional chaos that typified the National Socialist system also existed in Serbia. The coexistence of individual agencies whose competencies overlapped, and were never clearly spelled out, consistently produced often bitter power struggles and turf battles between various occupation authorities.[59] All the more noticeable, then, the seamless way in which the various occupation elements augmented one another, and their smooth cooperation, in the area of Jewish policy.

The Holocaust in Serbia, then, was a collective deed of all the occupation agencies in which immediate responsibility shifted from one agency to another. Whoever took the momentary lead in the various phases of the persecution—the Wehrmacht or the *Einsatzgruppen*, the military administration or the embassy—depended on the situation at hand. To the extent that general guidelines from central headquarters in Berlin were even necessary, they were immediately adapted to the situation on the ground. In the process, the political police and the civil and military occupation authorities succeeded or supplemented one another as needed in taking the lead on Jewish policy. From the beginning, all occupation agencies were in complete agreement over the common goal to make the Jews "disappear." And they were able to come to quick agreement over precisely what means should be used to accomplish that goal as the situation demanded.

Notes

1. Holm Sundhaussen, "Jugoslawien," in *Dimension des Völkermords: Die Zahl der jüdischen Opfer des Nationalsozialismus*, ed. Wolfgang Benz (Munich, 1991), p. 329.
2. Walter Manoschek, "'*Serbien ist judenfrei*': Militärische Besatzungspoltitik und Judenvernichtung in Serbien 1941/42," in *Schriftenreihe des Militärgeschichtlichen Forschungsamtes* (Munich, 1995, 2nd edition), Vol. 38.
3. The exact number of Jewish victims cannot be established. Of the approximately 12,500 Serbian Jews, 4,200 Jews from the Banat, and approximately 1,000 foreign Jewish refugees, only a tiny number managed to survive, either by fleeing in time or going into hiding as "U-boats."
4. Bundesarchiv-Militärarchiv Freiburg (from hereon BA-MA), RH 26-718/3 and RH 20-12/121; Georg Tessin, *Verbände und Truppen der deutschen Wehrmacht und der Waffen-SS im Zweiten Weltkrieg 1939-1945* (Osnabrück, 1976), Vol. 13, pp. 127-132.
5. Interrogation statement of the former general plenipotentiary for the economy in Serbia, Franz Neuhausen, while in the Yugoslavian military prison in Belgrade, 20 September 1947; cit. from Venceslav Glisič, "*Der Terror und die Verbrechen des faschistischen Deutschland in Serbien von 1941 bis 1944*" (Ph.D. Thesis, Berlin, 1968), p. 31.
6. Directive of the Supreme Commander of the Army on the Regulation of the Engagement of the Security Police and the SD in Association with the Army during the Invasion of the Soviet Union, 28 April 1941, citation from *Deutsche Besatzungspolitik in der UdSSR*, ed. Norbert Müller (Cologne, 1988), pp. 42-44.
7. OKH, GenStdH/GenQu., Abt. Kriegsverwaltung (Army Supreme Command, General Staff of the Army/General Quartermaster, Department War Administration), Nr. 11/0308/41 g.K. Chefs. bis zum "Operationsbeginn," from 2 April 1941, cit. from Helmut Krausnick and Hans-Heinrich Wilhelm, *Die Truppe des Weltanschauungskrieges: Die Einsatzgruppen der Sicherheitspolizei und des SD 1938-1942* (Stuttgart, 1981), p. 137.
8. Military Historical Archive in Belgrade, German Archive, 50-4-4.
9. VO from 23 April 1941, Nbg. Dok. NOKW 1100.
10. Military Historical Archive in Belgrade, German Archive, 12-1-66.
11. Central Office of the Landesjustizverwaltungen Ludwigsburg (from hereon ZStL), 503 AR 12/62, Beiakte Bd. 6, Witness statements of Willi J. and Anton W.
12. Field mail letter of Lieutenant Peter G., 24 May 1941, Bibliothek für Zeitgeschichte, Stuttgart, Sammlung Sterz (Library for Recent History, Stuttgart, Sterz Collection).
13. Situation and Activity Report of the "*Propagandaabteilung S(erbien)*" (Propaganda Department S[erbia]), May-August 1941, BA-MA, RW 4/v.231.
14. Directive concerning the Jews and Gypsies, 30 May 1941, Jewish Historical Museum, Belgrade, 21-1-1/20.
15. Henceforth, the fate of the Gypsies in Serbia unfolded only partly parallel to that of the Jews. Thus, in July 1941, those Gypsies whose ancestors had been settled since 1850 were excepted from these measures; the women and children were released from the camp before the gassing operation. The decisive reason why the Gypsies were only partially exterminated lay in the impossibility of categorizing them in accordance with their religious affiliation. The Gypsies who in the fall of 1941 were interned in the "hostage camps" in Belgrade and Šabac were executed as well as the Jews. For the extermination of the Gypsies

in Yugoslavia, see Donald Kenrick and Grattan Puxton, *The Destiny of Europe's Gypsies* (London, 1972), reference is to German edition, *Sinti und Roma: Die Vernichtung eines Volkes im NS-Staat* (Göttingen, 1981); Karola Fings, Cordula Lissner, and Frank Sparing, *"… einziges Land, in dem Judenfrage und Zigeunerfrage gelöst": Die Verfolgung der Roma im faschistisch besetzten Jugoslawien 1941-1945* (Cologne, n.d.); and most recently Michael Zimmermann, *Rassenutopie und Genozid: Die Nationalsozialistische Lösung der "Zigeunerfrage"* (Hamburg, 1996), pp. 248ff.

16. Politisches Archiv, Auswärtiges Amt Bonn (from hereon PA-AA), *Botschaft Belgrad, Judenangelegenheiten Bd 62/6, Aufzeichnung über Besprechung über Judenfragen beim Militärbefehlshaber in Serbien am 14.5.1941* (Embassy in Belgrade, Jewish Matters Vol. 62/6, Memorandum on discussion of Jewish questions in the office of the military commander in Serbia, 14 May 1941).

17. Supporting documents in BA-MA, RH 26-718/3 and RH 20-12/121.

18. Directive concerning the engagement of the Security Police and the SD, 17 July 1941, BA-MA, RW 40/79. For concurrent developments in France (where many of the same conditions prevailed), compare the contribution by Ulrich Herbert, "The German Military Command in Paris and the Deportation of the French Jews" in this volume.

19. On 22 June 1941, the head of the military administrative staff, Privy Counsel (*Staatsrat*) Harald Turner, ordered the arrest of all leading Communists and veterans of the Spanish Civil War. Concurrently, the Jewish community in Belgrade had to provide forty men on a daily basis, who would be shot as hostages in the event of partisan attacks; Bundesarchiv Koblenz (BA-K), 70 Jugoslawien/33, *Anklageschrift gegen den Befehlshaber der Sipo-SD (BdS) Belgrad, Dr. Emanuel Schäfer* (70 Yugoslavia/33, Indictment against the Commander of the Security Police and SD in Belgrade, Dr. Emanuel Schäfer), p. 19.

20. Field mail letters of Lieutenant Peter G., 9th Company/Infantry Regiment 721, 714th Infantry Division, 27 July 1941, 29 July 1941, and 3 August 1941, Bibliothek für Zeitgeschichte Stuttgart, Sammlung Sterz.

21. Chief of the Wehrmacht Supreme Command (OKW) to military commanders in Serbia, 9 August 1941, BA-MA, RW 40/5.

22. Chief of the Higher Command LXV, General Bader, to all companies, 23 August 1941, BA-MA, RW 40/5.

23. Führerweisung Nr. 31a., 16 September 1941, cit. from *Hitlers Weisungen für die Kriegsführung 1939-1945: Dokumente des Oberkommandos der Wehrmacht*, ed. Walter Hubatsch (Munich, 1965), pp. 149f.

24. Teletype message from General Field Marshal List to Wehrmacht Supreme Command (OKW) and Army Supreme Command (OKH), 12 September 1941, NOKW-Dokument 1898.

25. Böhme to all units of the 342nd ID, 25 September 1941, BA-MA, RH 26-342/8.

26. Omer Bartov, *Hitler's Army: Soldiers, Nazis and War in the Third Reich* (New York, 1991), reference is to German edition, *Hitlers Wehrmacht: Soldaten, Fanatismus und die Brutalisierung des Krieges* (Reinbek, 1995) p. 109.

27. Keitel's order of 16 September 1941, BA-MA, RH 26-104/14.

28. Situation report by Turner, NOKW-Dokument 892, 21 September 1941.

29. Telegram from Veesenmayer and Benzler to the Foreign Office, 8 September 1941, PA-AA, Inland IIg.

30. See correspondence between Benzler, Veesenmayer, and the Foreign Office in Berlin (PA-AA, Inland IIg).

31. Luther to Benzler, 16 September 1941, NG-Dokument 3354.

32. Böhme's telephonic order to Quartermaster Section, 4 October 1941, BA-MA, RH 24-18/213.
33. Böhme's order, 10 October 1941, BA-MA, RH 26-104/14.
34. Activity report from the 704th ID, 1 November 1941, BA-MA, RH 26-104/15.
35. Report on the shooting of Jews on 9 and 11 October 1941, BA-MA, RH 24-18/213.
36. Walter Manoschek, *"Serbien ist judenfrei": Militärische Besatzungspolitik und Judenvernichtung in Serbien 1941/42* (Munich, 1995, 2nd edition), pp. 155-158.
37. Ibid., pp. 158-168.
38. Turner's order to all district and field commands, 26 October 1941, NOKW-Dokument 802.
39. Ibid.
40. Compare Gabriele Anderl, Walter Manoschek, *Gescheiterte Flucht: Der jüdische "Kladovo-Transport" auf dem Weg nach Palästina 1939-42* (Vienna, 1993).
41. Rademacher's notes on the results of his official visit to Belgrade, 7 November 1941, PA-AA, Inland IIg.
42. Turner's order to all district and field commands, 26 October 1941, NOKW-Dokument 802.
43. Turner's letter to Hildebrandt, 17 October 1941, NO-Dokument 5810.
44. Author's interview with A.A. on 22 February 1990 (tape recording excerpt).
45. Aktennotiz Sühnemaßnahmen bis 5.12.1941 (file note "atonement measures" until 5 December 1941), BA-MA, RW 40/23.
46. For estimates of the number of victims, compare Manoschek, *"Serbien ist judenfrei,"* p. 166, note 60.
47. Memorandum from Turner, 20 October 1941, NO-Dokument 3404.
48. Comments on the occasion of the visit of the Deputy Supreme Commander to Belgrade, 5 December 1941, NOKW-Dokument 1150.
49. Partial copy of Turner's letter to Wolff, 11 April 1942, ZStL, 503, AR-Z 372/59.
50. Menachem Shelach, "Sajmište: An extermination camp in Serbia," *Holocaust and Genocide Studies* 2 (1987): 243-260.
51. Christopher Browning, *Fateful Months: Essays on the Emergence of the Final Solution* (New York; London, 1985), p. 71.
52. Unless otherwise noted, the reconstruction of the gassing operations is based on proceedings against the BdS Serbia, Emanuel Schäfer (ZStL, AR 1256/61), and against Herbert Andorfer (Landesgericht Wien, 27e, Vr 2260/67), and the judgment against Herbert Andorfer (ZStL, 503 AR 2656/67); in addition, see Manoschek, *"Serbien ist judenfrei,"* pp. 169-184.
53. Witness statement of Edgar Enge, 2 May 1966, Landesgericht Wien, 27e, Vr 2260/67.
54. Witness statement of Karl W., 24 November 1964, ZStL, AR 1256/61.
55. Witness statement of Dr. Walter U., 5 April 1952, ZStL, AR 1256/61.
56. Witness statement of Anton W., 9 August 1962, ZStL, AR 12/62.
57. Investigation of members of "Sonderkommando 1005," ZStL, AR-Z 115/77.
58. 29 August 1942, NOKW-Dokument 1486.
59. Compare Christopher Browning, "Harald Turner und die Militärverwaltung in Serbien 1941-1942," in *Verwaltung contra Menschenführung im Staat Hitlers,* ed. Dieter Rebentisch und Karl Teppe (Göttingen, 1986).

– Chapter 7 –

THE NATIONAL SOCIALIST "SOLUTION OF THE GYPSY QUESTION"[1]

Michael Zimmermann

Gypsies, Roma, Sinti

The members of the group whose persecution under National Socialist rule I want to describe are known as "Gypsies," as "Roma," and in the German-speaking world, as "Sinti and Roma." The concept "Gypsy" is particularly complex. A sociographic concept that equates Gypsies with an itinerant population, and in many countries with a foreign itinerant population, forms one extreme; the other is based on categories such as "ethnicity" (*Ethnie*), "people" (*Volk*), "family" (*Stamm*), or "race" (*Rasse*). This second view itself exists in a more cultural variation that assumes a particular life style and culture—one that differs from that of the majority population—as well as in a biological expression that defines Gypsies as a group united by descent and "blood." Either the cultural or the biological construction can become the basis for a racial concept of "Gypsy." In one case the cultures of non-Gypsies and Gypsies are juxtaposed, the cultural differences are declared unbridgeable and the Gypsy culture intolerable. In the other case,

Gypsies are not only defined as "alien-blooded" (*Fremdblütige*), but also stigmatized as "inferior."

In general, the "Gypsy" concept that uses the categories "ethnicity," "people," "clan," or "race" is both narrower and broader than the one that argues from sociography. It is narrower in that it excludes itinerants who cannot be counted among the Gypsies according to ethnicity, broader in that it includes settled and partially settled individuals who define themselves as Gypsies, Roma, or Sinti in an ethnic or cultural sense. Thus, despite a common aggregate, a more ethnic understanding of the concept gives the group of persons who are classified as "Gypsies" a different composition than does a sociographic definition.

The modern civil rights movements among Gypsies in Europe and the United States have proposed the self-definition "Roma" as a concept inclusive of all Gypsy groups. In the German-speaking world in particular, the combination "Sinti and Roma" has become accepted as a common designation. The Sinti are the largest living Gypsy group residing in the German linguistic area. Their presence there goes back some 600 years. In this same area, Roma is used for Gypsy groups from eastern and southeastern Europe.

"Roma" and "Sinti" were originally self-identifications used as elaborations on, or alternatives to, the term "Gypsy." Identity as Roma or Sinti, determined by inner group cohesion as well as stigmatization from outside, is thus decided in different ways. Familial relationships and the original common language, Romany, play a role, as does the group's own culture, the distance from non-Gypsies, and, for a minority, the itinerant way of life. The civil rights movements and political organizations of Roma and Sinti also point to the common fate of persecution suffered under National Socialism.

The thesis of a continuing and super-historical identity among Gypsies cannot, however, be verified. The self-understanding among those concerned is influenced by varying degrees of alienation and acculturation relative to the respective majority society, as also by the varying structure and strength of a particular culture.[2] Only a few individuals stress an encompassing common political consciousness, for example as a "folk" or "nation."

When the non-Gypsy majority population adopts concepts such as "Roma" or "Sinti" or "Sinti and Roma," they become foreign identifications. Their introduction is in itself attributable to the Roma and Sinti civil rights movements. Compared to the concept "Gypsy," these ascriptions demonstrate a new development. Derived from the Romany language, they signal an evolved self-consciousness, as well as a growing interest among the subjects themselves in how they are seen by non-Gypsies.

In short, the terms "Gypsy," "Roma," or "Sinti," in themselves include a variety of meanings. If the specific National Socialist policy toward Gypsies is to be stressed in contrast to the prior German policy, it is important to analyze the various discourses about "Gypsies" in terms of their origins and influence. Thereby one has to query the continuities and breaks to be found in this discourse.[3]

Hitler and the "Gypsy Question"

Under National Socialist rule, the Gypsies were abandoned to genocide. This genocide at first seems to stand in odd contrast to the fact that the "Gypsy Question" played a totally subordinate role in Hitler's phantasmagorias and political considerations. Characteristic for the dictator's notions about this group are comments during a conversation on 2 October 1941 with Reinhard Heydrich, head of the Reich Security Main Office (Reichssicherheitshauptamt, RSHA). It concerned military service for German Gypsies. Heydrich, who brought up the subject, operated with the racialist terminology of the allegedly "asocial" Gypsy *"Mischlinge"* (persons of mixed race), a concept with central significance for National Socialist Gypsy policy. Hitler limited himself to repeating received clichés. At the outset, he called Gypsies a "plague" on the rural population, then he clothed the stereotype of the Gypsy thief in the guise of an absurd anecdote about thousands of Gypsies from Romania and Hungary who—"schooled" as pickpockets—had "flocked" to Vienna for *Kaiser* Franz Josef's sixtieth jubilee in 1908. Finally he located Gypsy romanticism in the "bars of Budapest" and declared all Hungarians to be Gypsies. After this comment, probably intended to make a point, he changed the subject.[4]

The dictator's scant interest in the "Gypsy Question" has had significant consequences for the writing of history. In particular, those historians who placed Hitler and his antisemitism at the center of their research on National Socialist extermination policies hardly paid attention to the murder of Gypsies, since they had become accustomed to looking *at* the dictator and thus to a certain extent *from* the dictator's perspective. The question why Sinti and Roma were killed in Auschwitz-Birkenau and elsewhere is, however, important precisely in light of the slight importance of these groups in Hitler's personal world-view. This is so, first for the consequences in regard to our picture of the Nazi system and the role of the dictator that follow from the gap between this mass murder and Hitler's slight interest in the "Gypsy Question." Implicitly it also concerns the weight that historians choose to place on all marginalized groups under National Socialist rule.

The Inconsistencies of Assimilation

The dominant policy toward Gypsies in Germany during the nineteenth and early twentieth centuries was based on concepts that went back to the period of late absolutism, which reached a high point of development at the Viennese Court. Expressed in a 1783 decree of Josef II, this concept forbade Gypsies—who could no longer, as outlaws (*Vogelfreie*), be murdered without consequences—from moving, changing their names, or living in the woods. They would practice agriculture and live in houses. Use of the Gypsies' language, Romany, was punishable with beatings. Gypsies were not to marry one another nor live together out of wedlock; their children would be taken from them and given to non-Gypsies. This coercive view, which aimed at permanent settlement of the Gypsies and their adaptation to peasant society, had only a limited effect given inadequate state enforcement powers and the isolated lifestyle sought by the Roma at whom it was aimed. Several states in the later small-German empire adopted this view, but they lacked adequate enforcement mechanisms.

The arguments with which men of the Enlightenment such as Heinrich Grellmann[5] legitimized Habsburg Gypsy policies influenced the discourse on "the Gypsies" for a long while. In 1783, Grellmann's "Historical Essay on the Gypsies" argued that education and a settled existence could transform them into "useful citizens." Grellmann wavered on the question whether one must first make this "people" (*Volk*), which has "wandered about aimlessly in the wilderness for centuries," into humans or whether Gypsies were already humans. But he did concede that one must take into consideration the "circumstances" under which they had previously lived, in addition to their origins and the "related manner of thought," which he tried to document with an amalgam of common anti-Gypsy clichés. If "the roots of degradation" were still too deep among the first generation of pupils, the effort would "be repaid by the second or third generation." By that point, at the latest, one would notice "how little profit" would come from "throw[ing] the Gypsies away as dross."[6]

During the next 150 years, the demand for settlement and adaptation contained in this concept was, however, able to achieve

a practical political consensus only to the extent that virtually all
communities assumed that they would not be the place where the
Gypsies established themselves. The abstract demand for a settled
existence for Gypsies was from this viewpoint quintessentially a
policy of expulsion. Nevertheless, the majority of Gypsies carried
on their occupations in the late nineteenth and twentieth centuries
from permanent, often urban quarters.[7]

The police held the monopoly on Gypsy policy. They declared
those affected—in Germany a group of perhaps 20,000 persons, or
not quite 0.03 percent of its population in 1910—to be a "plague,"
which was to be "combatted." Police practice was influenced by a
sociographic definition of "Gypsies and persons moving about in
the manner of Gypsies." Viewed as such were those who in fact or
according to police suspicion were on the road at least part of the
year in a family group—almost always within a very small geographic area. The "combat against Gypsies" (*Zigeunerbekämpfung*),
the discriminatory character of which is obvious, nonetheless
remained without apparent effect, since the various authorities
aimed only to keep the Gypsies out of their own domain. Thus they
got in one another's way in their "combat against the Gypsy plague."

After 1933, the police and the ministerial bureaucrats of the
Reich and the *Länder* (states) at first remained wedded to this model
of Gypsy policy, which alternated between the goals of "expulsion"
and "settlement" (*Seßhaftmachung*). Nonetheless, discrimination
against and oppression of Gypsies in the first years of National
Socialist rule were not simply a continuation of policy. In the *Länder*, laws and regulations were in many instances made more severe.
Benefits were considerably reduced. A number of communities created centralized camps for Gypsies, which distinguished themselves
from previous Gypsy camp sites by their strict supervision.

Enlightenment and Racial Hygiene

The discourse about Gypsies which developed under late absolutism had ultimately viewed its objects as deficient beings, whose
ostensible backwardness was connected not merely with the "character of their origins." It was also social in nature, and to this
extent could be affected by social policies. Modern racism, on the
other hand, asserted Gypsies' fundamental and constant "inferiority," which was attributed to an unalterable "genetic fate." This
was the view of the neurologist and psychiatrist Robert Ritter,
whose Research Institute for Racial Hygiene (*Rassenhygienische*

Forschungsstelle, RHF) greatly influenced National Socialist Gypsy policy. Ritter denied the Gypsies any individuality and declared them to be "typical primitives," who were "without history" and "culturally impoverished."[8]

Although this view was based on common clichés about Gypsies, it nonetheless marked a significant conceptual change. For despite the influence that biological racial thought had already gained over the view of Gypsies, until the first third of the twentieth century their inclusion in bourgeois society, their schooling and cultural adaptation was not basically contested. Racial hygienists such as Ritter now recommended making "primitives" sterile and thus biologically "harmless" (*unschädlich*). If, in 1783, Heinrich Grellmann emphasized the need, aside from their "origins," to give the Gypsies credit for the "circumstances" in which they had been living, Ritter declared that their "unique racial character" (*rassische Eigenart*) "could not be changed by environmental influences."[9] While Grellmann wanted to fit the Gypsies into bourgeois society, Ritter wanted to "hinder" their "further rise."[10] The possibility for change, which presupposed the concept developed in late absolutism of a distinction between the simple life of a Gypsy and the influences of society, was no longer a concern for modern racism.

The juxtaposition between Grellmann and Ritter, between Enlightenment and racial hygiene, was nonetheless rooted in a common perspective. The "Solution to the Gypsy Question" would consist of the dissolution of the Gypsies as a societal group. Ritter referred to exactly this goal in 1938, when he declared that previous attempts by police and social policy "to solve" the "Gypsy Problem" had failed. In "recognition of their unique racial character," "new paths must be taken."[11]

Ritter's notions were characteristic for the racial paradigms that became official state policy in National Socialist Germany. Thus, already in 1933, Gypsies were sterilized after passage of the "Law to Prevent Genetically Deficient Offspring." They were also covered under the Law for the "Protection of Blood," the ban on marriage between "Aryans" and "members of alien [*artfremden*] races," and also under the "Marital Health Law," also passed in 1935, which denied marriage to allegedly "inferior" individuals. In the scientific world, Ritter, whose research institute within the Hereditary Medicine section of the Reich Health Office was founded in 1936, was not alone in making Gypsies the object of racial hygiene research. Similar if less ambitious efforts were planned or realized at the universities in Giessen, Münster, Berlin, Frankfurt am Main, Munich, Vienna, and Königsberg.

Ritter's Institute for Racial Hygiene began its actual research on Gypsies in the spring of 1937. "Provisional working groups" of "experts [who were] linguistically qualified as well as having special genealogical and racial biological training"—so they described themselves—looked for Gypsies "in camp sites, as well as in traveling wagons, hospitals, prisons, and concentration camps" and interviewed them "unrelentingly."[12] With help of on-site "research results" and evaluation of the extensive police files, as well as genealogical material from archives, parish records, and municipal offices in the Research Institute's Gypsy Clan Archive (*Zigeunersippenarchiv*), so-called hereditary charts (*Erbtafe*) were created. They in turn were evaluated for certificates for "Gypsies" and "Gypsy *Mischlinge*" which, for a consideration, were made available to the Reich Criminal Police Office. In this way a scientific-police complex grew out of the Criminal Police and the Racial Hygiene Research Institute. Thereafter, despite competing institutional interests they exercised the decisive influence on the concept and practice of National Socialist Gypsy policy.

Like other researchers in this area of racial hygiene, Ritter directed his main attack against "Gypsy *Mischlinge*," in which category he included over 90 percent of "persons counted as Gypsies," and whom he stigmatized as a "riff-raft without form or character."[13] Ritter's suggestions for the "Solution of the Gypsy Question" culminated in the notion, which he set forth in numerous scientific articles,[14] of dispersing the Gypsies among various types of camps. For the small group of "ethnically pure wandering Gypsies" (*stammechte Wanderzigeuner*), he proposed limited and police-supervised freedom of movement, and winter internment in non-enclosed camps. For "Gypsy *Mischlinge*," however, he wanted sex-segregated "security detention" (*Sicherheitsverwahrung*). "*Mischling*" married couples would be allowed to live together only after prior sterilization, and then only if a Reich Gypsy Office, which was to be created, had granted permission. This was meant to accomplish the "disappearance" of the group that Ritter had stigmatized as an "asocial *Mischling* population."[15]

This extreme aversion to alleged "*Mischlinge*," to "miscegenation" (*Vermischung*) and "blending" (*Verfließen*) altogether, bespeaks the disposition of the *Freikorps* soldiers and early National Socialists as described by Klaus Theweleit, for whom the "the forbidding of any miscegenation" was at the center of psychosocial defenses, as well as the general hostility toward "miscegenation" that Albert Memmi has characterized as the fundamental characteristic of modern racism.[16] This cultural code should not be neglected, because

unconscious obsessions underlay the *völkisch* racism that determined the actions of such central institutions of the Nazi system as
the Reich Security Main Office.[17]

Racism and the "Prevention of Crime"

Racial hygiene-based research on Gypsies fit into the conception of
police intervention in society that was developed during the latter
1930s by the Reich Criminal Police Department (*Reichskrimi-
nalpolizeiamt*, RKPA), the supreme authority within the criminal
police.[18] Following similar comments by Himmler and Heydrich,
RKPA chief Arthur Nebe understood the police to be a "defense
corps [*Schutzkorps*], which is responsible for protecting society
domestically" as well as for "preserving and protecting" the "life
and development of the *Volk* from every disturbance and destruction." This assignment, which was simultaneously threatening,
tautological and expansive, was directed not just against "elements
hostile to the state," but also against those identified by the police as
"asocial," from whom the state also required "constant protection."
    Nebe further declared that police responsibilities included not
just "the elimination of criminals" but also "preserving the purity
of the German race." Because National Socialism put "the community in the place of the individual," for the RKPA the "preventive weapon to forestall damage to the individual member of the
Volk or the national wealth" was of equal importance to the investigation of crimes.[19] In accordance with this goal of the police state,
in late 1937 the RKPA designated as a "Fundamental Decree" its
first order for the "preventive combating of crime."[20] It attributed
crime to behavior "injurious to the community" by particular segments of society. This behavior was itself explained by genetic factors specific to certain groups.[21]
    Preventive detention (*Vorbeugungshaft*) functioned as the pri-
mary tool of "the preventive combating of crime," behind which
stood the biological motivation of a utopian "German *Volk* community" without crime and criminals. It was modeled on protective
detention (*Schutzhaft*) and similarly could not be nullified by the
courts. Preventive detention was to be ordered for persons identified by the criminal police as "professional criminals," "habitual
criminals," "common threats" (*Gemeingefährliche*), or "common
pests" (*Gemeinschädliche*). From among these highly elastic terms,
"professional" and "habitual criminals" were linked with the criterion of three valid prior convictions, and "common threat" with

the concept of "serious crime," but for "common pests" the criteria were totally arbitrary. It included those who showed themselves unwilling to "fit into the community."[22]

As a result of the social-biological "preventive combating of crime," beginning in 1938, in addition to other prisoners, more than 2,000 German and Austrian Gypsies who were stigmatized as "asocial" were incarcerated in the concentration camps at Buchenwald, Dachau, Mauthausen, Ravensbrück, and Sachsenhausen. Following Germany's occupation of the Czech lands, Poland, Alsace-Lorraine, and the Netherlands, the provisions of the "preventive combating of crime" were in modified form also imposed in these territories.

According to existing directions for the assignment of Gypsies to concentration camps, self-employment instead of working for wages was sufficient proof of "asociality." "As a Gypsy, [he] has never had regular employment," was the comment in a Cologne ruling, "since leaving school carried on as horse trader."[23] Artists and musicians were particularly endangered. Even the removal of their permit for itinerant work, which destroyed the basis for their professional existence, was used as proof of their "asociality." Thus in Magdeburg, a thirty-six year old musician, widower, and father of four children, was sent to the Buchenwald concentration camp with the following rationale: "In 1937, in this year the permit for itinerant work was denied him. Since this time he has had no employment. According to the determinations he is to be viewed as a work-shy person. He has not yet been engaged in criminality."[24]

Deportation and Gassing

In addition to the "preventive combating of crime," a decree entitled "On Combating the Gypsy Plague," a "regulation of the Gypsy Question based on the nature of this race," was formulated by the RKPA in consultation with Ritter, and signed by Himmler in late 1938.[25] For the criminal police leadership, this marked the definitive transition from a Gypsy policy that was understood as a component of the extirpation of "aliens to the community" (*Gemeinschaftsfremden*) to a persecution *sui generis*. In local police practice, the discourse of race and biology now totally replaced the prior sociographic view of Gypsies, which had placed the migrant lifestyle at the center and was directed against "Gypsies" as "persons who traveled about like Gypsies."

After the outbreak of war, this Gypsy policy was once again greatly intensified. In accord with the goal of a global expulsion of

Jews and Poles motivated by "the politics of the *Volk*," the criminal police thereafter favored the "out-settlement" of Gypsies away from the German Reich. Already in October 1939, the Reich Security Main Office, to which the RKPA belonged as Office V, ordered that "Gypsies who were later apprehended" were to be accommodated "in special group camps until their *final (endgültigen)* deportation."[26] After a failed attempt to deport at least the Berlin Gypsies to occupied Poland, in May 1940, 2,330 Gypsies—and by that fall some 500 more—were sent to the General Government.

The immediate impetus for the early decision to deport came from the Wehrmacht High Command. As a result of the imminent attack on France and the traditional clichés about "Gypsy spies," High Command suggested that the victims come from the western Reich regions. Most of the deportees were concentrated into unpaid forced labor columns in the General Government. Some survived as musicians or artists. Still others sought to return illegally to Germany. Estimates of the death rate among Sinti and Roma deported during 1940 are only available for Hamburg, according to which 80 percent of the deportees died.

Further deportations of Gypsies, which were planned for 1940, failed because of the contradictions and assumptions which also characterized National Socialist policy toward Jews after the outbreak of war. The deportation intentions of the Nazi leadership and RSHA were expressed in ever more short- and intermediate-term plans, according to which increasing numbers of Jews and Gypsies were to be crowded together in German-occupied or -annexed Poland. This effort, however, was delayed by resistance within the occupation administrations, whose own goal was removal of these groups, and their forced presence was seen as a temporary, but in the long-run "untenable situation."

When, in the fall of 1941, the systematic deportation of German Jews began, Gypsies, and especially Roma from Austrian Burgenland, were again affected as well. The ground for persecution of this particular Gypsy group, which had as its backdrop the interwar economic and political crises in the area, was prepared by Dr. Tobias Portschy, who in March 1938 was made Gauleiter of the NSDAP and *Landeshauptmann* for Burgenland. In this region, where Roma had already lived a settled existence under Maria Theresa and Josef II, Portschy gave the "Gypsy Question" priority over the "Jewish Question."[27]

In his memorandum "The Gypsy Question,"[28] Portschy declared that the Roma were "professional thieves," "do-nothings, work-shy, loiterers, and criminals," as well as "train-bearers" (*Schlepperträger* [*sic!*]) of the earlier Social Democratic and Bolshevist systems," who would "devour the industrious and plagued border Germans." Their numbers, according to Portschy's frightening vision, would grow within fifty years from 8,000 to at least 60,000 persons. Gypsy children, exposed to parents and older siblings living in "concubinage," would in no time be stimulated to sexual intercourse, thereby creating a separate Gypsy sexual morality, which would have a devastating effect on the German *Volk* because it would lead to prostitution and blackmailing of "wealthy German race-defilers." To this extent—this was the quintessential aspect of this memorandum, which was shot through with repressed sexual fantasies and anxiety regarding racial mixing—the Gypsies were a huge "danger" "to the preservation of pure German blood in the borderlands."

"Good and bad, Germans and Gypsies" were "not to be reconciled with one another." As a "National Socialist solution of the Gypsy Question," Portschy suggested sterilization, forced labor in work camps, subsequent deportation to eventual German colonies, and bans on elementary school education, military service, and hospital care. He would punish sexual intercourse between Gypsies and those with "German blood" as "race defilement" (*Rassenschande*).

The extraordinarily fervent local and regional witch-hunt against the Burgenland Roma explains why, after the first Gypsy deportation in May 1940, they, in particular, were made the priority group for a second transport to the General Government. When the RSHA and RKPA saw this possibility in the fall of 1941, 5,000 Burgenland Roma were deported to the Lodz Ghetto and crammed together there in a special sector. Even before the year's end, hundreds had fallen victim to spotted fever. The ghetto administration and the lord mayor of Lodz had predicted crowding, food shortages, and epidemics as a result of the deportations. Shortly after the transports arrived, the housing and food situation became ever more unbearable and epidemics spread. The German officials who predicted the catastrophe had arranged conditions so that it actually occurred. In the end, those confined in Lodz were so malnourished and sick that they appeared to those responsible for the situation as "subhumans", who must somehow be eliminated. The survivors of the epidemics were, like the Jews, suffocated in gas vans in Kulmhof.

Mass Shootings

The boundary between the acceptance of mass death and the systematic extermination of Gypsies had, however, been crossed months earlier, shortly after Germany's attack on the Soviet Union in summer 1941. Along with Jews, Soviet Communist party functionaries, partisans, and other "undesirable elements," Gypsies were among the victims of the SS *Einsatzgruppen*, the mobile killing units that operated behind the German front line. At first they killed Jewish members of the Soviet state and party apparatuses, the Jewish intelligentsia, and all those Jews who were considered potential opposition. Already in the first months of the war against the USSR, the *Einsatzgruppen* made the transition to selecting primarily male Jewish city dwellers of military service age as victims for execution, intended as "retaliation" for real or alleged public opposition.

When, in late July to early August 1941, the Nazi leadership believed that the USSR's collapse was imminent, Himmler and the RSHA radicalized the *Einsatzgruppen*'s list of duties with the order to murder as many as possible of the Jewish population in the occupied Soviet Union.[29] Simultaneously, the murder command was extended to the Gypsies. As a result of the phantasmagoria of "racially inferior," "spying Gypsies," Wehrmacht units also handed Roma over to the *Einsatzgruppen* or shot them themselves.

The statements by which Einsatzgruppen and Wehrmacht units sought to legitimize the shooting of Gypsies—often only after the fact—gave the common anti-Gypsy stereotypes an instrumental connection with the German warfare and occupation policy. In addition to the stigma of asociality, they cited the clichés of notorious thievery, "alien elements," the claim that Gypsies were a burden in every way, and above all, the clichés of espionage and partisan activity.

The Gypsies were turned over by the Wehrmacht to the *Einsatzgruppen* for shooting; they were also denounced by the Russian population, and killed during prison checks and in controls of the civilian population in the area near the front, or as a commando group was deployed to its next posting. The *Einsatzgruppen* themselves did not, however, conduct systematic searches for Gypsies. This is an important difference from the murder of Jews. The Jewish population centers were systematically fenced off and destroyed by *Einsatz-* and *Sonderkommandos* after the late summer of 1941. Similarly large Gypsy settlements did not exist. The Russian Roma lived in family groups, not in social configurations similar to the Jewish communities, which were based on the requirements of the *minyan*, the quorum of ten men for prayer. As a result of the cultural distance from non-Gypsies, Gypsies probably distrusted Germans more than did Jews, who had positive memories of the German military from the

First World War and who could hardly have learned much about National Socialist antisemitism from the Soviet media. With ties to the normal system of political and social regulations, Jews were also more easily deceived by summonses to assemble for "resettlement." The *Einsatzgruppen* would not have considered such a procedure for the Roma, since they could imagine the Gypsies only as a constantly wandering group, which nevertheless did not stop them from occasionally shooting settled Roma.

The *Einsatzgruppen* carried out their killing with an articulated picture of the enemy, at its summit the Jews, who were allegedly linked with Communism through a "Jewish-Bolshevik conspiracy," The Gypsies figured in this imaginary world as "racially inferior" "spies" and "agents" of the imagined "world enemy." As auxiliaries of "Jewish Bolshevism," they became murder victims whenever *Einsatzgruppen* learned of their presence. The murderers saw them merely as tools of the imagined world enemy, not a category of humans whose ferreting out was a priority. However when the mobile killing units lingered in an area, as did *Einsatzgruppe D* in the Crimea, or was augmented by units of the German Order Police, and could count on support from civil occupation authorities, as in the Baltic region, they proceeded to systematically kill Gypsies.

In the General Government, as in the USSR, more Gypsies were shot by German Security Police and Order Police than were killed in concentration camps. The geographic distribution of the murders, their extension over time, and the participation of different German units, especially of the Order Police, make clear that what happened was not a matter of individual excesses, but rather of killings that could affect all Gypsies who moved outside the cities. Based on eyewitness testimony and extensive court investigations, it has often been claimed that the Gypsies were shot in police raids on rural roads or in the woods. Some of these raids were directed against partisans or, if parachutes were found, against Germany's military enemies, or in still other cases against Jews who had fled or gone underground. As in the Soviet Union, police and Wehrmacht obviously considered the Roma to be spies and agents of an enemy which, in the imaginary world of the occupation administration, consisted primarily of Jews, resistance fighters, and Germany's military opponents. In the General Government, Roma were also in danger of being killed when they remained hidden within a village. Both settled and itinerant Gypsies were—often along with Poles, sometimes also with Jews and Soviet prisoners of war—shot in retribution for attacks they had not carried out on trains or gendarmes, Gestapo agents, and Gestapo spies. Such acts were pre-supposed by commands that saw every Gypsy as a potential enemy spy and a person whose life was, in any event, inferior.

In Serbia[30] it was the Wehrmacht command which, in the fall of 1941, took some 1,000 male Gypsies, like Jews, as hostages, and had them shot by special units in retribution for the deaths of German soldiers and German civilians. The rules of retribution policy issued by the commanding general for Serbia in early October 1941 prescribed the shooting of 100 hostages for every German soldier or ethnic German killed and 50 for every wound sustained by these groups. Because the Wehrmacht lacked victims for its retribution executions, *Einsatzgruppen* from the Security Police and the Security Service stationed in Belgrade were asked to provide the requisite number of hostages.

In the summer of 1941, the *Einsatzgruppen* had crammed together Jews from Belgrade and the Banat in a transit camp and a larger group of Jewish refugees in the Sabac concentration camp, where Gypsies were also interned. Thus Roma living in Serbia were, in the following period, included among the victims of the German "atonement" measures. This was in accord with the notion of the Wehrmacht command in Serbia that the arbitrary execution of Serbs would limit the maneuverability of occupation authorities. Because the military command, on the other hand, wanted to maintain the quota of 100 executed hostages for one dead German soldier, and 50 hostages for each one wounded, there were no qualms about killing Jews and Gypsies in the fall of 1941.

These executions did, however, raise a new question. What was to be done with the Jewish women, children, and elderly, as well as with the Gypsy women and children whose men had been shot? In late October 1941, a transitional solution was decided upon: the building of a camp in Semlin, on the banks of the Sava River, opposite Belgrade. The commandant was recruited in early 1942 from the Jewish Office of the local Gestapo. Along with the Jewish prisoners, 292 Roma women and children were confined. The Jews were killed in the spring of 1942 in a gas van brought from Germany. The Roma women and children, on the other hand, were released immediately before these murders began. This decision was probably based on the gradations of the racist world-view, in which Jews figured as Germany's most dangerous enemies.

 Altogether, the differences that became clear between Nazi Gypsy policy in German-occupied eastern and southeastern Europe and within the Reich were ultimately attributable to emphasis on different facets of the Gypsy "enemy image." Outside the Reich,

and above all in eastern Europe, the anti-Gypsy phantasmagoria
was primarily directed against the wandering Gypsy, whose pere-
grinations provided camouflage for spying as an agent of the "Jewish-Bolshevik world enemy," while in Germany the imagined threat
was primarily from "Gypsy *Mischlinge*," who, because partially or
fully settled, had close contact with non-Gypsies and thus allegedly
"penetrated" the "German *Volk* body."

Auschwitz-Birkenau

Through Himmler's order of 16 December 1942, what had been
the disjointed persecution and murder of Gypsies became more
coherent. This order foresaw the deportation of Sinti and Roma "to
a concentration camp." The RSHA, which was responsible for carrying out Himmler's order, chose the recently developed Auschwitz-
Birkenau. The deportation involved Gypsies from Germany,
Austria, Bohemia, and Moravia, from the Netherlands, Belgium,
and northern France. There were no deportation orders for French
Gypsies from outside the Nord and Pas-de-Calais departments,
which were under the control of the German Military Command in
Belgium. After 1940 numerous French Gypsies were interned in
camps under the authority of the German military administration,
on whose initiative they were created. Nor were there deportation
orders for Polish, Soviet, or Baltic Gypsies. Insofar as they survived
until 1943/44, they were still in danger of being hauled off to
Auschwitz-Birkenau.

Himmler's deportation order was the result of long discussions
during the fall of 1942 about the further development of Gypsy
policy. Participants, in addition to the SS Führer himself, included
the RKPA, the RHF, the Party Chancellery, the Race and Settlement
Main Office of the SS, and the SS Office for "Ancestral Inheritance"
(*Ahnenerbe*), which here for the first time, on Himmler's order,
intervened in Gypsy policy. This new competitor was viewed with
mistrust by the RKPA and the Research Institute for Racial
Hygiene, which attempted to outdo it with their own extremely
radical proposals.

Beginning with the question of proper behavior toward the
small group of Gypsies whom "Ancestral Inheritance" had classified
as "racially pure" and thus, because of their origins in India,
"Aryan," the discussion soon included what was to be done with
the remaining "Gypsy-like persons." Himmler's order of 16 December 1942 answered this question in the sense of a suggestion made

to him by the RKPA: have them deported. The small group of itinerant Gypsies who were declared "racially pure" and the "good Mischlinge in Gypsy terms" (*im zigeunerischen Sinne guten Mischlinge*) were to be exempted from concentration camp internment. The same was true of a few "Gypsy *Mischlinge*" who were deemed "socially adjusted," for whom forced sterilization was prescribed. Himmler also informed Hitler about the gist of this decision. There is no evidence of the dictator's intervention, not to mention initiative, after this point. What counted was only that Hitler had no objections to this Gypsy policy which he had not himself conceived.

The actual deportations, which began in the spring of 1943 and continued into the summer of 1944, did not entirely adhere to the text of the orders. In the German Reich, the criminal police and communal officials often used the latitude of these instructions to make the communities fully or largely "free of Gypsies." While the deportations of Jews reflected their depersonalization and social isolation, the continuing presence of the Sinti and Roma, which since the outbreak of war had resulted from a ban on free travel directed specifically against the Gypsies, led on the contrary to an increase in resentment among the population. This in turn often radicalized the attitude of local administrations and led to demands for the most complete deportation possible of local Sinti and Roma. Because the Gypsies were a small minority and were not initially stigmatized in 1933, they mostly found neither helpers nor allies. Considerably fewer voices were raised against their deportation than against that of the Jews.

In foreign lands under German occupation, without genealogical research it was impossible to distinguish between allegedly "racially pure" and "*Mischling* Gypsies." Here selections were based on a combination of racially influenced improvisation and various notions regarding "Gypsies" based on current national policy or legislation.

The deportation of Gypsies to Auschwitz-Birkenau, as to Lodz in 1941, would not have been possible without the active participation of communal administrations and police. Already during the Wilhelminian Empire and Weimar Republic, they had turned their attention to pushing those stigmatized as "Gypsies" from city or village and thus hindering as far as possible any permanent settled existence. When, after 1933, the political framework had fundamentally changed, it was no great distance to the demand for more consistent persecution measures. In fact it was now not only the criminal police leadership, but also mayors, welfare offices, health offices, police presidents, district presidents (*Landräte*), and governors (*Regierungspräsidenten*), who demanded concentration camp internment or permanent expulsion in order to definitively "solve" the "Gypsy Problem."

The deportations to Auschwitz-Birkenau, which were drawn out over more than a year, found widespread approval among police and administration officials as a radical continuation of the prior Gypsy policy. At the same time, the deportations were glossed over as the final maintenance of this policy. For example, police reports called the deportations not only "resettlements," "evacuations," and "deliveries"; characteristically they were also designated with the terms "removal" (*Abschiebung*) or "transport," which had long been accepted for police escorts of itinerants from place to place.[31]

There were, however, several indications that such euphemisms were not able to silence consciences totally. Among some members of the German police there were above all signs of shrinking back when small children were to be sent to Auschwitz by "separate transport" (*Einzeltransport*). In the end, these children, too, were nonetheless deported. On the whole, the wish to make one's own area "free of Gypsies," the police principles of command and obedience, and the bureaucratic chain of command, as well as the division of jurisdictions among various institutions and persons, which was both psychologically exculpating and practically constraining, all worked together so that opposition to the removal of Sinti and Roma remained minimal.

The criminal police were aware of the family structure of the Gypsies, for whose persecution they had primary responsibility. For this reason, as early as 1940 they had ordered the deportation of Gypsies to the General Government "in clan units."[32] Namely, when no consideration was given to the close family ties, the police experienced organizational difficulties that were recorded as negative. Thus in 1943 the Reich Criminal Police arranged to deport Gypsies to Auschwitz-Birkenau in families. In Birkenau, the Roma and Sinti were crowded together in an actual family camp, while otherwise, except for Jews deported from Theresienstadt, men and women were housed in separate camp sections.

National Socialist Gypsy policy categorized the Gypsies in three groups according to a racial hierarchy, of which only the first— "racially pure" and "good *Mischlinge* in a Gypsy sense"—was to have a future; the second group of "socially adjusted Gypsy *Mischlinge*" would be subjected to forced sterilization. Those deported to Auschwitz-Birkenau were regarded as the third group—

"inferior" in the eyes of police and racial hygienists to the ones who would be sterilized.[33]

This logic conformed to the intent of the persecuting authorities that the Gypsies confined in Birkenau would never leave the camp world. This was a death sentence—although one that was not proclaimed as such and which thus allowed those responsible to suggest that they were not accountable for the Gypsies' predictable deaths, because in Auschwitz the camp commandant was, after all, responsible. This silence about the foreseeable destruction permitted the rationalization of murder as concentration camp internment, as had in any case been intended for allegedly "asocial" Gypsies since 1938. To further quiet consciences they could persuade themselves they were even doing the Gypsies an additional favor by deporting them to Auschwitz-Birkenau in family groups.

In order to make space for the hundreds of thousands of Jews from Hungary and other countries whom the SS deported to Auschwitz-Birkenau beginning in the spring of 1944, not all of whom were immediately murdered, the Birkenau Gypsy camp was liquidated that summer. The 2,900 Sinti and Roma living there were gassed.

Altogether more than 19,300 of the roughly 22,600 individuals crowded together in the Auschwitz-Birkenau Gypsy camp were killed; more than 5,600 were gassed, more than 13,600 succumbed to hunger, illnesses, epidemics. But far from all of the 3,100 remaining survived the end of Nazi Germany. In the months before dispersal of the Birkenau Gypsy camp to other camps and satellite camps, many of them died while doing forced labor, especially at the Dora Mittelbau camp in Thuringia or in sterilization experiments at Ravensbrück. Others died on death marches during the last weeks of the war, or in the Bergen-Belsen concentration camp where, along with tens of thousands of other prisoners, Sinti and Roma were deported shortly before the war's end, or in the Dirlewanger unit, where German Gypsies who had survived the camps were forced, in the last weeks of war, to fight on the front line against the Red Army.

Parallel to the murders in Auschwitz-Birkenau and in German-occupied areas of eastern and southeastern Europe, the forced sterilization of Gypsies in Germany—the second part of the extermination policy and already being practiced—now became more systematic. Forced sterilization was a catastrophe of hardly describable dimensions for those affected. Their lives thereafter were tormented by illnesses and memories rooted in their traumatic experiences. In the traditional culture of the Sinti and Roma, a large number of children was considered the measure of happiness and respect. Thus those who were forcibly sterilized often felt like "trees that bore no fruit" or "living corpses."[34] The number of Sinti and Roma in the German Reich, inclusive of Austria, who were forcibly sterilized before 1943/44 is estimated at 500, the number following the Auschwitz Decree of 29 January 1943 is estimated at more than 2,000.[35]

The Preconditions for Genocide

The concept on which the murder and forced sterilization of Gypsies was based—not in the sense of a sole cause, rather in the sense of a necessary precondition—was not a product specific to the Nazi system. The social-biological racism that lay at the center of the murder found a certain agreement in Germany, as in many other European countries and the U.S., even before 1933, and not only on the *völkisch* right. In the Nazi system, however, these views were transformed into directions for political action, which governed such central institutions as the Reich Security Main Office. After the fall of 1939, the RSHA was the decision-making center for Gypsy policy inside Germany and beyond. The *Einsatzgruppen* in the German-occupied territories belonged to it, as did the RKPA, which conceived, coordinated, and implemented the persecution in the German Reich, in Austria, in the occupied Czech lands and also in extensive parts of German-occupied western Europe, and influenced the murder of Gypsies in eastern Europe.

The *völkisch* mentality employed a discourse that transferred measures traditionally taken to prevent from imaginary danger not only against Jews, but also against such groups as Gypsies to a racialist conception of society, which then after 1933 formed a central motivating force for National Socialist policy. The enemy image of this *völkisch* racism had variations in accent and balance. The Gypsies were stigmatized as both an "alien race" and at the same time as "alien to the community" in racial hygiene terms. According to National Socialist conceptions they seemed ready to "destroy" the "*Volk* community" from below. But the central threat was imagined to be "Jewry" (*Judentum*). Jews had been declared the "anti-race" (*Gegenrasse*): they were considered to be disproportionately represented within the intelligentsia and upper classes; for biological and historical reasons, they were said to possess inherited characteristics that were particularly "subversive" (*zersetzend*); moreover they were believed to have already made deep inroads into the "German *Volk* body."

This racism was not limited to antisemitism. Its pre-eminent importance to the policy to exterminate Gypsies also has consequences for the historiographic controversies between "intention-alists" and "structuralists" regarding the causes of National Social-ist genocide.[36] "Intentionalists" postulated as its determining cause an antisemitic murder program, which was inherent in Hitler's world-view. The existence of such an a priori fixed program is not provable toward the Jews, and likewise not for "euthanasia" of the disabled or toward the Gypsies—groups whom the "intentional-ists" do not really consider when they link genocide exclusively to antisemitism. "Intentionalists" do, however, have a particular need to clarify why Gypsies, who were so marginal to Hitler's world-view, were killed.

The "structuralist" proposition of the "cumulative radicaliza-tion"[37] of National Socialist persecution and extermination may come closer to understanding the dynamic of genocide. This propo-sition emphasizes the war, the competitive forces in the system of rule, and the political contradictions introduced by the Nazi system itself. In addition, it stresses explanatory factors that are not inten-tional in the most precise sense, such as careerism, obedience and faith in authority, group loyalties, economic interests, or the psy-chic denial of murder. But the extreme definition of "structuralism" is in danger of concealing the motive forces behind extermination by means of a problematic mechanical metaphor. "Once fully in motion, the extermination of those unable to work proceeded on its own dynamic. The bureaucratic machinery built by Eichmann and Heydrich functioned automatically."[38] Further, "structuralists" share with "intentionalists" the view that the heart of the National Socialist *"Weltanschauung"* was Hitler's "seemingly downright paranoid" and "fanatical pronouncements of racial antisemitism,"[39] resulting in their neglect of the murder of Gypsies.

From the perspective of this genocide, both Hitler's centrality in the "intentionalist" scheme and the insufficient consideration of murderous intent in the "structuralist" approach appear problem-atic. The limitations of these approaches may perhaps be overcome if one takes account of those reflections that view modern racism as a central motive behind the extermination policy, loosening inhibi-tions precisely because of its alleged scientific basis, with the RSHA as its most powerful instrument. For Gypsy policy, in particular, the RKPA, as Office V of the RSHA, and the RHF formed the institu-tional complex that above all translated racial theory into the prac-tice of persecution. This attempt at interpretation, which can be characterized as "conceptualist," emphasizes the intentions and institutions of mass extermination, without, like "intentionalism," placing all one's bets on the person of Hitler.

Beyond the existence of the institutional complex of RKPA and RHF, attention must be paid to the collapse of moral objections against the destruction of human beings, which characterized in particular the power aggregate of the SS leadership and the RSHA after the outbreak of war and, above all, after the attack on the Soviet Union. One must also consider the dynamics of National Socialist murder policy, which was not only polycratic but in some sense polycentric, for example in the cases of Serbian Gypsies and, in a particularly terrible manner, the Burgenland Roma. Contingent factors also influenced the murder of Gypsies, for example, Himmler's interest in Gypsy research, awakened in 1942; the construction of the Birkenau camp in late 1942/early 1943; and the deportation of Hungarian Jews beginning in the spring of 1944. Finally, one cannot ignore the competitive struggle sparked by the hostility of the RKPA and RHF to the SS "Ancestral Heritage" Office, whose entrance into Gypsy research and policy was fostered by Himmler. The "structuralist" view may add a more dynamic quality to the proposed "conceptualist" interpretation, by including in the interpretation of genocide the role of factors that are not in the narrow sense ideological.

In conclusion, it remains accurate to say that racially motivated genocide formed the essence of National Socialist Gypsy policy, when compared to the prior German variety. At the same time, the Nazi system was linked with the problematic of the traditional "combat against Gypsies," which found itself caught in a paradoxical conflict of goals: wanting to expel the Gypsies, but also make them lead a settled existence. No place could be found which simultaneously corresponded to both aims; the National Socialist synthesis led to murder. The only condition where expulsion and a settled existence were permanently united was death.

Notes

1. This article emphasizes newer research. For a more inclusive treatment, see Michael Zimmermann, *Rassenutopie und Genozid. Die nationalsozialistische "Lösung der Zigeunerfrage"* (Hamburg, 1996).
2. For an overview of the culture and history of the Gypsies, see Angus Fraser, *The Gypsies* (Oxford and Cambridge, MA, 1995); Katrin Reemtsma, *Sinti und Roma. Geschichte. Kultur. Gegenwart* (Munich, 1996).
3. My interpretation of the concepts "Gypsy," "Sinti," and "Roma" was greatly influenced by discussions with Leo Lucassen (University of Amsterdam) and Wim Willems (Centrum voor de Geschiedenis van Migranten, Amsterdam). See Lucassen, "'Zigeuner' in Deutschland 1870-1945. Ein kritischer historiographischer Ansatz," in *1999. Zeitschrift für Sozialgeschichte des 20. und 21. Jahrhunderts* 10, no. 1 (1995): 87-100; Willems, *In Search of the True Gypsy: From Enlightenment to "Final Solution"* (London, 1997) (orig. in Dutch, *Op zook naar de ware zigeuner. Zigeuners als studieobject tijdens de Verlichting de Romantiek en het Nazisme* [Utrecht, 1995]); Jacqueline Giere (ed.), *Die gesellschaftliche Konstruktion des Zigeuners. Zur Genese eines Vorurteils* (Frankfurt a.M. and New York, 1996); Wulf D. Hund (ed.), *Zigeuner. Geschichte und Struktur einer rassistischen Konstruktion* (Duisburg, 1996). See the recent English-language study, Lucassen, Willems, and Annemarie Cottaar, *Gypsies and Other Itinerant Groups: A Socio-Historical Approach* (New York, 1998).
4. Institut für Zeitgeschichte, FA 514, Dr. Koeppen über Hitlers Tischgespräche, Bl. 33ff. Bericht Nr. 39, Führerhauptquartier, 3.10.1941 (Abendessen 2.10).
5. On Grellmann, see Willems, *In Search of the True Gypsy*, pp. 22-92.
6. Heinrich M. G. Grellmann, *Die Zigeuner. Ein historischer Versuch über die Lebensart und Verfassung, Sitten und Schicksale dieses Volkes in Europa nebst ihrem Ursprunge* (Dessau and Leipzig, 1783), pp. 140, 10, 139, 6.
7. On the connections between these policies and poor relief and the professionalization of the police, see Leo Lucassen, *Zigeuner. Die Geschichte eines polizeilichen Ordnungsbegriffs in Deutschland 1700-1945* (Cologne, 1996); other valuable studies on pre-1933 Gypsy policies are Thomas Fricke, *Zwischen Erziehung und Ausgrenzung. Zur württembergischen Geschichte der Sinti und Roma im 19. Jahrhundert* (Frankfurt a.M., 1991) and *Zigeuner im Zeitalter des Absolutismus. Bilanz einer einseitigen Überlieferung* (Pfaffenweiler, 1996); Ulrich F. Opfermann, *"Daß sie den Zigeuner Habit ablegen." Die Geschichte der "Zigeuner-Kolonien" zwischen Wittgenstein und Westerwald* (Frankfurt a.M., 1996); Evi Strauss, "Die Zigeunerverfolgung in Bayern 1885-1926," in *Gießener Hefte für Tsiganologie* 3, nos. 1-4 (1986): 31-108, and "Die Diskriminierung von Sinti und Roma in Bayern vom Ende des 19. Jahrhunderts bis Anfang der 20er Jahre," in Ludwig Eiber, *"Ich wußte, es wird schlimm." Die Verfolgung der Sinti und Roma in München 1933-1945* (Munich, 1993), pp. 13-20.
8. Robert Ritter, "Die Asozialen, ihre Vorfahren und ihre Nachkommen," in *Fortschritte der Erbpathologie. Rassenhygiene und ihrer Grenzgebiete* 5, no. 2 (1941): 152, 137-155, and "Primitivität und Kriminalität," *Monatsschrift für Kriminalbiologie und Strafrechtsreform* 31 (1940): 204, 198-210. On Ritter, see Willems, *In Search of the True Gypsy*, pp. 197-283.
9. Ritter, "Primitivität und Kriminalität," p. 205.
10. Ibid., p. 210.

11. Ibid., p. 200, and Ritter, "Zur Frage der Rassenbiologie und Rassenpsychologie der Zigeuner in Deutschland," in *Reichsgesundheitsblatt* (1938): 425f.

12. Hans Reiter, *Das Reichsgesundheitsamt. Sechs Jahre nationalsozialistischer Führung* (Berlin, 1939), p. 357; Robert Ritter, "Die Bestandsaufnahme der Zigeuner und Zigeunermischlinge in Deutschland," in *Der Öffentliche Gesundheitsdienst* 6, no. 21 (1941): 480f., 477-489.

13. Robert Ritter, "Die Zigeunerfrage und das Zigeunerbastardproblem," in *Fortschritte der Erbpathologie. Rassenhygiene und ihrer Grenzgebiete* 3, no. 1 (1939): 15, 2-20; *Bestandsaufnahme*, p. 481.

14. Ritter, *Zigeunerfrage*, p. 18; also *Primitivität und Kriminalität*, p. 210; "Zigeuner und Landfahrer," in *Der nichtseßhafte Mensch* (1938), pp. 71-88, here 87.

15. Eva Justin, manuscript on "Zigeunerforschung," printed in Joachim S. Hohmann, *Robert Ritter und die Erben der Kriminalbiologie. "Zigeunerforschung" im Nationalsozialismus und in Westdeutschland im Zeichen des Rassismus* (Frankfurt a.M., 1991), pp. 469-500, esp. 482-484.

16. Klaus Theweleit, *Male Fantasies* (2 vols.; Minneapolis, 1989), pp. 73-77 (orig. in German, *Männerphantasien* (2 vols.; Reinbek, 1980); Albert Memmi, *Rassismus* (Frankfurt a.M., 1987), pp. 73f.; Pierre-André Taguieff, "Die Metamorphosen des Rassismus und die Krise des Antirassismus," in *Das Eigene und das Fremde. Neuer Rassismus in der Alten Welt?*, ed. Uli Bielefeld (Hamburg, 1991), pp. 221-268.

17. The relationship between history and psychoanalysis requires a new discussion. The volume *Geschichte und Psychoanalyse* (Cologne, 1971), edited and with an introduction by Hans-Ulrich Wehler, no longer represents the state of international discussion. In particular, psychoanalysis is now being discussed not just in terms of its function for the individual, but for its insights into the psychology of societies and thus its applicability to historical methodology, as is also the importance of ethno-psychoanalysis for the investigation of European societies and the relationship between discourse analysis and psychoanalysis.

18. On the criminal police, see the basic study by Patrick Wagner, *Volksgemeinschaft ohne Verbrechen. Konzeptionen und Praxis der Kriminalpolizei in der Zeit der Weimarer Republik und des Nationalsozialismus* (Hamburg, 1996), esp. pp. 254-298.

19. Arthur Nebe, "Aufbau der deutschen Kriminalpolizei," in *Kriminalistik* 12 (1938): 4-8, here 4f.

20. Bundesarchiv Koblenz, Erlaßsammlung "Vorbeugende Verbrechensbekämpfung" (following in BAK, VV), "Grundlegender Erlaß über die Vorbeugende Verbrechensbekämpfung durch die Polizei," Pol. S-Kr. 3 Nr. 1682/37-2098— v. 14.12.37; Ausführungsbestimmungen BAK, VV, RKPA, Tgb. Nr. RKPA 60.01 250/38, Richtlinien des RKPA über die Durchführung der vorbeugenden Verbrechensbekämpfung, 4.4.1938.

21. Nebe, *Kriminalpolizei*, p. 4; Paul Werner, "Vorbeugende Verbrechensbekämpfung durch die Polizei," in *Kriminalistik* 12 (1938): 60, 58-61.

22. "Grundlegender Erlaß über die vorbeugende Verbrechensbekämpfung," A II 1 d and e, B III 3; Werner, *Vorbeugende Verbrechensbekämpfung*, p. 60; Richtlinien des RKPA, über die Durchführung der vorbeugenden Verbrechensbekämpfung, A II 1 e B I, Abs. 9.

23. Hauptstaatsarchiv Düsseldorf, R 2034/20, Bl. 24.

24. Landeshauptarchiv Sachsen-Anhalt, Rep. C. 29, Anhang II, Z258, Bl. 50.

25. BAK, VV. RdErl.d. RFFSSuChdDtPol. I. RMdl. vom 8.12.1938-S-Kr. 1 Nr. 557 VIII 38-2026-6, A.I.4(1) and A.1.5(1).

26. BAK, VV, RSHA Tgb. Nr. RKPA 149/1939-g-, Schnellbrief, 17.10.1939, Betr.: Zigeunererfassung, Abs. 1 (author's emphasis).

27. Dokumentationsarchiv des österreichischen Widerstands (DÖW), 11.532, Grenzmark Burgenland, Wahlzeitung zum 10.3.1938. Portschy listed, in order, the most important problems in Burgenland as agriculture, the "Gypsies," and the "Jewish Question."

28. DÖW 4.969; also Staatsarchiv Nürnberg, ND, NG 845. Portschy's Memorandum is dated August 1938.

29. Ralf Ogorreck, *Die Einsatzgruppen und die "Genesis der Endlösung"* (Berlin, 1996).

30. See the chapter by Walter Manoschek in this volume.

31. See, for example, Generallandesarchiv Karlsruhe, 364/Zug 1975/3 II, Fasc. 24, Gendarmerieposten Oberschefflenz, 28.3.1943, I. Nr. 378, marked "Abschiebung," "Transport," "eingeliefert," and "Reise."

32. BAK, VV, RFSSuChdDtPol.i.RMDI., V B Nr. 95/40 g, 27.4.1940, Ausführungsanweisungen; BAK, VV, RFSSuChdDtPol.i.RMDI., V B Nr. 95/40 g, 27.4.1940, Richtlinien für die Umsiedlung von Zigeunern.

33. BAK, VV, RSHA, 29.1.1943, VA2, Nr. 59/43g.

34. Melanie Spitta and Karin Seybold, *Das falsche Wort. Wiedergutmachung an Sinti (Zigeunern), in Deutschland? Textbuch zum Film* (Munich, 1987), p. 32; P. Petersen and Ulrich Liedtke, "Zur Entschädigung zwangssterilisierter Zigeuner," in *Der Nervenarzt* 42, no. 4 (1971): 200, 197-205.

35. Hansjörg Riechert, *Im Schatten von Auschwitz. Die nationalsozialistische Sterilisationspolitik gegenüber Sinti und Roma* (Münster/New York, 1995), p. 135.

36. See also Michael Zimmermann, "Utopie und Praxis der Vernichtungspolitik in der NS-Diktatur. Überlegungen in vergleichender Absicht," in *Werkstatt Geschichte* 5, no. 13 (June 1996): 60-71.

37. Hans Mommsen, *Totalitarismus und Faschismus. Eine wissenschaftliche und politische Begriffskontroverse*, ed. Institut für Zeitgeschichte (Munich, 1989), pp. 18-27, here 24; and "Hitlers Stellung im nationalsozialistischen Herrschaftssystem," in *Der "Führerstaat": Mythos und Realität. Studien zur Struktur und Politik des Deutschen Reiches*, ed. Gerhard Hirschfeld and Lothar Kettenacker (Stuttgart, 1981), pp., 43-69, here 56. Etymologically derived from *cumulus* (hill) and *radix* (root), the concept "cumulative radicalization" is linguistically problematic.

38. Hans Mommsen, "Die Realisierung des Utopischen. Die 'Endlösung der Judenfrage' im 'Dritten Reich,'" in *Kontroversen um Hitler*, ed. Wolfgang Wippermann (Frankfurt a.M., 1986), pp. 277f., 248-298. Similarly, Martin Broszat: "Precisely this final and decisive stage [i.e., the mass extermination of Jews], which would surely not have been set in motion without Hitler's approval, but which independent of his interventions—which are not known in any detail—points to a fatally automatic process which had been set in motion. Clearly the question of Hitler's explicit commands in this connection is largely secondary." Remarks by Broszat in *Der Mord an den Juden im Zweiten Weltkieg. Entschlußbildung und Verwirklichung*, ed. Eberhard Jäckel and Jürgen Rohwer (Frankfurt a.M., 1987), pp. 179-184, here 184.

39. Mommsen, *Hitlers Stellung*, p. 63.

– Chapter 8 –

GERMAN ECONOMIC INTERESTS, OCCUPATION POLICY, AND THE MURDER OF THE JEWS IN BELORUSSIA, 1941/43

Christian Gerlach

No country in Europe was so severely affected by the Second World War as Belorussia. When liberated by the Soviet army in the summer of 1944, far fewer than 7 million of the original 9.2 million inhabitants remained in the country, and of these 3 million were homeless. Many villages and towns no longer existed. The enormous loss of state, community, and private property can scarcely be calculated. In Belorussia the Germans murdered about 700,000 Soviet prisoners of war, 500,000 to 550,000 Jews, 340,000 peasants and refugees as victims of the so-called "partisan struggle" and about 100,000 members of other population groups. In addition, more than 380,000 people were transported to the Reich as forced laborers.[1]

Three years earlier, in the summer of 1941, the German Army Group Center conquered Belorussia within a few weeks. Despite this rapid defeat, the Soviet authorities succeeded in evacuating 1.5 million people by train to the East, mostly out of eastern Belorussia, in an ad hoc evacuation campaign.[2] The evacuees included, above all, urban dwellers, particularly factory workers, civil authorities and functionaries, and perhaps 150,000 to 180,000 Belorussian Jews.[3] In the summer of 1941 the entire area of Belorussia fell under German military administration, which was replaced in the western half by various civil authorities between 1 August and 20 October 1941.[4] Though planned, the further expansion of the civil administration into the rest of Belorussia never occurred, and the eastern half of the country remained under military control for the duration of the occupation period.

Belorussia, never an independent state until 1991, for centuries occupied a difficult position in the field of political tension created by the politics of its large neighbors Poland and Russia. After 1920 it became a Soviet republic, with the exception of today's western Belorussia, which was part of Poland until the Soviet Union occupied and annexed east Poland in 1939.[5] A large Polish minority lived in the western districts, particularly in the cities. After this "reunification under socialist conditions" and at the time of the German invasion, Belorussia was in several ways a divided country: the Soviets persecuted the middle classes and the Poles—there were repeated waves of imprisonment and deportation from 1939 to 1941—while the Poles had repressed the Belorussians. Belorussia was even more divided economically and socially: in the west, industry was less developed, and by far the largest part of the agricultural economy was still in private hands. In the east, collectivized agriculture was the norm.

The German occupying powers divided Belorussia into no fewer than seven different large territories. The border between the areas under military and civil authority, although not identical with the prewar border between the USSR and Poland, ran directly through the country in a north-south direction. Almost all borders were changed or entirely redrawn and were more or less invented.

The so-called Generalkommissariat White Ruthenia, the sole administrative district under the Germans comprised solely of Belorussian territory, included the capital city Minsk and was part of the Reichskommissariat Ostland, with the capital city Riga. Larger parts of Belorussia, chiefly Polesje (the Pripyat Marshes), were divided between the Reichskommissariat Ukraine, the Generalkommissariat for Vohlhyn and Podolia, and the Generalkommissariat Shitomir. A further district, the Bezirk Bialystok, was annexed by the Reich and affiliated with East Prussia. The Bezirk Bialystok was not administered by the Ostministerium but by the East Prussian Gauleiter and Oberpräsident Erich Koch, who was also Reichskommissar for the Ukraine.

The eastern half of Belorussia was governed for the most part by the rear area of Army Group Center. Eastern Belorussia was divided into administrative districts controlled by the security divisions, field commanders, and district commanders. The General Quartermaster of the Army commanded administrative functions in the rear area of Army Group Center, while Army Group Center was responsible for military functions. In a military administrative district, economic organization required a special administrative body; in the area of Army Group Center, this task was fulfilled by the Economic Inspection Center, responsible to the Wirtschaftsstab Ost in Berlin.

In addition, there were Belorussian authorities at the city, Rayon (county district), community, and village levels, who were dependent on the German military and civil administrations. They were recruited in part from opponents to the Soviet system loyal to the Germans, in part from supposedly neutral persons; not a few secretly supported the Soviet powers and the political underground, and many maneuvered back and forth. But all-in-all the Belorussian support authorities "functioned," particularly in regard to anti-Jewish policies.

I begin the following essay with an analysis of the German plans, dating from 1941, to let millions of people in the Soviet Union starve to death, and the implications for Belorussia, particularly for Belorussian Jews. The second section examines how German units began to murder Belorussian Jews in 1941, and the step-by-step move towards total annihilation in the eastern part of the country. In the third section, I describe the liquidation campaigns in the different territories, which claimed as victims almost all Jews in western Belorussia in 1942. My analysis first concentrates on the course and to a certain degree on the structure of the mass murder of the Jews, and on its goals; second, I want to illuminate the connection between the overall concept of German occupation policies, which above all focused on economic interests, and the destruction of the Jews; and third, I examine the role played by the various occupation authorities in these events.

I

Toward the end of 1940, the Reich Ministry of Food and Agriculture prepared the annual report on the state of food for Hitler. State Secretary of the Reich Food Ministry Herbert Backe, who had already gained more power than his superior, Minister Darré, sent the report back two times, because its conclusions did not appear dramatic enough. Over the Christmas holidays of 1940, Backe simply sat down and wrote it himself.[6] His subsequent presentations to Göring and Hitler in January 1941 were the starting-point of the plan to use criminal occupation policies to obtain needed food stuffs from the Soviet Union. Göring immediately ordered a reduction in German meat rations for the summer, and in his meeting with Hitler, Backe for the first time argued that the Ukraine could be used as a "surplus area" for German food supplies, if deliveries to the remaining Soviet Union were stopped.[7] Shortly before this, on 18 December 1940, Hitler had signed the orders for the invasion of the Soviet Union.

After the failure of the attack on Great Britain in summer 1940, the strategic situation of Germany resembled that of the First World War, when the Reich was defeated because of its inferiority in capital, production capacity, raw materials, and food stuffs. Starvation had played a key role in the emergence of the revolutionary movement in 1918. In 1940, however, there was still no two-front war, larger territories had been occupied in comparison to the First World War, and Blitzkrieg campaigns had saved resources and war materials. But no Blitzkrieg existed for the economics of food and nourishment. By the end of 1939, almost entirely cut off from overseas transportation by the ocean blockade, Germany could no longer guarantee its own supplies of grain and oil-seeds. Victory in western Europe did not improve the balance of food stuffs—quite the contrary. Starvation was common in southeastern European countries, in part because they had already delivered so much food to the Reich. There was still no starvation in Germany. Supplies sufficed, but during 1940/41 grain stockpiles melted away. Because the end of the war was unforeseeable, this was a serious situation. During the summer of 1941, only a massive campaign brought in the new harvest without supply bottlenecks.[8] The campaign included measures for slaughtering fowl, because they required too much feed. This action took place under the official slogan "Eliminate the Bad Chickens!" (*Merzt die schlechten Hühner aus!*) Chickens were considered "bad" if they laid fewer than 100 to 120 eggs per year.[9]

Even with these domestic measures, the German government had difficulty supplying the population with food, and imports from the Soviet Union were also unreliable. Before the German invasion in 1941, the Soviet government had repeatedly declared that to avoid a drop in domestic consumption they did not want to raise appreciably grain exports to Germany. In any case, the Soviets demanded a high price, in highly valued industrial and military goods. The German government was moving towards a dependency that should not be underestimated,[10] and in response, the Reichs Food Ministry now drafted plans to let "*x* millions of people starve" after the invasion of Russia. This was the most extensive plan for murder yet known to history. It was aimed at two specific population groups: first, at the inhabitants of the agricultural "subsidy areas" of the "forest zones" in central and northern Russia, and with minor exceptions in Belorussia, where a "withering away (*Absterben*) of industry as well as a large part of the population" would need to be organized; and second, at the Soviet urban population as a whole. The occupation plans called for the re-establishment of large Russian agricultural exports as in the period before the First World War, and this required a return to the population conditions of that time. Although population levels in the USSR had remained static since 1918, the urban population had grown by some 30 million. To simply reduce rations for all inhabitants would have little effect, because of the uncontrollable black market. Nor could agricultural production be raised temporarily in the occupied Soviet territories, because planners realistically calculated that war-related destruction would result in considerable declines in production capacity.[11]

Besides these economic-agricultural motives, planners invoked a second tactical reason for instituting a policy of starvation against the Soviet population related to military strategy. The entire German operations plan had to deal with the difficulties caused by the enormity of the planned campaign.[12] For the army, this meant that the majority of the Red Army had to be destroyed in rapid maneuvers west of the Dniepr, to avoid its retreat into the inner reaches of the country and to prevent the establishment of a new, strong line of defense. The destruction of the remnants of Soviet resistance would require a deep attack into central Russian and the Caucasus before the onset of winter, and, as was foreseen, the range of German operations would be dependent on the provision of munitions, gasoline, and reserves. Maintaining supply lines in operations extending up to 2000 km was extremely difficult. This was well over the distances of about 400 km within which supplies could be easily transported by road, as in the war against France, and in the Soviet Union a large part of carrying capacity would be needed for the gasoline used by the trucks themselves. In addition, advances would require heavy rail support, but there were few extended east-west rail lines.[13] At the same time, a successful attack would require a rapid advance.[14] For these reasons, resupply transports would have to be relieved of everything that was not absolutely necessary.[15] The solution, in so far as there seemed to be one, was if possible to carry no food. The entire army on the Eastern Front, some three million men with extremely high ration requirements, would have to "live off the land," as it was called. In this way, the policy of starvation—in the logic of the German aggressor—became an unconditional military necessity. The plans implied that the greatest share of the extorted provisions would in practice be delivered to soldiers in the Wehrmacht rather than to citizens in the Reich, and this is in fact what happened. Reducing the supply of food stuffs to the Soviet population was thus entirely in the interest of the German army.

In response, the General Quartermaster of the Army, General Eduard Wagner, whose responsibility for both the organization of the military administration and lines of supply gave him a key position, had by February 1941 already devised guidelines for the future of the armed forces. The guidelines foresaw the relief of supply problems through the brutal enforcement of German interests and the "exploitation the countryside ... according to a well-thought-out plan." As if following the Backe plan, Wagner's order specifically states that "the individual countries are to be treated *differently*" and that Belorussia was to be handled particularly "ruthlessly."[16] After February 1941, the head of the Army Economics and Armaments Office of the High Command of the Armed Forces (OKW), General Georg Thomas, was one of the most passionate defenders and initiators of the starvation plan. By January, his office had already given up on plans to preserve the Soviet armaments industry by taking it into German possession.[17] From the beginning of March 1941, information folders for officers of the General Staff of the Army in the districts of the western Soviet Union illustrated the "disregard for the value of human life" in the region which seemed to allow brutal measures. The folders listed the number of Jewish inhabitants in urban areas, as well as other data on the "density of population" and the "density of the population in the countryside," which was irrelevant for military purposes. Such figures must have been included with the intent to change them.[18]

The starvation plan was approved by Hitler, co-initiated by Göring and the leaders of the Wehrmacht, and adopted by the responsible German State Secretaries on 2 May 1941. Experts at the German Reichsbank reviewed the economic considerations.[19] In June 1941 the economic guidelines in the "Green Folder," issued by Göring and signed by Chief of the OKW Keitel, became the basis for German occupation policies in the Soviet Union.[20] SS and police units were among others left responsible for realizing the guidelines, as demonstrated by surviving comments from Himmler and from Franz Six, Chief of the Vorkommando Moscow of Einsatzgruppe B. In July 1941, in the High Command of Army Group Center, Six declared that 30 million people would starve in "fire strips" (*Brandstreifen*) surrounding Moscow.[21] Himmler told a meeting of SS Group Leaders in the middle of June (the date is no longer a matter of doubt) that the Soviet population would be decimated by about 30 million people.[22] By chance or not: two days before that meeting occurred, Himmler spoke with Backe about agriculture in the Soviet territories planned for occupation.[23] It is noteworthy that Erich Koch, one of the most brutal of all National Socialist politicians, refused the post of Reichskommissar in Moscow because it was "an entirely negative task."[24]

We can thank the former Higher SS and Police Leader of "Russia Center" Erich von dem Bach-Zelewski for his confession in the Nuremberg trial about the Himmler statement cited above. Bach-Zelewski neglected to mention, however, that the plans called for the death of 20 million people in his region alone.[25] Bach-Zelewski's area of responsibility was initially Belorussia and later included central Russia. In the Wirtschaftstab Ost, one of the agricultural experts, most probably geographer Waldemar von Poletika, wrote "shall die" (*sollen sterben*) in the margins of a planning paper on Belorussia, alongside statements that 1,000,000 young, well-motivated, surplus workers could be transported from the region to Germany. Further marginal notes by von Poletika noted that the entire urban and half the rural population was supposed to die—a total of about 6.3 million people.[26]

Current scholarship makes isolated references to a *general* connection between the starvation plan and the suspected prewar plans for the destruction of the Soviet Jews, though we have virtually no sources to support this conclusion.[27] But the connection was quite concrete and direct: in Belorussia, for example, more that 90 percent of the Jews lived in towns and cities; they comprised a good 30 percent of the urban population.[28] This meant that the death of the mass of Belorussian Jews was planned beforehand. In addition, before 22 June 1941, besides the starvation plan, the most important elements of the German leadership had the *determined intention* to kill the vast majority of all Soviet Jews, who lived in the towns and cities of the western USSR—above all with starvation, supported by brutal occupation policies. But how and in what time period this mass murder could be actually carried out was still unclear. This is confirmed by postwar statements about the orders of the *Einsatzgruppen* Mitte in June 1941, which announced the general destruction of the Jews without comprehensive, concrete directives for the operation.[29] In addition, National Socialist ideology portrayed the Soviet Jews as potential enemies who should be fought with preventative measures, because they were the representatives and "wire-pullers" of the socialist system.[30] Supposedly Jews would offer particularly strong resistance to the destruction of socialism and the Soviet state apparatus, as well as to German plans for repression and exploitation.

To a great extent, plans for starvation and murder would quickly prove untenable. Nonetheless, the gain of agricultural surpluses at the cost of the population combined with de-urbanization and de-industrialization remained the main goal of German occupation policy in the Soviet Union until 1944.

II

In the first weeks after the German invasion, the SS and police units that entered Belorussia (*Einsatzgruppe* B and four police battalions) were not ordered to kill all Jews they encountered.[31] Nonetheless, they began to practice mass murder immediately; about 90 percent of their victims at this time were Jews. But as a report of *Einsatzgruppe* B stated,[32] the target group of these actions was "at first" limited: they killed men between about fifteen and sixty years of age, and not all of them, but rather those who could be labeled in Nazi jargon "Jewish intelligentsia"— teachers, lawyers, civil authorities, and state and party functionaries.[33] Broadly understood, these murders conformed to Heydrich's initial instructions to kill "Jews in state and party positions." There were practically no pogroms in Belorussia. In these first weeks, German liquidation operations were concentrated in the larger cities, above all Bialystok, Minsk, and Brest. The first Wehrmacht troops to enter Minsk interned all 40,000 men between fifteen and fifty living there—Jews and non-Jews—in a civilian prison camp. It was probably Generalfeldmarschall Günther von Kluge, the Commander in Chief of the (at that time) 4th Panzer Army, who authorized *Einsatzgruppe* B and the Army Secret Police to carry out the selection.[34] In the course of several weeks, they shot approximately 10,000 camp inmates, most of them Jewish. On the night of 7 July in Brest, Feldkommandantur 184 ordered police battalion 307 and part of the 162nd Infantry Division to undertake a mass internment. On the following day, the Police Battalion, a unit of the Security Police and SD from Lublin shot 4,000 Jewish men and 400 non-Jewish men. In Bialystok there were three mass shootings.[35] In smaller cities in July, SS and police "only" (meant relatively of course) carried out smaller massacres ranging from several dozen to several hundred Jewish men.

The military administration also ordered the first anti-Jewish regulations during these first weeks. These included forcing the Jews to wear a yellow badge or armlet, the establishment of Jewish Councils (which had to register Jewish inhabitants), the institution of various prohibitions (e.g., against buying food on the open market), and the establishment of ghettos. General orders for these actions came from regional authorities, the Army High Command, and the advancing commanders of the Army districts in the rear. The timing and course of implementation, however, was dependent on local military authorities. Ghettos were established because of local decisions, at first in particularly heavily damaged cities such as Minsk, Vitebsk, Bialystok, and Schklow, where there was an immense quartering and housing problem and where non-Jewish inhabitants were supposed to be helped at the expense of the Jews. The last ghettos in Belorussia were only established in May 1942 and some places never had one. General von Schenckendorff, the commander of the rear area of Army Group Center, issued the basic orders on 7 and 13 July 1941; at first the General Quartermaster of the Army, under whose jurisdiction this fell, gave no central orders to establish ghettos.[36]

The ghettos also served to limit the economic activity of the Jews as well as their consumption. After August 1941, their food ration was in most places set at 100 to 200 grams of bread per day, even smaller than that of the non-Jews.[37] This was not enough to live on, but the Jewish population survived, ensuring their supply of necessities through the black market, ersatz materials, and gardening. The numbers of dead from starvation remained *relatively* limited, although the Germans murdered many Jews for smuggling food. By August 1941, plans to let the Belorussian urban population starve to death had already been abandoned, in large part because the limited numbers of security troops could not prevent people from foraging in the countryside or buying food in the black market. And in this case, because the military could tolerate neither unrest related to hunger nor epidemics in the cities, the military administration worked in opposition to the agricultural authorities. In addition, the Wehrmacht required a working city infrastructure.

From the start, the use of Jewish labor was uncertain. In the beginning of July, the Wirtschaftsstab Ost frantically debated whether Jews would be allowed to work at all in the occupied Soviet territories in the future. If the Jews were denied work, their fate appeared grim indeed. After an initial inspection tour in Lithuania, leading economic functionaries declared that Jewish specialists were for the time being indispensable—as if before this, the assumption had been quite different.[38] On 15 July the Wirtschaftsstab Ost issued this order: "The local economic offices are to promote the maintenance of Jewish skilled workers in their posts in factories with production important to the war effort, when there is no available replacement and when production levels must be maintained." These orders were confirmed by Göring on 28 July and by the *Wirtschaftsführungsstab Ost* on 18 December 1941. By no means were all Jewish workers intended to be "retained"; instead there were numerous restrictions.[39] These orders also determined practice in Belorussia. In local negotiations, SS and police decided the life and death of Jewish people capable of work.

In actual fact, from the German point of view, the need for labor in the cities of Belorussia was very limited. German air attacks had destroyed many large cities and their factories. In eastern Belorussia, the Soviets had dismantled and transferred 109 factories and made others unusable. Many industrial areas lacked raw materials and energy. In addition, the German economic authorities shut down or cut back production in intact plants, when their products were meant "only" for the use of the civil population, as for example in the textile industry.[40] There was practically no real armaments industry. In many cities in 1941 and also into 1942, poor living conditions (a result of deliberate policy) forced non-Jewish inhabitants to move or flee, though the population had already dropped to about half of prewar levels because of evacuation, destruction, and flight.[41] Food, housing, and work shortages prevailed. Belorussian city administrators and the first German employment offices were hardly allowed to create new jobs. In the summer months of 1941 they saw only *one* practical means to lower high unemployment rates among non-Jews: to replace Jewish workers by the thousands.[42] The need for skilled labor was particularly low in Belorussia. Employment office statistics from 1941 and 1942 show that the share of labor in the general Jewish population was very low and that the quota of skilled laborers among all Jewish laborers was for the most part under 50 percent.[43] The reports of Jewish survivors show that they were rarely placed in the jobs they were trained for and often had to change positions. The authorities typically used Jews as short-term workers in periods when labor needs were particularly pressing.[44] For the criminal German authorities in Belorussia, most Jewish workers were by no means difficult to replace, despite historiographical assumptions to the contrary.

III

The question of why the mass murder of the Jews in the occupied Soviet territories was expanded in 1941 has been the focus of much discussion in the last decades. This expansion took place not in one step, as often assumed, but in two discernible phases. First, the killing units began to murder Jewish women and children, as well as men, in large numbers. The various killing units took this step at different times. *Einsatzkommando* 9, the first unit in *Einsatzgruppe* B, began this phase around July/August; the majority of *Einsatzkommando* 8, on the other hand, began to a great extent only in the beginning of September, likewise Police Battalion 322.[45] Because of the extensive source material, the SS Cavalry Brigade is a particularly good example. In mid-July 1941 Bach-Zelewski had asked Himmler if they could carry out a liquidation operation in Polesje. After a visit to Baranovitchi on 31 July, Himmler issued this radio message on the morning of 1 August: "Express orders for the RF-SS. All Jews must be shot. Drive Jewish women into the swamps."[46] By mid-August, the brigade had murdered at least 15,000 people between Baranovitchi and Pinsk—95 percent of them Jewish. In the most severely hit areas the "Jewish intelligentsia," broadly considered, were again particular targets for murder. The 1st SS Cavalry Regiment had killed all Jews in several small market towns, though they were spared in some other places. The 2nd Regiment shot 4,000 to 8,000 Jewish men in Pinsk on 5 August; two or three days later, in a separate operation, they killed 2,000 women, children, and elderly. In other places, this Regiment killed only Jewish men.[47] These actions marked the period of transition, but there was no clear break.

On 15 August 1941, Himmler visited Minsk, where Bach-Zelewski, Nebe (the head of *Einsatzgruppe* B), and *Einsatzkommando* 8 demonstrated a mass shooting action to their superior. It has recently been claimed, on the basis of statements made by accomplices, that Himmler gave the order for the "undifferentiated killing of all Jews encountered" at this meeting in Minsk,[48] but this is apparently wrong. In fact, Himmler had actually given orders for the expansion of the liquidation campaign to the 1st SS Infantry Brigade three days before, in a personal meeting with the HSSPF Rußland-Süd, Jeckeln. These orders were probably intended for broader implementation.[49] But the slightly decreasing number of murders committed by Einsatzgruppe B up to mid-September, and the remarks in several subsequent reports by Nebe on the "limited importance of the Jewish question," suggest that Himmler never gave the reputed order in Minsk.[50] Nor did his visit in any way mark the "birth of the gas chamber" or the mobile gas vans. Plans for these had already begun before this.[51]

The second step from mass murder to total destruction, scarcely noted in current research, was the start of the liquidation of entire Jewish communities. This step also took place in different regions at different times. After the end of August 1941, Section Troop Borisov of *Einsatzkommando* 8 first liquidated the Jewish communities between Borisov and Minsk.[52] Around the middle of September, *Einsatzkommando* 8 together with the Gendarmerie began a similar operation in the area of Mogilev, while *Einsatzkommando* 9 worked in the area around Vitebsk.[53] In September, the Security Police and the SD undertook a series of shootings of several hundred currently "unemployed Jews" in larger cities like Orscha, Bobruisk, Borisov, and Gomel.[54] An order of Keitel's forbidding the use of Jewish labor except in all-Jewish forced labor troops was now carried out.[55] On 2 October, the liquidation of the large ghettos in the rear areas of Army Group Center began with the shooting of 2,273 Jewish men, women, and children in Mogilev.[56] Within two months all of the ghettos had been liquidated: the Germans murdered 6,500 Jews in Mogilev, 4,000 in Vitebsk, 7,000 in Borisov, 2,000 in Orscha, 2,500 in Gomel, 7,000 in Polozk, and 7,500 in Bobruisk, where 7,000 had already been murdered by the SS Cavalry Brigade. During the same period, smaller ghettos were liquidated.[57] Only in a very few cities were several hundred Jewish workers allowed to stay alive. In the beginning of February 1942, only some 22,000 Jews remained alive, mostly in remote areas that the murder commandos had not yet been to.[58] These Jews were subsequently shot in early 1942. The liquidation was thus total very early on.

In any case, for organizational reasons the SS and police could not immediately begin the liquidation of the ghettos. The *Einsatzkommandos* in particular had first to complete several other tasks: inspecting local conditions, searching for political enemies and files, transmitting initial reports to Berlin, and collaborating with the rebuilding of the Belorussian supporting administration and police, whose existence as a functioning body was a necessary prerequisite for the larger liquidation operations. In addition, the commandos had to be stationed permanently in a fixed territory. Section Troop Borisov (noted above), under Werner Schönemann, was the first unit to achieve this in Belorussia at the end of July

1941.[59] In the entire occupied Soviet territories, *Einsatzkommando* 3 in Lithuania was the first to stay in a specific area and also the first to begin the liquidation of Jewish communities.[60] These different starting dates suggest not a single order for the expansion of murder, but rather a series of local, tactical orders.

The initial signal was given on 2 October by Higher SS and Police Leader Bach-Zelewski, on the same day—as he knew in advance—that Army Group Center began its offensive against Moscow.[61] Unlike the *Sonderkommandos*, most of the *Einsatzkommandos* were not moved forward in the military campaign, but were held back, obviously because they now had orders to kill all Jews in the rear area within a short period of time. At this point, the origin of this order is impossible to document. But the course of events shows that the resolution of the economic problems of the occupation authorities was the final, decisive impulse for the complete liquidation of the Jews in Army Group Center. For this reason, operations began in the large cities and ended in the outlying ghettos—in contrast to the situation in Lithuania. Local conditions likewise reveal the connections between economics and elimination: in Mogilev, at the time of both massacres, *non-Jewish* skilled workers escaped starvation and housing shortages by fleeing into the countryside, and *Einsatzgruppe* B reported that it had immediately afterwards returned the ghetto to the city administration.[62] Bobruisk experienced massive unemployment, and in Borisov food shortages were such that soon even local farmers were starving. Vitebsk suffered from a dire lack of provisions, and Jews there had received no food, with the result that most of them were actually starving by this time. Countless bodies lay in the ghetto, and *Einsatzkommando* 9 shot Jews who still lived because of the "danger of an epidemic."[63]

At the same time, large massacres of Jews in Generalkommissariat White Ruthenia took place. But in contradiction to many interpretations, these operations were not the product of blind rage, nor did they result in the total annihilation of the Jews in this region.[64] Despite ideological exhortation, these calculated acts of murder controlled by the regional Wehrmacht authorities actually had three limited, clearly defined goals. First, the 707th Wehrmacht Infantry Division was to murder all Jews in the countryside, or force them to emigrate from larger areas. Second, Reserve Police Battalion 11, with Lithuanian assistants, had the task of killing all Jews in the Soviet part of the Generalkommissariat, with the exception of Minsk. Third, the Jewish population was to be reduced in the small cities close to the major east-west roads and in the larger cities in formerly Polish areas, in order to relieve food and housing shortages. Indispensable Jewish labor, however, was to be spared; both operations were undertaken in the interests of the Wehrmacht troops quartered in the area. The 707th Infantry Division carried out these plans in towns; the Security Police and the SD from Minsk had responsibility for larger cities.[65] In Minsk, 12,000 Jews were shot to make room for in-coming transports of Jews from Germany. In Slonim, 9,000 "useless gobblers" (*unnütze Fresser*), in the words of the district commissar, were murdered. In both cases, the German authorities had determined an exact number of victims in advance. In Minsk, a second operation was planned and carried out, because the initial quota was not fulfilled.[66]

One element in particular stands out about the crimes in the Generalkommissariat White Ruthenia: in this area the Wehrmacht shot up to 19,000 Jews, clearly without a general from the OKW order to kill Jews,[67] but on the decision of a division commander. In this case, few other killing units were available. There was no Order Police Battalion, and only a weak commando of Security Police and SD in Minsk. On 4 October, at the request of the Wehrmachtbefehlshaber Ostland, Reserve Police Battalion 11 was transferred from Lithuania to Minsk by the commander of the Order Police.[68] The time parallels with events in the rear area under army control is remarkable, even more so when one notes the contemporaneous start of the mass shootings in east Galicia, in the Warthegau, and in Volhyn-Podolia.[69] The still limited character of the mass murder in the Generalkommissariat in 1941 (though 60,000 Jews were shot), in contrast to the rear area under army control, is explicable first because in eastern Belorussia, cities and factories were more heavily destroyed and practically no Jewish labor was needed. In addition, the pressures of starvation and housing shortages were greater in the cities because they had experienced direct assaults by the Wehrmacht. The larger picture showed similar tendencies: in September, because of the unforeseen conditions of war, Backe set up a new plan for wartime food supply that was sanctioned by Hitler and Göring. Backe, who demanded "extremely radical measures," exercised enormous pressure on the Wirtschaftsstab Ost, on the General Quartermaster of the Army, and on the OKW, and they unscrupulously passed it on.[70] A number of connected events occurred in the autumn of 1941: the transportation catastrophe of Army Group Center during the Battle for Moscow; the premeditated murder of prisoners of war incapable of work, which meant the starvation of the majority, especially in the rear areas of Army Group Center; the reduction of rations for non-Jewish city dwellers; and the intensification of the bloody struggle against "outsiders" (*Ortsfremde*)—starving refugees and scattered members of the Red Army.[71] Events in autumn 1941 marked the *transition from utopian plans for genocide to an implementable program of mass murder.* The initial criminal plans could still be realized, if only in part. In addition, to those responsible, it appeared more pressing to murder the Jews—seen as particularly "dangerous" political enemies—in the former Soviet territories than in the former Poland. This also explains the slaughter of the entire Jewish population in the small districts in the north of the Generalkommissariat of Shitomir (in the territory of the civil administration) between September 1941 and January 1942.[72]

In 1941 about 200,000 Belorussian Jews were murdered, practically all of those living in the eastern half of the territory. In the west, 300,000 were still alive. The military authorities above all shared political responsibility for these murders, because the intensification of the killing was directly connected to the implementation of plans to supply provisions to the Wehrmacht. In contrast to the liquidation of the prisoners of war, for which they were directly responsible, army agents themselves murdered Jews only in exceptional cases. Shootings of Jews by frontline troops during advances, which occurred in a number of cases, had the character of antisemitic attacks or brutal acts of retaliation. Killings by frontline troops, however, did not affect most cities; nor did they reach the massive dimensions of the massacres later carried out by the SS, police, and security troops.[73] After the advance, army participation was apparently limited: it is only possible to document the murder of so-called "country Jews" by several security divisions, the participation in massacres by Security Police with their own shooting commandos on the local level, and voluntary participation in shootings by numerous individual soldiers and officers.[74] The operations of the 707th Infantry Division are in fact an exception. It is of course clear that the army cooperated in and gave massive support to SS and police operations, for example in Bobruisk, Orscha, Borisov, Slonim, and Novogrodek,[75] and that they carried out ongoing transfers of captured Jews to the Security Police. In addition, army units made use of the police in mass murder operations or gave orders to carry them out, as in Brest or in the case of Reserve Police Battalion 11. But they rarely got their own hands dirty.

IV

The year 1942 was characterized by the implementation of campaign-style murder programs against the Jewish population of western Belorussia, above all in the Generalkommissariat White Ruthenia. On 2 and 3 March, for example, Security Police in Minsk, Baranovitchi, and Vilejka shot over 6,500 Jews, for the most part children, women, and unemployed. A crisis session of the Stadtkommissar in Minsk had earlier resulted in orders that despite the famine, the inhabitants could be "given no aid of any kind."[76] In a hearing after the war, Minsk Gestapo Chief Heuser remembered that "the main thing that was done in that severe winter crisis was saving lives 'worth living' [*lebenswertes Leben*], that is, White Ruthenians, at the expense of 'unworthy or sick' lives (Jews, Gypsies, the mentally ill, and prison inmates)."[77]

But these massacres did not seem to be sufficient for the authorities responsible for the murder campaigns. On 26 March, at a meeting in Riga (Kube was apparently present), the Generalkommissars of Reichskommissariat Ostland stated that "even though they may create a political inconvenience for us, it is seen as regrettable that the procedures pursued up to now [i.e., the mass shootings] have for the time being once again been abandoned. The current situation, in which the Jews receive no food whatsoever, is no solution." By November 1941, the Reichskommissariat had already de facto forbidden the murder of Jews through starvation because of the high risk involved, in so far as the Reichskommissariat was responsible for the prevention of epidemics spreading from the ghettos.[78] Negotiations now began between Kube, Zenner (SS and Police Leader of White Ruthenia), and Strauch (commander of the Security Police and SD), resulting in the selections of Jews, district by district, in all areas. Jews who, according to the Gebietskommissare (whose officials selected the Jews), could not be used as laborers were shot or murdered in gas vans. Kube ordered the district commissars to "select out all [Jews] not absolutely necessary to the national economy [*Volkswirtschaft*]."[79] The Reichskommissariat in Riga agreed; the local "Jewish expert" noted on a similar order, "corresponds to previous arrangements."[80] The selections first occurred in the region around Lida. In seventeen towns, between 8 and 12 May, the Security Police shot 16,000 Jews and let 7,000 live.[81] Because of partisan attacks, mass flight of refugees and Jewish uprisings, and a lack of police manpower, the operations in the other districts took place in a somewhat less tightly organized manner. Skilled workers in the remaining ghettos were only killed in the last quarter of 1942. Nonetheless, the overwhelming majority of the estimated 112,000 Jews murdered in Generalkommissariat White Ruthenia in 1942 were victims of the campaigns between May and August. On 31 July Kube wrote a report, apparently on the request of Lohse, his Reichskommissar. Lohse immediately presented the results to Göring in Berlin, at a large conference on the food question in occupied Europe. Lohse answered a question from Göring with the remark that "now only a small part of the Jews remain alive; umpteen thousands are gone."[82]

In May 1942, in the Generalkommissariat Volhyn-Podolia, 326,000 Jews remained alive, including over 80,000 in the Belorussian area. On the basis of postwar statements, Gerald Fleming has already established that Hitler, not Himmler, gave the order for their elimination to Erich Koch in July 1942. Various sources show that the operation, with the internal slogan "A Jew-Free Ukraine!" (*Ukraine judenfrei!*), was actually controlled by Koch and the civil authorities, and that Koch had received dramatic demands for food deliveries to the Reich.[83] The role played by these demands is also demonstrated by the acceleration of the murders in August and by the course of events, which moved from the south, where the richest agricultural areas lay, to the north. On 9 July, Himmler took over the operation to "secure the harvest" in the Reichskommissariat Ukraine.[84] In September and October 1942, units of the Order and Security Police shot all the Jews in southwestern Belorussia, including 16,000 to 18,000 in Brest and up to 26,000 in Pinsk, the largest remaining Belorussian ghetto. The liquidation of the Pinsk ghetto has been seen as a perfect example of actions taken under a short-term order from Himmler based on ideological grounds—even though Koch had personally given the order several weeks before, and the civil authorities had already determined the course of events.[85]

The operation in Pinsk ended on 1 November; on the following day, almost 100,000 Jews in the Bialystok district were forced into internment centers, so they could be quickly deported to the Treblinka and Auschwitz extermination camps. The smooth cooperation between Security Police and SD and the civil authorities, here also responsible to Koch, was again evident. Technical obstructions in rail transport were the sole source of disruption.[86] By February 1943, in the area belonging to today's Belorussia, all 60,000 to 70,000 Jews were victims of this operation.

Approximately 20,000 Belorussian Jews remained in Minsk, Lida, and Glebokie. They were shot or deported at the latest in the summer and autumn of 1943. The head of the finance branch in the Reichskommissariat Ostland, Vialon, had obtained a promise from the SS that skilled Jewish workers could remain employed, but the authorities in Generalkommissariat White Ruthenia did not allow this, because they could replace the Jews with Belorussians, with evacuees forced away from the front, and with new machinery.[87] In the end only several hundred Belorussian Jews were able to survive as forced laborers in the camps in Poland. In addition, about 30,000 to 50,000 Jews escaped from the Belorussian ghettos. However, fewer than half of them survived the so-called "Jew hunts" by Germans until liberation.[88]

In conclusion I would like to emphasize five main points:

1. The majority of Belorussian Jews were killed in regional murder campaigns. People were shot close to where they lived; relatively few were suffocated in gas vans. Thus the start, duration, and size of these programs was not determined by the distribution of rail transport or by the liquidation capacity of the death camps under the leadership of the Reichssicherheitshauptamt or the "Aktion Reinhard."

2. *Economic interests and crises* were far more important influences on the tempo of the liquidation of the Jews, *especially in the phases of acceleration.* The various liquidation programs in Belorussia, particularly those against non-Jewish population groups, were in large part responses to pressures related to food economics. This was the main interest of the occupying powers; on the central or regional levels, demanding food-delivery goals and local emergencies in the meager deliveries to non Jewish urban populations produced decisions to murder either unemployed Jews, or all of them. Antisemitism and anti-Bolshevism were necessary preconditions for these murders, helping to establish the possibility of such ideas in the first place—but only economic pressure led to the massive killing campaigns, to the horrible dynamics of mass murder.

3. Thus the liquidation of the Jews was directly connected with the progress of the war. This was a concrete, palpable connection that cannot be explained by overly simple conceptual models of euphoria versus defeatism. Though the National Socialists were prepared in advance to commit crimes, at the beginning of 1941, the starvation program was a bitter necessity of war, for both the collective strategic situation of Germany and for the unavoidable supply problems related to the new military campaign. In the fall of 1941, both problems were greatly intensified: by developments at the front, in the transportation sector; through the newly developed war food plan necessary for supplying the

Reich; and in the race for time in the battle for Moscow. Simplistic conceptions of the starvation policy now collapsed. In order to keep the situation in control, the burdens that emerged from the general intensification of the war were passed on more sharply to the inhabitants of the occupied territories, above all to specific, delimited, stigmatized population groups. The undisguised mass murder of Jews and Soviet prisoners of war was the result. In spring and summer 1942, the new deliveries demanded by the Reich Food Ministry from the occupied areas to improve food supplies in the Reich were at the very least decisive for the acceleration of new murder programs against the Belorussian Jews.

4. The participating institutions—the military and civil authorities—did not act with restraint, nor did they simply give their consent. They were one of the driving forces behind the destruction of the Jews. The murder of the Jews and other population groups in Belorussia was hardly an exception in German occupation policies, but rather its means, and an essential part of its organization. As the liquidation of the Jews increasingly became a key part of the general strategy of occupation policies, the role of the SS and police declined in importance; they rarely determined the course of these policies. They did repeatedly seize the initiative in the mass murder of the Jews, their killing was unbelievably gruesome and hateful (which cannot be described here), and they at times exceeded the measures asked for by the authorities. But the massive liquidation campaigns took place only when they accorded with the combined interests of the administrative authorities. For example, in autumn 1941 Einsatzgruppe C did not succeed in carrying out their original goal of immediately killing all Jews in Volhyn-Podolia for political reasons, because the civil authorities still wanted to keep reserves of Jewish skilled laborers.[89] The well-known conflicts between Kube and the SS dealt only with how to proceed with the murders and was in any case limited to a personal level.[90]

5. In the search for explanations, above all for the events of 1941, the orders giving the commands for mass murder have up to now been represented somewhat too simply and directly, almost theatrically in the case of Minsk in August 1941. The expansion of the murders was a result of tactics, a response to regional possibilities for killing and so-called "killing requirements". The mass murder was carried out in

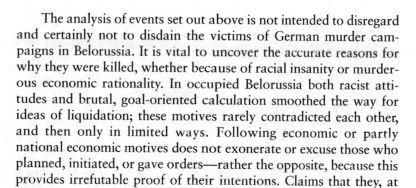

a cold and calculated fashion, as the great majority of statements by perpetrators show, although few witnesses could clearly comprehend all the economic calculations that lay behind these actions. One *single* general order to kill all Jews was not enough to set the liquidation everywhere in motion. Mass murder always required supplementary local or regional planning, and it required interest, consensus, and initiative to ensure that the far-reaching destruction became a reality.

The analysis of events set out above is not intended to disregard and certainly not to disdain the victims of German murder campaigns in Belorussia. It is vital to uncover the accurate reasons for why they were killed, whether because of racial insanity or murderous economic rationality. In occupied Belorussia both racist attitudes and brutal, goal-oriented calculation smoothed the way for ideas of liquidation; these motives rarely contradicted each other, and then only in limited ways. Following economic or partly national economic motives does not exonerate or excuse those who planned, initiated, or gave orders—rather the opposite, because this provides irrefutable proof of their intentions. Claims that they, at least, acted out of some sort of madness or insanity are indefensible.

Notes

1. The figures are based on the postwar territories of Belorussia and are from my dissertation "Die deutsche Wirtschafts- und Vernichtungspolitik in Weißrußland 1941-44" (Technical University of Berlin, 1997). The population figures before the German invasion agree with those those from Belorussia, see Jerzy Turonek, *Bialorus pod okupacja niemiecka* (Warsaw, 1993), p. 236. The figures I use for the number of "Ostarbeiter" transported to the Reich agrees almost exactly with the official data (376,362): *Collected Data on the Victims of German-Fascist Crimes in White Russia* (July 1945, in Russian), ZStA Minsk 845-1-58, Bl. 10. The number of homeless is from M. P. Baranowa and N. G. Pawlowna, *Kurze Geschichte der Belorussischen Sozialistischen Sowjetrepublik* (Jena, 1985), p. 124; Norbert Müller, *Wehrmacht und Okkupation* (East Berlin, 1971), p. 262.

2. See Klaus Segbers, *Die Sowjetunion im Zweiten Weltkrieg* (Munich, 1987), p. 183; Lothar Kölm, "Zur Standortverlagerung von Produktivkräften zu Beginn des Großen Vaterländischen Krieges der Sowjetunion (1941-1942)," in *Jahrbuch für die Geschichte der sozialistischen Länder Europas* 26, no. 2 (1983), p. 128; Turonek, *Bialorus*, p. 54.

3. My own figures, and see Mordechai Altshuler, "Escape and Evacuation of Soviet Jews at the Time of the Nazi Invasion," in *The Holocaust in the Soviet Union*, ed. Lucjan Dobroszycki and Jeffrey S. Gurock (Armonk and London, 1993), pp. 77-104, esp. 97.

4. The Bialystok district was established on 1 August 1941, the Generalkommissariat (GK) White Ruthenia as well as Volhynia and Podolia on 1 September 1941, the GK Shitomir on 20 October 1941.

5. Including the district around Bialystok, which was returned to Poland after 1945 and is not discussed here.

6. Backe to Darré, 9 February 1941, BA R 14/371, Bl. 19.

7. Backe's presentation to Göring was on 13 January, to Hitler before 29 January 1941; see Backe to Darré, 9 February 1941; see also the Reichsmarschall des Großdeutschen Reiches, Beauftragter für den Vierjahresplan V.P. 510/3g, 13 January 1941, BA R 14/371, Bl. 10/R and 16-20; for the meeting with Hitler, *KTB WiRüAmt/Stab*, 30 January 1941, BA-MA RW 19/164, Bl. 126. General Thomas (WiRüAmt) was informed during a high-level meeting with Göring and others including Backe, *Terminkalender Göring*, 29 January 1941, Institut für Zeitgeschichte (IfZ) ED 180/5.

8. See Akte BA R 14/128, especially *Vermerk* 24 May on a meeting on 20 May 1941 in RMEuL (Abschrift), Bl. 44-47.

9. NSDAP-Partei-Kanzlei, *Anordnung 32/41r*, 12 July 1941, with RMEuL, II B 4, *Betr.: Ausmerzung der schlechten Hühner*, BA NS 6/821; RMEuL, II B 4, an die Landesbauernführer, 9 September 1941, BA R 43 II/613, Bl. 260/R.

10. See Rolf-Dieter Müller, "Von der Wirtschaftsallianz zum kolonialen Ausbeutungskrieg," in *Der Angriff auf die Sowjetunion*, ed. Horst Boog et al. (Frankfurt a.M., 1991), pp. 141-245, esp. 144-156; Ludolf Herbst, *Das nationalsozialistische Deutschland 1933-1945* (Frankfurt a.M., 1996), pp. 339-42; Andreas Hillgruber, *Hitlers Strategie: Politik und Kriegführung 1940-1941* (Frankfurt a.M., 1965), pp. 242 ff., esp. 256, on a new German-Soviet accord dated 10 January 1941 requiring increased deliveries to Germany of 2.5 million tons within fifteen months. See Herbst, *Deutschland*, p. 350. His conclusion that this "was enough to mask the [German] need for imports until 1943" is incom-

prehensible. See also Heinrich Schwendemann, *Die wirtschaftliche Zusamme-narbeit zwischen dem Deutschen Reich und der Sowjetunion von 1939 bis 1941* (Berlin, 1993). The German leadership did not see this as an alternative to the emerging starvation plan. On the uncertainty of Soviet deliveries, see Generaloberst Halder, *Kriegstagebuch, Bd. II*, ed. by Hans-Adolf Jacobsen (Stuttgart, 1963), pp. 207, 311 (3 December 1940 and 13 March 1941).

11. Wirtschaftsstab Ost, Gruppe La, "Wirtschaftspolitische Richtlinien für Wirtschaftsorganisation Ost, Gruppe Landwirtschaft, 23 May 1941," in *IMT* (German edition), Vol. 36, pp. 135-157; "Aktionnotiz [of General Thomas] über Ergebnis der heutigen Besprechung mit den Staatssekretären über Barbarossa," 2 May 1941, in IMT, Vol. 31, p. 84. On the German starvation plan in general, see Müller, *Von der Wirtschaftsallianz*, pp. 184ff.; Götz Aly and Susanne Heim, *Vordenker der Vernichtung* (Hamburg, 1991), pp. 365-393.

12. See the analysis of Albert Beer, *Der Fall Barbarossa: Untersuchung zur Geschichte der Vorbereitungen des deutschen Feldzuges gegen die Union der Sozialistischen Sowjetrepubliken im Jahre 1941* (Ph.D. Thesis, Münster, 1978), esp. pp. 27-82.

13. Fundemental in this regard is Klaus A. Friedrich Schüler, *Logistik im Ruß-landfeldzug: Die Rolle der Eisenbahnen bei Planung, Vorbereitung und Durch-führung des deutschen Angriffs auf die Sowjetunion bis zur Krise vor Moskau im Winter 1941/42* (Frankfurt a.M., 1987), here pp. 106ff.

14. See Beer, *Barbarossa*, p. 194; Klaus Reinhardt, *Die Wende vor Moskau* (Stuttgart, 1972), p. 35; and Alfred Philippi, *Das Pripjetproblem* (Frankfurt a.M., 1956), esp. p. 10.

15. See Ihno Krumpelt, *Das Material und die Kriegführung* (Frankfurt a.M., 1968), pp. 140ff.

16. OKH, GenStdH, GenQu, Qu I/II Nr. I/050/41g.KdoS. Chefsache, February 1941, *Anlage 15: Anordnungen über militärische Hoheitsrechte, Sicherung und Verwaltung im rückwärtigen Gebiet und Kriegsgefangenenwesen*, BA-MA RH 3/132, here Bl. 78f. (author's emphasis).

17. Müller, *Von der Wirtschaftsallianz*, pp. 165f.; on the role of Thomas see idem, "Das Unternehmen "Barbarossa" als wirtschaftlicher Raubkrieg," in *Der deutsche Überfall auf die Sowjetunion*, ed. Gerd R. Ueberschär and Wolfram Wette (Frankfurt a.M., 1991), pp. 125-157, esp. 137.

18. Military-geographical data on European Russia, Mappe A: General Survey (GenStdH, Abt. IV [Mil-Geo.], Berlin, 2nd, corr. printing/closed on 1 March 1941), Textheft, p. 36, and Anlage/Große Kartenskizzen zum Textheft, Enclo-sure 8, with printed note on the slip cover: "Enclosure 8—recorded at the last moment." In addition see Mappe E: Weißrußland. Closed on 27 March 1941.

19. On Hitler, see WiStab Ost, Gruppe La, "Wirtschaftspolitische Richtlinien für Wirtschaftsorganisation Ost, Gruppe Landwirtschaft, 23 May 1941," in *IMT*, Vol. 36, p. 140. On Göring and the Wehrmacht, see the following passages and Müller, *Von der Wirtschaftsallianz*, 172ff. and 184ff. On the State Secretaries, see "Aktennotiz über die Besprechung am 2.5.1941," in *IMT*, Vol. 31, p. 84. On the German Reichsbank, see Referat A 4, Dr. Stamm, *Zur Möglichkeit, den großdeutschen Fehlbedarf an Getreide in Höhe von jährlich 3 Millionen t aus Sowjetrußland sicherzustellen*, 13 June 1941 (copy), BA 25.01, Nr. 7007, Bl. 233-256.

20. Der Reichsmarschall des Großdeutschen Reiches, *Richtlinien für die Führung der Wirtschaft in den neubesetzten Ostgebieten (Grüne Mappe), Teil 1* (2nd printing, July 1941), "Aufgaben und Organisation der Wirtschaft," Nbg. Dok.

NG-1409, with a cover letter from the Chief of the OKW, WFSt/WiRüAmt, 16 June 1941; various summaries of the permanent, in-use "Grüne Mappe" in BA-MA RW 31/128D and /130-133.

21. Rudolf-Christoph Freiherr von Gersdorff, *Soldat im Widerstand* (Frankfurt a.M., 1977), p. 93; Wilfried Strik-Strikfeldt, *Gegen Hitler und Stalin: General Wlassow und die russische Freiheitsbewegung* (Mainz, 1970), p. 32. According to the reference label, the visitor was the leader of a "Vorauskommando Moskau" (v. Gersdorff), although both authors tried to leave uncertainties about his identity. Six was the leader of the "Vorkommando Moskau" of *Einsatzgruppe B*.

22. Examination of Erich von dem Bach-Zelewski, 7 January 1946, in *IMT*, Vol. 4, pp. 535f.; *Terminkalender Himmler* for 12-15 June 1941, OSOBYI Archives, Moscow 1372-5-23, Bl. 445; *Terminkalender* of Himmler's personal Referenten Rudolf Brandt for 12-15 June 1941, BA NS 19/3957, Bl. 87R-89R (inc. names of participants). Also see [Karl Hüser] *Wewelsburg 1933 bis 1945: Kult- und Terrorstätte der SS* (Paderborn, 1982), pp. 3, 323. Peter Whitte et al. (eds.) *Der Dienstkalender Heinrich Himmlers 1941/42* (Hamburg, 1999), pp. 172-74.

23. Himmler to Greifelt, 11 June 1941, BA NS 19/3874, Bl. 9.

24. According to the account in Rosenberg to Lammers, 5 July 1941, BA R 6/21, Bl. 101.

25. Examination of Friedrich Jeckeln, 2 January 1946, BA Zwischenarchiv Dahlwitz-Hoppegarten (hereafter BA D-H) ZM 1683, A.1, Bl. 105. Six had mentioned similar things including Bach-Zelewski's responsibility; see v. Gersdorff, *Soldat*, p. 93.

26. Eugen v. Engelhardt, "Die Ernährungs- und Landwirtschaft der Weißrussischen Sozialistischen Sowjetrepublik," BA F 10772, Bl. 5895-6051, also BA-MA RW 31/299 and /300, here RW 31/299, Bl. 11 and 72. Bernhard Chiari has already discussed the marginal comments without making their full meaning clear in "Deutsche Zivilverwaltung in Weißrußland 1941-1944," in *Militärgeschichtliche Mitteilungen* 52, no. 1 (1993): 67-89, 78f., note 72. For the identity of the author of the marginal comments, see the accompanying text, Dr. Buchholz, "Kriegsverwaltungsrat beim WiStab Ost, zur Rückübersendung an Waldemar v. Poletika," 7 October 1941, BA-MA RW 31/299; *Kürschners Deutscher Gelehrten-Kalender, 8.-14. Ausgabe* (Berlin-W., 1954-83). Poletika (b. 1888) was a professor in Petrograd from 1919-23, emigrated in 1923 to Germany, was professor at the Berliner University from 1934/45, and for a number years the director of the Agrarwissenschaftlichen Forschungsstelle für die Oststaaten in Bonn after 1950.

27. See above all Ulrich Herbert, "Arbeit und Vernichtung: Ökonomisches Interesse und Primat der 'Weltanschauung' im Nationalsozialismus," in *Ist der Nationalsozialismus Geschichte?* ed. Dan Diner (Frankfurt a.M., 1993), pp. 203f. But, in view of the sequence of events—to the extent they can be reconstructed—one cannot share the view that "intentional destruction" (*Vernichtungsabsicht*) was "rationalized" by the agricultural experts only after the events. In any case, this was a selective program for murder. The same goes for assumptions based on the "primacy of the 'Weltanschauung.'"

28. See Mordechai Altshuler (ed.), *Distribution of the Jewish Population of the USSR 1939* (Jerusalem, 1993), pp. 38-41, 69-73 (I thank Dieter Pohl for calling my attention to this publication); *Bevölkerungsstatistik Weißrutheniens*, edited by the Publikationsstelle Berlin-Dahlem (Berlin, 1942).

29. See the examination of Alfred Filbert, 9 June 1959, Staatsanwaltschaft [hereafter StA] Munich I 22 Ks 1/61, Bl. 966-67R; and also 11 and 14 May 1959, StA Berlin 3 Pks 1/62, Vol. 1, Bl. 171 and 200f.; examination of Walter Blume, 2 July 1958, StA Munich I 22 Ks 1/61, Bl. 254, and also 20 May, 1960, StA Berlin 3 PKs 1/62, Vol. 6, Bl. 264R; examination of Ernst Ehlers, 17 April 1959, StA Munich I 22 Ks 1/61, p. 843/R. See Alfred Streim, *Die Behandlung sowjetischer Kriegsgefangener im "Fall Barbarossa"* (Heidelberg and Karlsruhe, 1981), pp. 88f.; for a different view see Ralf Ogorreck, *Die Einsatzgruppe und die "Genesis der Endlösung"* (Berlin, 1996), pp. 68-76.

30. The racist thinker who developed the supposed connections between Jews and their particularly active involvement in revolutionary politics is described by Fritz Nova, *Alfred Rosenberg: Nazi Theorist of the Holocaust* (New York, 1986), 103-24.

31. Ogorreck, *Einsatzgruppen*, pp. 110-27; Andrej Angrick and Martina Voigt, et al., "'Da hätte man schon ein Tagebuch führen müssen.' Das Polizeibataillon 322 und die Judenmorde am Bereich der Heeresgruppe Mitte während des Sommers und Herbstes 1941," in *Die Normalität des Verbrechens: Festschrift für Wolfgang Scheffler*, ed. Helge Grabitz, et al. (Berlin, 1994), pp. 325-385.

32. *Ereignismeldung* [hereafter EM] *43 des Chefs Sipo/SD*, 5 August 1941, BA-MA SF-01/28930, Bl. 1787.

33. Heydrich to the HSSPF im Osten, 2 July 1941, BA R 70 SU/32. Here Heydrich informed the HSSPF about the orders that he had already given the *Einsatzgruppen* before 22 June 1941.

34. See Paul Kohl, *"Ich wundere mich, daß ich noch lebe": Sowjetische Augenzeugen berichten* (Gütersloh 1990), p. 77, 84f., and 261f.; "Bericht Ministerialrat Dorsch (Zentrale der Organization Todt) 10 July 1941," in *IMT*, Vol. 25, pp. 81-83 (according to the report Kluge reserved the right to allow dismissals for himself); EM 20, EM 21, and EM 23, 12, 13 and 15 July 1941, BA-MA SF-01/28929, Bl. 1479ff., 1493, 1513 (Meeting btw. Nebe and Kluge); GFP-Gruppe 570, Einsatzplan for 6-12 July, 1941, BA-MA WF-03/30429, Bl. 347-349.

35. For Brest, see EM 32, 24 July 1941, BA-MA SF-01/28930, Bl. 1637; Letter exchange 221st Sich. Div.-HSSPF Rußland-Mitte 7 and 8 July 1941, BA-MA RH 26-221/12a, Bl. 307 and 315; *Vermerk LKA* Baden-Württemberg/ZStL 23 February 1962, ZStL 202 AR-Z 52/59, pp. 3646-3676. For Bialystok, see Heiner Lichtenstein, *Himmlers grüne Helfer: Die Schutz- und Ordnungspolizei im Dritten Reich* (Cologne, 1990), pp. 69-93; Angrick and Voigt et al., *Tagebuch führen*, pp. 331-336.

36. Befehlshaber rückwärtiges Heeresgebiet Mitte, Abt. VII/Mil.-Verw., *Verwaltungs-Anordnungen Nr. 1 und 2, 7. und 13.7.1941*, ZStA Minsk 409-1-1, pp. 71-73/R; RK Ostland, *Vorläufige Richtlinien für Behandlung der Juden im Gebiet des Reichskommissariats Ostland*, 18 August 1941, Ifz Fb 104/2; *Bekanntmachungen "Der Oberbefehlshaber der deutschen Armee,"* BA-MA WF-03/25645, Bl. 806 (Panzergruppe 3), WF-03/14270, Bl. 242 (4th Army) also printed in Kohl, *Ich wundere mich*, p. 197 (9th Army). For the order of the GenQu 19 August 1941, see Befehlshaber rückwärtiges Heeresgebiet Mitte, Abt. VII/Kr.-Verw., in *Verwaltungsanordnungen Nr. 6, 12.9.1941*, BA F 40540, Bl. 795.

37. 403rd Sich.Div., Abt. Ib, *Besondere Anordnungen für die Versorgung Nr. 23, 13.7.1941* (copy), ZStA Minsk 409-1-1, Bl. 14; Stadtkommissar Brest, *Lagebericht*, 21 November 1941, BA F 13752, Bl. 9; WiStab Ost, *Besondere Anordnungen Nr. 44*, 4 November 1941, BA-MA (BArchP) F 72745, Bl. 478-480.

38. Compare various reports in BA-MA RW 31/90b; *KTB WiStab Ost*, 3, 4, and 8 July 1941, BA-MA (BArchP) F 43384, Bl. 15, 17, 25; Chef WiStab Ost, Reports of 10 and 12 July 1941, BA-MA (BArchP) F 43390, Bl. 832, 836.

39. WiStab Ost, Fü/Ia, *Betr.: Beschäftigung jüdischer Facharbeiter*, 15 July 1941, BA-MA (BArchP) F 72745; Verbindungsstelle OKW/WiRüAmt bei Göring to Thomas, 29 July 1941, BA-MA (BArchP) F 44544, Bl. 103; *Niederschrift über die Sitzung des Wirtschaftsführungsstabes Ost* on 18 of 21 December, 1941, BA-MA (BArchP) F 42743, Bl. 623.

40. E.g., WiStab Ost, 2. *Vierzehntagesbericht (20.7-28.8)*, 9 August 1941, BA-MA (BArchP) F 43390, Bl. 870; Wiln Mitte, Chefgruppe Wirtschaft, *Besondere Anordnungen Nr. 1*, 12 July and also *Nachtrag* 13 July and *Anlage 1*, 19 July, 1941, BA-MA (BArchP) F 42747, Bl. 677, 685.

41. See e.g., *KTB Verbindungsoffizier IV* Wi OKW/WiRüAmt of the 4th Army, 5 and 6 July 1941, BA-MA (BArchP) F 42872, Bl. 9f; EM 21 and EM 145, 13 July and 12 December 1941, BA-MA SF-01/28929, Bl. 1489, 1491; and /28934, Bl. 3391.

42. Wiln Mitte, *KTB-Tätigkeitsbericht* for 20-27 July 1941, BA-MA (BArchP) F 42858, p. 668; Ortskommandantur Minsk, *Befehl Nr. 8*, 21 August, 1941, ZStA Minsk 379-2-4, p. 109; Gebietskommissar Slonim, *Lagebericht*, 25 January 1942, StA Hamburg 147 Js 29/67, Sonderband D.

43. See *Anzahl der Arbeitskräfte, die in mit Wehrmachtaufträgen belegten Betrieben beschäftigt sind, Stand: 10.10.1942*, BA-MA (BArchP) F 42898, Bl. 966f.; Kreiskommissar Grodno, "Kreiswirtschaftsamt, Bericht 9.12.1942," in Serge Klarsfeld (ed.), *Documents Concerning the Destruction of the Jews of Grodno*, Vol. 6 (Paris, 1992), p. 241.

44. For regulations against this, see e.g. the "Verordnung über Arbeitseinsatz, Verpflegung und Entlohnung der Juden des Stadtkommissars Minsk vom 25.8.1942" in *Minsker Zeitung*, 2 September 1942.

45. Urteil LG Berlin 3 PKs 1/62, 22 June 1962, in *Justiz und NS-Verbrechen*, Vol. 18 (Amsterdam, 1977), p. 616; see on the transitional phase e.g. B. *KTB Pol.Btl.322*, 31 August and 1 September 1941, BA F 56753, and *Bericht der Untersuchungskommission des Rayons Dribin*, 5 November 1944, Der Bundesbeauftragte für die Unterlagen des Staatssicherheitsdienstes der ehemaligen DDR [BStU] ZUV 9, Vol. 20, p. 17.

46. *Reitende Abteilung, SS-KavRgt. 2*, 1 August, 1941, 10:00 a.m., BA F 6296, Bl. 936; *Terminkalender Brandt*, 31 July 1941, BA NS 19/3957.

47. See the court proceedings ZStL 204 AR-Z 393/59 and LG Braunschweig 2 ks 1/63, in Staatsarchiv Wolfenbüttel, 62 Nds Fb. 2, No. 1264ff. See in general Yehoshua Büchler, "Kommandostab Reichsführer-SS: Himmler's Personal Murder Brigades in 1941," in *Holocaust and Genocide Studies* 1, no. 1 (1986): 11-25; Ruth Bettina Birn, "Zweierlei Wirklichkeit? Fallbeispiele zur Partisanenbekämpfung im Osten," in *Zwei Wege nach Moskau*, ed. Bernd Wegner (Zurich, 1991), pp. 275-290.

48. Ogorreck, *Einsatzgruppen*, pp. 179-183, 211 and 220 (for the citation).

49. Himmler was "very annoyed" and demanded daily case reports and increased brigade activity. On this, see the radio message from Grothmann (adjutant to Himmler) to Hermann (commander of the 1st SS-Inf. Brigade), 11 August (for the citation); and Knoblauch (Chef Kommandostab Reichsführer-SS) to Jeckeln and SS-Obersturmbannführer Wander to Knoblauch, both 12 August 1941, BA NS 33/312, Bl. 18 and 26 and also NS 33/292 Bl. 23. See also the court procedure ZStL 202 AR-Z 1212/60 (1st SS-Inf. Brigade) and Ogorreck, *Einsatzgruppen*, pp. 190ff.

50. In July 1941, *Einsatzgruppe* B murdered on average 346 people per day, between 1 and 20 August 295 people per day, between 21 August and 13 September 285 people per day, between 14 and 28 September 419 people per day. Totals based on *Einsatzgruppe* B's own data in EM 31, EM 43, EM 73, EM 92, and EM 108, 23 July, 5 August, 4 September, 23 September, and 9 October 1941, BA-MA SF-01/28929-33, Bl. 1627, 1792, 2201, 2558, and 2863. Citation in *Einsatzgruppe* B, *Polizeilicher Tätigkeitsbericht für 17-23.8.1941*, BStU, ZUV 9, Vol. 31, Bl. 35.

51. See Christian Gerlach, "Failure of Plans for an SS Extermination Camp in Mogilev, Belorussia," in *Holocaust and Genocide Studies* 11, no. 1 (1997): 60-78, here 65.

52. See Res. Pol.Btl. 11, *Lagebericht*, 21 October 1941, ZStA Minsk 651-1-1, Bl. 4; judgement of LG Köln 24 Ks 1/63, 12 May 1964, in *Justiz und NS-Verbrechen*, Vol. 20 (Amsterdam, 1979), pp. 173ff.

53. See EM 92 and EM 124, 23 September and 25 October 1941, BA-MA SF-01/28932-33, Bl. 2552-54 and 3042; various court records of witnesses and perpetrators in ZStL 202 AR-Z 179/67, Dok.Bd. 1, Bl. 156ff., 199ff., 236ff., and Bd. 2, Bl. 27ff. and 170ff.; examination of L.A.M. 12 March and S. G.Z. 13 March 1949 as well as *Bericht der Untersuchungskommission des Rayons Dribin*, 5 November 1944, BStU ZUV 9, Vol. 20, Bl. 17, 111, 126.

54. EM 90, 21 September, EM 92, 23 September, EM 108, 9 October, EM 124, 25 October 1941, BA-MA SF-01/28932, Bl. 2479, 2552, /28933, Bl. 2859 and 3042f.

55. OKW/WFSt/Abt.L (IV/Qu), "Betr: Juden in den neu besetzten Ostgebieten" 12 September 1941, in *Deutsche Besatzungspolitik in der UdSSR*, ed. Norbert Müller (Cologne, 1982), p. 72; Wiln Mitte, *Lagebericht Nr. 8-10*, 6 November, 22 November, and 2 December 1941, BA-MA (BArchP) F 42862, Bl. 966, 1003, 1034.

56. For the course of events see Angrick et al., *Tagebuch führen*, pp. 346-350.

57. For an overview with at times different figures see Wila Orbach, "The Destruction of the Jews in the Nazi-Occupied Territories of the USSR," in *Soviet Jewish Affairs* 6, no. 2 (1976): 14-51.

58. Beauftragter des RMO beim Befehlshaber rückwärtiges Heeresgebiet Mitte, *Bericht Nr. 6*, 10 February 1942, BA-MA FPF-01/8212, Bl. 595.

59. Judgement of LG Köln 24 Ks 1/63, 12 May 1964 in *Justiz und NS-Verbrechen*, Vol. 20, pp. 173f.; Statements of Schönemann and of his translator R.L. (1962), StL 202 AR-Z 81/59, Vol. 3, pp. 598, 605f., 628, 695, 702, 773.

60. See the contribution by Christoph Dieckmann in this volume.

61. See AOK 9, Ic/A.O., to Panzergruppe 3, AOK 9/Ia, and Sonderkommando 7a, 28 September 1941, BDC, SL 47 F, p. 236. See also Helmut Krausnick, "Die Einsatzgruppen vom Anschluß Österreichs bis zum Feldzug gegen die Sowjetunion," in *Die Truppe des Weltanschauungskrieges*, ed. Krausnick and Hans-Heinrich Wilhelm (Stuttgart, 1981), pp. 179ff.

62. EM 133, 14 November 1941, BA-MA SF-01/28934, Bl. 3178 and 3188-90; Tätigkeits- und Lagebericht der Einsatzgruppen Nr. 7 for 1-30 November 1941, ZStL UdSSR Bd. 401.

63. See *KTB Wirtschaftskommando Bobruisk* for 1-15 October and 15-31 October 1941, BA-MA (BArchP) F 42901, Bl. 24; *KTB Gruppe IV Wi zb V Nr. 38* (Borisov) for 20-27 October and 3 December 1941, BA-MA (BArchP) F 43063, Bl. 955 and 958; *Rayonverwaltung Borisov* 23 December 1941, 23 January, 23 February, and 18 March 1942, Gebietsarchiv Minsk 624-1-1, Bl.

17, 20f., and 25; on Vitebsk e.g. examination of W.I.B., 29 August 1944, ZStL
USSR Vol. 423, contents data to p. 65f.; *Berichte der Untersuchungskommis-
sion Vitebsk*, ZStA Minsk 861-1-5, Bl. 15, 23; Leni Yahil, *The Holocaust* (New
York and London, 1990), p. 271.

64. See for another view Hannes Heer, "'Killing Fields': Die Wehrmacht und der
     Holocaust," in *Mittelweg 36*, no. 3 (1994): 7-29, here 23-26.

65. On goals and the order of command, see Kommandant in Weissruthenien des
     Wehrmachtbefehlshabers Ostland, Abt. Ia, *Monatsbericht* 11 October-10
     November, 1941, BA-MA RH 26-707/2, Bl. 1 (although here reports that the
     "total eradication of these alien [volksfremden] elements was carried out" are
     included alongside of descriptions of local limitations on the operations and
     the evacuation of "country Jews" [Landjuden]); for the Res. Pol.Btl. 11 see
     Fschr. HSSPF Rußland-Nord to Himmler et. al., 6 and 10 October 1941, BA
     D-H ZB 6735, O.II, Bl. 111 and 115; and Akte ZStA Minsk 651-1-1.

66. See Gebietskommissar Slonim, *Lagebericht 25.1.1942*, StA Hamburg 147 Js
     29/67, Sonderband D; a Jewish survivor received information on the motive
     and the planned number of victims from the deputy *Ortskommandant*, see
     court proceedings of A.O., 26 October 1960, ibid., Sonderband C1, Bl. 19, 22;
     also see the remarks of a perpetrator on the above mentioned appeal in the
     examination of X.H., 1 February 1974, ibid., Vol. 54, Bl. 10326f.; on the sud-
     den halt of the operation when the "quota" had been reached see the statement
     by J.M. (1946), ibid., Vol. 1, Bl. 140, 142; and Nachum Albert, *The Destruc-
     tion of Slonim Jewry* (New York, 1990), p. 87. On Minsk, see EM 124, 1
     December 1941, BA-MA SF-01/28934; judgement of LG Koblenz 9 Ks 1/61,
     12 June 1961 in *Justiz und NS-Verbrechen*, Vol. 17, pp. 510-14; Wassili Gross-
     man and Ilja Ehrenburg (ed.), *Das Schwarzbuch*, pp. 242-45; Anna Krasnop-
     erka, *Briefe meiner Erinnerung: Mein Überleben im jüdischen Ghetto von
     Minsk 1941/42* (Haus Villigst, 1991), pp. 22-27.

67. In this regard, see Herbert Jäger, *Verbrechen unter totalitärer Herrschaft*
     (Frankfurt a.M., 1982), p. 343.

68. BdO Ostland to Lohse, 17 October 1941, ZStA Minsk 651-1-1. Bl. 28.

69. See Dieter Pohl, *Nationalsozialistische Judenverfolgung in Ostgalizien 1941-
     1944* (Munich, 1996), pp. 139ff., and the contribution by Thomas Sandküh-
     ler in this volume; Götz Aly, *"Endlösung": Völkerverschiebung und der Mord
     an der europäischen Juden* (Frankfurt a.M., 1995), p. 355; Shmuel Spector,
     The Holocaust of Volhynian Jews 1941-1944 (Jerusalem, 1990).

70. [WiRüAmt] Chef des Stabes, *Aktennotiz: Besprechung bei Staatssekretär
     Körner am 4.9.1941, 12:00*, BA-MA RW 19/177, Bl. 117-19; letter from
     GenQu Wagner to his wife, 9 September 1941, BA-MA N 510/48; Ver-
     bindungsstab des OKW/WiRüAmts bei Göring to Thomas 16 September 1941,
     in *IMT*, Vol. 36, pp. 107f.; *KTB WiStabOst* 23 September 1941, BA-MA
     (BArchP) F 43384, Bl. 146. Citation in Elke Fröhlich (ed.), *Die Tagebücher von
     Joseph Goebbels, Teil II., Bd. II* (Munich, 1996), 132 (17 October 1941). I am
     grateful to Peter Witte, Hemer, for pointing me to that source. See also ibid. on
     23 October 1941 (p. 161).

71. See my dissertation (as in note 1).

72. For this, see the court proceedings ZStL 204 AR-Z 117/67, 119/67, 121/67,
     and 122/67; the reports of the investigation commission of the Polesje district,
     20 June 1945, of the Kreis Kalinkowitschi, 15 December 1944, and Mosyr 12
     January 1945, ZStA Minsk 845-1-12, Bl. 1-4, and 861-1-12, Bl. 25-30 and
     71-76.

73. Frontline units murdered 20 Jewish people in Lida, 73 in Baranovitchi, 16 in Pinsk, several in Grodno and Lenin, at one time 10 and then 20 in Slonim, and 100-300 in Stolbzy. For details see my dissertation (note 1); for a different interpretation, see Heer, *Killing Fields*, pp. 7ff.

74. In February 1942 alone, Wehrmacht units killed 2,200 Jews in the area of Army Group Center, see Abwehrkommando III (B), *Tätigkeitsbericht Feber, 12.3.1942*, BA D-H FW 490, A, 28, Bl. 10; also see Hannes Heer, "Die Logik des Vernichtungskrieges, Wehrmacht und Partisanenkampf," in *Vernichtungskrieg: Verbrechen der Wehrmacht 1941-1944*, ed. H. Heer and Klaus Naumann (Hamburg, 1995), pp. 104-38, here 117. The statements in Heer, "Killing Fields", on a general "Wehrmacht liquidation program" beyond the actions of the 707th Inf. Div. should be relativized: the 354th Inf. Rgt. took part in large massacres "only" in operations of the section troop Borisov of Einsatzkommando 8 and did not carry them out alone (see Zentralstelle Dortmund 45 Js 9/64, e.g. Vol. 1, pp. 165f.; Vol. 2, pp. 3ff., 11f., 43f.; Vol. 3, pp. 102ff.; Vol. 6, pp. 131f.; Vol. 7, pp. 54f.; Vol. 9, pp. 106f.; Vol. 10, pp. 132; see ZStL 202 AR-Z 81/59, esp. Vol. 3). The at least 3,500 victims of the "fight against the partisans"—Operation "Bamberg" in early 1942—were not "mostly Jews" but rather for the most part non-Jewish farmers; only about 200 were Jews (see *Tagesmeldung der Einheiten der 707th Inf. Div.*, BA-MA RH 26-707/5 and BA-MA WF-03/7364, Bl. 471-94; and eyewitness accounts in Ales Admovitch, Yanka Bryl, and Wladimir Kolesnik, *Out of the Fire* (Moscow, 1980), pp. 31-56). In the Glebokie district (Glubokoje), in May and June 1942, 13,000 Jews were murdered not by the Wehrmacht but by the section troop Lepel of Einsatzkommando 9 under Heinz Tangermann with the assistance of the local German Gendarmes (Gebietskommissar Glebokie to GK Weißruthenien, 1 July 1942, ZStA Minsk 370-1-483, Bl. 15; in this regard see also Jürgen Matthäus, "'Reibungslos und planmäßig': Die zweite Welle der Judenverfolgung im Generalkommissariat Weißruthenien (1942-1944)," in *Jahrbuch für Antisemitismusforschung* 4 (1995): 258f.; Heinz Tangermann, SS-Unterstürmführer, *Bericht, Betr.: Bandenkampfabzeichen*, 30 March 1944, BA D-H ZM 635, A.1, Bl. 73-76 [fragment]).

75. See ZStL 202 AR-Z 64/60 against employees of the Bobruisk field airport; for Orscha, see Heer, *Vernichtungskrieg*, p. 122; for Borisov see Hans-Heinrich Wilhelm, "Die Einsatzgruppe A der Sicherheitspolizei und des SD 1941/42," in Krausnick and Wilhelm, pp. 576-81; on Slonim and Nowogrodek see Heer, *Killing Fields*, p. 25.

76. EM 178, 9 March 1942, BA-MA SF-01/28936, Bl. 3966; *Schwarzbuch*, pp. 249f.; on Baranovitchi, see also *Vermerk* ZStL 2 July 1969, StA Munich 1 113 Ks 1/65a-b, Vol. 7, Bl. 1203. On the meeting of 12 February, see EM 169, 16 February 1942, BA-MA SF-01/28935, Bl. 3846.

77. Examination of Georg Heuser, 1 March 1966, StA Hamburg 147 Js 31/67, Bl. 4291.

78. For this citation, see "Bericht des ständigen Vertreters des Ostministeriums beim RK Ostland 12. 5. über eine Besprechung bei Lohse" on 26 March 1942, IfZ Fb 104/2. There were massive murder "actions" in the following months in GK White Ruthenia alone, see RMO, 20 September 1941 (Durchschlag), BA R 6/387, Bl. 1; RKO, Abt.IIa4, *Betr.: Einsatz jüdischer Ärtze (gez. Trampedach)* 3 November 1941, ZStA Minsk 370-1-141a, Bl. 183. It is especially noteworthy that this report was written not by the Health Department *(Gesundheitsabteilung)* but by the specialist for Jewish questions or "Jewish

expert" (*Judenreferenten*) in the Political Department (*Abteilung Politik*) of the RKO.
79. GK White Ruthenia to the Gebietskommissare, 10 July 1942, IfZ Fb 104/2.
80. GK White Ruthenia, Abt. IIa, *Betr: Auftreten von Juden bei den Banditen*, 8 September 1942 (with Trampedach's marginal note), OSOBYI Archives, Moscow 504-1-7.
81. See court proceedings StA Mainz 3 Ks 1/67.
82. For the citation, see *Stenographisches Protokoll der Besprechung Görings mit den Reichskommissaren und den Militärbefehlshabern der besetzten Gebiete, 6.8.1942*, in *IMT*, Vol. 39, p. 402. See Kube to Lohse, "Betr.: Partisanenbekämpfung und Judenaktion im Generalbezirk Weißruthenien," 31 July 1942, printed in Ernst Klee, Willi Dreßen, and Volker Riess, "*Schöne Zeiten*": *Judenmord aus der Sicht der Täter und Gaffer* (Frankfurt a.M., 1988), pp. 169-71. On the different districts, see e.g. the court proceedings StA Hamburg 147 Js 29/67 (Slonim); StA Munich 1 113 Ks 1/65a-b (KdS-Außenstelle Baranovitchi). The figure of 112,000 Jews murdered in 1942 in GK White Ruthenia is based on data in my dissertation (see note 1).
83. See the figures in note 82; StA Frankfurt a.M., Anklageschrift 4 Js 901/62, 28 March 1968, ZStL 204 AR-Z 393/59, Vol. 17, Bl. 4629; Koch's remarks on the note about the meeting in Rowno on 26-28 August 1942 in *IMT*, Vol. 25, p. 318. See Gerald Fleming, *Hitler und die Endlösung: "Es ist des Führers Wunsch ..."* (Wiesbaden and Munich, 1982), pp. 141-148. For figures on the Jewish population, see *Meldungen aus den besetzten Ostgebieten des Chefs Sipo/SD, Nr. 5, 29.5.1942*, BA-MA SF-01/28937, Bl. 430.
84. Himmler to Keitel 9 July and OKW (Warlimont) to Backe, 13 July 1942, BA-MA (BArchP) F 43386, Bl. 507, 510; and Spector, *The Holocaust of Volhynian Jews*, pp. 172ff.
85. See Himmler to HSSPF Ukraine 27 October 1942, in Helmut Heiber (ed.), "*Reichsführer ...!*" *Briefe von und an Heinrich Himmler* (Stuttgart, 1968), p. 165; see also e.g. Raul Hilberg, *Die Vernichtung der europäischen Juden* (Frankfurt a.M., 1991), p. 400; in contrast see WFSt/Qu, *Betr.: Besprechung beim WBfh. Ukraine am 12.9.42*, notation of 14 September 1942, BA-MA RW 31/59b, Bl. 365 ("the Reichskommissar ordered the liquidation of these Jews"); GK Wolhynien-Podolien (KdS Rowno?) to various KdS-Außenstellen, 31 July 1942 (copy), Archiv der Polnischen Hauptkommission Warsaw, *Sammlung von Aktensplittern von SS- und Polizeieinheiten*, Vol. 77. I am grateful to Dieter Pohl for copies from these files.
86. See court proceedings LG Bielefeld 5 Ks 1/65, Nordrhein-Westfälisches Staatsarchiv Detmold D 21 A, Nr. 6134-6360. For an overview of the German "actions" see Yitzhak Arad, *Belzec, Sobibor, Treblinka: The Operation Reinhard Death Camps* (Bloomington and Indianapolis, 1987), pp. 131-135.
87. Reuben Ainstein, *Jüdischer Widerstand im deutschbesetzten Osteuropa während des Zweiten Weltkrieges* (Oldenburg, 1993), p. 89 and 233f.; court proceedings StA Mainz 3 Ks 1/67 (Lida); RK Ostland, II Fin, *Betr: Zusammenfassung der Juden in Konzentrationslagern*, 31 July 1943, BA D-H ZR 945, A.2, Bl. 22f.; on the "seamless replacement" [*reibungslose Ersetzung*] see WiIn Mitte, *Aktenvermerk über Besprechung mit GK Weißruthenien, 20.9.1943*, BA-MA (BArchP) F 42860, Bl. 1044; for a retrospective view see Gebietskommissar Glebokie, *Räumungsbericht 9.8.1944*, BA R 93/14.
88. This evaluation in Moshe Kaganowitsch, *Der Anteil der Juden an der Partisanenbewegung Sowjetrußlands* (contents summary), StA Hamburg 147 Js

29/67, Vol. 3, Bl. 594/R; Hauptkommissar Baranowitsche, *Bericht 27.8.1942,* Nbg.Dok. NG-1315; Shmuel Spector, "Jewish Resistance in Small Towns of Eastern Poland," in *Jews in Eastern Poland and in the USSR, 1939-1946,* ed. Norman Davies and Antony Polonsky (London, 1991), pp. 138-144, here 143f.; Kohl, *Ich wundere mich,* p. 75.

89. EM 133, 14 November 1941, BA-MA SF-01/28934, Bl. 3196.

90. See Helmut Heiber (ed.), "Aus den Akten des Gauleiters Kube," in *VfZ* 4 (1956): 67-92.

– Chapter 9 –

THE WAR AND THE KILLING OF THE LITHUANIAN JEWS

Christoph Dieckmann

O n 24 June 1941, only two days after the war with the Soviet Union began, in the small Lithuanian town of Gargždai, the first killings of Jews in the German-occupied Soviet Union took place. That afternoon, a commando from the German Security Police and the security service (the SD) from Tilsit and a division of the Security Police from Memel shot 201 people.[1] After this massacre of civilians, a series of further shootings followed along the Lithuanian border. In this way, by 18 July 1941, more than 3,300 people had been killed.

The killings on June 24 in Gargždai have been described by the Stuttgart historian Eberhard Jäckel, according to whom the head of Einsatzgruppe A, Dr. Walter Stahlecker, did not stop at the killing of adult men but allowed "also Jewish women and children" to be shot. This led Jäckel to the conclusion that Stahlecker received verbal instructions on 17 June 1941, during a conversation with his commanding officer Reinhard Heydrich, the head of the Reichssicherheitshauptamt (RSHA, the headquarters of the security service of the Reich), "that he had to, or had permission to, kill all Jews."[2]

This view, which has great significance for the analysis and interpretation of the development of the genocide of the Jews as a whole, rests on the opinion given by the Munich historian Helmut Krausnick as an expert witness in the Federal German court proceedings in Ulm in 1958 with reference to statements from those charged with the killings in the Lithuanian border regions. According to Krausnick, on 23 June 1941, Stahlecker had instructed the local police leaders in Tilsit to "implement the special treatment of all Jews, including women and children, as well as of Lithuanians suspected of Communism."[3]

This assumption appears questionable, both in the light of more recent sources and from the evidence given in the records of the Ulm *Einsatzgruppen* trial itself. The approximately 10,000-12,000 (predominantly Jewish) victims of the first wave of killings in German-occupied Lithuania were in the first place Jewish men and Communists. Jewish women and children were as a rule excluded from these shootings. The first half of this chapter reappraises this discussion of the context and the issuance of orders for the first killings in Lithuania.

In August 1941, a new phase was launched. The German civil authorities, already established at the end of July 1941, switched over to a policy of massacring very nearly the entire Jewish population—men, women, children—in the rural areas. From August 1941 on, the Jewish population in the larger towns of Lithuania were subjected to mass selections to which tens of thousands of Jews fell victim. Within a few months at least 120,000 Jews were shot and killed by German and Lithuanian police, who carried out their task with an inconceivable brutality. The Lithuanian police were established by the German occupation authorities in the very first days of the war, and came under German control. Approximately 45,000-50,000 Jews survived these selections. They were confined to ghettos in order to be put to work for a short period for the German war industry.[4]

The second part of this chapter focuses on the background to this transition from the first to the second phase of the murderous German policy in Lithuania in August 1941. If, as I am trying to show, no order had been given for the total annihilation of the Lithuanian Jews by the beginning of the war in June 1941, how did it come to be that only six weeks later the German leadership then decided to kill not only Jewish men as previously envisaged, but also women and children, in hundreds of mass shootings? In comparison to other regions in occupied Soviet territory, what happened in Lithuania came especially early and amounted to a policy of almost total annihilation—but why? In order to investigate questions about the motives and the timing of the radicalization of the anti-Jewish policy in Lithuania, a reconstruction of the German decision-makers' views of the events is needed. How did the regional German authorities perceive the situation, and how did it appear to the leadership of the Reich?

The war with the Soviet Union, launched with high expectations, took center-stage in the thinking of the National Socialist regime. It is common to argue that there was a close ideological connection between German war aims, the conduct of the war, and the killing of the Jews. By early 1941, the German leadership, as Andreas Hillgruber argued as long ago as 1972, was depicting this war against the Soviet Union as a *"Weltanschauungskrieg"* to exterminate "Jewish Bolshevism" and to procure *"Lebensraum"* for the German people.[5] In this light, the killing of Eastern Jewry during the course of the war would appear at the very least to have already been decided at the outset of the war. Other authors have laid more emphasis on the unexpectedly poor progress of the war, which led the National Socialists to switch their focus, influenced by their antisemitic *Weltanschauung*, to killing the Jews at once, as a "sacrifice and an act of vengeance" for the difficulties encountered in the pursuit of the war and for the prospect of the defeat of the Third Reich: an act of vindictiveness, one might say.[6]

The doubt as to whether these arguments give a satisfactory analysis of the concrete relation between war, antisemitism, and the killing of the Jews in occupied Soviet territory marks the starting point for the following considerations about the structures and motives of the German murder campaign in Lithuania in the summer and fall of 1941.

The Initial Phase: The First Shootings and Pogroms of June–July 1941

The 176th Infantry Regiment under Major General Robert Sattler, part of the 61st Infantry Division, was given the task, as part of Army Group North, of conquering the town of Gargždai on the first day of the attack on the Soviet Union. Through Gargždai ran the only road in the entire region covered by the corps. The bridge there over the Minija was of important strategic significance and could be quickly secured by skirting around Gargždai. However, the Second Battalion's intention "to take the place by surprise" was thwarted because Russian frontier troops defended the area obstinately.[7] In the battle, which lasted until the afternoon of 22 June, probably about 100 Germans lost their lives. Of the approximately 3,000 inhabitants of the small town, there were 1,000 Jews, living particularly in the area to the west of the town, which was most heavily fought over, where the Soviet frontier troops had their emplacements.[8] German troops reported that "civilians had also" taken part in the battles.[9] On 23 June, many of the townspeople, who had tried for the most part to take shelter in cellars, were driven onto the marketplace. There the Jewish population and alleged Communists were probably separated from the rest of the population by frontier police from Memel and the helping hands of Lithuanians from Gargždai. Some 600-700 Jews had to remain overnight in the town gardens. The frontier police officials took those Jewish men above fifteen years of age away to a meadow to the west of the town, where they were guarded by German customs officials.[10] Following the directive to impose collective punishments against the civilian population in places which resisted,[11] a German company leader, with the agreement of the division leadership, informed the nearby frontier police position of the situation in Gargždai. The case was handed over to the frontier police, since the company had to make haste in order to catch up with the regiment, which had already moved on. The mobile units of the Wehrmacht were not themselves to carry out "special search and cleansing actions," since their priorities were to engage in "battle and [forward] movement."[12] The frontier police commissariat at Memel informed their superiors at the state police station in Tilsit, which then made a request to the RSHA in a special priority telex for directions as to what was to be done in view of the fact that the numbers of people arrested by the Wehrmacht had grown appreciably.[13]

On 24 June, the leader of the state police station, Hans-Joachim Böhme, and the head of the SD, Werner Hersmann, met with Stahlecker. Whereas Böhme and Hersmann, as they put it when charged in 1958, said that they had received the order to kill the Jews of Gargždai from Stahlecker, their report to the RSHA of 1 July 1941, read quite otherwise. There it was stated that they had discussed the situation with Stahlecker on 24 June, who "in principle" gave his "agreement to the cleansing actions in the area around the German borders."[14] In this document there is no question of an order, but rather of Stahlecker's "agreement," which therefore suggests that Stahlecker was reacting to the recommendations of Böhme and Hersmann. Seventeen years later, the State Court of Ulm mistakenly took these statements to mean that the accused had been given an "imperative order" (*Befehlsnotstand*).

In fact, however, the state police station at Tilsit instructed Gestapo Chief Dr. Erich Frohwann and SD-Chief Edwin Sakuth from the frontier police commissariat at Memel to prepare for the shooting of 200 able-bodied men. On 24 June, 200 men—Communists and predominantly Jews—were shot under the direction of the state police station in Tilsit and of the frontier police commissariat in Memel, their valuables having been taken before the shootings. A woman who had married a Russian commissar was also killed. The remaining Jewish women and children were locked up in barns guarded by Lithuanian police at the other end of the town and the women were put to work. Almost three months later, on 14 and 16 September, these approximately 300 women and children were then shot by German and Lithuanian police in two "actions" in a forest six to seven kilometers northeast of Gargždai.[15]

The state police station in Tilsit received Stahlecker's agreement not only to shoot Communists and Jews in Gargždai but also to further killings in the Lithuanian border region. Already on the following day, 25 June, the same Kommando shot 214 men and a woman in Kretinga, and 111 men two days later in Palanga. In Kretinga on 25 June, Jewish women and children were explicitly excluded from the killings, according to the state police report.[16] In Palanga, the local commander, also commander of the airbase there, placed at the Kommando's disposal a firing squad of sixteen to twenty men from the 6th Air Training Company of a fighter squadron from the airfield nearby.[17] Luftwaffe soldiers from Airfleet 1 had already driven the Jewish men into the synagogue, where they guarded them while the women were isolated in the Pryšmančiai Farmyard. As in Gargždai, the Jewish women and children from Palanga and Kretinga were shot by Lithuanian and German units two months later, at the end of August and the beginning of September 1941.

In the process of the first killing actions, a further Einsatzkommando was formed, grouping Wehrmacht units with the frontier police commissariat at Memel and the state police station in Tilsit, under their ambitious leader Hans-Joachim Böhme.[18] This Kommando had received extensive authorization for "cleansing actions" in the Lithuanian border area for which Sonderkommando 1b under Erich Ehrlinger and Einsatzkommando 3 under Karl Jäger had already been assigned. On 4 July, Heydrich's authorization was transmitted to the other *Einsatzkommandos*. According to Heydrich, in order to secure and ensure the freedom of movement of the *Einsatzgruppen* and *Einsatzkommandos* he had given state police stations the "authorization to carry out cleansing actions in newly-occupied territories across the border from their sectors."[19]

The defense strategies of the accused in the trials in Ulm of 1958 gave rise to the myth that Stahlecker and Heydrich had issued an order for the killing of Jewish men, women, and children to the state police station at Tilsit at the beginning of the war. As in the Nuremberg Einsatzgruppen trials, here it was a question not of historical fact, but of the "defense line" with which the accused sought to exonerate themselves.[20] Stahlecker's "agreement," Heydrich's "authorization," and the fact that it was above all Jewish men of an age for military service and Communists who were murdered contradict the supposition that at the beginning of the war precise instructions were given for the murder of the whole Jewish population in occupied Soviet territory. When on 30 June 1941, the Lithuanian police chief of Alytus, a town in the south of Lithuania, offered to kill all of the Jews in the whole region with a squad of 1,050 Lithuanian police and partisans in a few days, it was rejected by the German side.[21]

There are some rather clearer hints in another set of instructions given to the *Einsatzkommandos* in Lithuania at the beginning of the war. Hans-Joachim Böhme, the head of the Tilsit state police station, who used the situation in the first days of the war to become the head of one of the *Einsatzkommandos*, was apparently instructed by Stahlecker and Heydrich "to shoot Jewish men aged sixteen or over as well as dangerous Communists." Böhme himself named one such order in defending himself in court, when he sought to deflect the charge that he was responsible for the murder of Jewish women and children.[22] A similar instruction is documented for the region bordering Kaunas. On 15 August, SS-Hauptsturmführer Joachim Hamann of Einsatzkommando 3 in Kaunas instructed the head of the Lithuanian constabulary to seize and isolate all Jewish men older than fifteen in the provincial commissariat of Kaunas, as well as all Jewish women who had been active Communists.[23] The testimony of Böhme was of course given in connection with the question of his responsibility for the shooting of women and children, and the instruction from Hamann to the Lithuanian police was issued at a later time, but the presumption that there was an instruction for the killing of Jewish men over fifteen years old as well as all persons suspected of being Communists is confirmed by the practice of the killings in these first weeks of the war.

Only those Jewish men who were seen as absolutely necessary for the continued operation of industries central to the war effort were explicitly excepted from these killings, in particular Jews who were skilled workers. They were allowed to live after the intervention of the German industrial detachments for whom they worked in ghettos under German control. The general instruction in this regard was sent from the Economic Directorate of the East (Wirtschaftsstab Ost, WiStab Ost) to the regional industrial units on 15 July 1941. These received an order "to leave Jewish skilled laborers in service [where working on] production important for the war effort [and] where no substitute is available and the maintenance of production depends on it."[24]

The systematic action of the Tilsit state police station *Einsatzkommando* in the Lithuanian border region—involving the targeted arrest and murder of specific groups of Communists and of Jewish men and the isolation of the Jewish population, gathering them for the most part into places on the outskirts of the areas in which they lived—was typical of the campaign of the German and Lithuanian police against the Jews before mid-August across the whole of Lithuania. Einsatzkommando 3 in Kaunas and the part of Einsatzkommando 2 active in northern Lithuania up to the beginning of October also focused on these groups.

SS-Unterführer Krumbach from the state police station in Tilsit, under interrogation for his role in the shooting of Jewish men in Kretinga, described the situation in June 1941 with greater clarity than his superiors did when defending their action in court on the ground that they were only following "imperative orders." To the question "How and why was the shooting of all of the Jews to take place, as it was explained to you? Were women and children also discussed?" Krumbach answered "Böhme and Hersmann explained to me then that according to an order from the Führer, the whole of Eastern Jewry had to be exterminated so that there would no longer be Jewish blood available there to maintain a world Jewry, thus bringing about the decisive destruction of world Jewry. This affirmation was by itself not new at that time and was rooted in the ideology of the Party. The *Einsatzkommandos* of the Sipo [Security Police] and of the SD were instituted for this task by the Führer.... To my question what should happen to the Jewish women and children who remained and to the families of the Soviet officers, who after all had to be taken care of and supported, I received the reply that these would in all probability be accommodated in specially constructed camps. Full particulars of these were however still not known, and the time was also not yet ripe for a decision to be made."[25]

In an analysis which appeared in 1991, Peter Longerich argued that the "commanders of the extermination units" had received a "kind of general authorization to kill the Jewish population in the conquered territories, without numerical restriction, which was leveled to begin with essentially against men."[26] Even if Longerich's thesis "of a technique of instruction based on interaction" were to hold true,[27] the assumption that the heads of the *Einsatzgruppen* were given a "general authorization" is too vague. One should rather speak of a specific conception of terror and murder on the part of the Security Police as a systematic means of waging war, which determined the activities of the German death squads formed in the first months of the war. Many statements made before and after 22 June 1941, point to the fact that to the German political, military, and Security Police leadership this was a matter above all else of quickly eliminating the "Jewish-Bolshevik leadership strata," which from the National Socialist point of view constituted the core of the Soviet state. The concept rested on the line laid down by Hitler: "The Jewish-Bolshevik intelligence must be removed since up until now they have been "oppressors" of the people."[28] The German leadership believed that the murder of these most important "*Weltanschauungsträger*" [carriers or vehicles of an ideological world-view] would greatly accelerate the collapse of the Soviet state.

The model for this concept was provided by the murderous progress of the Security Police in Poland after September 1939 against the Polish leadership stratum.[29] In spring 1940, it was used by the General Government as a means to secure the "complete control of the Polish people in this area" as a permanent feature of the German occupation regime, when Hitler gave the following instruction to General Governor Frank: "What we have now identified as the leadership level in Poland, that is to be liquidated; [if a new leadership were to] grow again, it is to be apprehended and done away with in an appropriate period of time."[30] In a more extreme and expanded form this concept was to be executed during the war against the Soviet Union and now took in those Jewish men "fit for military service."

The discussion of the plans for killing campaigns in the spring of 1941, i.e., before the war, shows that the "commissar instructions" and the "legal decree" dealt with not only the political commissars in the Red Army but also the entire group defined by the National Socialists as the "leadership strata" of the Soviet state, whose murder was eventually undertaken both by the army and by the *Einsatzgruppen*. On 25 April 1941, Alfred Rosenberg turned— in view of the lack of personnel—against the option "of a *general* elimination of all state, communal, and local functionaries.... A *general* extermination, as both one of the first acts of battle and also later through the use of civil authorities, would be a measure which, politically and socially, would later inevitably be revenged terribly."[31] There was however no dissent with respect to the "senior and the highest commissars." It was self-evident, according to Rosenberg, "that naturally tens of thousands of oppressors of the peoples of the East would have to be wiped out."[32] The Wehrmacht leadership by contrast turned against the restriction that "only high and very high functionaries should be executed," since it appeared to be difficult to have to separate "the different levels of officials," and it would also be a waste of time.[33]

In the last draft of these "Directions for the treatment of political commissars" of 6 June 1941, there was, then, no further mention of the "treatment of political functionaries"; the Wehrmacht was now only concerned about the political commissars, but only in a broad sense.[34] The rest of the "carrier stratum" in the occupied regions of the Soviet Union was to be turned over to the security divisions and *Einsatzgruppen*, who would thus have more time for "sorting" and investigating those with political responsibilities. General Quartermaster Eduard Wagner had negotiated this division of responsibilities with Heydrich, with the result that the security divisions were to concentrate on the big transportation roads while "the forces of the Reichsführer SS in the hinterlands would mainly take charge of the areas between the runways."[35] The German forces' short- and long-term goals no longer appeared to be in conflict with each other, since the killing of Communists and Jewish men would create "the basis for the final removal of Bolshevism," and at the same time would "secure the areas lying between the supply routes."[36]

The well-known statements made by Heydrich in his letter to the leadership of the SS and the police of 2 July 1941, accordingly envisaged "hitting the Jewish-Bolshevik leadership strata as effectively as possible."[37] Heydrich's instructions took account of Rosenberg's objections of April 1941 to the murder of persons "still useful for industry, union work, and trade." Of the lower levels of officials, "solely" the "radicals" were to be done away with, while all middle-ranking and senior political functionaries were to be killed immediately.

Heydrich's orders to the Security Police and the criminal instructions of the Wehrmacht should be seen as an expression of a process of the division of labor in a "war of *Weltanschauungen*" to which both were committed. Both series of instructions were linked by a concept which emerged from within the Security Police: to kill off the leadership of the Soviet state so as to be able to subjugate the whole country quickly. In the RSHA and Security Police leadership group around Heydrich, but also far beyond that group as well, Jewishness was seen as the "racial" basis of Bolshevism. The murder of the Jewish men was seen as a way of executing the order to "liquidate" the Soviet leadership stratum.[38]

During these initial phases, the male members of the "Jewish intelligence strata" were to be wiped out, not only in the border areas of Lithuania but in the whole of Lithuania.[39] The systematic progress of the German and Lithuanian police in the towns and villages of Lithuania, registering, arresting, and finally killing the upper class of the Jewish community of the day, came out of this concept of radical preventive terror. In addition, the numerous "pogroms" which took place in many parts of Lithuania in the first weeks after the outbreak of war were as a rule of a systematic character: frequently Lithuanian, but also German, police made targeted arrests. In some areas, and above all in Kaunas, the head of Einsatzgruppe A, Stahlecker, instigated deadly pogroms in which the entire Jewish quarter of a town was attacked. In two nights in Kaunas alone, over 2,000 Jews were barbarically murdered. Although Einsatzkommando 7A notified the RSHA from Vilnius (Vilna) that the "self-cleansing efforts" had been intensified there, they did not succeed in organizing a manhunt as murderous as the one in Kaunas.[40] One objective of the pogroms was nevertheless achieved: a "campaign of arrests" was immediately introduced and Communists and Jewish men were taken into custody.[41]

Heydrich's calculation, however, had still further ramifications. The leaders of the *Einsatzgruppen* had to give these pogroms the appearance that Lithuanians had "spontaneously" begun them, taking revenge on "the Jews" in brutal massacres and wild mass shootings for their supposed Bolshevik activity,[42] so that in this way they might prevent the responsibility of the German Security Police for these killings from becoming known "outside."[43] In the wake of these "wild" pogroms, the Security Police could even appear to be a guarantee of order—and here there are clear parallels with the utilization of the pogroms in Germany of 9 November 1938, by the Security Police and SD.[44] Heydrich wanted to set up a basis for legitimizing—in the eyes of "German circles"—the implementation of anti-Jewish policy by force. The Jews had to disappear from the occupied territories on the grounds of peace, order, and coexistence with the indigenous population in these areas, ruled by relatively few German personnel. The Security Police wanted to secure its position as an institutional check on the "wild wrath of the people" and claimed sole responsibility for anti-Jewish policy in the occupied Soviet Union, against the claims of other

German bodies, and above all that of the civil administration. Nevertheless, the Security Police only received an all-encompassing authority for this area in 1943.

Before the beginning of the war, the German leadership had planned on a quick Wehrmacht victory over the Soviet Union, a matter of a few months. After this victory, the Jews were to be deported "to the East," as it was generally said; in June and July 1941, this referred more concretely to the northern regions of the Soviet Union around the Arctic circle, where a large proportion of the Soviet Gulag were. Beyond such vague hints, there were thus far, however, no written plans or material on this project; all deliberations on it thus stand on an insecure foundation.[45] From March 1941 on, all previous planning undertaken by the RSHA and the Reich Commissar for the "resettlement" of the Jewish population could not be implemented to the expected extent. The war for "loot, *Lebensraum*, and annihilation" had also to make it possible for National Socialist population policy planners to overcome the difficulties they were facing in making the "ethnic cleansing of the land" a reality.[46]

As absurd as such a plan for the deportation of European Jewry "to the East" may seem today, in June 1941 the National Socialist leadership clearly took it to be a real possibility. The living conditions there, whether it be in the Pripyat marshes or in the camps of the Gulag Archipelago, were so abject and cruel that in this scheme the prospect of a genocide was visible.

It can thus be asserted that with respect to the first seven weeks of the war in the areas under German occupation, there was in June 1941 still no order envisaging the total elimination of the Jewish population during the war. In expectation of a speedy military defeat of the Soviet Union, vague but exceedingly brutal plans were laid to deport the Jews living in the area under German control to more easterly areas of the occupied Soviet Union after victory. For those people seen by the National Socialists as the most dangerous potential opponents of German rule—the "carrier class" of the Soviet state, Jewish men of fighting age, and especially "the intelligentsia"—an immediate killing campaign was discussed and adopted. This killing program followed from a racist preventive-policing concept and was tuned to the interests of the military. The defeat of the other side in the war was thus to be accelerated and the risk of potential resistance minimized. To this end, a division of labor was discussed and set out between the Wehrmacht, Security Police, and the leaders of the future civil authorities of the occupied Soviet Union. The first instructions given to the Einsatzgruppen were to arrest and kill all Communists and Jewish men over fifteen years of age. The first killings also then took place in those areas from which there had been reports of actual resistance.

The Second Phase: August to November 1941

In mid-August 1941, in contrast with the earlier period covered above, the killings suddenly developed on a greater scale. In the north and northeast of Lithuania, German and Lithuanian units began to kill Jewish women and children. Within three months, by the end of November 1941, at least 120,000 Jews were shot.

A review of the literature on the German occupation regime in Lithuania makes clear that the background for the extension of the killing program to include Jewish women and children has rarely been investigated.[47] Aside from the later works of H.-H. Wilhelm,[48] there has been no more intensive reflection on the question because studies have proceeded from the assumption that a decision to kill *all* of the Jews in the Soviet Union had been taken before the war against the Soviets began. To be sure, Yitzhak Arad did describe the different phases of the anti-Jewish policy but merely conjectured that this was a product of a "technical" problem: the capability of the *Einsatzkommandos* to undertake a planned and graduated process.[49]

In order to trace the question of the radicalization of the anti-Jewish policy at this time in Lithuania, the developments of summer 1941 will now be examined in more detail, and above all from the perspective of the German decision-makers. What had changed for German decision-makers in the region and for those in Berlin? In pursuing this line of inquiry, it is necessary to contrast German expectations of the war with the Soviet Union and the actual progress on the ground. As a result of the unexpected turn in the war, two core areas of German occupation policy were now of the utmost importance: military security and the issue of supplies.

The overall objective of the German war plans was to encircle the main troop divisions of the Red Army in the first weeks of combat, in order that, according to the constantly-repeated formulation of Hitler, the "vital force of the enemy be annihilated."[50] The Commander-in-Chief of the Army, von Brauchitsch, envisaged the initial phase thus: "Presumably heavy battles at the borders, lasting up to four weeks. Subsequently there would only be a small amount of resistance left to be dealt with."[51] The Red Army would already be defeated before the German army reached the Dvina and Dniepr rivers, in the Baltic this meant a decisive conflict while still in Lithuania and west of Latvia.[52] Without considering any alternative whatsoever, every plan proceeded from the assumption "that they would in fact succeed in preventing the Red Army from escaping to the interior of the Soviet Union."[53] Army Group North, comprising twenty-eight divisions, was given the task of "preventing Russian forces capable of fighting from retreating from the Baltic to the east and creating conditions for further speedy advances in the direction of Leningrad."[54]

In the event, however, the military campaign did not develop as expected. Despite the speedy progress of Panzergruppe 4 and parts of the 18th and 16th Armies—Lithuania was fully under German occupation within five days—the main forces of the 8th and 11th Soviet Armies succeeded in pulling back behind the Dvina, partly in an unplanned retreat, partly on the order of their commanding officers. Although the 11th Soviet Army failed to establish lasting defensive positions either at the Dvina or in the area of Pskow and Ostrow, many of its divisions remained battleworthy, and in the Luga sector there was enough time for the Soviet troops to erect defensive lines.

This overturned the assumption underpinning German strategy that, after fierce battles at the beginning of the war behind the old borders of Russia, the path to Leningrad would essentially be free. Following similar developments in the area covered by the Germans' 16th and 18th Armies, the easy possession of the land which had been expected failed to materialize across the entire area covered by Army Group North. From mid-July 1941, it proved particularly difficult for Panzergruppe 4 and the 16th Army to stabilize their sectors at the front in the face of counterattacks from the Red Army.[55] On 26 July, the Chief of the General Staff, Halder, already foresaw the position over the entire frontline "ending in stable [entrenched] warfare," and two weeks later he declared, "What we are undertaking now are the last desperate attempts to prevent stable warfare setting in."[56] The "Blitzkrieg" had failed, since the main fighting forces of the Red Army in the north of the Soviet Union had not been defeated in the first weeks of the campaign.[57] The Germans' underestimation of the "Russian Colossus" became clear in the second half of July, the German attack having already failed to achieve its objective.[58]

However, the Soviet retreat and the German strategists' underestimation of the fighting power as well as the equipment of the Red Army were only one aspect of the impending collapse of the German military's tactical plans. Personnel and material requirements had not been calculated generously and supply and provisioning problems proved to be of major significance for the military situation of the German troops.

Starvation Policy as a Tool of War

Before the war against the Soviet Union a starvation policy of incredible proportions was planned against the Soviet population.[59] A central goal of the war against the Soviet Union was to tackle the economic constraints faced by Germany, in particular with respect to grain and oil, through the exploitation of Soviet resources. In order to attain this objective, it was decided with "approval from the highest level," that "many tens of millions" would have to be allowed to starve to death.[60] At the same time, the starvation policy was conceived of as a weapon of war. Within the shortest time, two-thirds of the entire German army was no longer to rely on the Reich for provisions, but—as it was put in the instructions of 23 May 1941, which laid the basis for the policy—they "had to be provisioned entirely from the East."[61]

In concrete terms, for the supply of Army Group North, in particular in relation to fuel and provisions, a supply base was to be constructed on the Lithuanian-Latvian border in Dvinsk (Daugavpils in Latvian), to replace delivery from the Reich with goods to be found in the occupied Baltic as quickly as possible. It was clear from the outset that east of the Dvina the supply operation would become more difficult.[62] In the event, however, Panzergruppe 4, racing ahead of the 16th and 18th Armies, faced far greater supply problems than expected. The distance which had grown between the Panzergruppe and the infantry armies behind it was enormous, the roads in an exceptionally poor condition and, on top of that, they were constantly overused. In this situation, the intervening areas were "not exploited economically"—as the Head of WiStab Ost, General Wilhelm Schubert, reported, "the population robbed energetically" and the Panzergruppe demanded "motorized economic guard troops," which could not be deployed.[63] From the outset, supply questions were seen as a problem of control and security and not only as a question of requisitioning, procuring, and transporting goods.[64] Already on 1 July, General Quartermaster Wagner noted that "The pacification of the hinterland is causing considerable trouble. The singularity of our military strategy has resulted in far-reaching insecurity in the hinterland, where there are isolated enemy detachments."[65] Moreover, both the infantry units of the 16th Army—which were to be supplied from Lithuania and parts of Latvia—and the units of the 18th Army in Estonia took to the field under conditions in which, as industrial detachments reported, the basic supply process was out of control. The orderly securing of goods to which the army had aspired was thus aggravated. The attempt to bypass the supply problems encountered on land by using supply ships in the Baltic also collapsed, since the German battle fleet had failed to capture the Baltic islands, which, still occupied by the Soviets, lay in the way.[66]

The supply and provisioning situation came further to the fore in mid-July together with the worsening military position on the front. On 17 and 18 July, the head of Panzergruppe 4, General Erich Hoepner, forcefully reproached those responsible for army supplies.[67] Hoepner's units often received only one train per day from the supply base at Dvinsk, instead of the planned ten trains. The whole of Army Group North, instead of receiving the thirty-four trains it claimed to need each day, only exceptionally received as much as eighteen trains per day. For the attack planned in the second half of July by Panzergruppe 4 on Leningrad the whole supply capacity of Army Group North would have had to be placed at their disposal, which would have brought the 16th and 18th armies to a complete standstill.[68] In the following weeks, the attack on Leningrad had to be postponed seven times solely because of supply problems.[69] At the same time the military position of the 16th and 18th armies was in a critical state.[70] On 23 July, Hitler had stressed that what interested him above all else was the attack on Leningrad, to which end "everything possible" should be dedicated.[71] However, General Quartermaster Wagner could not make the necessary supplies available to Panzergruppe 4.[72] For this reason in July 1941 it was already decided not to try to capture and destroy Leningrad and Moscow immediately, but instead to seal off and starve both cities.[73] Supply was not only increasingly endangered by transport conditions; in addition, the procurement of essential goods was already proving to be far more difficult than had been expected. The whole German war effort seemed to be threatened by this. At the end of July, a staff officer in the Economic Armaments Office (Wirtschafts-Rüstungs-Amt, WiRüAmt) summarized his view of the position in the areas covered by Economic Inspection Groups North and Center and outlined the limitations on troop movements caused by supply problems: "We have to be able to count on not finding any supplies in place. If the advance only goes this slowly, and with the ever-greater supply problems it will hardly be possible to go any faster, Russia will systematically burn everything down (viz. Minsk), as it has so masterfully accomplished in every campaign for hundreds of years."[74]

Supply Difficulties in the Area Covered by Army Group North

The German organizations responsible for the supply of the Wehrmacht knew beforehand that the military's objectives rested essentially on whether they succeeded in securing the necessary supplies quickly enough. In the first days of the war, reports came from Lithuania that rich sources of basic provisions had been found. The picture changed very quickly however. The liaison officer with the General Quartermaster reported to the WiRüAmt: "On 27 June incoming reports corrected the previous picture. In Lithuania army stocks almost totally destroyed. Planned destruction of the remaining stocks prepared. Realization prevented by Lithuanian self-defense. For that reason, such large stocks as that in Kovno can generally not be counted on."[75] The various bodies dealing with procurement and transport were increasingly finding it difficult to procure the amounts of goods demanded of them and to transport them to the front.

The 16th Army, for instance, then constantly engaged in fighting with the Soviets, depended for its supplies on the Dvinsk supply center. As early as 17 July the Chief Quartermaster of Army Group North, Major Alfred Toppe, had arranged for this supply base to be established, "as far as possible using booty and supplies from the land," and to procure and secure resources in the area southwest of Dvinsk.[76] At the same time the first reports came in from the liaison officer of Wirtschaftsstab Ost at Army High Command 16 which appeared to affirm the supposition that east of Latvia and Lithuania a "famine, with all its consequences," had set in. The Russian officials had fled, German troops requisitioned supplies without being subject to any control, and the harvest was endangered. "The civilian population was threatened by the specter of starvation!"[77] The geographical spread of the famine was of course from the outset a calculated development. It was intended to facilitate the German war effort and not—as now in practice proved to be the case—to endanger it. German soldiers were often badly supplied, as a letter from the field of 23 July from the area near Dvinsk illustrates: "This war requires iron nerves and composure. That we are often short of provisions is only to be blamed on the bad rail and street connections. Often we are very tight with our provisions, but despite this we must endure. We must at this time last the whole day with half a loaf of bread.... How often I have longed for a proper meal, but unfortunately ..."[78]

Hitler was informed by Halder of the great difficulties faced by the 16th Army.[79] Yet on 27 July, the whole of Panzergruppe 3 from Army Group Centre further south was also ordered to go to the supply base at Dünaburg for provisions, albeit not yet to support Army Group North militarily.[80] The Army Group leaders were clear that they were thus faced by "barely solvable problems" of supply.[81]

In mid-August the branch office responsible for the provisioning of Army Group North under General Quartermaster Wagner, Supply Region North (Versorgungsbezirk Nord), established that in the whole area covered by the 16th Army there was no more livestock left to be taken.[82] Reports came in that the farmers were already totally impoverished and lacked all provisions, even lacking nourishment for themselves.[83] From October all reports spoke of a catastrophic food situation northeast of the Baltic states.

In the wake of food shortages in the rural areas east of the Baltic frontiers, the food shortage came to a head particularly quickly in the Baltic cities. At the beginning of July, Kaunas had supplies of flour and meat for six weeks, and from Vilnius it was reported that remaining foodstuffs would last two weeks.[84] On 9 July, Wirtschaftsstab Ost reported to Wirtschaftsinspektion Nord in Kaunas that in order to secure the hinterland it would be necessary to feed the most needy of the native population. In pursuit of this aim, the "residues" of foodstuffs from the newly-established indigenous authorities were to be released.[85] Finally in Kaunas and Vilnius ration cards were given out, with the proviso that "the amount given out would not be fixed at the outset ... but determined after each daily restocking."[86] Any right the inhabitants of the towns then held to specific quantities of provisions was to be disregarded. The stores that had been taken were low. Only 5,000 to 6,000 tons of grain were left in the depots from which the towns of Kaunas and Vilnius also had to be supplied.[87] In August and September, however, 6,500 tons were delivered to the Wehrmacht,[88] and the towns officially ran out.

Since the German troops, as predicted, were provisioned "off the land," the food situation in the Lithuanian towns next to the rural areas northeast of the borders was "extraordinarily difficult" at all times.[89]

Supply Region North made great efforts—in vain—to be informed of the extent of the "direct provisions taken for troops from the land," in order to be able to determine the magnitude of the provisions still needed.[90] In July 1941, the repeated strongly-worded instructions of Keitel and Wagner to the effect that the economic service centers should at least be kept informed of the involvement of German soldiers in obtaining provisions and live-stock holdings, remained unheeded.[91] The quantity of consumers, on the other hand, was easier to record. In mid-July 1941, the Lithuanian administration responsible for the food industry in Kaunas arranged that by 1 September all mayors and regional directors count those of their inhabitants who did not grow their own food, meaning those "living in the villages and towns and not possessing a plot of land." This would help to determine "how many inhabitants needed to be provided with food centrally."[92] The German authorities eventually made their food provision budget on the basis of 803,000 inhabitants.[93]

At the end of July, the leadership of the Reich turned its attention to the economic problems faced in the war, since the "assumption that operations would be very quick could no longer be made."[94] The previous plans for the starvation policy and the economic exploitation of the occupied regions had to be modified.[95] On 22 July, Herbert Backe, State Secretary in the Reich Supply Ministry, gave a "Report on Provisions" to the main figure responsible for the war economy, Hermann Göring.[96] Göring then, on 27/28 July, summarily ordered that "agricultural products in the occupied regions of the East be centrally registered and be taken to the troops according to the advice given by German supply bases." Only those people "performing important tasks for Germany" were to receive provisions.[97]

From now on, in consequence, labor capability and potential decided who received provisions and who did not. The previous geographical division of the occupied lands into "contributory zones," condemned "to die off," and "surplus zones," which would become "production areas," was modified.[98] Those people from whom no more work in the service of German war industry could be expected were exposed to a merciless starvation policy.

Likewise on 28 July 1941, Wagner and the chief quartermasters of the three army groups decided to refill the holdings of the supply bases by 15 August. After 15 August, they were even to begin stockpiling.[99] Eventually on 12 August, two weeks later, Wagner laid down the requisitioning targets, the delivery quantities for each quarter of the year, to be made available from 1 September 1941, to 31 August 1942 under the jurisdiction of Supply Region North.[100] These targets were very high and amounted to 250,000 tonnes annually in grain for bread alone.[101] From that, at

least 120,000 tonnes were to be supplied from Lithuania.[102] This
amount was the equivalent of some 15 percent of the expected
Lithuanian harvest of 800,000 tonnes of wheat and rye.[103] The economic departments of the German occupation authorities made the
Lithuanian administration responsible for compliance with the
delivery demands and for allocating individual districts with specific requisitioning demands. Nevertheless, these orders, too,
proved far too difficult to fulfill.[104]

The German civil occupation administration was clear that this
would aggravate the food problem for the population in the Baltic.
The food and agriculture department of the Reichskommissariat
pointed out that Göring "decided ... that the Wehrmacht takes
absolute precedence as a consumer ... over the indigenous civilian
population. The deficit in meeting the procurement needs of the
Wehrmacht, which you know full well, will thus be fulfilled under
all circumstances, in an emergency at the expense of the native civilian population."[105] On 31 July, a meeting was recorded in the
records of the body with overall responsibility for economic policy
in the occupied Soviet Union, Wirtschaftsführungsstab Ost: "Backe
asked about the possibility of sending a letter from the Reich Marshal [Göring] to the places concerned. Körner informed the meeting
that the clear instructions of the Reich Marshal were that the interests of the food industry of Greater Germany clearly were to take
priority in all supply questions in the newly-occupied area."[106] In
the same conversation, Backe and Hans Joachim Riecke, leader of
Chefgruppe Landwirtschaft (agricultural economics) in WiStab Ost
and at the same time the division leader for food and agriculture in
the Ministry for the East, stressed that the civil administration also
had "from now on to begin to supply the population with [only]
the smallest rations." The delivery of food supplies was thereby
directly connected to basic questions of not only a medium-term
production increase, but also a fear of growing resistance in the territories which had been plundered.

The Supply of Provisions for Jews

The German occupation authorities in Lithuania sought from the
outset to set up a racist hierarchy for the supply of food, which at
the end of July 1941 was again intensified on the instructions of the
leadership of the Reich. This hit the Jews on the one hand, where
they did not appear useful to the Germans as skilled workers, and
on the other the Soviet prisoners-of-war. Over 200,000 prisoners-

of-war died in Lithuanian camps under the supervision of the Wehrmacht during the first six months of German occupation.

In the first half of July the military administration had already arranged food rationing for the whole of Lithuania. This established a distinction between Jews and non-Jews. The non-Jewish population was supposed to get the parsimonious amount of 1750 grams of bread, 200 grams of flour, 150 grams of grits, 400 grams of meat, 125 grams of lard and 125 grams of sugar per week. The Jewish population by contrast received practically nothing. For them, the allotted amounts each week totaled only 875 grams of bread, 100 grams of flour and 75 grams of grits.[107] Jewish quarters were cut off from the stocks of the town administration and from the kitchens of large factories.[108] When quotas were fixed for the stocks and coupons introduced on 12 July, Jews could only buy at specific times and from special shops, "in order to shorten queues."[109] In the registration of the population for their nutritional allowance, "persons of Jewish origin ... were to be registered separately."[110] On 5 August, the *Deutsche Zeitung im Ostland* (the German Newspaper in the East) summed up the most important orders of the civilian authorities under the heading "The new norms in this industrial area": "Goods must only be handed out to Jews if adequate stocks exist to meet the needs of other inhabitants."

In contrast to the starvation rations in the more easily-controlled prisoner-of-war camps, the draconian food rationing for the Jewish population could not be enforced in this way: insufficient personnel meant they could not control the procedure. The instructions nevertheless document the intention of the German regional occupation authorities to reduce the problems of supplying provisions at the cost of the Jewish population and rapidly to force this population into profound misery. The connection between National Socialist provisions policy and anti-Jewish measures did not only affect Lithuania. On 28 July, Göring instructed that the policy be applied by the entire German occupation administration in the Soviet Union. Moreover, in reply to a query from WiStab Ost he added "that the Jews in the areas administered by Germany had no business to be there any longer. Where they have to be put to work, this must take place in the form of work units.... Provisions must be particularly regulated and overseen."[111] With these words the overall guidelines of the anti-Jewish policy of the Reich leadership at this time were formulated.

The civil administration established in Lithuania at the end of July was given the task of translating this policy into action, together with the SS and police authorities. The Reichskommissar for the

East (*Reichskommissar für das Ostland*, RKO), Hinrich Lohse, spoke briefly afterwards, noting that "the decision of the Führer ... [was that the] Germanization of Reichskommissariat Ost should be the ultimate goal" and that the Jews should be "completely removed from this area."[112] However, what was really meant by the guidelines given by Hitler and Göring—that the Jews be "completely removed from this area," and that the Jews had "no more business to remain in areas occupied by Germany"—was still unclear. In the course of the discussion between the Security Police and the civilian administration in the next week-and-a-half over the "Provisional Guidelines on the Jewish Question in Reichskommissariat Ostland" issued on 13 August, a number of contradictory interventions were made on the subject. What is clear however is that a revision of the previous plans was under discussion. On 6 August, the head of Einsatzgruppe A, Stahlecker, observed in the margin of a letter giving his view of the draft guidelines for the civilian administration: "The draft foresees resettlement from the open country into the towns. If, now, resettlement is to be tackled, this must take place in a fundamental sense, as follows."[113] Stahlecker then outlined, evidently on the basis of previous plans, his conception of "areas reserved for Jews" into which the Jews could be "pumped" so that they could be "profitably used for work" there. Stahlecker's formulation with the emphatic "now" made clear that the Security Police were also having to change their plans with respect to the Jewish population as a whole. The "resettlement" had clearly been planned for later, probably after a speedy victory. This victory was retreating, however, farther and farther into the distance.

What were the results of the discussion between the civilian administration and Einsatzgruppe A? It is possible to reconstruct the decision-making process, in part from eyewitness statements from the postwar trials (which were sometimes very detailed), and partly from examining the policy as it actually developed at the time.

After the end of July 1941, the position of the Jews of Lithuania became more and more difficult. Those Jews who lived on the land were mostly isolated outside populated areas, in synagogues, barracks, barns and abandoned farms. Many thousands of men had already been arrested or murdered. Since women, children, and older men were basically forbidden to leave these improvized camps, they suffered from hunger and disease spread easily. A number of the women were put to work. The Lithuanian police and administration were responsible for guarding them and supplying provisions.

On both the local level and the level of regional commissariats, the worsening supply situation was now discussed *ad infinitum*. At this stage, as many witnesses recalled, it was already clear that with respect to the nutritional wants of Jewish women and children no further allocations were to be made. They were rather to be killed.[114] Thus a Gestapo official from Memel explained in the course of these discussions that Jewish women and children in any case did not work and, as useless consumers of food, had therefore to be done away with.[115] In response, the Lithuanian administration had refused to give food coupons to Jews. In July 1941, the mayor of Kretinga complained to the SD that he did not know how the Jews should be fed.[116] The Lithuanian mayor installed by the Germans in Gargždai pressed for foodstuffs to be provided for the Jewish women and children in Kretinga, the county seat. The German administration explained, however, that the Jews were "useless eaters" and instructions were for them to be killed.[117] The Regional Commissar of Šiauliai, Hans Gewecke, instructed the Lithuanian district president and mayors that they should have the Jewish women and children shot by Lithuanian police, overseen by Germans.[118]

All in all, the witness statements are largely in agreement; by contrast, the surviving records from the civilian administration only give a few signs of this, and these moreover require careful scrutiny. On 13 August, the order was issued for the ghettoization of all Jews in the Šiauliai regional commissariat within the next fourteen days: the rural Jews were to be concentrated in county towns and were to be supplied with provisions from the Lithuanian town administrations.[119] Because of the state of the sources, this must leave open the question of whether or not the statements of the leader of the Tilsit state police station, Böhme, made in connection with a massacre of over 500 Jewish women and children in Batakiai, are true. At the trial, he maintained that SS-Hauptsturmführer Hans Merten, the town commissar charged with overseeing provisions for Tauragė (Tauroggen), had said of these killings that a "definitive solution" of this kind followed from the civilian administration's guidelines of 13 August on the "Jewish Question," according to which the Jews "were to be ghettoized and at the same time subjected to a limitation of their food provisions."[120]

On 3 September 1941, the first clear reference found in the sources thus far was made to the effect that the German Security Police in an area in Lithuania had now been instructed "to liquidate all Jews."[121] Since the discussion between the civilian administration and the Security Police turned solely on the question of Jewish workers and their families, an agreement must have already taken place in the course of August that the remaining Jewish population be killed. The provisional guidelines "for the handling of the Jews in the area of Reich Commissariat East" of 13 August give some information about this arrangement: "The open country is to be cleared of Jews."[122] This took place in the next three months. The inclusion of Jewish women and children in the killings was not a subject of controversy between the civilian authorities and the SS, in contrast to the question of Jewish workers, as the events of the following weeks and months showed.

The killing of the Jewish women and children of Lithuania began on 15 August in the rural regions of northeast and north Lithuania and was then pursued in and around Kaunas. Of the over 90,000 Jews killed up to the middle of October 1941, over 40,000 had lived in the northern Siauliai regional commissariat and over 30,000 in the region of Kaunas.[123] On the basis of the witness statements above, largely in agreement on this point, it is clear that provisions problems in Lithuania and in the region of Army Group North in general constituted an important, and possibly a decisive, factor in the decision to kill, instead of feeding, "useless" Jewish women and children.

Results

This examination of anti-Jewish policy in the Baltic has shown that first the military and six weeks later the civilian occupation apparatus in this region came under massive and increasing pressure to act. The unexpectedly difficult position for the armies in the regions at the front, east of the borders of the Baltic, impacted in particular in two respects on the area which was now the "*hinterland* of the front." On the one hand, more and more goods from the occupied countries had to be requisitioned solely for supply and in the face of logistical transport difficulties be quickly placed at the disposition of the German troops. On the other hand, as the decision-makers saw it, supply and transport problems were inescapably tied to questions of security. The order from Wirtschaftsstab Ost of the beginning of July noted above, to feed only the most needy of the indigenous population, was motivated by the need to "secure the hinterland." In addition to this, the transports were not to be exposed to attacks, a risk which appeared to be a potent one because of the relatively thin security forces of the German occupation regime. Both of these problem areas—the procurement of foodstuffs and the securing of the "hinterland of the front"— appeared to the National Socialists to be resolvable through a more radical policy with respect to the Jewish population. In January

1942, Einsatzkommando 3 correspondingly recounted the murderous deeds of the so-called Hamann Kommando, responsible for the killing of some 60,000 Jews: "In the course of the work of this commando, which covered the whole of Lithuania, it was seen that it would not be possible to stabilize the sectors lying to the rear of the front through the liquidation of a few Jews."[124]

The killing of the Jews could be rationalized according to supposedly real constraints. A higher amount of foodstuffs was left for the remaining population and, most important of all, for German soldiers. At the same time it was said that this would improve the security position. The prospect envisaged before the war that the whole Jewish population would be deported "to the East" presupposed a victory over the Soviet Union and appeared for the time being to be unrealizable.

Facing a war which was claiming many victims, the National Socialist occupation authorities now confronted the question of whether foodstuffs should be placed at the disposition of the Jewish population isolated at the rural margins or go rather to the soldiers fighting at the front. The Lithuanian administration was made formally responsible for the provision of food to Jews in the country and in the ghettos, but the Lithuanian administration depended on the apportioning of foodstuffs under German control. The German administration was, however, unable to make deliveries to the soldiers of its armies and tank divisions without falling back on the Reich for supplies. Its instructions nevertheless read otherwise, and within weeks they became more and more urgent: the administration had to substitute increasing quantities of supplies from the Reich with supplies from the occupied territories. In addition, they faced the instructions issued by Wagner that from 15 August they were to begin to increase the stocks in the supply bases and shortly thereafter achieve very high quarter-yearly deliveries of bread, grain, meat, etc., to the armies. In this context, Göring's order to feed only those working for the German war industry clearly implied that the Jewish section of the population was to be denied the right to live. It was left to the regional occupation administration to determine how exactly the decrees of Hitler and Göring were translated into action.

In reconstructing the perspective of the German decision-makers in Lithuania during this period, it becomes evident that after mid-July 1941 their position appeared to come to a head in unexpected and—in terms of their objectives—threatening ways. The administration was soon placed under increasing time pressure and faced with increasing demands for greater supplies. In this situation the immediate killing of the Jews of Lithuania increasingly appeared from their antisemitic viewpoint to be a real option. The personnel for carrying out such a killing campaign was available thanks to the radical representatives of the German Security Police in the Baltic and Lithuanian policemen who were prepared to collaborate. This was even more true after the SS had widened its network of support bases and personnel in Lithuania at the beginning of August. Himmler had visited Kaunas on 29 July, and on 2 August ordered the SS posts to expand.[125] The Lithuanian police units were assimilated into the constabulary under the SS and police station chiefs,[126] who for their part were placed under the SS leaders, the heads of the police force, and the General Commissar for "police security."[127]

The regional occupation authorities, however, needed the authorization of the Reich leadership for the systematic murder of the Lithuanian Jews. This was a question of systematic mass murder on a scale which ultimately only Hitler could have authorized. Like the German authorities in Lithuania, the Reich leadership also saw that their objectives were increasingly sliding into the distance and that the time available for the campaign was running short. Before the war against the Soviet Union began, Hitler had stressed that it was essential that there be no delays.[128] In July 1941, Hitler therefore asked for an up-to-date timetable: "How much time do I still have before I have to be finished with Russia, and how much time do I still need?"[129] Canaris wrote of the situation in Hitler's headquarters "that the atmosphere there was very nervous, since the Russian campaign—as is increasingly the case—is not drawing to a close 'according to the rules of the game.' The signs are increasingly clear that the war has not led to the internal collapse we expected, but rather to a strengthening of Bolshevism."[130]

The delays caused by the unexpectedly poor military progress of the war effort not only raised a question mark over the implementation of previous strategic planning: it also affected "Hitler's entire program."[131] The "serious crisis"[132] evident from mid-July to mid-August 1941 endangered the cornerstone of National Socialist war diplomacy, the hope of dragging England onto the German side through control of the European continent, and above all else the aspiration to stop the United States from entering the war. Indeed, exactly the opposite began to appear likely. Instead of a "lightning victory" over the Soviet Union, a long drawn-out war of attrition was emerging,[133] which would moreover in all likelihood have to be conducted against an alliance of states which would gradually cooperate more closely and which also had a greater military potential.

The exact date of the eventual conversation between the Reich leadership and the regional occupation authorities in the Baltic about the killing of the Jews in this part of the occupied Soviet Union has thus far not been pinned down. The leaders of the bodies responsible for the civil administration, the economy, the Security Police, and the Wehrmacht had many opportunities to make arrangements orally at the end of July or in early August.[134] The result of these conversations has already been shown above: Lohse spoke on August 1 of the "decision of the Führer" that the Jews be "completely removed from this area."[135] Two weeks later it finally became clear that there was no longer a question of deporting the Lithuanian Jews "to the East," but rather that they were to be exterminated by the German occupation authorities with Lithuanian assistance. On 15/16 August 1941, German and Lithuanian units killed 3,200 Jewish men, women and children in Rokiškis near Dvinsk, which fell within the regional commissariat of Šiauliai under Hans Gewecke, a close friend of Hinrich Lohse.[136] With respect to the date, it is probable that the note by Goebbels on a meeting with Hitler on 19 August also related to the killing campaign against the Lithuanian Jews which had now been embarked upon on a large scale: "We also spoke about the Jewish problem. The Führer is of the conviction that his earlier prophecy in the Reichstag—that if the Jews succeeded in provoking a world war once again, it would end with the extermination of the Jews—was coming true. In these weeks and months it has proven accurate with an almost uncanny certainty. In the East the Jews have to pay the price; in Germany they had in part already paid and they would in the future have to pay still more."[137]

This examination of the situation in the north of the occupied Soviet Union in summer 1941 lays bare a multitude of factors in the political process which contributed to the speed with which the Lithuanian Jews were killed. Already before the war the National Socialist leadership had planned that all of the Jews would, as soon as possible, be completely "transferred" out of the Reich Commissariat of the Eastern Territories. The plans also implied the very rapid and thorough pauperization of the Jewish population: the supposed "Jewish-Bolshevik intelligence" had to be destroyed immediately. National Socialist security policy was the most important element in this calculation. Nevertheless, it was not foreseen at this early date that the decision to kill all of the Jews would be taken during the war.

The fundamental historical context in which the racist and economically-motivated plans to exploit and expel the Jews developed into the sudden murder of the majority of the Jewish population was primarily the unexpectedly unfavorable course taken by the war. There can be no doubt that the Germans' anti-Jewish policy had already escalated before the war against the Soviet Union to such an extent that the killing of the Jews had moved into the realm of the possible. The intent to exterminate the Jews was clear from the plans for deportations. The analysis of the policy as it actually developed makes it seem possible that further factors were also necessary. The modification of the racist starvation policy targeted at large parts of the Soviet population in Lithuania meant first and foremost the pauperization of the Jewish population, which was to be denied the right to live. The mass killings were in this connection legitimized on the grounds of National Socialist security policy, which saw in the Jewish population per se a threat to the "stabilization of the rearwards sections of the front." Food and security policy appear thereby to have been the two crucial aspects which led to a radicalization of anti-Jewish policy and made the decisive changes and transitions possible.[138]

With regard specifically to Lithuania, the sudden murder of a large part of Lithuanian Jewry while the war was still underway appeared to the National Socialist decision-makers in the occupation administration to be a means of reducing a threatening and unexpectedly difficult situation, first and foremost with respect to the German war industry, and at the same time as a way of minimizing security and policing concerns. With respect to the increasing time pressures and the rapidly-intensifying pressures to take action it was decided that "the Jews have to pay the price." In the antisemitic perception of National Socialist decision-makers this could even be portrayed as a legitimate "emergency defense" against the Jews, alleged to be the "mortal enemies" of the German people.[139]

It seems to me for these reasons to be questionable to claim that the basic frame of mind in which these decisions arose was chiefly a product of the intoxication with victory of the National Socialist leadership, rather than of more pragmatic considerations.[140] Perhaps it would be better to say that the successful radicalization of the policy was a product of the situation in which decision-makers were allegedly facing extremely threatening shortages and constantly increasing time pressures. These problems were then to be overcome by virtue of National Socialist "pragmatism," meaning with politically-motivated violence, the terror of a "racial deterrence policy," and targeted killing campaigns motivated by the argument that some must die so that others can live or fight better.

Notes

1. Incident reports, USSR (Ereignismeldungen UdSSR, abbreviated EM below) No. 26, 18 July 1941, Bundesarchiv (BA) R 58/214.
2. Eberhard Jäckel, "Die Entschlußbildung als historisches Problem," in Eberhard Jäckel and Jürgen Rohwer (eds.), *Der Mord an den Juden im Zweiten Weltkrieg: Entschlußbildung und Verwirklichung* (Frankfurt a.M., 1987), pp. 9-17, here pp. 16f.
3. Helmut Krausnick, "Hitler und die Befehle an die Einsatzgruppen," in Jäckel and Rohwer, *Mord*, pp. 88-106, here p. 99.
4. An overview of the killing of the Lithuanian Jews is given by Yitzhak Arad, "The 'Final Solution' in Lithuania in the Light of German Documentation," in *Yad Vashem Studies* 11 (1976): 234-272. The figures given for Jewish victims and survivors are both minimum numbers. Exact statistics are not likely to be found. The figure given by Dina Porat of 175,000 Lithuanian Jews killed by the end of 1941 is probably somewhat too high. Dina Porat, "The Holocaust in Lithuania. Some unique aspects," in David Cesarani (ed.), *The Final Solution: Origins and implementation* (London/New York, 1994), pp. 159-174, here p. 161.
5. Andreas Hillgruber, "Die 'Endlösung' und das deutsche Ostimperium als Kernstück des rassenideologischen Programms des Nationalsozialismus," in *VfZ* 20 (1972): 133-153. Compare Gerd R. Ueberschär, "Der Mord an den Juden und der Ostkrieg: Zum Forschungsstand über den Holocaust," in Heiner Lichtenstein and Otto R. Romberg (eds.), *Täter—Opfer—Folgen: Der Holocaust in Geschichte und Gegenwart* (Bonn, 1995), pp. 49-81.
6. See Philippe Burrin, *Hitler und die Juden: Die Entscheidung für den Völkermord* (Frankfurt a.M., 1993), p. 172, and Arno J. Mayer, *Krieg als Kreuzzug: Das Deutsche Reich, Hitlers Wehrmacht und die "Endlösung"* (Reinbek, 1989), p. 660.
7. Proceedings of the State Court of Ulm against Bernhard Fischer-Schweder and others, Staatsarchiv Ludwigsburg EL 322, Vol. 8, p. 1955. Testimony given on 30 January 1957, by the company commander of the 3rd/I.R. 176.
8. Statement of one inhabitant from Gargždai, Feliksas S. Ibid., Vol. 8, pp. 2095-2097.
9. Walther Hubatsch, *Die 61. Infantrie-Division 1939-1945. Ein Bericht in Wort und Bild* (Friedberg, 1983), p. 18.
10. Bill of indictment against Fischer-Schweder and others, ibid., Vol. 13, p. 3374. Rabbi Meir Levin and a Jewish doctor, Dr. Uksmann, who had been the district doctor under the Soviets, were cruelly mistreated and murdered. See Dov Levin (ed.), *Pinkas HaKehillot, Lita* (Book of the Communities) (Jerusalem, 1996), p. 190.
11. Decree of Hitler of 13 May 1941 about the exercise of martial law in the "Barbarossa" region and giving particular measures taken by the troops. Printed in *Anatomie des SS-Staates*, Vol. 2 (Munich, 1989), pp. 182f.
12. Covering letter of 24 May 1941 from Brauchitsch for the martial law decree of 13 May 1941. Printed in ibid., Vol. 2, pp. 185f.
13. See EM No. 2, 23 June 1941. BA R 58/214.
14. Registered letter from the Tilsit state police station of 1 July 1941 to the Reichssicherheitshauptamt (RSHA) IV A 1. Re: Cleansing campaigns on the other side of the former Soviet-Lithuanian border. Zentrale Stelle der Lan-

desjustizverwaltungen zur Aufklärung von NS-Verbrechen in Ludwigsburg (ZStL), Sammlung UdSSR, File 245 Ag No. 254-257, pp. 2-5.

15. Only Rachel Jamai survived this massacre. See Pinkas HaKehillot, p. 190.

16. "A decision was taken not to renew the action since only Jewish women and children remained in Krottingen." Registered letter from the Tilsit state police station to the RSHA of 1 July 1941, see n. 14.

17. ZStL 207 AR-Z 72/60, Proceedings against H.-H. St. In these proceedings there are explicit descriptions of the murders, committed by Luftwaffe members. The degree of the participation of Wehrmacht units in the shootings at Kretinga is still not easy to clarify.

18. See also Jürgen Matthäus, "Jenseits der Grenze. Die ersten Massenerschießungen von Juden in Litauen (June-August 1941)," in ZfG 44 (1996): 101-117. Matthäus has not considered the role of the Wehrmacht correctly, since he had not seen the trial records in the Ludwigsburg State Archive and the appropriate evidence did not appear in the bill of indictment or in the text of the judgement.

19. Einsatzbefehl No. 6 from Heydrich to the heads of the Einsatzgruppen, 4 July 1941. Sonderarchiv Moskau 500-5-3, p. 48.

20. See Alfred Streim, "Zur Eröffnung des allgemeinen Judenvernichtungsbefehls," in Jäckel and Rohwer, Mord, pp. 107-119, here p. 111.

21. Letter from the "Self-Defense Leader" of the Alytus region, the chair of the executive committee of the regional authorities, and the regional police chief, to the German commanders of the town in Alytus, 30 June 1941, Lietuvos Centrinis Valstybes Archyvas (LCVA) (Central State Archive of Lithuania) R 1436-1-29, Bl. 12f.

22. Judgment of 28 August 1958, against Fischer-Schweder and others. Printed in C.R. Rüter and Adelheid L. Rüter-Ehlermann (eds.), Justiz und NS-Verbrechen, Sammlung deutscher Strafurteile wegen nationalsozialistischer Tötungsverbrechen 1945-1966 (Amsterdam, 1976), Vol. 15, p. 201.

23. Circular letter from Hamann to Reivytis, 15 August 1941. LCVA R 693-2-2, Bl. 2.

24. Telegram from WiStab Ost to Verteiler B of 15 July 1941, Re: Employment of Jewish skilled workers, Latvijas Valsts Arhivs (Staatsarchiv Lettlands) (LVA) P 70-2-52, Bl. 202.

25. ZStL 207 AR-Z 51/58. Proceedings against A. Krumbach and others. Interrogation of A. Krumbach on 7 October 1958, Vol. 1, pp. 86-87.

26. Peter Longerich, "Vom Massenmord zur 'Endlösung'. Die Erschießungen von jüdischen Zivilisten in den ersten Monaten des Ostfeldzuges im Kontext des nationalsozialistischen Judenmords," in Bernd Wegner (ed.), Zwei Wege nach Moskau: Vom Hitler-Stalin-Pakt zum "Unternehmen Barbarossa" (Munich, 1991), pp. 251-274, here p. 267.

27. Ibid., p. 269.

28. Entry for 3 March 1941, Percy E. Schramm (ed.), Kriegstagebuch des Oberkommandos der Wehrmacht (KTB OKW) (Munich, 1982), Vol. 1, p. 341.

29. See Uwe Adam, Judenpolitik im Dritten Reich (Düsseldorf, 1972), p. 305.

30. Werner Präg and Wolfgang Jacobmeyer (eds.), Das Diensttagebuch des deutschen Generalgouverneurs in Polen 1939-1945 (Stuttgart, 1975), pp. 211f.

31. Nuremberg document PS 1020. Memorandum No. 3. Re: UdSSR, p. 7f. Italics in original.

32. Ibid., pp. 6f.

33. Discussion notes made by Tippelskirch OKW/WFSt/Abt. L (IV/Qu) of 12 May 1941. Published in Anatomie des SS-Staates, Vol. 2, pp. 179f.

34. Directions for the treatment of political commissars from the OKW, 6 June 1941. Printed in *Anatomie des SS-Staates*, Vol. 2, pp. 188-191.

35. Thus Wagner on 15/16 May 1941, in a speech to Security Division 285, which was later active in the Baltic. Cited by Ralf Ogorreck, *Die Einsatzgruppen und die "Genesis der Endlösung"* (Berlin, 1996), p. 42.

36. Statements on 6 June 1941, by Nockemann, the leader of RHSA Amt II, made in a conversation with General Quartermaster Wagner, representives from the Security Police, army officers and the counter-espionage department of the OKW. Cited by Ralf Ogorreck, "Die Einsatzgruppen der Sicherheitspolizei und des SD im Rahmen der 'Genesis der Endlösung'. Ein Beitrag zur Entschlußbildung der 'Endlösung der Judenfrage' im Jahre 1941," unpublished Ph.D. dissertation (FU Berlin, 1992), p. 42. The published version of Ogorreck's dissertation mentioned in n. 35 unfortunately omits 51 pages of the dissertation (pp. 36-87), which describe and analyze in the most thorough way to date the history of the genesis of the instructions which were later considered to have been criminal acts.

37. This is the formulation in EM No. 43 of 5 August 1941. BA R 58/214. Heydrich's letter of 2 July 1941, is published in Peter Longerich (ed.), *Die Ermordung der europäischen Juden* (Munich, 1989), pp. 116-118.

38. See Ulrich Herbert, *Best: Biographische Studien über Radikalismus, Weltanschauung und Vernunft, 1909-1989* (Bonn, 1996), pp. 163-180 and pp. 237-245.

39. See EM No. 32 of 24 July 1941. BA R 58/214.

40. EM No. 9 of 1 July 1941. BA R 58/214.

41. EM No. 10 of 2 July 1941. BA R 58/214.

42. Heydrich discussed this (orally) on 17 June, recalling it once again on 29 June and drawing up instructions for it in writing on 2 July 1941. Longerich, *Ermordung*, pp. 116-119.

43. See the full report of Einsatzgruppe A of 15 October 1941. There it appears as: "It was however not undesirable that they, [the German Security Police] at least initially, did not give the appearance of using the clearly unusually harsh measures, which would certainly elicit a stir in German circles. It must be shown to the outside world that the native population itself took the first measures, of its own accord, in a natural reaction against centuries of oppression by the Jews and the terror of the Communists in former times." Sonderarchiv Moskau, 500-4-93.

44. See Ulrich Herbert, "Von der 'Reichskristallnacht' zum 'Holocaust'. Der 9. November und das Ende des 'Radauantisemitismus'," in idem., *Arbeit, Volkstum, Weltanschauung: Über Fremde und Deutsche im 20. Jahrhundert* (Frankfurt a.M., 1995), pp. 59-79.

45. See Götz Aly, *"Endlösung": Völkerverschiebung und der Mord an den europäischen Juden* (Frankfurt a.M., 1995), pp. 268-279; Burrin, *Hitler und die Juden*, pp. 114-116; Hans Safrian, *Die Eichmann-Männer* (Vienna/Zurich, 1993), p. 169.

46. Aly, *"Endlösung,"* p. 319. Already at the end of March 1941, a plan put forward by Heydrich to Göring for the "Solution of the Jewish Question" faced jurisdictional questions from the future Ostministerium (Ministry for the East); memorandum of 26 March 1941, from Heydrich after meeting with Göring. Sonderarchiv Moskau, 500-3-795, Bl. 145. Until the end of September, Adolf Eichmann thought of the "occupied Soviet Russian territories" as a "territory for the establishment of clearance contingents"; see Aly, *"Endlösung,"* pp.

268-279. In October 1941, General Governor Hans Frank finally asked Alfred Rosenberg whether the Polish Jews could not now be deported to the occupied Soviet Union, since Hitler had already authorized Frank to make a general deportation of the Polish Jews in the second half of March and once more on 19 June 1941; memorandum of 14 October 1941, on the visit of Rosenberg to Frank of 13 October 1941. Diensttagebuch, p. 412; see Aly, *"Endlösung,"* pp. 334-336, 338, and 351f.

47. Seppo Myllyniemi, *Die Neuordnung der Baltischen Länder, 1941-1944: Zum nationalsozialistischen Inhalt der deutschen Besatzungspolitik* (Helsinki, 1973); Roswitha Czollek, *Faschismus und Okkupation: Wirtschaftspolitische Zielsetzung und Praxis des faschistischen deutschen Besatzungsregimes in den baltischen Sowjetrepubliken* (Berlin, 1974); Hans-Heinrich Wilhelm, *Die Einsatzgruppe A der Sicherheitspolizei und des SD 1941/42* (Frankfurt, 1996); Knut Stang, *Kollaboration und Massenmord: Die litauische Hilfspolizei, das Rollkommando Hamann und die Ermordung der litauischen Juden* (Frankfurt et al., 1996); Juozas Bulavas, *Vokiškuju Fasistu Okupacinis Lietuvos Valdymas 1941-1944* (German Fascist Occupation Rule in Lithuania) (Vilnius, 1969); Kazys Rukšenas, *Hitlerininku Politika Lietuvoje 1941-1944 Metais* (Hitlerite policy in Lithuania in the years 1941-1944) (Vilnius, 1970); Yitzhak Arad, *Ghetto in Flames: The Struggle and Destruction of the Jews in Vilna in the Holocaust* (Jerusalem, 1980); Dov Levin (ed.), *Pinkas HaKehillot: Lita* (Jerusalem, 1996).

48. Hans-Heinrich Wilhelm, "Offene Fragen der Holocaust-Forschung: Das Beispiel des Baltikums," in Uwe Backes et al. (eds.), *Die Schatten der Vergangenheit: Impulse zur Historisierung des Nationalsozialismus* (Frankfurt a.M., 1992), pp. 403-425.

49. "The rate of extermination [was] dictated by the physical capability of the murder squads." Arad, *Final Solution,* p. 239.

50. As Hitler for instance put it on 23 July 1941, KTB OKW, Vol. 1, p. 1030; on 18 August 1941, KTB OKW, Vol. 1, p. 1054; on 22 August 1941, KTB OKW, Vol. 1, p. 1063ff. Hitler's formulation should be understood in military terms and refers to the destruction of the military potential of the Soviet Union with respect to human and material resources.

51. Note by von Brauchitsch of 1 May 1941, in conversation with Chef L on 30 April 1941, PS 873. International Military Court, Nuremberg, *Der Nürnberger Prozeß gegen die Hauptkriegsverbrecher vom 14. November 1945–1. Oktober 1946: Urkunden und anderes Beweismaterial,* Vol. 26, pp. 399-401; Andreas Hillgruber, *Hitlers Strategie: Politik und Kriegführung 1940-1941* (Bonn, 1993), p. 508.

52. Rolf-Dieter Müller, "Das Scheitern der wirtschaftlichen 'Blitzkriegsstrategie'," in Horst Boog et al. (eds.), *Der Angriff auf die Sowjetunion, Aktualisierte Ausgabe von Das Deutsche Reich und der Zweite Weltkrieg,* Vol. 4 (Frankfurt, 1991), pp. 1116-1227, here p. 1138.

53. Klaus Reinhardt, *Die Wende vor Moskau: Das Scheitern der Strategie Hitlers im Winter 1941/42* (Stuttgart, 1972), p. 35.

54. Deployment instructions of the OKH for "Barbarossa," 31 January 1941, Colonel-General Halder; *Kriegstagebuch: Tägliche Aufzeichnungen des Chefs des Generalstabes des Heeres 1939-1942,* Vols. 2 and 3, Stuttgart 1963/1964 (KTB Halder). Here Vol. 2, Appendix 2, p. 464.

55. See KTB Halder, Vol. 3, 17 July 1941, p. 88; KTB OKW, Vol. 1, p. 1029, and Hitler's "Ergänzungen zur Weisung Nr. 33" of 23 July 1941, in Walther

Hubatsch (ed.), *Hitlers Weisungen für die Kriegsführung* (Munich, 1965), pp. 166-168.

56. Entries for 26 July 1941 and 8 August 1941. KTB Halder, Vol. 3, pp. 121 and 170.

57. Moreover, Army Group South did not succeed either, and the initial successes of Army Group Center were put in question in the battle around Smolensk which dragged on from mid-July 1941. See Reinhardt, *Wende*, pp. 28-35.

58. Müller, *Scheitern*, p. 1167; Gerhard L. Weinberg, *A World at Arms: a global history of World War Two* (Cambridge, 1994), p. 269. Weinberg was referring to the first weeks of August, by which time this failure was clear.

59. Götz Aly and Susanne Heim, *Vordenker der Vernichtung: Auschwitz und die deutschen Pläne für eine neue europäische Ordnung* (Hamburg, 1991). See esp. the chapter "Der Krieg gegen die Sowjetunion und die Vernichtung von 'zig Millionen' Menschen," pp. 365-393. See the contribution by Christian Gerlach in this volume.

60. Industrial policy guidelines of 23 May 1941, for Wirtschaftsorganisation Ost, Gruppe Landwirtschaft. *IMG*, Vol. 36, pp. 135-157, citing pp. 140 and 145.

61. Ibid., p. 148.

62. See Walter Chales de Beaulieu, *Der Vorstoß der Panzergruppe 4 auf Leningrad 1941* (Neckargemünd, 1961), pp. 21f.

63. Weekly report WiStab Ost 6-12 July 1941. Bundesarchiv-Militärarchiv Freiburg (BA-MA) RW 31/11.

64. The basic text on logistical questions relating to supplies is Klaus A. Schüler, *Logistik im Rußlandfeldzug: Die Rolle der Eisenbahn bei Planung, Vorbereitung und Durchführung des deutschen Angriffes auf die Sowjetunion bis zur Krise vor Moskau im Winter 1941/1942* (Frankfurt a.M., 1987).

65. KTB Halder, Vol. 3, p. 32.

66. The command to capture the Baltic islands was issued on 11 July 1941. Werner Haupt, *Heeresgruppe Nord 1941-1945* (Bad Nauheim, 1966), p. 46.

67. Hoepner complained 'most strongly' to all of the commanders on the Eastern Front about the inadequate supply of provisions. Müller, *Scheitern*, p. 1170. In his original plan Hoepner wanted to be in Leningrad by 13 July. Heinrich Bücheler, *Hoepner: Ein deutsches Soldatenschicksal des XX. Jahrhunderts* (Herford, 1980), p. 136.

68. Müller, *Scheitern*, p. 1146.

69. Ibid., p. 1147.

70. See Hitler's Directive No. 33 of 19 July 1941, in Hubatsch, *Hitlers Weisungen*, p. 163.

71. Notes by Halder on lecture by Hitler, 23 July 1941. KTB Halder, Vol. 3, p. 108.

72. Müller, *Scheitern*, p. 1147.

73. The Army High Command made the shift on 25 July 1941. KTB OKW, Vol. 1, p. 1036. Hitler had already told Halder on 8 July that he aimed to use the Luftwaffe on Leningrad and Moscow "to raze them to the ground in order to prevent men remaining there who we would have to nourish in winter." KTB Halder, Vol. 3, p. 52.

74. Report of 28 July 1941, by Gusovius for General Thomas on his journey in the area covered by industrial inspection teams (Wirtschaftsinspektionen, Wi In) Center and North of 23-27 July 1941. BA-MA, WiID 86.

75. Daily report to the WiRüAmt from the Liaison Officer (Verbindungsoffizier, VO) with the General Quartermaster (GenQu). Thomas saw this on 1 July 1941. BA-MA RW 31/90a.

76. Letter from branch office GenQu Nord Dept. II B to distributors on 17 July 1941, re. Registration of captured property and rural resources for the sustenance of operations. LVA P 70-1-3, Bl. 1.

77. Enclosure 52 (23 July 1941), war diary of the VO of OKW/WiRüAmt (IV Wi) at the Army High Command (Armeeoberkommando, AOK) 16. 22 June–14 February 1942. BA-MA RW 46/261.

78. Letter from the field of 23 July 1941 from Private First Class M.F. of the 256th Inf. Div., which as part of the 9th Army (Army Group Center) had conquered the south of Lithuania. Extracts published in Hans Manoschek (ed.), "Es gibt nur eines für das Judentum: Vernichtung": Das Judenbild in deutschen Soldatenbriefen 1939-1944 (Hamburg, 1995), p. 37.

79. Notes by Halder of 23 July 1941, for a report to Hitler. KTB Halder, Vol. 3, p. 127.

80. General Wagner to Halder on 23 July 1941. KTB Halder, Vol. 3, pp. 103 and 106. On 15 August 1941, Hitler decided to assign Army Group North three divisions from Panzergruppe 3 for military purposes too. KTB Halder, Vol. 3, p. 179.

81. Discussion between all three Army Group heads on 25 July 1941. KTB Halder, Vol. 3, p. 120.

82. Enclosure 96, KTB IV Wi AOK 16. BA-MA RW 46/261.

83. Enclosure 80, ibid.

84. EM No. 12, 4 July 1941, and No. 14, 6 July 1941. BA R 58/214. Report from Marrenbach on July 6 about journey of 1-4 July 1941, to Vilnius and Kaunas. BA-MA, RW 31/90b.

85. Telegram from WiStab Ost to Wi In Nord of 9 July 1941. LVA P 70-1-2, Bl. 2. On 11 July 1941, this instruction, in exactly the same wording, was sent as "Special Instruction No. 7" to all economic offices. LVA P 70-2-52, Bl. 190.

86. Report of 31 July 1941, from Captain Reiner and Kriegsverwaltungsrat Ihde of WiStab Ost about a reconnaissance trip to Riga, Dvinsk, and Kaunas. Sonderarchiv Moskau, 1458-40-221, Bl. 68-72.

87. Statement of account of IV Wi AOK 18 relative to stocks on 20 July 1941. LVA P 70-2-40, Bl. 2.

88. Statement of account re. Requirements of Army Group North (16th and 18th armies, Panzergruppe 4) for meat, lard, and flour in August and September 1941. LVA P 70-1-16, Bl. 39.

89. Full report of Einsatzgruppe A of 15 October 1941. Sonderarchiv Moskau 500-4-93, p. 68.

90. Branch Office Gen.Qu. Nord II B to AOK 18 on 4 July 1941, re. Guidelines for the management of the economy in the newly-occupied regions. LVA P 70-2-1, Bl. 14-15.

91. Entry of General Thomas on 18 July 1941, "Ergebnis der Vorträge beim Reichsmarschall und bei Keitel am 17.7.1941." BA-MA RW 19/512, Bl. 37-39. GenQu Wagner re. Land use in the hinterland. Copy to WiRüAmt, Stab 1a, on 1 August 1941. LVA P 70-1-2, Bl. 16.

92. The Kaunas food industry administration to the mayors of all towns and villages and community directors. 16 July 1941. LCVA R 1444-1-13, Bl. 162.

93. Note by the head of the agricultural economics directorate (Chefgruppe Landwirtschaft, Chefgr. La) of WiStab Ost re. Report on working trip around Riga, Kaunas, and Minsk in the period 24 October to 2 November 1941. LVA P 70-2-38, Bl. 83-88.

94. "Richtlinien für die Führung und den Einsatz der Wirtschaftsdienststellen in den neu besetzten Ostgebieten" of 11 August 1941. Published in Rolf-Dieter Müller (ed.), *Die deutsche Wirtschaftspolitik in den besetzten sowjetischen Gebieten 1941-1943* (Boppard, 1991), pp. 418-420.

95. Meeting of Wirtschaftsführungsstab Ost on 31 July 1941. BA-MA RW 31/11, Bl. 99-109. Brief by KTB WiRüAmt of 31 July 1941, entitled "Organisationsfragen Russland." BA-MA Wi-ID/1222.

96. Entry for 22 July 1941, in Göring's desk diary. IfZ Ed 180/5.

97. Order of Göring on 27 July 1941, "Schwerpunkte und Methoden der wirtschaftlichen Ausbeutung der Sowjetunion." BA-MA RW 31/188, Bl. 74-76. Report of 29 July 1941, from General Nagel giving the replies of Göring to questions put by WiStab Ost. BA-MA RW 31/97.

98. Economic policy guidelines of 23 May 1941 (n. 62), p. 156f.

99. KTB Halder, Vol. 3, pp. 125 and 129.

100. This is made clear in a letter from Supply Region North of 11 September 1941, to the Chief Intendant with the Wehrmacht Commander-in-Chief in the East, re. Supply requirements for rations for Army Group North, 15 September to 15 December 1941. LVA P 70-1-4, Bl. 54.

101. Owing to the poor harvest, the distribution of bread grain was lowered by 55,000 tonnes in the autumn. 195,000 tonnes of supply needs remained to be delivered. Statement of account for Food and Agriculture Department in the RKO of 31 January 1942: provision conditions and delivery to the Wehrmacht. LVA P 70-1-16, Bl. 119.

102. Memorandum of a member of Chefgr. La. of WiStab Ost re. Report on working trip to Riga, Kaunas, and Minsk in the period 24 October to 2 November 1941. LVA P 70-2-38, Bl. 83-88.

103. Note by Krauss (RKO): conversation with the General Commissar in Kaunas, Food and Agriculture Department, 16-18 October 1941. Latvijas Valsts Vestures Arhivs [Latvian Historical State Archive) (LVVA) P 1018-1-155, Bl. 24.

104. Supply Region North, 1 October 1941, to Wi In Nord, re. Release of rationed food and luxury goods from the country to the food rationing offices. LVA P 70-1-7, Bl. 26.

105. Letter from Martin Matthiessen, leader of the economics department in the RKO, 5 November 1941, to division leaders in Kaunas, Riga, and Minsk, re. Utilizing the land for the Wehrmacht. LVVA P 69-1a-10, Bl. 537.

106. In the record for the head of WiStab Ost, this passage has been emphasized. RW 31/11, Bl. 99-109. The State Secretary responsible for the four-year plan, Paul Körner, was charged by Göring with the direction of Wirtschaftsführungsstab Ost.

107. Order of the garrison in Alytus to the civil authorities, 14 July 1941. LCVA R 1436-1-38. On 16 July the Lithuanian police were ordered to keep an eye on this food rationing. LCVA R 1436-1-29, Bl. 19-20. In the town garrison in Vilnius, at the beginning of July it had already been decided to leave only half as much rations for the Jews as for the rest of the population. Report from Marrenbach of 6 July on a trip to Vilnius and Kaunas, 1-4 July 1941. BA-MA, RW 31/90b.

108. EM No. 33, 25 July 1941. BA R 58/214.

109. EM No. 17, 9 July 1941. BA R 58/214.

110. Kaunas food industry administration to the mayors of all towns and villages and community superintendents. 16 July 1941. LCVA R 1444-1-13, Bl. 162.

111. Report of 29 July 1941, from General Nagel over the replies from Göring to the questions which WiStab Ost had submitted. BA-MA RW 31/97.
112. Record of 5 August 1941, of the "Discussion of the political and economic situation in the East in the meeting with Reichsminister Rosenberg on 1 August 1941." BA R 6/300, Bl. 1-5, here p. 2.
113. LVVA P 1026-1-3, Bl. 237-239. Noted by Stahlecker on the left side of Bl. 238. In the published version of this document this was wrongly transcribed as "If resettlement is now to be tackled 'here'." In Hans Mommsen and Susanne Willems (eds.), *Herrschaftsalltag im Dritten Reich: Studien und Texte* (Düsseldorf, 1988), pp. 467-471, here p. 469, fn. 17.
114. Rüter, *Urteil*, Vol. 15, pp. 194-203. Proceedings against Fischer-Schweder et al., Bills of Indictment, Vol. 13, pp. 3466-3484.
115. Rüter, *Urteil*, Vol. 15, p. 200ff. Proceedings against Fischer-Schweder et al., Supplementary documents, Böhme memorandum, p. 48.
116. Proceedings against Fischer-Schweder et al., Bills of Indictment, Vol. 13, pp. 3468 and 3484.
117. Proceedings against Fischer-Schweder et al., Vol. 8, Statement by F.-S., p. 2100.
118. See in particular the statements of the Lithuanian Security Police Chief of Kretinga, Pranas Lukys. Proceedings against Fischer-Schweder et al., Vol. 10.
119. Šiauliai Regional Commissariat to the district heads and mayors of the municipalities on 14 August 1941 re. Directions and Guidelines from the Regional Commissar of 13 August 1941. LCVA R 1099-1-1, Bl. 153-155.
120. Proceedings against Fischer-Schweder et al., Supplementary documents, Böhme memorandum, p. 52.
121. Note by Gewecke on 3 September 1941, re. Jewish concerns in Schaulen [Šiauliai]. ZStL 207 AR-Z 774/61, Vol. 3, Bl. 529-530.
122. Provisional guidelines for the handling of Jews in the area under Reich Commissariat East. Printed in IMG, Vol. 27, pp. 19-25, here p. 24.
123. Full report of EG A up to 15 October 1941. Sonderarchiv Moskau 500-4-93.
124. Preliminary instalment of the second Stahlecker report, probably composed in January 1942. BA R 90/146.
125. Letter from Himmler of 2 August 1941, to HSSPF 101-103 and HSSPF East in Krakau, re. SS and police station leaders in the army regions [*Heeresgebieten*] as representatives of the HSSPF. LVVA P 1026-1-17, Bl. 279.
126. The corresponding order of 2 August 1941, for the Lithuanian units in Vilnius can be found in LCVA R 689-1-223, Bl. 16.
127. Himmler announced this on August 9, 1941. "Betr.: SS- und Polizeiorganisation in den besetzten Ostgebieten." Sonderarchiv Moskau 1323-1-50.
128. "We must have successes from the outset. There must be no setbacks." KTB Halder, Vol. 2, pp. 318f. On 4 June 1941, the commanders of the Army Groups were again addressed collectively by Halder: "Important: Speedy Accomplishment of Operation Barbarossa." KTB Halder, Vol. 2, p. 438.
129. Hitler's concern was reported by Keitel when he visited the leadership of Army Group Center in Borrisow at the end of July 1941. Cited by Reinhardt, *Wende*, p. 35. I am grateful to Christian Gerlach for this reference.
130. Diary of Erwin Lahousen, entry for 20 July 1941. IfZ Fd 47.
131. Reinhardt, *Wende*, p. 13.
132. Elke Fröhlich (ed.), *Die Tagebücher von Joseph Goebbels*, Part II Diktate, Vol. 1 (Munich et al. 1996), entry for 19 August 1941, pp. 257 and 261ff. On 29 July 1941, Goebbels noted for the first time that there was a "crisis." On 2 August 1941, he concluded from this that the German people must be pre-

pared for a "hard and eventually a long war." Ibid., p. 139, 164. On 8 August 1941, he believed it was "highly unlikely" that the war against the Soviet Union could still end in 1941. Ibid., pp. 194f.

133. The ever more drastic orders on the security position in the occupied territories were all directed against the Jews, although this early on there was still hardly any resistance on the part of the Jews. On 16 July 1941, Hitler had stated that everyone was to be shot who only looked out of line. On 23 July 1941, Keitel declared: "The troops available for the security of occupied eastern regions will only be sufficient in terms of the breadth of the area ... if the occupying power spreads such a terror which would by itself be sufficient to wipe out all desire on the part of the population to resist." Note for the record by Bormann about conversation between Hitler, Rosenberg, Lammers, Keitel, Göring, Bormann. IMG Vol. 38, 221-L, pp. 86-92; IMG, Vol. 34, pp. 258-9, 052-C.

134. On 24 July 1941, Lohse, the Reich Commissar for the Eastern Territories, before beginning his activities in the Baltic, was informed by General Quartermaster Wagner about the situation there; on 25 July he saw the Wehrmacht's Commander-in-Chief for the Eastern Territories, Walter Braemer; and he spoke on 26 July with Hitler. Shortly thereafter Lohse met with Himmler, the senior SS and police leader Adolf Prützmann and the head of the constabulary Karl Daluege, during Himmler's three-day journey in the Baltic between 29 and 31 July. Stahlecker had likewise "made contact" with the Reich Commissar "immediately after his installation." See the war diary of the diplomat Otto Bräutigam, in *Biedermann und Schreibtischtäter. Materialien zur deutschen Täter-Biographie: Beiträge zur nationalsozialistischen Gesundheits- und Sozialpolitik*, Vol. 4 (Berlin, 1987), p. 138ff. EM No. 35 (27 July 1941), BA R 58/214. Richard Breitman, *The architect of genocide: Himmler and the Final Solution* (Hanover/New England, 1991), p. 190. Landesarchiv Schleswig-Holstein, Lohse papers, Section 399.65, No. 10. Full report of EG A on 15 October 1941. Sonderarchiv Moskau 500-4-93, Bl. 3ff.

135. See above, n. 112.

136. "Gesamtaufstellung der im Bereiche des EK 3 bis jetzt durchgeführten Exekutionen" of 10 September 1941. BA R 70 SU/15, Bl. 78.

137. Goebbels, *Diktate*, entry for 19 August 1941, Vol. 1, Bl. 269.

138. See Ludolf Herbst, *Das nationalsozialistische Deutschland 1933-1945* (Frankfurt a.M., 1996), esp. chapters 12 and 13, here p. 378.

139. First fortnightly report WiStab Ost, 22 June–5 July 1941. BA-MA RW 31/90b.

140. See, for e.g., Christopher R. Browning, "The Euphoria of Victory and the Final Solution: Summer-Fall 1941," in *German Studies Review* 17 (1994): 473-481; Weinberg, *Eine Welt in Waffen*, p. 334.

– Chapter 10 –

IN THE SHADOW OF AUSCHWITZ
The Murder of the Jews of East Upper Silesia

Sybille Steinbacher

At the largest of the National Socialist concentration and exter-mination camps, Jews from throughout Europe were gassed, shot, hanged, poisoned, and killed in medical experiments. At the outbreak of the Second World War, roughly 100,000 Jews were liv-ing within thirty kilometers of the future site of the gas chambers, in the province immediately surrounding Auschwitz. Their fate has never been the subject of historical research; nor has the concrete political history of the area around Auschwitz been examined.[1] And yet East Upper Silesia served as an advanced outpost for National Socialist policies of race and conquest. Not only was the region one of the principal sites of the murder of Jews in eastern Europe, as one of the four annexed eastern areas, it also played a significant role in policies of resettlement and Germanization. Along with the Ruhr, East Upper Silesia was also one of the most important centers of arms production in the German Reich. Unlike in the Warthegau, East Prussia, and Danzig–West Prussia, anti-Jew-ish policy was guided largely by economic principles. As the focus of conflicting economic interests and ideological dogmas, extermi-nation policy in the province underwent a unique evolution. Given the immediate proximity of Auschwitz-Birkenau, certain questions

Notes for this section begin on page 296.

all but clamor for answers: What became of the Jewish population? What were the consequences of the policies of race and conquest, resettlement and forced labor? Was the "Final Solution," in its organization and dynamics, attuned to the concentration and extermination camp?—or to put the matter another way: Were the Jews of East Upper Silesia delivered especially swiftly and thoroughly into the machinery of destruction?

A wealth of newly released empirical material serves to focus our inquiries into "Jewish policy"[2] and the murder of the Jews of East Upper Silesia on several key connections within the context of a sophisticated study of the details of National Socialist extermination policy.[3] Against a background examination into the impetus toward increasingly radical measures arising in the occupied territories and affecting the decisions of the Berlin government, we shall investigate how resettlement policy and "Jewish policy" were functionally related, as well as how the anti-Jewish campaign was conceptually integrated into occupation policy. In addition, the role of agents operating at middle and lower administrative levels of persecution and extermination policy, their freedom of action, and their individual initiatives are of great interest in connection with an investigation of relevant bureaucratic processes of decision-making and implementation. Moreover, the issue of the influence exerted by individual circumstances on the long-range planning of anti-Jewish policy is of great importance, as is the issue of the role played by economic factors in the process of the "Final Solution." Not the least of our concerns is the role played by ideological factors in setting the murder of the Jews in motion.

I

Anti-Jewish policy was in no sense purposely steered toward mass murder in carefully prepared, increasingly radical phases. At least in the initial phase, a definitive program contrived to culminate in "eradication," destruction, and murder did not exist. On the contrary, interruptions and fluctuations were typical, with expulsion being the underlying aim of "Jewish policy" in East Upper Silesia in the early stages. That the occupying forces were ready to resort to open violence was clear from the beginning. Even the early days of September 1939 were marked by terror, when Einsatzgruppe z.b.V. under SS-Obergruppenführer Udo von Woyrsch began to advance from Kattowitz behind the rear guard of the 14th Army of Wehrmacht Army Group South. The force had been rapidly assem-

bled from mixed units of security and regular police specifically for
duty in Upper Silesia on Himmler's teletyped order of the evening
of 3 September.[4] Due to the Silesian uprisings at the beginning of
the 1920s, it was assumed that an especially large number of
activists in the resistance would be operating in the region.
Although the SS-*Einsatzgruppen* in the Polish campaign clearly
had no orders to target Jews, Einsatzgruppe z.b.V., in contrast to
other special units, unleashed a wave of systematic violence against
the Jewish population, which included mass executions and attacks
on Jewish institutions.[5] Presumably those acts were carried out on
the personal initiative of SS-Obergruppenführer Udo von Woyrsch,[6]
who, as one of Himmler's favorites, clearly enjoyed broad freedom
of action in "Jewish matters."[7] A genocidal mentality had already
manifested itself in German units in the first days of the war. The
brutality of their behavior is clear enough in those few but eloquent
entries in the daily reports of Einsatzgruppe z.b.V. referring to
"synagogues catching fire," "incidental shootings," "pacification
actions," and "shooting insurgents."[8]

Even those East Upper Silesian Jews who initially managed to
flee from the marauding troops were subjected to openly capricious
violence. At least, 2,000 Jews, and possibly many more, were permanently forced into the Soviet sphere of influence when Eduard
Wagner, General Quartermaster of the Army High Command,
closed the border at the San.[9] Those who remained in the German
sphere of influence suffered the full weight of racist policy. As early
as 4 September, the Head of the Civilian Administration (CdZ)
issued a decree concerning "the property of persons who have
fled."[10] The exclusion of the Jewish population from the economic
life of East Upper Silesia introduced by that decree was the first act
of state-sponsored anti-Jewish policy. "Jewish policy" began so
swiftly and with such vehemence that the Jews were already economically and socially marginalized before the administrative
structure was fully in place. Within days the occupying forces had
confiscated Jewish-owned landed property, houses and lots, businesses and shops, as well as closing and padlocking shops, freezing
security bonds and bank accounts, and blocking access to safety
deposit boxes. When German trustees, acting on orders from Georg
Brandt, military commander for Upper Silesia, confiscated Jewish
business enterprises, economic "aryanization" became systematic.
Jews were dispossessed, deprived of legal rights, humiliated, and
reduced to a state of panic from the very outset.

In September 1939, Jews comprised barely 5 percent of the
entire population of the province. With its 7.46 million inhabitants,

Silesia was the most populous of the four annexed territories in the East; covering roughly 48,000 square kilometers, it was also the largest. In a complicated administrative restructuring in October 1939, the two newly established administrative units in Oppeln and Kattowitz were added to the existing Silesian government districts of Breslau and Liegnitz, which had been part of the Old Reich.[11] Silesia was thus expanded to include not only the formerly Prussian industrial area around Kattowitz, Beuthen, Hindenburg, and Königshütte, along with the coal mines in the Dombrowa and Olsa region, but also territories lying far beyond the once disputed territory that had been awarded to Poland in accordance with the arbitration agreement reached in Geneva in May 1922. Thus, the Reich was expanded to include areas populated exclusively by Poles and Polish-speaking Jews. These were districts that, prior to the First World War, had been part of Russian-controlled Congress Poland and the Austro-Hungarian Kingdom of Galicia; they had never before belonged to the German—or Prussian—sphere of influence.[12] These areas, bordering directly on the Government General, were added to the Kattowitz government district and officially annexed by the German Reich.

The administrative relationships in the new territories were of primary importance for the evolution of "Jewish policy," because plans for ethnic restructuring were strongly influenced by the location of the borders. The so-called police line, which was drawn at the end of November 1939, was of incomparably more importance for the Kattowitz district than its customs and administrative border with the Government General. It not only ran through the middle of the district but also created two legally distinct areas, each of which had its own political priorities.[13] Throughout the entire occupation, the Kattowitz district remained deeply divided both ethnically and administratively. To the west of the police line lay so-called East Upper Silesia—the main industrial "plebiscite" area. This area had been the bone of contention in the border dispute between the German Reich and Poland after the First World War. It contained about a million Poles, along with approximately 600,000 people of "varying ethnicity—the mixed population typical of Silesia, which was bilingual and could not be definitively assigned to a single nation. In addition, there were about 300,000 Germans and people of German descent, as well as roughly 5,000 Jews. East of the police line, however, in the newly acquired, purely Polish areas, the population consisted almost exclusively of "people of alien ethnicity," totaling about 750,000 Poles and between 90,000 and 100,000 Jews. That area—which included Auschwitz,

then a city with 7,000 to 8,000 Jews—was condescendingly referred
to as the "East Strip." Auschwitz had second-class status for a short
period following its annexation at the end of October 1939, but
was, from May 1941 on, legally equivalent to cities in the Old
Reich.[14] The Auschwitz of the "Final Solution"—and historical
studies of the period have not registered this fact—did not lie in a
geographically nebulous "East," but was a city on what was at that
time German soil.

Because the Jewish portion of the Silesian population had been
small to the point of being undetectable prior to the annexation of
the East Strip,[15] the so-called Jewish question became an issue for
the province only with its eastward expansion in the fall of 1939.
The almost exclusively orthodox Jews in the East Strip had virtually nothing in common with the largely assimilated, German-
speaking Jewish population living west of the police line. Bound by
traditional rites and customs, with their ear locks and long beards,
typically dressed in kaftans, they corresponded precisely to the
stereotypes subscribed to by the German occupiers, who had been
indoctrinated in antisemitism.

 The occupation forces saw the large concentrations of Poles
and Jews in the East Strip as posing serious risks to the Upper Silesian industrial area with its rich coal deposits, and its iron, zinc,
copper, and steel works. In terms of economic and ethnic policy,
the police line was intended to prevent ostensibly negative influences from coming in from the eastern districts. The line, which
separated from the Old Reich all of Danzig-West Prussia and the
Warthegau but only those parts of Silesia and East Prussia comprising the newly acquired regions, was not a national border.
 Nevertheless, as far as police matters and passport control were
concerned, it effectively turned the annexed regions into foreign
territories—or into Reich territories of second-class status.[16] In the
Kattowitz district the police line was intended to secure the western part economically and promote its development as a self-contained, independent economic area. The line was supposed to
protect the economy by reducing unwanted immigration from the
East Strip, preventing smuggling and illicit trade, and safeguarding
the western zones' labor force. The police line was an ethnic wall
separating a western zone marked for Germanization from an area
that was to be isolated and exploited in accord with ethnic policy.
 The line held the "ethnically alien" inhabitants within the East
Strip, prevented free movement and flight, and thus had an important logistic function in the pursuit of the overarching political goal
of "ethnic reordering."

In his new capacity as Reich Commissar for the strengthening of the German Nation (RKF), to which Hitler had appointed him on 7 October 1939, Reichsführer SS (RFSS) Heinrich Himmler was in charge of Germanization in the territories in western Poland.[17] Now responsible for the systematic expulsion of the "racially inferior" Poles and Jews, he succeeded in combining his existing authority in security matters with his new responsibilities so as to establish an enormous power base in the conquered East. The goal of the planned population transfers, for which Himmler created an independent SS apparatus, was to create through resettlement policy a durable core population of Germans cleansed of "racially alien elements" that would serve as a basis for the racial-biological restructuring of all of Europe under German hegemony. The ideological program was to pursue Germanization by radically denationalizing the occupied areas in the East, reconstituting them both economically and socially, and systematically repopulating them with "racially valuable" *volksdeutsch* and *reichsdeutsch* immigrants.[18]

That three-step master plan for implementing ethnic policy envisioned the liquidation of the intellectual and political elite along with property owners, the expulsion of all Jews and most Poles, and the strict segregation of the remaining Polish population from the settlers, who would be German or of German descent. That racist program, euphemistically called "resettlement," was organized in the annexed eastern territories through the so-called short-term plans (*Nahpläne*) and began to be implemented between October 1939 and March 1941. The violent methods employed in the name of "ethnic reordering" impacted the indigenous Jews and Poles in East Upper Silesia in equal measure. In this phase, anti-Jewish policy and anti-Polish policy were based on exactly the same political premises, pursued the same goal, and were organized by the German bureaucracy as being essentially indistinguishable.[19]

II

During the tenure of Gauleiter and Oberpräsident Josef Wagner, relations between the civilian authorities on the one hand and the SS and police on the other were characterized by vigorous conflict over policies of ethnic restructuring. Wagner, a "veteran of the party's political struggle," hence a close confidant of Hitler, had governed in the province since 1935.[20] With the outbreak of the war, due to the constitutionally unique status of the annexed eastern territories,[21] his already far-reaching authority was expanded to embrace additional responsibilities. Together with Fritz Dietlof Graf von der Schulenburg, who served as deputy Oberpräsident in Breslau from 1939, Wagner developed ambitious measures for Germanizing the province. This area was an especially prestigious one because the *gauleiters* were carrying out a personal commission of the "Führer." Hitler proclaimed at the end of September 1939 that, "at the end of ten years," he demanded from them "just one announcement": "namely that their districts were German, and in fact pure German. He would not, however, ask what methods they had used in order to make their districts German, and he would not care if it was later demonstrated that the methods employed to secure control of the area had been neither nice nor exactly legal."[22]

In the area of Germanization policy, Himmler's desire to establish the SS in the conquered East as his own territorial regime independent of civilian authority stood in diametric opposition to the ambitions of Wagner and Schulenburg. In their struggle with the SS, however, the civilian authorities were never motivated by an inclination to object to the forcible expulsion of Poles and Jews on humanitarian grounds. Neither Schulenburg, who at a later stage was one of the leaders of the nationalist conservative opposition and one of the architects of the attempted coup of 20 July 1944, nor Wagner was likely to put up any opposition.[23] Both men were convinced that the "Aryan" race represented a superior level of civilization; they struggled with the SS solely over administrative control of ethnic matters while their interest in the racial and economic protection of the German people was quite in accord with the goals of the SS.

In the fall of 1939, full authority over resettlement policy lay with Gauleiter and Oberpräsident Josef Wagner. Wagner implemented the resettlement program ruthlessly until forced to surrender his authority to the SS once and for all after Himmler's intervention and, along with Schulenburg, officially to step aside for Himmler's favorite, Fritz Bracht.[24] Wagner was already a leading figure in the first deportation project—the so-called Nisko plan.[25] At the beginning of October 1939, as part of the projected establishment of the "Reichsghetto Lublin," Adolf Eichmann, who was at that time still directing the Central Office for Jewish Emigration in Vienna and Prague, prepared on his own initiative for the removal of 70,000 to 80,000 Jews from East Upper Silesia, along with additional Jews from Vienna and Mährisch-Ostrau. Wagner had already been considering expelling the Jewish population from his province's East Strip "beyond Cracow."[26] Once drawn by Eichmann into the Nisko plan, he played a prominent role in the planning but was unable to prevent the collapse of the entire project by the end of October 1939 due to organization and logistical difficulties.

From that point on, the shifting of populations in East Upper Silesia was the task of *Arbeitsgruppe Umsiedler* under the direction of Fritz-Dietlof Graf von der Schulenburg. Initial plans focused on the area west of the police line—the area that seemed to lend itself to immediate Germanization thanks to the large number of inhabitants who were either German or of German ancestry. The East Strip, on the other hand, was considered more of a problem area for ethnic policy due to the large number of "ethnically alien" inhabitants and was temporarily exempted from Germanization. This meant the roughly 100,000 Jews in the East Strip were temporarily spared deportation. Even so, Wagner's office regarded the area east of the police line as crucial to the Germanization program. The East Strip was quickly turned into an internal dumping ground for "racially undesirable" inhabitants of the area west of the police line.[27] That measure became necessary in early 1940, when the Government General reduced the numbers of Poles and Jews that it would accept from the annexed regions, and then later stopped such immigration altogether. Due to difficulties in implementing resettlement policy, the East Strip came to serve as an internal dumping area for "racially inferior" elements from within East Upper Silesia, much as the Government General did for the annexed areas in the East. Subsequently, there developed in that relatively small area a space problem that was to impact massively on the continued evolution of "Jewish policy." German authorities simply left the care and shelter of all the Jews of East Upper Silesia to the existing Jewish communities while herding all the Jews into the East Strip. The largest "deportation destinations" were three cities in the formerly Russian Congress Poland in which Jews had been living for a long time: Bendzin (Polish, Bedzin; Germanized after 1941 as Bendsburg), Sosnowitz (Polish, Sosnowice), and Dombrowa (Polish, Dabrowa). In Bendzin alone, 24,495 of 54,000 inhabitants were Jews; in Sosnowitz, 26,249 of 114,774; and in Dombrowa, 15,663 of 42,000.

III

When Fritz Bracht became the new Gauleiter and Oberpräsident of Upper Silesia, first on temporary, then on permanent appointment,[28] the change in administrative leadership brought a shift in the principles underlying resettlement and Jewish policy. Very much the protégé of the Reichführer SS, Bracht permitted Himmler to exercise the unfettered influence on the province's population policy that he had always craved. Jewish and resettlement policies, which civilian authorities had treated as one and the same, came under the permanent control of the SS in the fall of 1940. The two strands of ethnic policy were immediately separated and assigned to different departments: Fritz Arlt, a twenty-eight year old SS-Untersturmführer who held a doctorate in anthropology, took over as part of his job as Himmler's RKF representative the responsibility both for deporting the Polish population and for settling *volksdeutsch* and *reichsdeutsch* immigrants.[29] "Jewish policy," which was now elevated to the level of a separate department, became the province of SS-Oberführer Albrecht Schmelt, former chief of police in Breslau. Schmelt's office, which was established in October 1940 with headquarters in Sosnowitz, was a unique institution in conquered Poland. Created by Himmler himself, the office probably reported to him either directly or through the *Höherer SS- und Polizeiführer*.[30] Acting as special deputy of the Reichsführer SS, Schmelt created a new kind of system of forced labor "for exploiting and directing the ethnically alien work force in East Upper Silesia." He organized the system, quite in the spirit of the SS, so effectively that within a short period of time roughly 17,000 exclusively Jewish forced laborers, male and female, were being exploited in physically demanding labor a minimum of twelve hours per day. Deprived of social benefits as well as unemployment pay, pensions, health benefits, and birth and death benefits, the Jews were forced to contribute a large portion of their paltry wages to Schmelt's office.

In East Upper Silesia economic interests controlled anti-Jewish policy. Pragmatic labor policy and economic efficiency long took precedence over "racial" dogma. This was characteristic for the evolution and dynamic of the extermination policy, and it distinguished developments in the region from the processes at work in the other annexed regions in the East. Except for the Ruhr, East Upper Silesia had an all but unique status in the armament economy of the German Reich. Rich deposits of zinc, minerals, and lead, huge production sites for iron and steel, and one of the largest coal fields in Europe made the province "an armament factory for the Reich."[31] Himmler's specific interest in securing influence in the very center of the arms industry through the "Jewish investment" makes it clear that he was out to add to his control of security and resettlement policy unlimited economic power in the conquered eastern territories. "Jewish policy" was guided by the premise that the war economy was not to be enfeebled by population experiments, but rather productivity was to be enhanced through the recruitment of a Jewish work force that could be used as desired and exploited to the maximum. In the name of economic efficiency, the use of Jews as forced labor began in East Upper Silesia much earlier than anywhere else in the German occupied regions.[32] From the fall of 1940 on, anti-Jewish policy no longer aimed at expulsions but rather at the systematically organized use of forced labor. Jews were explicitly exempted from the rigorous deportations controlled by RKF Representative Fritz Arlt. Thus, the 17,993 victims of the Saybusch Action, the first resettlement of inhabitants of East Upper Silesia into the Government General, were exclusively Polish.[33] Between September 1940 and January 1941, 4,125 farmers from Galicia were moved into Polish houses, apartments, and farms.[34] Concerning the roughly 560 Jews in the Saybusch district, the order of the Gestapo in Kattowitz stated explicitly: "Jews must not be evacuated."[35]

Under the supervision of Schmelt's office, Jews worked in specially established camps at construction sites along the Silesian strip of the Reichsautobahn between Berlin and Cracow, in forced labor camps attached to various private businesses in open country or in the vicinity of large industrial sites, and in work areas of the Wehrmacht's factories, so-called "shops," which were established under German management in the Jewish cities in the East Strip.

The idea of employing Jews as forced labor in guarded camps was not new. It had been practiced in the Old Reich by the Reich's Institute for Employment and Unemployment Insurance since December 1938,[36] and even a few weeks longer in the Ostmark.[37] Since the outbreak of the war, forced labor had also been a core element of anti-Jewish policy in conquered Poland. Immediately following the invasion, Jews were forced as punishment and "for educational reasons" to clear away rubble, lay railroad tracks, dig anti-tank ditches, sweep streets, and perform ameliorative tasks. On the very day that the Government General was established, Hans Frank decreed forced labor to be obligatory for Jewish males from the age of fourteen, which was later extended to include women and children.

While in other areas the "Jewish investment" was primarily an instrument of social isolation and humiliation, in East Upper Silesia its purpose from the very outset was to achieve economic efficiency. Under Schmelt's monopoly, the use of forced labor was for the first time systematically organized as an instrument of anti-Jewish policy. In the late autumn of 1940, Himmler's special representative

anticipated the practice of renting out prison labor; the IG Farben
Works in Auschwitz was the first private business to adopt the practice in the spring of 1941.[38] It was ultimately introduced throughout
the Reich with the founding of the SS Office of Economic Management (WVHA) in March 1942. Schmelt developed and personally
controlled, independently of the Board of Concentration Camps, a
blanketing network of more than 200 individual camps with exclusively Jewish inmates stretching from East Upper Silesia to Lower
Silesia. In essence, he was already practicing in his area what would
be introduced throughout the Reich under the aegis of the Board of
Concentration Camps in the middle of 1944 when around 500,000
concentration camp inmates in a dense system of camps were forced
to perform forced labor in arms production.

Although Schmelt subjected the Jews of East Upper Silesia to a
rigid system of control, repression, and exploitation, he had a calculated economic interest in maintaining their capacity to work. Pragmatic economic considerations had a retarding effect on dogmatic
interpretation of "racial" principles. Consequently, anti-Jewish policy at first had less harsh consequences in the province than elsewhere in the occupied East. Of course, little is known about the
productivity of the Jews in the forced labor system run out of
Schmelt's office. Given the miserable living conditions, especially in
the Schmelt camps located along the Reichsautobahn, the use of
forced labor there may have been economical but can hardly have
been profitable. One must assume that it proved about as nonsensi-
cal as the practice of recruiting concentration camp inmates for
forced labor. The latters' productivity was less than 50 percent of
that of a German worker, at times as low as 20 percent. But quite
apart from the program's actual efficiency, Schmelt collected fees
from firms for the loan of Jewish workers. The office realized such
high profits that the forced labor program financed, among other
things, a special fund established by Gauleiter and Oberpräsident
Fritz Bracht to underwrite resettlement projects for Volksdeutsche[39]
as well as supplementary aid for the families of fallen SS men.[40]
Additionally, Schmelt's office was a main contributor to the state
purchase of the Gau's "model estate," Parzymiechy, which was to be
used to "set up" Volksdeutsche as farmers.[41] Schmelt also made personal use of the monies derived from the "Jewish investment," building a private residence for himself in the idyllic Parzymiechy region,
and depositing around 100,000 marks in his private bank account.[42]

Anti-Jewish policy in East Upper Silesia, while simultaneously
embodying the principle of complete bureaucratic control and rigorously exploiting the work force, was tricked out in legal garb and

legitimized with the aid of formal legislation. Its goal was isolation and "racial" segregation while simultaneously establishing legal practices in the area that would comport with the "Jewish policy" in the Old Reich. The first step was the introduction of the Nuremberg Laws, which went into effect on 11 June 1941.[43] In that same month, it was decreed that Jews must adopt the given names of Sara and Israel, which had been mandatory in the Old Reich since August 1938.[44] In September 1941, simultaneously with the Old Reich, East Upper Silesia introduced the requirement that Jews wear the yellow Jewish star; the armband that had been required before then was abolished.[45] Additional decrees introduced numerous minor harassments. Beginning in the spring of 1941, Jews might enter government offices only with special permission[46]; in Sosnowitz a special post office for Jews had to be established.[47] Jews were not permitted to perform in or attend concerts.[48] Jews were forbidden to shop in grocery stores owned by non-Jews, and they might not engage in trade.[49] Jews were not permitted to use trains or busses.[50] Exceptions were made only for those who had to commute to and from work in the East Strip. For a time, a special streetcar for Jews, which displayed a blue Star of David and a sign reading "Only for Jews," ran between Sosnowitz and Bendzin.[51] As part of the "Pelzaktion" [fur drive] Jews were compelled to contribute their winter clothes and skiing equipment to German soldiers on the Eastern Front.[52] Ultimately, they were no longer permitted to keep cows or work animals.[53] Even their bicycles were taken away from them,[54] and—in an epitome of absurdity—they were permitted to walk only on the right side of the sidewalk moving in the direction of traffic.

IV

In the euphoria of victory, amid grandiose delusions of power politics, as part of its campaign against the Soviet Union, the National Socialist regime also plotted its course for dealing with ideological enemy number one—the Jews. The ideological equation of Bolshevism and Jewry, which was typically mentioned in the same breath as plans for a "racial" war of extermination, was of decisive significance for the increasingly radical evolution of "Jewish policy."[55] Up until then deportation and resettlement strategists had been forced to endure inertia, obstructions, and impasses in their planning; now the dream of conquering a "gigantic empire in the East" opened a new dimension in the racial and political "reordering of

Europe." Expulsion and extermination now became intermingled. Jewish deaths became a numerical value calculated into plans to "create space for Germans." From then on, the strategy underlying "Jewish policy" was to combine deportations with forced labor leading eventually to exhaustion and death. Those too old, too ill, or too young to work were to be driven into extinction centers near the Arctic Ocean, there to die.[56] When mass shootings of Jewish men began in the occupied areas of the Soviet Union at the end of June 1941, and when women and children were targeted for liquidation in many locations a month later, a "quantum leap"[57] in "Jewish policy" had been reached.

In all probability, systematic extermination resulted from a combination of more or less directed contingency plans that grew harsher in fits and starts. In the planning phase, decisions of the Berlin government were less decisive than the individual initiatives of lower-level officials in the regional civilian and police occupation authorities. Extermination policy was not centrally planned and organized according to the same rules in all areas; it was rather a normal component of each region's system of governance. Mass murder, although it cannot be explained in a way that is entirely free of contradictions, was in all probability the result of an exceedingly complex, long-term political process that for a long time was played out in public. Events were not controlled by a self-regulating, automatic process but rather by real people taking actions at all levels of the apparatuses of occupation in the individual territories.

 A situation of enormous implications arose in the East Strip in March 1941, when, for logistical reasons, preparations for the Russian campaign led to the premature termination of resettlements into the Government General. The existing concentration of Jews now blocked the funneling in of other population groups. Thousands of Poles had to be assigned to mass housing, so-called Polish camps, east of the police line, while simultaneously people of German descent were streaming into the East Strip from the Romanian Buchenland. In the conflict over living space, the province's internal dumping ground became so crowded that the very existence of the Jews concentrated in that area became a source of conflict. Against this background, before Auschwitz-Birkenau became an extermination camp, an atmosphere of collapsing inhibitions and a latent readiness to commit murder was spreading throughout East Upper Silesia.

Among all the diverse causes leading to the murder of the East Upper Silesian Jews, obstacles to the implementation of resettlement policy played an essential role. Deporting and importing ethnic populations, though synchronized in theory, did not stay balanced in

practice. Responsible officials in the RKF and the Reichssicherheitshauptamt (RSHA) insisted on bringing masses of people into the
province without arranging for housing and feeding. All these shifts
of populations were going on simultaneously, and all of them were
emptying into the same area. In the hierarchy of those to be provided for, the Jews were "racially" the least valuable. In the charged
atmosphere of the war against the Soviet Union, the conflict over living space became a ready-made justification for local politicians,
resettlement strategists, architects, and development planners to not
even include Jews in their plans for the future. In the transition from
a policy of deportation to mass murder, the logistical muddle in the
East Strip provided an ostensibly rational pretext for causing the
Jews simply to "vanish." When all activity relating to resettlement
policy degenerated into a series of frantic attempts to control the
chaos following the premature termination of resettlements in
March 1941,[58] pushing the Jews out became about all the authorities could agree on.

Contrived justifications were part of the program of murder
throughout the eastern occupied regions. Homicidal intentions
were concealed beneath the weighing of practicalities, and rationalizations were put forward as excuses for increasingly radical
actions. Thus, circumstances peculiar to a given situation, which
civilian and police functionaries took to be insoluble dilemmas,
provided an additional impetus for setting mass murder in motion.
Utopian schemes for "sanitizing" society provided the driving force
and the conceptual foundation of the program of murder. Those
responsible justified their own actions as harsh but, given the goal
of Germanization, unavoidable. Making cities and communities
German, along with an expanding program for refurbishing the
cities and modernizing the economy, provided the conceptual
framework for setting mass murder in motion.[59]

Antisemitism, posturing as a master race, and the concept of
Lebensraum coalesced in the hubris of planning for Germanization.
But seeking the sole explanation of mass murder in that complex of
supposedly rational justifications does not do justice to the com-
plexity of the causal chain. The destruction of the Jews—and this
must be stressed—was not a by-product of rationally devised plans
for reordering Europe.[60] And yet the processes at work in East
Upper Silesia demonstrate unambiguously that, against the conceptual background of Germanization, long-range plans for economic and social restructuring played a central role in setting the
destruction of the Jews in motion—and that there existed a functional connection between Germanization and genocide. From the

interplay of ideological motivations and the situational "necessity" of Germanizing the Polish and Jewish cities in the East Strip, there arose the dynamic of systematic mass killing.

Josef Wagner and Fritz Dietlof Graf von der Schulenburg had already created the logistical preconditions, when, in one of their last official acts, they permitted the East Strip, which had hitherto been exempted from the Germanization program, to be included in the area marked for ethnic reordering. The upgrading of the region's status was decreed on 10 October 1940 and, after details were clarified, approved by Himmler on 16 January 1941.[62]

At the same time, the number of Jewish inhabitants in Sosnowitz and Bendzin was constantly rising, because in the process of recruiting forced laborers, SS-Oberführer Albrecht Schmelt had caused small Jewish communities in the East Strip to be dissolved and their inhabitants moved to the large collection points.[63] The uninterrupted influx of Jews provoked massive criticism from Oberbürgermeister Franz-Josef Schönwälder in Sosnowitz and Bürgermeister Kowohl in Bendzin. Both municipal executives saw the Germanization program being seriously jeopardized, and both initiated measures to increase the pressure on the Jews. Schmelt's forced labor policy enjoyed the support of the municipal heads of government only when Jews were being moved to camps to work on the Reichsautobahn or in industries,[64] but not when they were being recruited as workers for the Wehrmacht "shops" in Sosnowitz and Bendzin. With the support of Police Chief Alexander von Woedtke, Kowohl and Schönwälder seriously impeded this usage of forced labor. Kowohl justified his position on the grounds that the German population should no longer have to "put up with" being thrown together with "Jewish parasites."[65]

In East Upper Silesia, anything that disrupted Germanization— from ramshackle houses to "racially" undesirable human beings— was ruthlessly swept aside. Rationalizations that stigmatized the Jews as harmful, disruptive, or superfluous and thus justified their disappearance did not, however, serve the purpose of overcoming any psychological inhibitions on the part of the officials. To assume as much would be to concede that they were aware of the injustice of their actions. Rapid Germanization was a political mandate, and the professional horizon of the local politicians was correspondingly narrow. Now that moral inhibitions had collapsed during the weeks of military rule, the responsible authorities lacked any awareness of the injustice of their actions. Their practice of justifying the disappearance of the Jews on ostensibly rational grounds reveals less a need for self-justification than a conscious conviction that what they were doing was right.

In the name of Germanization, mid- and lower-level officials set in motion a mechanism that was directly linked to the crimes of the SS in Auschwitz-Birkenau. Mass extermination—erroneously characterized after the war as a "regression to barbarism"—was motivated to a considerable degree by a desire to colonize and civilize. Simply put: The mass murder of the Jews was committed in order to bring "German culture" to the conquered eastern territories.

The labor policy of Schmelt's office, which gave priority to economic efficiency and strove to maintain the Jews' ability to work, conflicted with the eagerness of civilian administrative authorities to rid themselves of the Jews at once. The worse the military situation became following the German defeat before Moscow in December 1941, the more intensively the "Jewish investment" was exploited for the sake of arms production. A violent disagreement arose between Schmelt and the civilian authorities over the issue of the "working Jews." The conflict did not come about due to actions by the leadership of the regime, but rather developed locally—which indicates just how much freedom of action the local functionaries enjoyed. It appears most likely that Himmler laid down the basic tenets of "Jewish policy" relating to arms production, then granted his special representative Albrecht Schmelt the freedom to act on his own authority. Schmelt was supported by economic and Wehrmacht enterprises that were profiting from Jewish labor. The pressure to proceed more radically definitely came from the civilian authorities.

In connection with the Speer program, Schmelt stepped up his use of Jewish labor. Beginning in the spring of 1942, he had Jews trained for arms production, even as skilled laborers in concrete and construction.[66] Later, thanks to the serious labor shortage throughout the Reich, they became indispensable to the war effort. In the spring of 1942, 6,500 Jews were employed in forty armament factories crucial to arms production. In addition, numerous new Schmelt camps were established to support the production of submarines, airplanes, munitions, ceramics, freight cars, heavy machinery, tiles, light bulbs, and sugar—even highway construction and structural engineering. How successfully the SS strove to amass economic power is clear from an April 1942 communication from Higher SS- and Police Leader (HSSPF) Ernst Heinrich Schmauser to Himmler, in which Schmauser proclaimed himself especially pleased by the fact that Jews working in construction were being used in an area, "for which other workers are hardly available at all anymore."

The integration of Jews into arms production led to a slowing of the process of murder that was peculiar to the region. In contrast to what one might expect given the close proximity of Auschwitz-Birkenau, the Jews of East Upper Silesia were delivered into the machinery of murder neither remarkably rapidly nor especially thoroughly. On the contrary, most Jews were still alive after the Jewish populations of whole cities and regions in occupied Poland had already been exterminated. As late as November 1943, according to the figures of Richard Korherr, Chief Statistician for the Reichsführer SS, Schmelt still had at his disposal a total of 50,570 Jews. Thus, East Upper Silesia contained roughly a third of the Jews in the entire Reich who were still being employed as forced laborers.[68]

From the victims' perspective, working under the supervision of Schmelt's office offered protection and security against being transported to the extermination camps. For that reason, the province surrounding Auschwitz became a haven for Jews fleeing from other parts of occupied Poland. Several hundred Jews, especially from the Government General, tried to insinuate themselves into the East Upper Silesian forced labor camps in an effort to save their lives.[69]

In the final analysis, the labor program under Schmelt merely postponed murder; it did not prevent it. The first wave of systematic exterminations in East Upper Silesia began on 12 May 1942. From then until August, when mass murder temporarily reached a record pace, a total of roughly 38,000 Jews had been transported. More than half were judged unfit for work and transported directly to the Auschwitz-Birkenau camp; the rest went to the Schmelt camps.

Between October 1942 and March 1943, the Jewish quarters of Sosnowitz and Bendzin were sealed off as closed ghettos. Unlike the Jews in the Warthegau and the Government General, the Jews of East Upper Silesia had not previously been subjected to comprehensive ghettoization. Nor had starvation—an important tool of anti-Jewish policy in Warsaw and Lodz—been applied due to the economic interest in the Jews' productivity.

Presumably in response to the uprising of the Warsaw ghetto, Himmler ordered the destruction of all Jewish communities in the East Strip at the end of May 1943. The labor policy thus became obsolete; the extermination program could proceed unimpeded. A special supplement to an order of the Reichsführer SS of 21 May 1943 providing for all Jews to be deported from the Reich and from the protectorate of Bohemia and Moravia "to the east, or to Theresienstadt," made it clear that SS-Obersturmbannführer Adolf Eichmann, Chief of the Jewish Council in the RSHA, was to discuss with SS-Oberführer Schmelt "at once" "the issue of removing" the Jews of East Upper Silesia.[70] Four weeks later the death trains began running from Sosnowitz and Bendzin to the extermination camp at Auschwitz-Birkenau. By mid-August 1943 the ghettos had been liquidated, and more than 30,000 additional Jews had been taken away and killed. An order of the local SS command in Auschwitz read: "In recognition of work performed by all members of the SS in recent days, the commander has ordered that all service units shall have leave from 1300 hours on Saturday, 7 August 1943, through Sunday, 8 August 1943."[71] This directive related to the murder of East Upper Silesian Jews; it meant simply that the SS in the camp were being rewarded with a free weekend. The last transport from an East Upper Silesian forced labor camp, carrying a total of twelve Jews, pulled into Auschwitz-Birkenau on 23 July 1944.[72]

Roughly one of every ten inhabitants of the East Strip had been killed after the ghettos were dissolved; in Bendzin, more than half; in Sosnowitz, around a third of the city's population. The Executive Committee (Oberpräsidium) in Kattowitz under Fritz Bracht reported these figures to the chancellery of the NSDAP in September 1944. The "Jewish element," it was prosaically reported, had been "deported, which is to say, eliminated." That was demonstrated in two columns of figures showing former and current population counts under the terse headings: "formerly" and "now."[73]

In September 1943, Schmelt moved his offices to Annaberg in the region west of the police line, where he held civilian authority as Chairman of the Regional Council (Regierungspräsident) in the district of Oppeln.[74] On Himmler's instructions, between September 1943 and July 1944, the largest camps were removed from Schmelt's control and incorporated into the state system of concentration camps; the concentration camp at Groß-Rosen took over twenty-eight Schmelt camps, and Auschwitz-Birkenau absorbed at least fifteen;[75] Schmelt camps with fewer than 800 inmates were abolished at once.[76] Schmelt, however, retained both his title and, though considerably reduced in size, his system of forced labor, which he now operated with Polish workers. At the end of the war, however, Schmelt fell out of favor with Himmler when it was discovered that he was guilty of embezzlement. He was brought before an SS- and Police Court on charges of enriching himself through his office, but details of the proceeding are not known. Albrecht Schmelt committed suicide at the beginning of May 1945.

Although the use of forced labor ultimately proved to be but a stage in the process of murder that delayed, but did not prevent, extermination, subordinating "Jewish policy" to economic criteria was responsible for the fact that mass extermination in East Upper Silesia—despite the close proximity of Auschwitz-Birkenau—came relatively late. The majority of Jews stayed alive under comparatively "better" conditions for a relatively long period. The province's unique status in the Reich's economy and the consequent value placed on maintaining the Jews as a workforce were crucial in retarding the dynamic of the extermination policy within the province. That was the unique feature of the process of the "Final Solution" in the province. As the focus of conflict between, on the one hand, practical exigencies of the war economy, which required trouble-free operation and efficiency, and, on the other hand, ideological "racial" dogma, economic motivations could exert a retarding influence during a certain phase of the extermination policy—and this is shown clearly by conditions in East Upper Silesia. The lethal course of events relied on smooth cooperation between SS and civilian authorities. As far as extermination policy was concerned, the conflict between the apparatuses at the beginning of the war, which was already reduced with the appointment of a Gauleiter and Oberpräsident subservient to Himmler in the person of Fritz Bracht, faded fully into the background. In proceeding against the Jews, the SS and the civilian authorities acted in concert. The importance of regional initiatives in the overall context of mass murder, which originated in East Upper Silesia with functionaries at the bottom of the administrative hierarchy, cannot be overestimated.

The system of differentiated functions, division of labor, and isolation of areas of responsibility, which had already been established during the deportation program at the beginning of the war, became one of the most important organizational bases for systematic extermination after the shift to a policy of murder. The functional connection between resettlement policy and Jewish policy derived largely from experience in structure, organization, and personnel that had been gained during the period of short-term planning. The cooperation between the authorities had long proven effective by the middle of 1942, when murder replaced expulsion as the instrument of "Jewish policy." And yet psychological behavior models that interpret the radicalization of "Jewish policy" as the result of responsible officials in the RSHA having grown "disappointed" and "angry" at the difficulties of resettlement policy and then resorting to more and more brutal methods until mass murder was the sole instrument of anti-Jewish actions—such models are not very plausible.[77] Nor does it seem appropriate to speak of a "breakdown" of ethnic resettlement plans; rather it was a question of resettlement being set aside in favor of other priorities. Those plans were consistently pursued by the RSHA with great tenacity in the face of all obstacles until, in the atmosphere of war against the Soviet Union, they were transformed into projects that foresaw murder as a means of solving problems that plagued population policy.

Antisemitic convictions played an essential role in setting mass murder in motion. Ideology supplied the framework of justifications that permitted civil authorities and police to resort to drastic measures based on emergencies that had ostensibly arisen in the confusion of resettlement. In the name of Germanizing the East Upper Silesian cities, the systematic mass murder of Jews became part of a problem-solving strategy. The measure was justified as necessary to prevent German ethnicity (*Deutschtum*) from being compromised. The Jews of East Upper Silesia were certainly not shipped to the Auschwitz-Birkenau extermination camp in secret. On the contrary, violent expulsion was carried out so openly in the increasingly Germanized province that the regional press carried reports about it. The *Oberschlesische Zeitung*, for example, published in April 1944 under the headline "How Bendzin Became Bendsburg" an article accompanied by many photographs about the transformation of the ugly "nest of Jews" into an small, up-and-coming German city. It was reported with satisfaction that the once "almost completely Jewish" Bendzin, where "the most depraved discards of that race" had lived, was "now German and clean."[78]

Notes

1. This presentation is based on the results of my dissertation, "'Musterstadt' Auschwitz. Germanisierungspolitik und Judenmord in Ostoberschlesien." The study will be published by K. G. Sauer Verlag (Munich) in 2000 as part of a research project on the social history of Auschwitz, which was directed by Norbert Frei at the *Institut für Zeitgeschichte, München* (Institute of Contemporary History, Munich). In the absence of recent research, the two early studies by Martin Broszat and Czeslaw Madajczyk continue to be basic texts as far as occupation policy is concerned, although East Upper Silesia receives little attention in either work; see Martin Broszat, *Nationalsozialistische Polenpolitik 1939-1945. (Schriftenreihe der Vierteljahrshefte für Zeitgeschichte Nr. 2)* (Stuttgart, 1961); Czeslaw Madajczyk, *Die Okkupationspolitik Nazideutschlands in Polen 1939-1945* (Berlin, 1987) (first published in Polish in Warsaw, 1970). Surprisingly, studies of specific geographic areas are not available—a circumstance that may be due to difficulty in accessing documentation, but which presumably also derives from the fact that the events in Silesia after the war, described as "flight and expulsion," obscured our view of National Socialist extermination policy. Inadequate in this regard: Norbert Conrad (ed.), *Deutsche Geschichte im Osten Europa, Vol 4: Schlesien* (Berlin, 1994). Frank Golczewski touches briefly on the situation in East Upper Silesia in his survey of the process of the "Final Solution" in occupied Poland; see Frank Golczewski, "Poland", in Wolfgang Benz (ed.), *Dimension des Völkermords. Die Zahl der jüdischen Opfer des Nationalsozialismus* (Munich, 1996) (first published as vol. 33 of *Quellen und Darstellungen zur Zeitgeschichte*, Munich, 1991), pp. 411-497, especially 412, 422, 450, 457, 460, and 468. Deborah Dwork and Robert-Jan van Pelt, *Auschwitz von 1270 bis heute* (Munich, 1998) (first published in English, New York, 1996), do not treat the structure and dynamic of extermination policy in East Upper Silesia in their study. The empirical content of the research on Auschwitz in recent years has remained extremely paltry due to a lack of grounding in facts; hence, despite a wealth of publications, scientific studies based on source materials are, astonishingly, hardly in evidence.

2. Since this term cannot be reconciled with the classical concept of public policy, it will appear in quotation marks here.

3. For a survey of the most recent regional studies, see Ulrich Herbert (ed.), *Vernichtungspolitik 1933-1945. Neue Forschungen und Kontroversen* (Frankfurt a.M., 1998).

4. Himmler to Woyrsch, 3 September 1939, Institut für Zeitgeschichte (IfZ), *Nürnberger Dokumente* (Nürnb. Dok.) NOKW-1006.

5. More than 100 Jews died in Bendzin when the fire spread from the synagogue to the Jewish quarter. Another 30 Jews were shot in the middle of September for having allegedly set the fire themselves. ZStLu. V 206 AR-Z 394/67, 48-52. Notation of the Zentrale Stelle on the results of the investigation, 11 March 1968. In Trzebinia, Dulowa, and Krzeszovia, 43 Jews were killed, another 30 in Sosnowitz; ZStLu [Zentrale Stelle der Landesjustizverwaltungen, Ludwigsburg], 205 AR-Z. 1617/62. Proceeding against Fritz Stolz, unpaginated, Zentrale Stelle an Oberstaatsanwaltschaft am Landgericht Amberg, 6 December 1962. Between the beginning of September and the second half of October 1939, 40 synagogues were demolished and 45 completely destroyed by fire, BAK (Bundesarchiv Koblenz), Zeitgeschichtliche Sammlung 122/24; in addi-

tion: the Jewish cultural center in the Blachownia district to the office of trustees in Kattowitz, 19 November 1940, including a list of destroyed synagogues in the district, WAP Kat (Archivum Panstwowe w Katowicach), HTO 2876, Bl. 5. There are no exact figures of the total numbers of victims of Einsatzgruppe z.b.V. Estimates run between 1,400 and 1,500 (Madajczyk, *Okkupationspolitik*, 17) and 2,000 dead (Czeslaw Luczak (ed.), *Grabiez polskiego mienia na Ziemaiach Zachodnich Rzeczypospolitej "wcielonych" do Rzeszy 1939-1945*, (Poznan, 1969), p. 74).

6. See Broszat, *Polenpolitik*, p. 28; also: Helmut Krausnick and Hans-Heinrich Wilhlem (eds.), *Die Truppe des Weltanschauungskrieges. Die Einsatzgruppen der Sicherheitspolizei und des SD* (Stuttgart, 1981), pp. 13-278, specifically 54.

7. Woyrsch was in the vanguard of the struggle for National Socialist rule in Silesia. He played a leading role in building the party in 1925, then expanded the SS until it was the largest National Socialist formation in the eastern part of Germany, and also acted as a leader in the brutal suppression of the "Röhm Putsch" in the province. Woyrsch, who repeatedly entertained Himmler at his estate in Lower Silesia, enjoyed the privilege of addressing the Reichsführer SS with the familiar *"Du."* For a brief biography: "Zeugenschrift Woyrsch," IfZ, ZS 1593; see Ruth Bettina Birn, *Die Höheren SS- und Polizeiführer. Himmlers Vertreter im Reich und in den besetzten Gebieten* (Düsseldorf, 1986,) p. 349.

8. The reports date from 6 to 22 September 1939; see Krausnick, *Einsatzgruppen*, p. 41, 52.

9. *Kriegstagebuch der Rüstungsinspektion VIII Breslau* (War Diary of Arms Inspection VIII Breslau), pp. 96-98, specifically 98, 12 September 1939, BA-MA (Bundesarchiv-Militärarchiv Freiburg), RW 20-8/1. The closing of the border was announced on 12 September 1939, *Sammelbericht* [Summary Report] Nr. 4 of CdZ Fitzner, 5 September 1939. BA-MA, RW 20-8/17, Bl. 69-95, specifically 73. The report refers to a "large number" of Jews who were turned back "again."

10. Order of the CdZ, 5 September 1939, GStAPK (Geheimes Staatsarchiv Preußischer Kulturbesitz Berlin) HA XVII, BA Ost Reg.Kat./3, Bl. 116.

11. The government district Oppeln covered 11,694 square kilometers and had 1.35 million inhabitants. The government district Kattowitz was somewhat smaller, covering 8,923 square kilometers, but was more densely populated, containing 2.43 million inhabitants. For developments in the territory, see Madajczyk, *Okkupationspolitik*, p. 35, which contains slightly different figures; also Dieter Rebentisch, *Führerstaat und Verwaltung im Zweiten Weltkrieg. Verfassungsentwicklung und Verwaltungspolitik 1939-1945*, Vol. 29 of *Frankfurter Historische Abhandlungen* (Stuttgart, 1989), pp. 196f.

12. Specifically the districts Saybusch (Zywiec), Wadowitz (Wadowice), Krenau (Chrzanow), Ilkenau (Olkusz), Warthenau (Zawiercie), Bendzin (after 1941 also Bendsburg, Polish, Bedzin), and Bielitz-Biala (Bielsko-Biala), from spring 1941 also Blachstädt (Blachownia); see Broszat, *Polenpolitik*, pp. 31ff., 36f.; see also Walther Hubatsch (ed.), *Grundriß der deutschen Verwaltungsgeschichte 1815-1945*. Reihe A: *Preußen*, Vol. 4: *Schlesien* (Marburg a.L., 1976), pp. 285-313.

13. Order of BdO Paul Riege for the exercise of police authority east of the existing toll border, order number 11, 16 November 1939, AGK (Archiwum Glownej Komsisji Badania Zbrodni przeciwko Narodowi Polskiemu Instytut Pamieci Narodowej, Warszawer), CA 850/6, Bl. 16-20, especially 20.

14. The term "Old Reich" refers to areas lying within the German borders of 1937.

15. In May 1939 a total of 17,257 Jews lived in the parts of Silesia belonging to the Old Reich, which amounted to 0.7 percent of the entire population; far and away the most Jews lived in Breslau (11,172 in all), which was at that time, the third largest Jewish community in the German Reich after Berlin and Frankfurt am Main. Since the Jewish population in the area of Silesia that belonged to the Old Reich fell under the Old Reich's laws, it is not the subject of this study.

16. See Broszat, *Polenpolitik*, p. 37; Rebentisch, *Führerstaat*, p. 172; Ludolf Herbst, *Das nationalsozialistische Deutschland 1933-1945. Die Entfesselung der Gewalt: Rassismus und Krieg* (Frankfurt a.M., 1996), pp. 281f.

17. Decree of the Führer and Reichschancellor for the Protection of German Ethnicity, 7 October 1939, BAB (Bundesarchiv Berlin), R 49/1, Bl. 1-2; also BAB, R 58/242, MF 6, Bl. 246-248; also IfZ, Nürnbg. Dok. Dok. NG-962 and NG 1467; reprinted in NMT, Vol. 13, p. 138.

18. Inhabitants of the German Reich were called "Reichsdeutsche." "Volksdeutsche" was the term for members of German minorities in foreign states.

19. Concerning the operation and personnel of "Jewish" and resettlement policy up to the radicalization of anti-Jewish measures, using especially the Warthegau as an example, see Götz Aly, *"Endlösung." Völkerverschiebung und der Mord an den europäischen Juden* (Frankfurt a.M., 1995); also Götz Aly, "'Judenumsiedlung'—Überlegungen zur politischen Vorgeschichte des Holocaust," in Herbert (ed.), *Venichtungspolitik*, pp. 67-97. The connection between Jewish and resettlement policies was first established by Christopher Browning; see Christopher Browning, "Nazi Resettlement Policy and the Search for a Solution to the Jewish Question," in *German Studies Review* 9/3 (1986): 497-519; in German translation under the title "Die nationalsozialistische Umsiedlungspolitik und die Suche nach einer 'Lösung der Judenfrage' 1939-1941," in Christopher Browning, *Der Weg zur "Endlösung." Entscheidungen und Täter* (Bonn, 1998), pp. 13-36.

20. For a brief biography of Wagner, see Peter Hüttenberger, *Die Gauleiter. Studie zum Wandel des Machtgefüges in der NSDAP. (Schriftenreihe der Vierteljahrshefte für Zeitgeschichte* Nr. 19) (Stuttgart, 1969), p. 219; see in addition Karl Höffkes, *Hitlers politische Generale. Die Gauleiter* (Tübingen, 1986), pp. 367ff.

21. In the annexed eastern regions, a unique constitutional arrangement developed through the promulgation of special legislation that differed from the laws of the Old Reich. The Gauleiters governed nearly autonomously and largely independently of the Reich Ministry of the Interior; see Broszat, *Polenpolitik*, p. 34. Broszat, *Der Staat Hitlers. Grundlegung und Entwicklung seiner inneren Verfassung* (Munich, 1981), pp. 162ff.; Rebentisch, *Führerstaat*, pp. 175ff.

22. Bormann to Lammers, 20 November 1940, where a statement made by Hitler on 25 September 1939 is quoted, BAB, R 43 II/1549, Bl. 47-50; also IfZ Fa 199/51, Bl. 47-50.

23. The postwar myth surrounding Schulenburg also contributed to a transfiguration of Wagner. In the scholarly literature, Wagner is presented surprisingly uncritically as "thoughtful statesman" and an especially "mild" politician on the resettlement issue. And yet his policy appears relatively "restrained" only in comparison to the racial policies of the zealot Arthur Greiser in the Warthegau. It would certainly be wrong to speak of opposition to the Germanization policy on humanitarian grounds on either his or Schulenburg's part. On Schulenburg, see the glorifying and strongly apologetic biography by

Albert Krebs, *Fritz-Dietlof Graf von der Schulenburg. Zwischen Staatsraison und Hochverrat.* (*Hamburger Beiträge zur Zeitgeschichte Nr. 2*) (Hamburg, 1964); see also the more recent and more critical study by Ulrich Heinemann, *Ein konservativer Rebell. Fritz-Dietlof Graf von der Schulenburg und der 20. Juli* (Berlin, 1990).

24. The background of Wagner's dismissal cannot be precisely reconstructed. Himmler's machinations may have been decisive, but Hitler's territorial plans for Silesia may also have been the cause. Since Wagner was an avowed opponent of the recent subdivision of Silesia into *Gaus* for Upper and Lower Silesia, which Hitler had desired, Hitler's knowledge of that fact may have moved him to recall Wagner from Breslau. He did, however, leave Wagner as Gauleiter in South Westphalia with offices in Bochum for more than a year, and Wagner was also permitted to retain his authority as *Reichspreiskommissar* for the entire Reich. Wagner's ultimate fall at a meeting of *Gau* leaders in Munich in November 1941, though its details are equally impossible to reconstruct, had nothing to do with his policy in Silesia. Perhaps Wagner's critical statements concerning Germany's chances of victory in the Russian campaign persuaded Hitler to strike at his former confidant with unaccustomed harshness.

25. Eichmann's note of 6 October 1939. A facsimile appears in *Nazi-Dokumente sprechen*, published by the Rat der jüdischen Gemeinden in den böhmischen Ländern (Council of Jewish Communities in the Bohemian Lands) (Prague) and by the Zentralverband der jüdischen Gemeinden in der Slowakei (Central Association of Jewish Communities in Slovakia) (Bratislava), Prague (no year of publication), no pagination; also reprinted in Hans-Günther Adler, *Der verwaltete Mensch. Studien zur Deportation der Juden aus Deutschland* (Tübingen, 1974), p. 128; also in Miroslav Karny, "Nisko in der Geschichte der 'Endlösung'" in *Judaica Bohemiae* 3 (1987), no. 2: 69-84, especially 74. On the deportation plans, see Seeve Goshen, "Eichmann und die Nisko-Aktion im Oktober 1939. Eine Fallstudie zur NS-Judenpolitik in der letzten Epoche vor der 'Endlösung.'" in *Vierteljahrshefte für Zeitgeschichte* 29 (1981): 74-96, especially 79ff.; Seev Goschen, "Nisko—Ein Ausnahmefall unter den Judenlagern der SS," in *Vierteljahrshefte für Zeitgeschichte* 40 (1992): 95-106; see also Jonny Moser, "Nisko. The First Experiment in Deportation," in *Simon Wiesenthal Center Annual* 2 (1985): 1-30; Hans Safrian, *Die Eichmann-Männer* (Vienna, 1993); second edition with the title: *Eichmann und seine Gehilfen* (Frankfurt a.M., 1995), here pp. 68-85.

26. Notation on the conversation between Eichmann and Wagner, 11 October 1939; reprinted in *Nazi-Dokumente sprechen*, unpaginated.

27. Confidential memorandum of the Kattowitz Gestapo to the regional councils, mayors, district administrative heads, chiefs of police, Chief of Staff of the Security Police, and all Gestapo offices on foreign soil, 23 February 1940, containing information on the target area of the planned deportations, WAP Kat. RK 2833, Bl. 21-23, especially 21, also WAP Kat. HTO 62, Bl. 225.

28. Following the partition, the newly established *Gau* of Lower Silesia, with its capital in Breslau, was governed by Oberpräsident and Gauleiter Karl Hanke.

29. For Arlt's biography, see Götz Aly and Susanne Heim, *Vordenker der Vernichtung. Auschwitz und die deutschen Pläne für eine neue europäische Ordnung* (Frankfurt a.M., 1993) (first published in Hamburg, 1991), especially pp. 168-187, 207-222; see also Götz Aly and Karl Heinz Roth, *Die restlose Erfassung. Volkszählen, Identifizieren, Aussondern im Nationalsozialismus* (Berlin, 1984), pp. 71-74, 84f.

30. While the office's internal correspondence did not survive, important parallel documentation is available. Of central importance are the legal communications of public prosecutors of the Federal Republic after the war. Because of difficulties with documentation, Schmelt's office has not been systematically studied in scholarly research. For an important, albeit cursory, treatment, see Alfred Konieczny, "Die Zwangsarbeit der Juden in Schlesien im Rahmen der 'Organisation Schmelt,'" in *Beiträge zur nationalsozialistischen Gesundheits- und Sozialpolitik* (1983), no. 3: *Sozialpolitik und Judenvernichtung. Gibt es eine Ökonomie der Endlösung?*, pp. 91-110; Schmelt's unit is also mentioned briefly in Wolf Gruner, *Der Geschlossene Arbeitseinsatz deutscher Juden. Zur Zwangsarbeit als Element der Verfolgung 1938-1943*, Vol. 20 of *Dokumente–Texte–Materialien des Zentrums für Antisemitismusforschung der Technischen Universität Berlin* (Berlin, 1997), p. 264 note 293 and passim.

31. Robert Ley, NSDAP-Reichsorganisationsleiter, wrote in his greeting on the occasion of the first anniversary of Upper Silesia's independence, which appeared under the title "*Ein Jahr Gau Oberschlesien* [Upper Silesia After One Year]" in the *Kattowitzer Zeitung* on 1 February 1942: "As one of our mightiest arms producers, the *Gau* of Upper Silesia has the task of contributing to the strengthening of the German armament industry and thus to the achievement of the final victories of our arms."

32. On forced labor as an instrument of "Jewish policy," see Gruner, *Arbeitseinsatz*.

33. Transport list of the *Umwandererzentralstelle (UWZ)* of Litzmannstadt, 23 September to 14 December 1940; reprinted in Biuletyn Głównej Komisji Badania Zbrodni Hitlerowskich w Polsce (BGKBH) (1960) 12. Document 106. Broszat calculates 17,413 deportees but does not include the last transport of 29 January 1941; see Broszat, *Polenpolitik*, p. 99.

34. Himmler's instructions of 1 August 1940. BAB, 17.02/428, unpaginated.

35. Guidelines for the Evacuations in the Saybusch Area, 14 September 1940; reprinted in *Documenta Occupationis Teutonicae*, Vol. 11, *Polzenie Ludnosci w Rejencji Katowickiej w latach 1939-1945*, Waclaw Dlugoborski (ed.) (Posnan, 1983), pp. 166-171.

36. See Dieter Maier, *Arbeitseinsatz und Deportation. Die Mitwirkung der Arbeitsverwaltung bei der nationalsozialistischen Judenverfolgung in den Jahren 1938-1945*, Vol. 4 of *Publikationen der Gedenkstätte Haus der Wannsee-Konferenz* (Berlin, 1994), pp. 18, 22ff., 29; also Gruner, *Arbeitseinsatz*; Ulrich Herbert, "Arbeit und Vernichtung. Ökonomisches Interesse und Primat der 'Weltanschauung' im Nationalsozialismus," in Dan Diner (ed.), *Ist der Nationalsozialismus Geschichte? Zu Historisierung und Historikerstreit* (Frankfurt a.M., 1987), pp. 198-236; also in Ulrich Herbert (ed.), *Europa und der "Reichseinsatz." Ausländische Zivilarbeiter, Kriegsgefangene und KZ-Häftlinge in Deutschland 1939-1945* (Essen, 1991), pp. 384-426, especially 392.

37. See Gruner, *Arbeitseinsatz*, pp. 48ff.

38. See for now the dissertation by Bernd Christian Wagner, *IG Auschwitz. Zwangsarbeit und Vernichtung von Häftlingen des Lagers Monowitz 1941-45*. This study is also part of the research project on the social history of Auschwitz directed by Norbert Frei at *Institut für Zeitgeschichte*.

39. Note by Rudolf Höß (unpublished parts), IfZ. F 13/1-8, Bl. 31f.; excerpts published in *Faschismus-Ghetto-Massenmord*, Document 173, Bl. 226. War diary of the office of armaments inspection of defense district VIII in Breslau, 1 January–31 March 1941. Notation on the employment of "Schmelt Jews" in the

clothing industry, along with a reference to the special fund. BA-MA, RW 20/8-6, Bl. 87.

40. Correspondence between the *Hauptamt für Verwaltung und Wirtschaft* (Main Office for Administration and Economy) (later WVHA) and HSSPF Schmauser of the NSDAP-Reichsleitung and Himmler about Schmauser's request for funds ("schwarze Kasse [black fund]"), 17 November 1941–26 January 1944, IfZ, MA 303, 2589715-25898758.

41. IfZ, Nürnb. Dok. Nr. 3182. Greifelt to Brandt, personal staff of the RFSS; contains notes relating to a presentation at the headquarters of the Reichsführer SS on 28 May 1942, and notation of the use of "surplus funds deriving from the Jewish work program (Schmelt) in Upper Silesia."

42. Testimony of Schemlt's former secretary, Anneliese F. before the state office of criminal investigations in Hannover, 23 November 1971. Public Prosecutor's Office (StA) Dortmund, 45 Js 27/69, Vol. 18, pp. 213-216, Proceeding against Fritz Arlt.

43. RGBl (Reichsgesetzblatt) 1941, no. 50, 4 June 1941, Bl. 297, Decree for the Introduction of the Nuremberg Laws in the Annexed Territories, 31 May 1941. AZIH (Achiwum Zydowskiego Instytutu Historycznego, Warszawa). Jewish Council of Bendzin, 212/1, Bl. 14. Announcement by the representatives of the Jews of Bendzin of the introduction of the Nuremberg Laws, June 1941.

44. Official journal of the Regierungspräsident of Kattowitz, 26 April 1941; official journal of the Regierungspräsident of Kattowitz, 17 May 1941; police order of 9 May 1941, effective as of 1 June 1941. IfZ, Dd. 56.14. Announcement of the assumption of an additional given name, undated, probably in the middle of June 1941, AZIH, Jewish Council of Bendzin, 212/1, Bl. 5.

45. Announcement regarding the obligation to obtain and wear the Jewish star, 20 September 1941, AZIH, Jewish Council of Bendzin 212/1, Bl. 48. Announcement regarding how the Jewish star is to be displayed, 2 October 1941, AZIH, Jewish Council of Bendzin 212/1, Bl. 52. The badges had to be bought for ten pfenning at specially designated shops in the East Strip.

46. Decree of Woedtke, Chief of the Sosnowitz Police, to the Central Jewish Council in Sosnowitz, 17 April 1941, AGK CA 171/32, Bl. 14. Announcement of the representatives of the Jews of Bendzin regarding Woedtke's order of 28 May 1941 banning Jews in Bendzin, 30 May 1941, AZIH, Jewish Council of Bendzin, 212/1, Bl. 3.

47. See contemporary eye-witness account of Nathan Eliasz Szternfinkiel, *Zaglada Zydow Sosnowca* (Katowice, 1946), p. 20 (German translation: *Die Vernichtung der Juden von Sosnowitz* in the investigative documents of the public prosecutors office in Dortmund. StA Dortmund 45 Js 27/69, enclosures. Proceeding against Fritz Arlt.)

48. Chief of the Sosnowitz Police to the Gestapo in Kattowitz, 17 December 1941, WAP Kat. Sosnowitz Chief of Police 315, Bl. 1.

49. *Kattowitzer Zeitung*, 30 November 1940, police order regarding conducting business with Jews, promulgated 23 November 1940, effective as of 1 December 1940.

50. Order of the Sosnowitz Chief of Police excluding Jews from public transportation, 6 February 1941, amended 19 March 1941, AGK, CA 171/32, Bl. 5, 11. Announcement of the Police Command regarding the use of trains by Jews, 30 April 1941, AGK, CA 171/32, Bl. 15.

51. See Szternfinkiel, *Zaglada*, p. 20.

52. Circular from Moshe Merin, Chairman of the Central Jewish Council in Upper
     Silesia, to all local councils of elders, 20 December 1941, AZIH, Jewish Coun-
     cil of Bendzin 212/1, Bl. 58; see Szternfinkiel, *Zaglada*, p. 31.
53. Chief of Sosnowitz Police regarding the confiscation of cattle owned by Jews,
     8 May 1941, AGK, CA 171/31.
54. Situation report of the NSDAP District Directory in Bendzin to the NSDAP
     Provincial Directory, October 1941, undated, WAP Op. NSDAP Gauleitung
     207, Bl. 22. Report of the NSDAP District Directory in Bendzin to the NSDAP
     Provincial Directory, October 1941, undated, WAP Op. 2481/281, Bl. 22.
55. The close ideological connection is explicitly established in Andreas Hillgruber,
     "Die 'Endlösung' und das deutsche Ostimperium als Kernstück des rassenide-
     ologischen Programms des Nationalsozialismus," in *Vierteljahrshefte für Zeit-
     geschichte* 20 (1972): 133-153. While Hillgruber assumes that the murder of
     the Jewish population had already been planned by the beginning of the Russ-
     ian campaign, in a more recent study Burrin expresses the view that the bleak
     course of the military campaign was decisive; see Philippe Burrin, *Hitler und
     die Juden. Die Entscheidung für den Volksmord* (Frankfurt, 1993) (first French
     edition, Paris, 1992).
56. For the basic details, see Aly, *Endlösung*, pp. 273ff., 392.
57. Christopher R. Browning, *The Final Solution and the German Foreign Office*
     (New York, 1978), p. 8.
58. Notation by Butschek, RKF Ansiedlungsstab [Resettlement Staff] in Kattowitz,
     regarding a discussion on 19 March 1941 in Berlin on how to solve settlement
     problems, 20 March 1941, BAB. Film 16786, Deutsches Auslandsinstitut,
     unpaginated.
59. The relationship between municipal development and the murder of the Jews
     has not hitherto been explicitly investigated. For general information on city
     planning under National Socialism, especially in the Warthegau, see Niels
     Gutschow and Barbara Klein, *Vernichtung und Utopie. Stadtplanung
     Warschau 1939-1945* (Hamburg, 1994), especially pp. 21-41; Werner Durth
     and Niels Gutschow, *Träume in Trümmern. Stadtplanung 1940-1950*
     (Munich, 1993), especially pp. 75-112.
60. See the controversial theses of Götz Aly and Susanne Heim concerning the rela-
     tive importance of economic considerations of population policy in setting
     mass murder in motion; Aly and Heim, *Vordenker*; on the controversy, see
     Wolfgang Schneider (ed.), *"Vernichtungpolitik." Eine Debatte über den
     Zusammenhang von Sozialpolitik und Genozid im nationalsozialistischen
     Deutschland* (Hamburg, 1991); on the importance of racism, see in the afore-
     mentioned volume, Ulrich Herbert, "Rassismus und rationales Kalkül. Zum
     Stellenwert utilitaristisch verbrämter Legitimationsstrategien in der national-
     sozialistischen Weltanschauung," in Schneider (ed.), *"Vernichtungspolitik,"*
     pp. 25-35.
61. Schulenberg to Himmler via *Reichsstelle für Raumordnung*, 20 May 1940,
     BAB, R 49/902, unpaginated.
62. Note of the RKF-Planungshauptabteilung (Main Planning Office) on a conver-
     sation between Himmler, Bracht, and Bach-Zelewski, 11 September 1940, BAB,
     R 49/902, unpaginated; Arlt's list of suggestions to the RFK-Planungshaupt-
     abteilung, 5 October 1940; note of a discussion on 10 October 1940 at the
     invitation of the HSSPF in Kattowitz; participants included Bach-Zelewski,
     Ziegler, Springorum, and a representative of the RKF-Planungshauptabteilung,
     14 October 1940; note on the same discussion, 26 October 1940, BAB, R

49/902, unpaginated; Himmler's general directive RKF No. 10/I I, 16 January 1941, IfZ, MA 125/13, No. 38718. A similar recommendation had already been discussed on 30 July 1940 in the Oberpräsidium, minutes of the meeting, WAP Kat, OPK 1810, Bl. 3-4; on subdividing into zones, see also Greifelt's communication to Bracht, 23 November 1940, BAK, R 113/7, Bl. 117; also BAK, R 113/7, Bl. 147-148; *Kattowitzer Zeitung*, 10 November 1940, "Raumplanung in den Ostgebieten [Development Planning in the Eastern Territories]." Development, organization, and performance of the Office of the Gauleiter and Oberpräsident as representative of the Reichsführer SS, Reich Commissioner for the Protection of German Ethnicity in Upper East Silesia, September 1939 to January 1943, Bl. 55; includes a sketch of the zones of settlement I and Ia, BAB, 17.02/318; the sketch is also reproduced in Robert-Jan van Pelt, "A Site in Search of a Mission," in Yisrael Gutman and Michael Berenbaum (eds.), *Anatomy of the Auschwitz Death Camp* (Washington, 1994), pp. 93-155, especially 107.

63. File memorandum on a discussion at police headquarters in Sosnowitz, 12 November 1941, WAP Kat, RK 2780, Bl. 95-99, especially 97; Woedtke's note on resettling Jews as discussed on 19 November 1941, written on 25 November 1941, AGK, CA 171/32, Bl. 41; order of the Sosnowitz police, also WAP Kat, Chief of Sosnowitz Police, Bl. 316, 78.

64. Schönwälder to Springorum, situation report for November 1940, 30 November 1940, GStAPK, HA XVII, BA Ost. Reg. Bez./13, Bl. 112-121, especially 116. Schönwälder expresses satisfaction in the fact that the "idly lounging about, shadily dealing" Jews have "finally" disappeared.

65. Kowohl to the District Council of Bendzin, 24 June 1941, WAP Kat, RK 2785, Bl. 18.

66. Notes by Rudolf Höß (unpublished part), 1 November 1946, IfZ, F 13/1-8, pp. 31ff.; excerpts published in *Faschismus-Ghetto-Massenmord*, Dok. 173, p. 226. In contrast to Höß's assertions, there were no efforts to abolish the Schmelt camps in 1941. Quite to the contrary, the camps became more important than ever due to the Speer program. Also false, because based on Höß's memoirs: Israel Gutman editor-in-chief, Eberhard Jäckel, Peter Longreich, and Julius Schoep, editors of the German edition, *Enzyklopädie des Holocaust. Die Verfolgung und Ermordung der europäischen Juden* (Munich, 1995), p. 1071.

67. Schmauser to Himmler, 20 April 1942, IfZ, Nürnb. Dok. NO-1386, excerpts reprinted in Adler, *Mensch*, p. 230.

68. *Die Endlösung der europäischen Judenfrage. Statistischer Bericht des Inspekteurs für Statstik beim Reichsführer SS. Geheime Reichssache* (The Final Solution to the Jewish Question. Statistical Report of the Chief of Staff for Statistics for the Reichsführer SS. Secret Matter of State), 1 January 1943, BAB, NS 19/1570, Bl. 4-10, or 12-28, especially 8, 25; Korherr spoke of the "use of Schmelt camps," counting among the 50,570 East Upper Silesian Jews some 42,382 "stateless" Jews, by which he meant Jews who had always lived in the province. Of these 8,188 were treated in the subcategory of "foreign" Jews; these were Jews whom Schmelt caused to be removed from the transports on their way from Holland and France to Auschwitz-Birkenau. Additional extensive networks of forced labor camps existed from the summer of 1941 under the control of SSPF Friedrich Katzmann in east Galicia and also under the authority of SSPF Odilo Globocnik in the Lublin district of the Government General, including the camps along *Durchgangsstraße IV*, the axis connecting central Poland and the Crimea. There has been to date no systematic study of

the major forced labor projects. See (for the present) Thomas Sandkühler, _"Endlösung" in Galizien. Der Judenmord in Ostpolen und die Rettungsinitiative von Berthold Beitz 1941-1944_ (Bonn, 1996), pp. 46f.; Dieter Pohl, _Nationalsozialistische Judenverfolgung in Ostgalizien 1941-1944. Organisation und Durchführung eines staatlichen Massenverbrechens_, Vol. 50 of _Studien zur Zeitgeschichte_ (Munich, 1996), pp. 132ff., 331-355; lacking in new contributions: Daniel Goldhagen, _Hitlers willige Vollstrecker. Ganz gewöhnliche Deutsche und der Holocaust_ (Berlin, 1996) (first American edition, New York, 1996, pp. 335ff.).

69. Circular of the Kattowitz Gestapo, 26 February 1942; includes an announcement of "illegal Jews," APOSW (Archiwum Panstwowe Muzeum w Oswiecimiu), Bürgermeister Oswiecim, 1, Bl. 34; also the contemporary, eye-witness account by Szternfinkiel, _Zaglada_, pp. 46f.

70. Telex of the RSHA, 21 May 1943. ZstLu, 205 AR Z 308, Bl. 67. Proceeding against Baucke et al., volume of enclosures without pagination. No documents relating to the discussion between Eichmann and Schmelt have survived.

71. Headquarters and garrison orders of the Auschwitz concentration camp 1940-1945, edited manuscript, StB 31/43, 6 August 1943.

72. See Franciszek Piper, _Die Zahl der Opfer von Auschwitz. Aufgrund der Quellen und der Erträge der Forschung 1945 bis 1990_ (Oswiecim, 1993), pp. 183-186, Table 15.

73. Director of the Gau office for municipal policy at the Kattowitz Oberpräsidium in Bracht's name to the NSDAP Party Chancellery, 6 September 1944, WAP Kat, RK 1654, Bl. 103-107, specifically 104; also _Akten der NSDAP Parteikanzlei_, Teil II, Bd. 3/4, Bl. 12118-12122, especially 12119, containing the statement: "The Jewish element, which accounts for most criminals, the anti-German Polish intelligentsia, and the criminal element, have been resettled, i.e., eliminated, so that extraordinary levels of criminal activity are no longer a prospect." In addition: Reich Ministry of the Interior (RMI) to the Headquarters of Police, 10 October 1944, IfZ, Nürnb. Dok., NG-2660; the statistics were used by the Ministry of the Interior in a communication to the Headquarters of Police. Following the murder of the Jews, the number of inhabitants in Sosnowitz dropped from 130,000 to 101,788; in Bendzin, from 54,739 to 25,595; in Dombrowa, from 41,491 to 29,018; in Czeladz, from 23,000 to 20,571; in Zagorze, from 16,400 to 12,556; in Nikwa, from 12,550 to 11,083; and in Schümenschütz, from 28,560 to 24,669.

74. Schmelt to Arlt, 13 September 1943, announcement of the office's new address and telephone number, AGK 865/7, 75.

75. Unpublished parts of the notes of Rudopf Höß, IfZ, F 13/1-8, Bl. 31f.; excerpts printed in _Faschismus-Ghetto-Massenmord_, doc. 173. Höß again errs in dating the absorption of the Schmelt camps by the concentration-camp bureaucracy in the spring of 1943 and in saying that the process was "completely accomplished" by that time.

76. _Vierteljahresbericht der Rüstungsinspektion im Wehrkreis VIII_ [quarterly report of the Armament Inspectorate in Military District VIII] October-December 1943, especially "Judeneinsatz," undated, presumably January 1944, BA-MA, RW 20-8/32, Bl. 49.

77. This is Aly's interpretation, which was generally anticipated in Browning, _Nazi Resettlement Policy_ (in German translation: Browning, _Umsiedlungspolitik_). The shortcoming of this interpretation is that it fails to explain why the "failure"

of population plans led to mass murder only in the case of the Jews, but not in the case of the Polish population.

78. *Oberschlesische Zeitung*, 4 April 1944, "Wie aus Bendzin Bendsburg wurde. Ein Bildarchiv erzählt von der Wandlung einer Stadt" (How Bendzin Became Bendsburg. Pictures Show the Transformation of a City).

– Chapter 11 –

THE CONCENTRATION CAMP SS AS A FUNCTIONAL ELITE[1]

Karin Orth

The total number of victims killed in the concentration camps is estimated at 1.9 million people.[2] The question as to who in the camps—and in responsible positions—carried out the murders has remained unclear until now.

In his overview of the history and organization of the SS, the American historian Robert Lewis Koehl coined the term "concentration camp SS." This concept refers to a group within the camp SS, which was—so speculates Koehl—characterized by the fact that they were stationed permanently in the camps. Koehl assumes, that even during wartime members of the concentration camp SS were not deployed to the combat troops of the Waffen SS.[3] This is remarkable in that throughout the war there were regular exchanges between concentration camp guard troops and the Waffen SS. Research by Miroslav Kárný, Heinz Boberach, and Bertrand Perz has provided persuasive documentation to this effect.[4]

To test Koehl's thesis empirically—and answer the question posed at the outset—I have investigated two groups of SS officers in the concentration camps that were under the authority of the Concentration Camp Inspectorate (Inspektion der Konzentrationslager, IKL), which after 1942 was attached as Department

D (Amtsgruppe D) to the SS Economic Administration Main Office (SS-Wirtschafts-Verwaltungshauptamt, WVHA). The two groups were, on the one hand, the so-called "division heads" (*Abteilungsleiter*), who occupied in the SS hierarchy the level directly under the camp commanders; and on the other hand, the commanders themselves. SS officers who were "division heads" included,[5] in addition to the adjutants, the protective custody, work detachment, and administrative officers, the officers in command of guard units, (*Wachmannschaften*) and heads of the political division.[6] In the case of the division heads it can be proven that there was, in fact, a permanent group attached to the concentration camps. On this level of the hierarchy, historical reality conforms to Koehl's notion: the concentration camp SS can be characterized as a National Socialist "functional elite" differentiated by four career paths.[7]

Social-structural analysis has been able to delineate a "key group" of division heads, comprising adjutants, protective custody, and work detachment officers, as well as the commanders of the guard units. The majority of camp commanders were recruited from this "key group" after the mid-1930s.

Commanders and division heads occupied the top positions in the camp SS. Due to their different work roles and functions, collaboration by these two groups was the basis for the concentration camp's ability to function as an instrument of terror and oppression. This article will describe the fundamental features of the concentration camp SS. Its central questions concern the origins and generation of this unit's members, the constitution and self-presentation of the group itself, turning points in the collective use of force, as well as the careers of its members after the "collapse" of the Third Reich.

The Wartime Youth Generation

The overwhelming majority of members of the concentration camp SS belonged to the youth of the "wartime generation."[8] They are part of that generation that itself did not experience the First World War, but did grow up with its mythology. A segment of the male youth incorporated this mythology into their identity.

By far, the greatest number of these individuals grew up in middle-class families. Most finished their education at the elementary or middle school level, and a large percentage went on to complete an apprenticeship in either a merchandising or artisan trade.

Thus, these men came from the heart of Weimar society, not a socially déclassé milieu. They belonged to the social strata most affected by the economic, political, and social crisis of the Weimar Republic, the ones that felt threatened by social decline. In fact, the consequences of the economic crisis partially—but by no means disproportionately—affected both division heads and camp commanders. Some of them lost their jobs during the 1930s, either short-term or indefinitely.

Members of this group generally established contact with right-wing radical-völkisch circles as youths or young adults. These associations led them at a relatively early point to the National Socialists and their Sturmabteilung (SA) and Schutzstaffel (SS). They supported the National Socialist Movement long before the "seizure of power"; on the average they were already members of the NSDAP in September 1931.[9] It is not the early point in time that is remarkable—after all, the middle class provided the NSDAP with some of its earliest adherents—rather it is the correlation of their ages with their respective dates of joining the party and its divisions. Every second person was a member of both the NSDAP and the SS by his mid-twenties.

Soon after the "seizure of power," the SS offered them a regular position—and thus the chance to escape an often precarious employment situation. At the same time, it offered the possibility of professionalizing their political engagement with the Movement to which they had devoted themselves since their youth.

With the accession to political power, they immediately moved from a situation that was politically marginal and often professionally uncertain into the center of National Socialist society. They grasped at the chance to give their political engagement a professional perspective and a soldierly aura. That they would find a regular job with the SS, which historians have interpreted to be biographical happenstance,[10] was actually no accident, rather seems very plausible given their early presence in the right milieu.

Placement within the SS

Most members of the concentration camp SS joined the camp SS by the mid-1930s. The decisive element in their deployment to the early camps—to Dachau, Lichtenburg, Esterwegen, Sulza, or Sachsenburg—was either a coincidence or some close, service-related and "comradely" tie to SS officers already stationed there. These officers tried to bring along former subordinates and "comrades" to secure their own positions of power.

As a rule, most of the later division heads and camp commanders served initially in a guard unit. This fact is less noteworthy—
by the end of 1935 more than 2,500 other SS men[11] had shared this
duty—than their rapid professional success. As young as their early
to mid-thirties, they moved into leadership positions on the command staffs of the National Socialist concentration camps. They
proved themselves to be more qualified and/or more engaged than
the average guard troop. They also established early contacts with
the people who made career decisions, such as commanders, officers of the guard troops, who had a similar prominent position in
the prewar camps, or those in responsible positions in the highest
offices of the IKL.

Through their rise to the top of the camp SS these men achieved
positions of prominence that would have been unattainable by
someone of their family background, education, and intellectual
abilities during the Weimar Republic. Only because of the altered
power relationships were they able to attain the rank of officer
(which most of them reached with no training or schooling) and
establish a position of enormous power. This, however, was limited
to the camp system. In regard to the SS as a total organization, it
must be stressed that, almost without exception—and until the
war's end—members of the concentration camp SS remained in the
lowest third of the SS leadership hierarchy, thus in positions of
little influence.

The Social Network of the Concentration Camp SS

The concentration camp SS represents a novel "professional group."
It developed after the mid-1930s as the exclusive personnel core for
the existing National Socialist concentration camps.[12] With the
establishment of the camp system, Dachau, Buchenwald, and in particular Sachsenhausen and the IKL—which after 2 August 1938 was
located in Oranienburg, in the immediate vicinity of the Sachsenhausen camp—became centers of terror as well as meeting places for
the concentration camp SS.[13] The majority of the subjects of this
study had by this point already advanced to division head status. A
finely meshed network of professional, service-related, and personal
relationships developed within the SS officer corps at these camps.
The connections and patronage relationships formed after the late
1930s within the SS officer corps at Oranienburg (comprising officers from the Sachsenhausen camp as well as the IKL) proved to be
especially influential for hiring policies in the following years.

Integral components of the complex social network were personal friendships, as well as disagreements, a societal context oriented toward the ideology of the "SS Clan Community" (*SS-Sippengemeinschaft*), and an idiosyncratic linguistic argot. The revealing "camp language" could easily be deciphered by members of the camp SS and by camp inmates, but not by those outside the camp world.

Essentially, however, the entire fabric was held together by mutual crimes, by common service-related socialization, and the exercise of duties, which produced forms of habitual violence. Complicity in deed formed the group and welded it together. All members of the concentration camp SS had to undergo an "initiation ritual," which desensitized them to their own feelings, as well as to the torments of the tortured. Above all, however, it was meant to integrate them into the group of perpetrators. It was through practice, and not the infrequent "*weltanschauliche Schulung*," that members of the concentration camp SS gained the knowledge that informed their treatment of camp inmates and their running of a concentration camp. In the course of Nazi domination, the camp SS developed into an "expert group" in terror. Its "expertise" consisted in the capacity and readiness to translate the extermination policy of the Nazi regime into practice.

The concentration camp SS can also be described as a peer group. The subjects of this investigation oriented their actions and behavior toward normative notions of what an SS officer should be and do. The "SS-appropriate behavior" (*SS-mäßige Haltung*) that SS officers strove for and routinely examined in personnel reports involved the entire person: "orderly family relationships" (that is, a marriage that met "racial" and *weltanschauliche* criteria as well as producing numerous offspring), "healthy common sense," in addition to "faultless behavior" within one's circle of comrades, and "strict, but correct" relations with subordinate SS officers and SS men.

The "comradely" relationships of SS officers among themselves, which was not at all free of personal conflicts and disagreements, was not restricted to service-related activities. Rather social and cultural events for the officer corps, such as rallies (*Kameradschaftsabende*) or organized visits to the theater or movies, as well as social conventions, were elementary constituents of the SS community. Through these activities, SS men were connected in multiple ways to the cities and villages near the concentration camps. They visited local pubs, movie theaters and swimming pools, they appeared at parades and dances. Contacts and friendships were made, marriages planned and celebrated. A concentration camp's registry office often certified marriages, and a bridegroom's "SS comrades" acted as "guarantor for the bride" for the obligatory questionnaire from the SS Race and Settlement Main Office (SS-Rasse- und Siedlungshauptamt) or as best men.

The wives of SS officers, who usually lived where their husbands were stationed, had an essential function within the SS community. In a typical concentration camp, most SS officers and their families lived in an SS settlement located not far from the protective custody camp. SS families often used inmates as servants, gardeners, or other help. The women and children of SS officers were connected through close personal contacts; they met one another while shopping or during leisure activities. The familial and social context also facilitated intermarriage among camp SS families, which the Reich SS Command did not view unfavorably, and possibly even encouraged.

The primary importance of the familial and social context was to create a sense of normality and stability. For members of the concentration camp SS, the family symbolized the continuity of the German *Volk*, for whose well-being they believed they were serving. Thus they saw no conflict between carrying out their murderous duty and their leisure activities and family life. The intricately interwoven social network of the concentration camp SS, which despite the many personal disagreements lasted until the end of the war, the male society (*Männerbund*) of concentration camp SS members, and the wives and children who themselves acted as stabilizers, all provided an important foundation for their activities.

"Initiation": Violence in the Prewar Camps

Common service-related socialization shaped the concentration camp SS. By no means did the forms of violence and terror developed by this group lack subject or object as the analysis by Wolfgang Sofsky suggests.[14] Rather they were far more connected to structural relationships and precisely describable events. In addition, the victims of terror were purposively, not arbitrarily selected.

The initial murder in each of the early camps proved to be a collective watershed of applied terror and a moment of group- and identity-formation. In Dachau, for example, it can be shown that the first use of excessive force by SS men, which can be dated to the 11th and 12th of April 1933, was directed, if not exclusively, then especially against the Jewish prisoners. The violent excesses of that night culminated in the murder of four Jewish prisoners. Of the 21 prisoners killed in Dachau by the SS during 1933, a disproportionate number—namely two-thirds—were Jews.

These initial murders showed, first, that SS men did not yet have a routine for murder. Those killed were victims of excessive violence, an orgy of beating in which several SS men, in a drunken state, goaded one another to use deadly force. The SS men did not kill regardless of circumstances or without scruple. Secondly, however, these events show that the men were willing to translate the antisemitic world-view of the SS, which until the "seizure of power" had been largely limited to writings and words, into violent and murderous practice. They acted out what in their circles—and within the SS—was a consensus that "the Jews" harmed the German *Volk* and thus must be "eradicated" (*ausgemerzt*). Without reference to their world-view, one cannot explain why Jewish prisoners, in particular, constituted an extraordinarily high—and disproportionate—percentage of the victims of their murderous terror.

A further collective experience contributing to group and identity formation has to be dated to the second half of 1938 when the general preventive conception of the political police, formulated in 1936, was made the official practice of the concentration camp SS. That is the principle that Ulrich Herbert has called "racial deterrence policy" (*rassische Generalprävention*), which then replaced the battle against political enemies.

In the so-called "Operations Against Asocials" in the spring and summer of 1938, more than 10,000 people ended up in the hands of the camp SS, incarcerated at Buchenwald and Sachsenhausen, and after its establishment in August 1938, in Flossenbürg. (The SS continued to use the "traditional camp" at Dachau primarily to imprison political opponents of the regime.) In addition, immediately after the November pogrom approximately 30,000 Jewish men were taken to the camps. Together the "Operations Against Asocials" and the November pogrom, completely transformed the inmate population. At Sachsenhausen, for example, the camp SS registered a total of 8,207 prisoners at the end of 1938: only 20.3 percent of camp inmates were classified as being in political "protective custody," while 63.4 percent were "criminals" or "asocials"; the camp register listed an additional 16.3 percent as "Jews."[15]

The eruption of violence that can be documented in the second half of 1938 and the sharp rise in the death rate did not affect the political prisoners, or did so only to a slight extent. The treatment of Jewish prisoners, on the other hand, was characterized by a brutality and cruelty which was unprecedented in the history of the concentration camps. That SS men made Jewish inmates (rather than political prisoners) the objects of their violence can be explained only with reference to their antisemitic beliefs. From among the entire group of concentration camp inmates, they picked out specifically the Jewish prisoners. The SS men considered themselves justified in humiliating, torturing, and killing these—the Jewish, not the political—prisoners. The National Socialist world-view functioned as a screen that allowed the functional elite to target their victims.

"Internal" and "External Front"

The ideological conviction of the Reich SS Command at the beginning of the war, that they must proceed like a "state defense corps" (*Staatsschutzkorps*) against the "internal" and "external enemy" is also reflected in the deployment of the camp SS. Since the fall of 1938, the members of the police reinforcement had been increasingly incorporated into the guard troops—mostly older men from the General-SS. At the beginning of the war, they, as well as most of the functional elite of the concentration camp SS, remained stationed in the camps, because Himmler needed them for maintaining the internal front and for the planned expansion of the camp system. The members of the SS Death's Head units were, however, deployed to what they understood as the "external front." Both groups demonstrated specific qualitative advances in the use of force and terror, forms of the collective use of violence.

A few days after the beginning of the war, the SS Death's Head units entered Poland. At the rear, they acted in collaboration with the SS Task Forces, which had also been newly constituted when the war began. Members of the SS Death's Head units humiliated, beat, and killed defenseless Polish civilians in their path. From available sources it is known that they terrorized Polish Jews in particular. The crimes committed over a few days in Poland cannot be compared in extent and form with those of the concentration camp SS in the prewar years.

Shortly after the invasion of Poland, Hitler approved the consolidation of armed SS units in separate divisions. In October 1939 Himmler ordered Theodor Eicke, Inspector of Concentration Camps and Commander of the SS Death's Head Units, to withdraw these troops from Poland and create an independent force with them—the SS Death's Head Division.[16]

Within the SS officer corps were seven members of the concentration camp SS, who were promoted to camp commander between 1942 and 1945; at times they constituted a third of the acting commanders. As part of the SS Death's Head Division they had participated in the "Western campaign"—the war against France—which assumed mythic dimensions. They experienced this military victory of only a few weeks over the French "arch-enemy" as a military and personal triumph. In particular, the young SS men who themselves had not experienced the First World War, but had grown up with its mythology, exulted in the awareness that they themselves, in the same place where an earlier generation had lost the World War, had redeemed the shame of their fathers.

After the capitulation of France, the SS Death's Head Division constituted part of the occupation troops in southwest France. In the summer of 1941, it was among the first German formations to invade the Soviet Union. Its defeat proved decisive for the history of the SS Death's Head Division on the Eastern Front—as for the consciousness of its members. Between the fall of 1941 and October 1942 the division was nearly completely wiped out in the area around Demjansk, south of Leningrad. As early as the late fall of 1941, it recorded death rates of nearly 50 percent—disproportionately high compared to other German units deployed on the Eastern Front. It is not known how many Soviet soldiers were killed in the Demjansk area. However, there is evidence that the few successes of the SS Death's Head Division culminated in mass killings of Soviet soldiers in barbaric massacres.

For the few SS men who survived the so-called "Demjansk pocket," the battlefield "in the East," which differed fundamentally from the experiences and later interpretations of the Western campaign, provided an affirmation of their world-view. Because of the "hardness" (*Härte*) of the conflict and the immense losses, including their own casualties, the Eastern Front seemed to be the anticipated "racial" struggle for survival. In the summer of 1942, some SS Death's Head men returned to concentration camp service.

On the "internal front," camp commanders and division heads translated the extermination policies of the Nazi regime into actions against particular groups of prisoners. Some division heads first rose to the top of the command staff when the war began; they advanced to commander rank when the camp system was expanded. The first phase of the war, during which both the number of those incarcerated rose and mortality rates increased considerably, proved to be significant for the camp system and typified the collective use of force by the concentration camp SS.

A first systematic killing operation can be dated to the spring of 1941. The murder of sick and weakened camp prisoners designated as "Special Treatment 14 f 13" (*Sonderbehandlung 14 f 13*) began in early April 1941 in the Sachsenhausen camp, when a committee of "I 4" doctors selected sick and injured inmates whose condition identified them as "ballast" in the overcrowded camp. Inmates designated for death were killed in "euthanasia facilities." The concentration camp SS also used the killing operation to murder politically unpopular and/or Jewish prisoners. Moreover, this killing operation proved to be important for two reasons: for the development both of applied killing technologies within the camp system and—closely related to it—of "expertise" within the concentration camp SS.

The decision over life or death was gradually shifted to the concentration camp SS after the fall of 1941; SS men themselves now killed alleged or actually sick and weakened prisoners. Terms in the "camp jargon," such as "injection" (*abspritzen*), "poison drink" (*Gifttrinken*) or "death bath" (*Todbaden*) denoted the excesses of force. In addition, "Special Treatment 14 f 13" became a model for the far more extensive killing operation carried out by the concentration camp SS beginning in the summer of 1941: the mass murder of Soviet prisoners of war. Available research indicates that after the summer of 1941 at least 34,000 Soviet soldiers were killed in the concentration camps.[17] Critical for the connections discussed here is the fact that the murders were devised through collaboration between the "bureaucrats" of the IKL and the "practitioners" in the concentration camp SS—leading members of the Sachsenhausen command staff—who put them into practice. The staging of the murders, by deceiving the Soviet prisoners of war through a "medical examination," shows that the minds of the Sachsenhausen command staff reached back to experiences they had gathered a few weeks earlier with "Special Treatment 14 f 13." Here prisoners had also gone unsuspecting to their deaths because they did not recognize the danger of the alleged "medical examination" by "T 4" doctors.

The murder procedure developed by the SS officer corps at Oranienburg—the killing of Soviet prisoners of war in a special facility where they were shot in the nape of the neck—was "demonstrated" to other camp commanders as a "successful" method of killing in the fall of 1941. This killing facility was subsequently copied in several IKL concentration camps. The initial murders with Zyklon B at the Auschwitz camp must be linked to these two murder operations. Evidence indicates that members of the SS officer corps at Auschwitz, on their own initiative, devised an experiment that would be their own contribution to killing operations then being "carried out" within the camp system.

The victims of the often described first killing of humans with Zyklon B in Auschwitz in early September 1941 were 600 Soviet prisoners of war and 250 sick concentration camp prisoners.[18] The killing technology—asphyxiation by means of poison gas—was familiar to several SS men on the command staff. They had themselves viewed the "euthanasia" facility at Sonnenstein a few weeks earlier when they had transported selected concentration camp prisoners there as part of "Operation 14 f 13."[19] In Auschwitz the SS men—and this was the novelty—applied Zyklon B as a killing method. From their perspective, the choice of Zyklon B as a poison—as cynical as it may sound today—was obvious since it was available in large quantities in the camps, where the SS had used it after 1941 to combat epidemics, above all spotted fever and typhus.

The creation of the Sachsenhausen facility for shooting prisoners, which after the fall of 1941 was copied in numerous other concentration camps, as well as the development of a gas chamber at Auschwitz, which soon was "professionalized" at Auschwitz-Birkenau and used for the systematic extermination of European Jewry, demonstrate one thing: the development of killing technologies and their transfer among the extermination sites occurred not by means of written commands, but rather through historical actors.

Personnel Transfers in the Summer of 1942

The utilization of concentration camp prisoners in the war economy, which was being advanced by the SS in order to maintain its imperium, led on 16 March 1942 to the IKL's incorporation as Department D in the WVHA, which had been established on 1 February of that same year. Cooperation between industry and concentration camps had not yet been adequately tested, because by early 1942, only a few camps were "pilot projects" for the envisioned collaboration. Nor did WVHA chief Oswald Pohl believe that he could push through necessary changes in the function of the camps with SS personnel who were then in responsible positions.

Pohl undertook three actions. First, on 20 February he revoked jurisdiction over the deployment of workers[20] from officers of the work units (whom Pohl himself had established as independent division heads in the camps). He did so in order, second, to place responsibility directly on the commanders.[21] The deployment of (non-Jewish) concentration camp prisoners to work in the war economy was thus assigned the highest priority, while at the same time the extermination of European Jews assumed systematic form. From Pohl's perspective, only some of the acting commanders seemed to be in a position to meet the new demands placed upon the concentration camps by the wartime economy. As the third measure, he replaced a third of the acting commanders with SS officers who promised to carry out the new line in accord with his "profile of requirements."[22]

Pohl's personnel changes among camp commanders in the summer of 1942 make two things clear: first, that the appointment of camp commanders cannot simply be personalized, nor can it be considered in the context of a single concentration camp. The personnel policies regarding appointments set by the responsible office (and ultimately by Himmler) were linked to a far greater extent to changes in the function of the concentration camps. Second, and at the same time, they should be interpreted as a reaction to commanders' behavior and personalities.

As Pohl saw it, the SS officers who were removed from service in the WVHA's domain in the summer of 1942 were apparently unable to handle the responsibilities of a commander. They had also, in the SS context, misused their power. As varied as the reasons for transfer were—they included above all corruption and alcoholism—ultimately they could all be attributed to the same cause. The men who were suspended had committed a flagrant offense against the SS world-view; in a variation on Himmler's declaration, they had not remained "decent" (anständig) in the face of the "difficult task" (schwere Aufgabe) they had to perform.[23] It should be stressed that such a "misdemeanor" (Vergehen) did not lead to an inevitable or mandatory transfer or loss of rank. At a time when functions were in flux, it was, however, often the catalyst.

In the summer of 1942 (and in later years) Pohl and Himmler resorted to more or less drastic means to punish the "failure" (Versagen) of acting camp commanders. They ranged from transfer out of the WVHA camp system (as in the case of Sachsenhausen Commander Hans Loritz), to initiation of a criminal process, or (as in the case of Dachau Commander Alex Piorkowski) to cashiering from the SS, and on (as with Buchenwald Commander Karl-Otto Koch) to execution.

The SS officers who were appointed commanders in the summer of 1942 had earlier either served in the concentration camp SS, the IKL or WVHA, or in Eicke's SS Death's Head Division. This closed the split between the "internal" and "external" fronts which had opened up when the war began. Those commanders who had shared the combat experience of the SS Death's Head Division and who all (except one) had been wounded in the "Demjansk pocket," returned to concentration camp service in the summer of 1942. Pohl's decision to appoint as camp commanders several officers from the SS Death's Head Division who were wounded at Dem-

jansk can be explained by the existence of the social network within
the concentration camp SS. It developed in the mid-1930s and had
not been damaged by the deployment of some of its members to the
"external front." The close personal ties and patronage relationships that had developed within the SS officer corps in Oranienburg
or Dachau in the 1930s contradicted the notion that the return to
the "internal front" had been a coincidence, as some commanders
construed in retrospect.[24]

Thus in the summer of 1942 Pohl arranged for a personnel
change at the highest level of concentration camp leaders, but he
did not introduce entirely new leadership personnel. Rather, in
installing new personnel he relied almost entirely on members of
the concentration camp SS. Pohl's personnel decisions showed that
he himself had numerous ties with the camps.[25] On 1 February
1942, the joint office "Household and Construction"/"Administration and Economy," which was headed by Pohl, was consoli-
dated into the WVHA. This development signified the expression
and culmination of Pohl's steadily increasing influence over administration, personnel, construction activity, and "labor deployment"
in the concentration camps, as did his confirmation as WVHA chief
and the integration of the IKL as Department D. Pohl's subsequent
ability to determine who would fill commander positions resp. the
entire concentration camp command staff concluded a development
that can be traced back to 1934: Pohl's steadily expanding authority over the concentration camp system.

Researchers have often inferred from Pohl's growing power a
conflict between him and Eicke, ending with Eicke's separation
from the IKL at the outbreak of war.[26] In regard to personnel policy, this hypothesis cannot, however, be confirmed. The relationship
between Eicke and Pohl is better described as cooperative rather
than confrontational. Moreover, the concrete decision in the summer of 1942 regarding new appointments (and the question of who
would be placed where) was obviously not made without Eicke,
who during this phase of decision-making was in Oranienburg in
order to convince Himmler and Hitler to withdraw the SS Death's
Head Division, which by this point had been decimated.[27]

Because of the division's military importance on the Eastern
Front, its commander Eicke was then at the zenith of his power, as
well as in Hitler's favor. Regardless of whether—as Stutthof Camp
Commander Paul Werner Hoppe reported at the end of the war[28]—
Himmler actually solicited Eicke's recommendations on commander replacements, one can assume that Eicke attempted to gain
influence over the central decision made in summer 1942 for the

camp system. There is evidence for his success, first, in his continuing dominant influence over Richard Glück, his successor as Inspector of Concentration Camps and later chief of the WVHA's Department D. Second, Eicke and Pohl obviously agreed on their assessment that particular SS officers—for example, Hoppe, Fritz Suhren, or Anton Kaindl—were well-suited as commanders. On the other hand, in the summer of 1942 Eicke either did not want to, or was unable to retain his long-time protegés Hans Loritz and Karl-Otto Koch.

On 23 August 1942, Himmler accepted Pohl's recommandations for "transfers and removals of command" among camp commanders.[29] Those who retained their offices, as well as the young SS officers who were designated,[30] distinguished themselves by their administrative or organizational abilities and their "faultless" behavior, above all by their solidarity with the social network of the concentration camp SS. They actually began their service in October or November 1942. The reason for the delay cannot be derived from the postwar testimony of these SS officers. Their silence is, however, eloquent. Their unanimous and stubborn taciturnity regarding the period between their formal appointment in late August 1942 and the actual beginning of their service that October or November can be interpreted as an attempt to hide a critical event.

One surviving document may be the key to the answer. In a personnel request of 3 December 1943 in the dossier of Johannes Hassebroek, commander of the Groß-Rosen concentration camp, one can read that Hassebroek was "assigned to the service of the c.c." in Sachsenhausen between the 29th of August and mid-November 1942.[31] This assignment possibly involved not only him, but all the SS officers who were to assume their posts as concentration camp commanders: Anton Kaindl, Fritz Suhren, Max Pauly, Josef Kramer, and Paul Werner Hoppe. It would then be understood not as a traditional "training period," but rather as a swearing-in along the new lines Pohl intended to carry out with his personnel changes of the summer of 1942. Assuming that this evidence is not misleading, Sachsenhausen in the summer of 1942 can be seen as the staging area for, and constituting of, what was understood to be a new "generation" of camp commanders.

The Construction of "Decency"

The professionalization of commanders that was being attempted in the summer of 1942 entailed a specific self-awareness on the part of those camp commanders who were confirmed in office or newly appointed and who in the period until the war's end "proved" themselves in the eyes of their superiors. The subjects of this study made claims for having executed their responsibilities with "decency" and for belonging to the "most faithful" adherents of the Nazi regime. In postwar statements, a number of men who had served under them confirmed that the camp commanders in question behaved—in the jargon of the concentration camp SS—"strictly, but correctly" (*streng, aber gerecht*), and had forbidden any mistreatment of camp prisoners. Such testimony, because made in court, should be seen primarily as an attempted diversion from crimes committed and the guilt of those testifying.

The positive tenor of comments by camp survivors is nonetheless noteworthy and requires considerable explanation. The subjects of this study—for example, Hermann Pister, Martin Weiß, Paul Werner Hoppe, Johannes Hassebroek, Richard Baer, and Rudolf Höß—were not remembered as sadists or "beasts" by former prisoners who were interviewed. Rather they were described as "decent" and "correct" camp commanders—among the reported appellations were "Mr. Camp Commander" (*Herr Lagerkommandant*) for Pister, the "people's commander" (*Volkskommandant*) for Weiß, "gentleman in uniform" for Hoppe, or the "camp commander at Groß-Rosen who was most humane and most beloved by the prisoners" for Hassebroek.[32]

The mosaic of testimony by numerous witnesses, their admissions in postwar trials, as well as the findings of historical research, which provide information about camp reality and thus the concrete behavior of the SS officers under consideration, allows us to paint a picture of men who not only believed in the principles of the National Socialist *Weltanschauung*, but made them the foundation of their behavior. It was precisely on this point that they distinguished themselves, at least in their self-image, from their predecessors.

Among the principles of "order" by which the concentration camps oriented their procedures were the organization of prisoner society according to "racial" criteria, the total exhaustion of prisoners in armaments production, as well as the "punishment" of camp prisoners who dared to elude this "order." The lowest ranks of the prisoner hierarchy, namely Jewish, Polish, and Soviet inmates, were mercilessly worked to death or killed for the slightest reason. Camp commanders like Höß, Kramer, or Baer, who were installed at Auschwitz, carried out what in Höß's words was the "hardest command" (*härteste Befehl*), the killing of defenseless people with gas because they were Jewish prisoners, who it was certain harmed the German *Volk* and thus must be exterminated. They considered the murder of Jews to be necessary and right. In addition, they thought themselves to be "hard" enough to transform into deeds a conviction internalized since their youth. As Rudolf Höß expressed this connection:

> "... and it was always stressed that if Germany was to survive, then world Jewry must be exterminated and we all accepted it as the truth. That was the picture I had in my head, so, when Himmler called me to him [to assign Höß the task of carrying out the Final Solution], I just accepted it as the realization of something I had already accepted—not only I, but everybody. I considered it to be absolutely correct, and although this order, which would have shocked even the strongest and coldest nature ... did frighten me momentarily, it fitted in with all that had been preached to me for years."[33]

At the same time, and by no means contrary to the treatment of Jewish and Slavic camp prisoners, the commanders did in fact behave relatively "decently" and "humanely" toward one inmate group: the German prisoners who, in keeping with their racist world-view, had a fundamentally different "worth" than Jewish, Polish, or Soviet camp inmates. Consistent with their self-perception, they styled this behavior as definitive of their basic attitude toward life, as their general "bearing" (*Haltung*)—what Hasse-broek described as the "clean [*sauber*] life of a person and the irreproachable leadership of a commander."[34]

As foils to their self-styled and self-legitimized identities, these men enlisted their predecessors, whom they viewed as an "older generation" of camp commanders: in Hoppe's term, "old timers" or, in Höß's words, "old Dachauites (*alte Dachauer*)."[35] As a negative example and counter-construct they chose the first commander at Buchenwald, Karl-Otto Koch, whom they portrayed as the incarnation of a sadistic and corrupt SS officer, or as alternatives, Hans Loritz or Arthur Rödl. They characterized the behavior of a Koch, Rödl, or Loritz as the personalization of cruelty, corruption, a lax sense of service, and alcoholism, to which they compared their own exercise of duties, which—in Pister and Hassebroek's precise words—ultimately "served" the "well-being" of concentration camp prisoners.[36]

The camp survivors who were questioned indeed remembered commanders such as Pister, Weiß, Hoppe, or Hassebroek as SS officers who at least had tried to mitigate the brutality and mistreatment and to reduce mortality in the camps. In order to make camp prisoners available for "labor deployment" in the war industry, they had taken care to make incarceration conditions more bearable. Reality, however, contradicts these recollections. While some groups among the persecuted did experience the post-1942/43 economic arrangements in the concentration camps—and thus the regimes of Pister, Weiß, Hoppe, or Hassebroek—as an easing of incarceration conditions, forced labor meant death within a few weeks for other groups of prisoners, in particular those of Jewish or Slavic origin.

In the second half of the war, the SS improved working and thus living conditions only for the minority of prisoners from whose professional qualifications they profited. These prisoners—skilled workers, as well as the mostly German prisoners with camp functions—also had a chance during the final stage of the war of surviving the camp. These prisoners were, however, also the majority of those who after the war were questioned about their imprisonment in Allied and/or German court proceedings. In their perceptions, SS officers such as Pister, Hoppe, Hassebroek, or Weiß distinguished themselves positively from the earlier commanders, who had persecuted all prisoners (including the Germans) with senseless drills, meaningless work details, and beatings.

Labor performed by the overwhelming majority of camp prisoners during the second half of the war was not valued very highly because it seemed to be so readily available. Thus the majority of camp prisoners was—with minimal provisions—deployed in debilitating work detachments, in which "work" and "extermination" became synonymous. The Jewish and Slavic prisoners were located on the bottom rungs of the prisoner society that was "ordered" according to racist criteria and had hardly a chance of surviving the camp. They were thus denied any chance of articulating their impression of Pister, Weiß, Hoppe, or Hassebroek. It cannot be assumed that, had they ever had the opportunity to bear witness, they would have acknowledged any "improvement" of prison conditions during the second half of the war. The few survivors among this group of inmates were not as a rule heard in court as witnesses, because they could not give a description of a camp commander. They remembered him only as the distant ruler over life and death, but not his face, a concrete act of murder, or his name. They merely described the camp as "hell."[37]

The construct of "decency" was an essential component of these SS men's self-perception. From both a private ("as a person") and a service-related perspective, they believed that their behavior had been "decent" and "correct." Their self-perception should also be understood as the foundation of their identity: only because they believed their behavior was "decent" and "correct," could they implement the extermination policy of the Nazi regime. The "decency" construct was required in order to legitimize their murderous acts to themselves and before the public.

Both behavioral maxims—namely that the commanders mercilessly murdered or ordered the murder of the Jewish, Soviet, and Polish camp prisoners, while on the other hand their treatment of German prisoners was "decent" and "correct"—are inseparably interrelated. The foundation of concentration camp "order," which they considered valid until their deaths and at no point in their lives questioned, was *völkisch* racism. The fact that the picture of the "correct" and "decent" SS officer was mirrored in the reports of survivors merely expresses one particular perspective and one camp reality, namely that of privileged German camp inmates. For the reasons cited, they disproportionately served as witnesses to the past. In fact, mass mortality in the concentration camps first began when these men assumed their positions.

Failure and "Collapse"

Development of the camp system during the second half of the war shows that the commanders who were appointed to or confirmed in office were not in a position to implement Pohl's new line, that is, the economic orientation of the concentration camps. They did not succeed in restructuring them as both useful and "effectively" organized reservoirs of labor for the armament industry. Their failure— in comparison with the task they had been assigned—can be attributed to biographical and structural reasons.

First, given their origins, education, and mental abilities, members of the concentration camp SS were not in a position to realize the ambitious plans. Since 1942/43, because cooperation with industry was required, camp commanders and some division heads were, to a large extent, forced to deal and cooperate with the management of various firms, administrative heads, and local party and government functionaries.

Two examples will make clear the discrepancy between milieu of origin and wartime position. The commander at Neuengamme, Max Paul, formerly the owner of a small grocery store in a village in Schleswig-Holstein, after 1943 negotiated the deployment of camp prisoners in war production with Hamburg's business and industrial elite. During his tenure in Auschwitz, Rudolf Höß, who neither finished school nor had any vocational training, made agreements with engineers and directors of IG-Farben. The few sources of information about their personal state show that they were extraordinarily impressed by the role and position in which they had found themselves and for which their education and intellectual abilities had in no way prepared them.

The assumption, however, that it would have been possible for the concentration camp SS, and in particular the camp commanders, to build a perfectly "functioning" camp complex, which could have been "run" like a machine—both industrial and "effective"—is internally contradictory. Their failure can further be explained by the structural development of the camp system.

The commanders began their service in the late fall of 1942, coinciding with a tremendous expansion of the camp system, a sharp increase in the number of camp prisoners, and the rapid establishment of satellite camps. After 1943, and especially after 1944, the camp system became considerably more chaotic, with a drastic worsening of prison conditions, and the beginning of a massive rise in mortality.

During the last year of the war, the armament industry's demand for workers increased tremendously, caused by the Nazi leadership's attempt to use all available means to avert the impending military defeat. This demand led to a renewed increase in both the number of camp inmates and the number of satellite camps. Massive and arbitrary waves of arrests (now also in western and northern Europe) accompanied the retreat of German troops, increasing the number of camp prisoners. In August 1944 there were 524,286 people subject to the authority of the camp SS; on 15 January 1945 there were 714,211 prisoners.[38]

The demand for workers had the additional consequence that the principle which had been followed after 1942, of making the Reich territory "Jew free" and murdering the European Jews "in the East," was abandoned in April 1944, accompanied by evacuation of part of the WVHA extermination complex "in the East." Within a short period of time, beginning in the early summer of 1944, several tens of thousands of Jewish prisoners ended up in concentration camps in the Reich interior. The dramatic overcrowding of the Reich camps—especially during the second half of 1944—was experienced by those incarcerated there as a life-threatening decline in the conditions of imprisonment. The majority of camp inmates was confronted with a dramatic shortage of resources, accompanied by increases in mistreatment and "punishment," as well as the expansion of "work deployment." Mortality rates began to reach mass dimensions previously unknown in the concentration camps of the Reich.

With few exceptions, the "efficiency" achieved by deploying camp prisoners in the war industry remained well short of expectations. The catastrophic conditions that developed after 1944, at the latest, stood in striking contrast to Himmler's and Pohl's intention to continue making camp prisoners available as useful and "effective" workers for the war industry. In fact, their demands were motivated not by any economic concept, rather by the effort to preserve their power and retain Hitler's favor.

The last year of the war was also characterized by the fact that the concentration camp SS became a minority within the camp SS, and was confronted with the rapid dissolution of its position of power. Its monopoly as sole authority over camp inmates, over conditions of incarceration, "work deployment," and the deaths of prisoners, crumbled.

Three reasons can be identified. First, since late 1943 the command staff had come under the scrutiny of several special commissioners of the Reich Security Main Office (Reichssicherheitshauptamt, RSHA), who were investigating the growing number of corruption cases and "illegal" murders.

Second, the concentration camp guard troops were augmented by persons who no longer embodied the model of the prewar SS, but rather who—in particular the "ethnic German" SS men—during the course of the war had been deployed in the Waffen SS. Others were not part of the SS: for example, the female camp wardens (*Aufseherinnen*), some of whom were contract personnel from firms that requested camp prisoners, and Wehrmacht and Luftwaffe troops who were transferred to the SS. In some cases, the latter group even assumed leadership responsibility for the satellite camps. By mid-January 1945 every second guard was a former Wehrmacht member. This development was accompanied by the delegation of guard and control responsibilities to prisoners with functional positions. The structural changes in the guard troops led to numerous conflicts between those assigned to guard duties and the established concentration camp SS. Sometimes it also resulted in milder treatment of camp prisoners.

The third factor was increased cooperation between the SS and the armament industry after 1943/44, which led to a considerable loss of power by both Department D of the WVHA and the concentration camp SS, whose members tried to initiate vigorous opposition to these developments.

Few surviving sources can be used to infer the subjective reactions of the SS officers when confronted with the impending catastrophe of the camp system's total breakdown. It is clear, however, that not one left his post. Rather these men believed they could halt the dissolution of power by means of increased terror against camp prisoners, as well as by initiating summary court-martial proceedings against their subordinates. Although, or even because the camp system was collapsing around them, Allied troops were moving dangerously near, and the concentration camps were turning into death camps, among themselves and in public the commanders held fast to the belief that they would continue to exercise total rule over their powerful domains.

Max Pauly and Rudolf Höß, for example, interpreted the impending catastrophe as a "challenge," which could be met only with "relentless exertion." Pauly confronted the chaos with his life principles: "power" and "work," through which alone he could find "inner satisfaction"—as he wrote on 30 December 1944 in a letter to a former superior.[39] The more chaotic reality became, and the nearer the collapse of their world approached, the more intensely they held to "effectiveness" and "decency." De facto, however, their power had long since become a chimera, and the propaganda ideals of "ceaseless work dedication" and "decency" a protective shield.

Without exception, camp commanders attempted to keep their world "functioning" until the "collapse." They blamed their lack of success on their superiors, the other camp commanders, their subordinates, or the camp prisoners, above all on "circumstances" or—in Höß's words—"the war." In the end, the war proved itself to be—as Höß interpreted the trajectory of his life—"the stronger one." The "will" of the individual had been unable to prevail against it.[40] This interpretation remained enmeshed in the National Socialist *Weltanschauung*, which interpreted reality not as the product of human actions, but rather as the enactment of immutable laws of existence, the victory of the strong over the weak.

Members of the concentration camp SS collaborated in organizing their escape. Two escape routes and destinations can be identified: the "Alpine Fortress" in the Ausseer region and the "Northern Fortress" in Schleswig-Holstein. Although the sources give no clues as to the existence of any further concrete plans relating to these destinations, or whether they were simply "castles in the air," two things are clear: first, beginning in March 1945 the concentration camp SS in fact attempted to move the mass of camp prisoners in those directions (in order, for whatever purpose, to keep them firmly under their power), and second, all (with two exceptions) of the still active camp commanders, along with their command staffs and their families, embarked on one of the two escape routes.

The northern route had particular significance in that it was also used by Department D of the WVHA and other key groups of the SS terror apparatus. In the spring of 1945 Schleswig-Holstein became the assembly point for the RSHA, WVHA, Gestapo, and SS Reich leadership. It can be shown that, in late April or early May, at least four camp commanders—Pauly, Hoppe, Kaindl, and Höß—met with Himmler for the last time in Flensburg. In line with their self-image as model SS officers, they described this meeting as a disappointment. Höß and Hoppe reported that Himmler did not demand the "self-sacrifice for the idea" that he had promoted,[41] but rather ordered them to disappear into the Wehrmacht, an order that seemed to Höß a mockery of his ideas, actions, and identity.[42] With the "collapse" of their world, members of the concentration camp SS went underground in Schleswig-Holstein or southern Germany, equipped with new names and false papers.

Integration in Postwar Society?

Since the late 1970s, there has been widespread consensus among the German public and historians that the Nazi elites were in large measure seamlessly integrated into the postwar society of the Federal Republic. This was, in fact, the case for a number of groups.[43] However, the concentration camp SS had a different experience.

Within a short time, a large percentage of the department heads and camp commanders were in Allied captivity. These men were held together in particular incarceration facilities, for example, the Neuengamme and Westertimke internment camps, or the military prisons at Landsberg and Werl. In this milieu, isolated from the outside world and pressured by Allied judicial inquiries, they cultivated a demeanor that was as pathetic as it was consistent with their world-view. They portrayed themselves as victims of Allied "victors' justice" and "world Jewry," and they imagined themselves in the role of martyrs. Their self-image drew heavily upon the ideal of the "decent" and "correct" SS officer, which they had claimed for themselves during their service in the camps. A number of individuals largely supported this "position": wives and other family members, former subordinates and "comrades," and last but not least, some camp survivors.

What Primo Levi called the "gray zone" of the concentration camp did not dissipate with the end of the Third Reich. Rather it persisted into the years of Allied military jurisdiction (and sometimes beyond). The former SS men and inmate functionaries encountered one another before Allied military tribunals, alternately as witnesses and defendants. Many surviving inmate functionaries testified on behalf of the SS men in order to divert attention from their own involvement in the crimes of the SS. Others were bribed by wives of former SS men. In addition, a number of (mainly German) survivors believed that a subjective sense of justice demanded they testify that the indicted commander—for example, Weiß, Pister, or Hassebroek—was relatively "decent" and "correct" in his treatment of them and in comparison with their respective predecessors, Piorkowski, Koch, and Rödl.

The nimbus of the "decent" and "correct" SS officer, which was sworn to in numerous court statements, enabled these men to demonstrate their "bearing" against the "victor powers." Moreover, in court the construct of "decency" and the image of a model SS officer—hard pressed by the weight of the facts that the court and survivors assembled about the mass crimes committed in the camps—was transformed and hardened into a strategy of excuse and defense. Self-awareness and self-legitimization, exculpation and defense were inseparably merged.

Even when Allied military judges were influenced to an extent by frequent testimony regarding the "decency" of camp commanders in particular, not one was acquitted of guilt and responsibility. Of the department heads, 18.4 percent, and of the commanders who had served in this post after 1939, some 39 percent had been tried before an Allied military court, condemned to death, and executed by the early 1950s.[44] To a large extent, members of the concentration camp SS were seen by the international public, Allied military judges, as well as by German society as symbols of National Socialist atrocities. Their crimes were committed in places located within the German Reich, and early on they were identified to the international public through the dissemination of pictures from Bergen-Belsen and Dachau.[45] For these reasons members of the concentration camp SS—in contrast to the many bureaucratic criminals or Nazis who committed their crimes "in the East"—were by no means allowed by the Allies to seamlessly join postwar German society.

After the early 1950s, however, the military justice administrations of the Western Allies were increasingly inclined to use pardons to revoke earlier judgments against German war criminals, successively reducing prior sentences. Pardons were even granted to those

who had been convicted of atrocities in the camps. Members of the
concentration camp SS who were released from Allied imprisonment (the overwhelming majority in the Federal Republic) confronted a fundamentally changed political and social reality. Initially
they assumed an occupational and social status appropriate to their
origin and education; in employment and social position they
returned to the middle class. Their status remained insecure, however, in light of active and continuing judicial inquiries by state
attorneys. By 1967, 16.5 percent of the department heads had been
investigated, as was the case for all camp commanders who served
in these positions after 1939.[46] The investigations frequently lasted
for several years, during which those affected were temporarily, or
for the duration, held under investigatory arrest. The overwhelming
majority of the trials, however, ended without result; only a fraction
concluded with an official conviction.

The Motivation of the Perpetrators

The question, what motivated National Socialist "perpetrators" to
commit their murderous deeds is—as the so-called "Goldhagen
debate"[47] has demonstrated—both passionately discussed and
unanswered, among historians as well as the general public. Compared to the theory-oriented and ultimately one-dimensional explanatory model, whether it is complex and inspired by the sociology of
power, such as Wolfgang Sofsky's "absolute power," or sweeping,
such as Daniel Jonah Goldhagen's assertion of an "eliminationist
antisemitism " unique to "the Germans," there are few empirical
works. Exceptions include Ulrich Herbert's study of Werner Best or
Hans Safrian's on Eichmann's men.[48]

An important precondition for an explanatory model that is
not only plausible in itself but empirically adequate to the motivations and actions of the perpetrators is that the historical actors
have transmitted convincing subjective accounts. In the case of
Werner Best or the leaders of the RSHA, the frequency of such
sources is great. A number of contemporary documents from the
pens of historical subjects provide biographical information, as do
numerous postwar court testimonies (marked by constructs and
strategies, but as such very revealing). For members of the concentration camp SS such sources are scarce. Contemporary documents
with subjective content are rare; statements in court (especially
before Allied military tribunals) by the subjects of this study are
wanting both in quantity and quality, especially regarding their

careers or the motives behind their actions. Given the state of the sources, biographies of these men that would meet the standards of biographical research cannot be written.

Insofar as motives can be distilled, they are gained inferentially from the mosaic of witness testimonies and the men's statements in postwar proceedings, as well as from the findings of historical research, information on the reality of camp life, and thus the concrete behavior of the concentration camp SS.

What at first sight seems a problem of the survival of sources, upon closer inspection leads to the key to understanding these men. The group being described were neither intellectuals nor academics, nor members of the educated middle classes, groups to which these premises of self-reflection, the conscious construction of one's identity, and maintaining it in written form belonged. In the case of the concentration camp SS, not only have no subjective sources that could reveal its members' motives been transmitted, there never were any such documents.

For just these reasons, silence about one's own life and actions is characteristic of these men, who to an overwhelming extent came from the middle strata of Weimar society; they were intellectually capable neither of reflecting on their motives nor of developing a concept for behavior, nor did they see any necessity to do so. Rather they saw themselves as "men of action," executors of the National Socialist *Weltanschauung*, which, diffuse though it was, governed their actions.

What proved to be decisive for their behavior was the intricately interwoven social network of the concentration camp SS. By means of shared socialization and exercise of duties, ideas coalesced about how to run a concentration camp and how to deal with the prisoners. These SS men put into ultimately murderous practice the notions that found a consensus within their group (and within the SS). The most important among these codes were that "criminals" and "asocials" were to be "secured" in concentration camps, that sick and weakened camp prisoners represented a "burden" from which one should be freed, that "Russian commissars" who murdered German soldiers in inhuman ways were to be "executed," that "the Jews" must be "exterminated," that "useless eaters" had to die, that camp prisoners who fled or proved to be "dangerous" as the Allies approached were to be "executed," and that prisoners "unable to march" hindered one's own escape and thus were to be killed.

Members of the concentration camp SS did not derive their motives or the knowledge that governed their actions from books, discussions, "schooling in the *Weltanschauung*," or intellectual analysis. Rather the orientation towards "healthy common sense" was decisive. When the state attorney questioned what had justified the hanging of two camp prisoners, Franz Hofmann, the long-term head of the Auschwitz protective custody camp, answered: "As already stressed several times, as an SS officer, I never received instruction in criminal law and procedures. The thing was, though, I already knew, *as a person*, which crimes had to be punished with death and which did not."[49]

"Healthy common sense" or "everyday understanding" describes the orientation of the historical subject towards principles that were felt to be "normal" and valid without examination, which could be reproduced with no reflection. On the contrary, a recourse to theoretical maxims or norms that were anchored outside the group seemed to be as unnecessary as it was largely suspect. In the Nazi period, in the ways discussed in this article, "healthy common sense," which personnel reports routinely remarked upon as a particular criterion (and confirmed with the stereotypical formula "present"), was given a terrible significance. It should be read as a code for the racist and antisemitic consensus of the concentration camp SS, towards which its members were reflexively oriented. This connection is the central key to understanding the concentration camp SS. By means of this consensus, which was always being created anew by common criminal acts, an individual "knew" how he should behave without having to acquire this "knowledge" through a discussion group, books, or "schooling in the *Weltanschauung*."

"The camp inmates," according to Höß, "were ... seen and treated as enemies of the German state. Accordingly, the camp was organized so that the majority of these enemies in them had to be exterminated. Himmler never expressly said this to his helpers. But they created such conditions for their prisoners' stay in the camp that this never officially expressed extermination order was nonetheless fully put into practice in the camps."[50] The members of the concentration camp SS knew—or believed they knew—that Himmler, and ultimately Hitler, demanded exactly that from them. In this sense, the case of the concentration camp SS demonstrates in an exemplary manner that which marked National Socialist despotism as a whole: that the terror apparatus was kept going by the efforts of its members "to fulfill ... the will of the 'Führer,' or what they considered it to be."[51]

Notes

1. This article summarizes the findings of my dissertation: Karin Orth, "Die 'Konzentrationslager-SS.' Sozialstrukturelle Analysen und biographische Studien einer nationalsozialistischen Funktionselite" (Ph.D. Thesis, Hamburg, 1997).
2. Karin Orth, *Das System der nationalsozialistischen Konzentrationslager. Eine politische Organisationsgeschichte* (Hamburg, 1999), pp. 345f. This number does not include Jews murdered in the extermination centers.
3. Robert Lewis Koehl, *The Black Corps: The Structure and Power Struggles of the Nazi SS* (Madison, 1983), p. 168. Raul Hilberg chose the term "administrative core" to describe this phenomenon. See *The Destruction of the European Jews*, 3 vols. (rev. ed.; New York, 1985), p. 900.
4. See Miroslav Kárný, "Waffen-SS und Konzentrationslager," in *Jahrbuch für Geschichte* 33 (1986):231-261; Heinz Boberach, "Die Überführung von Soldaten des Heeres und der Luftwaffe in die SS-Totenkopfverbände zur Bewachung der Konzentrationslagern 1944," in *Militärgeschichtliche Mitteilungen* 34 (1983): 1185-1190; Bertrand Perz, "Wehrmacht und KZ-Bewachung," in *Mittelweg 36*, no. 4 (Oct./Nov. 1995): 69-82.
5. For a definition and other concentration camp "division heads," including female division heads, see Orth, *Konzentrationslager-SS*, pp. 87f.
6. Garrison doctors *(Standortärzte)* occupy a special position, as the only division heads who were not permanently stationed in the concentration camps. See Orth, *Konzentrationslager-SS*, p. 90.
7. See the extensive discussion in Orth, *Konzentrationslager-SS*, pp. 87-119. Inclusion of the concentration camp SS in the "Nazi elite" is based on a definition by Ulrich Herbert, which determines membership by proximity to and responsibility for the terror and extermination policies of the Nazi regime. Herbert, "Rückkehr in die Bürgerlichkeit? NS-Eliten in der Bundesrepublik," in *Rechtsradikalismus in der politischen Kultur der Nachkriegszeit. Die verzögerte Normalisierung in Niedersachsen*, ed. Bernd Weisbrod (Hanover, 1995), pp. 159, 157-173.
8. On the problematic aspects and definition of this concept, see Ulrich Herbert, "'Generation der Sachlichkeit.' Die völkische Studentenbewegung der frühen zwanziger Jahre in Deutschland," in *Zivilisation und Barbarei. Die widersprüchlichen Potentiale der Moderne: Detlev Peukert zum Gedenken*, ed. Frank Bajohr et al., *Hamburger Beiträge zur Sozial- und Zeitgeschichte 27* (Hamburg, 1991), pp. 115-144; Herbert, *Best. Biographische Studien über Radikalismus, Weltanschauung und Vernunft* (Bonn, 1996), pp. 42-50.
9. Orth, *Konzentrationslager-SS*, p. 139.
10. See, e.g., Tom Segev, *Soldiers of Evil: The Commandants of the Nazi Concentration Camps* (New York, 1987), pp. 123-193.
11. Numbers in Klaus Drobisch and Günther Wieland, *System der NS-Konzentrationslager 1933-1939* (Berlin, 1993), Table 21, p. 195, and Table 31, p. 257.
12. For a definition, see Orth, *Konzentrationslager-SS*, pp. 39f.
13. Ravensbrück seemed to have similar functions for senior female camp overseers *(Oberaufseherinnen)* and groups of female overseers. From May 1939 to 1942 Ravensbrück was, at least according to the current state of research, the only incarceration facility for female camp inmates, as well as the only training facility for female guards. Not until 1942 did the WVHA begin to establish women's sections in other concentration camps, at first only in WVHA camps "in the East." Until the end of 1943, however, Ravensbrück remained the *only*

prison facility for female camp inmates in German Reich territory. The personnel of the new women's sections were recruited from there.

14. Wolfgang Sofsky, *The Order of Terror: The Concentration Camp* (Princeton, 1997) (orig. in German, *Die Ordnung des Terrors. Das Konzentrationslager* [Frankfurt, 1993]). For criticism of Sofsky, see Karin Orth and Michael Wildt, "Die Ordnung der Lager. Über offene Fragen und frühe Antworten in der Forschung zu Konzentrationslagern," in *Werkstatt Geschichte* 4, no. 12 (1995): 51-56; Omer Bartov, "The Penultimate Horror," *The New Republic* (13 October 1997), pp. 48-53.

15. Numbers in Drobisch and Wieland, *System*, p. 288.

16. On this unit, see the extensive treatment in Charles W. Sydnor, *Soldiers of Destruction: The SS Death's Head Division, 1933-1945* (2nd ed.; Princeton, 1990).

17. See the extensive discussion in Orth, *Konzentrationslager-SS*, pp. 209-214.

18. See the extensive treatment in Stanislaw Klodzinski, "Die erste Vergasung von Häftlingen und Kriegsgefangenen im Konzentrationslager Auschwitz," in *Die Auschwitz-Hefte*, ed. Hamburger Institut für Sozialforschung, 2 vols. (Weinheim and Basel, 1987), Vol. 1, pp. 261-275; Danuta Czech, *Kalendarium der Ereignisse im Konzentrationslager Auschwitz-Birkenau 1939-1945* (Reinbek, 1989), pp. 117-119; Eugen Kogon et al., *Nazi Mass Murder: A Documentary History of the Use of Poison Gas* (New Haven, 1993), pp. 145-147 (in German, *Nationalsozialistische Massentötungen durch Giftgas. Eine Dokumentation* [Frankfurt, 1983]).

19. Czech, *Kalendarium*, p. 106.

20. Pohl's decree (20 February 1942), Nuremberg Tribunal Document NO-2167.

21. Pohl's order (30 April 1942), printed in Dienststelle des Generalinspekteurs in der Britischen Zone für die Spruchgerichte (ed.), *Beweisdokumente für die Spruchgerichte in der Britischen Zone* (Hamburg, 1947), G.J. Nr. 110.

22. Hermann Kaienburg, "KZ-Haft und Wirtschaftsinteresse. Das Wirtschaftsverwaltungshauptamt der SS als Leitungszentrale der Konzentrationslager und der SS-Wirtschaft," in *Konzentrationslager und deutsche Wirtschaft 1939-1945*, ed. Hermann Kaienburg, *Sozialwissenschaftliche Studien* 34 (Opladen, 1996), pp. 29-60. He interprets the demotion of the work unit officers as Pohl's "strategy for avoiding conflict" (p. 56). According to Kaienburg, the conflicts of commandants with the work unit officers at their camps had led Pohl, after the IKL's consolidation, to assign commandants responsibility for labor utilization. He overlooks, however, that shortly thereafter Pohl exchanged a third of the commandants. Thus Pohl paid no attention to the conflicts, rather he demoted the work unit officers because he then (after the IKL's consolidation into the WVHA) could exercise direct influence over the commanders. The SS officers he had recently put in place were now to give highest priority to his plans for work deployment.

23. See Himmler's speech (4 October 1943), Nuremberg Tribunal Document PS-1919. Sadism and perversion were also considered "indecent" by the SS. See Hilberg, *Destruction*, pp. 904-907, 1109-1110; Hans Buchheim, "Command and Compliance," in Helmut Krausnick et al., *Anatomy of the SS State* (New York, 1968), pp. 261-264 (in German, *Anatomie des SS-Staates* 2 vols. [3d ed.; Munich, 1982], Vol. 1, pp. 263-268); Karin Orth, "Die 'Anständigkeit' der Täter. Texte und Bemerkungen," in *Sozialwissenschaftliche Informationen*, 25, no. 2 (1996): 112-115.

24. See, e.g., Hassebroek's testimony (16 March 1967), Zentrale Stelle der Landesjustizverwaltungen (ZSL), 405 AR 3681/65, Verfahren gegen Hassebroek, Beiheft, Bl. 10. See Segev's interview with Hassebroek, quoted in Segev, *Soldiers of Evil*, pp. 176-182; Baer's testimony (30 December 1960), Staatsanwaltschaft beim Landgericht Frankfurt (SLF), Verfahren gegen Mulka u.a., 4 Ks 2/63, Bd. 42, Bl. 7462; Pauly testimony (2 April 1946), Public Record Office (PRO), JAG 145, WO 235/163, Bl. 25.

25. On Pohl's influence on the administrative heads and the work unit officers, see Orth, *Konzentrationslager-SS*, pp. 102-111. Because Pohl influenced these decisions over a long period, no general personnel transfers were necessary when he became head of the WVHA. With few exceptions they met his expectations.

26. See, e.g., Kaienburg, *KZ-Haft*, p. 40; Hans-Günther Richardi, *Schule der Gewalt. Die Anfänge der Konzentrationslagers Dachau 1933-1934* (Munich, 1983), p. 246; Martin Broszat, "National Socialist Concentration Camps 1933-1945," in *Anatomy*, pp. 397-504, esp. 461-462.

27. Sydnor, *Soldiers of Destruction*, pp. 236f., and p. 241, n. 39.

28. Hoppe interrogation (29 December 1953), Nordrhein-Westfälisches Staatsarchiv Münster (NSM), StA Bochum, Bd. 9041, Bl. 679; see Hoppe's interrogation (30 April 1953), NSM, Bd. 8996, Bl. 88; see Hoppe's interrogation (24 April 1953), NSM, Bd. 9040, Bl. 745.

29. Brandt's letter to Pohl (23 August 1942), Nuremberg Tribunal Document NO-1994.

30. The designated commanders were younger than their predecessors: the five who were removed were, on average, born in 1899, the new commanders on average in 1905. The youngest was just thirty-two at his appointment, the oldest forty-four years old. He, however, was suspended after only one year of service. Neither age nor administrative experience was, in any case, a sufficient condition for passing "probation" in the reality of the camp. Even very young commanders "misused"—in SS terms—their authority, nor did trained administrative officers always prove themselves capable of fulfilling the responsibilities of a commander.

31. Personal request (8 December 1943), Bundesarchiv Außenstelle Lichterfelde (BAL), Personalakte Hassebroek, OSS.

32. Letter from four former prisoners to Pister, Archiv Gedenkstätte Buchenwald (AGB), Buchenwald Prozesse, USA vs. Ilse Koch, roll 1; letter of L.W. (3 May 1946) to the Supreme Military Court, Forschungsstelle für Zeitgeschichte, Hamburg (FZH), Nachlaß Martin Weiß, Nachtrag; testimony by Hanswalter Nitsche about Hoppe (13 October 1953), NSM, StA Bochum, Bd. 9042, Bl. 523; indictment (30 May 1967), ZSL, 405 AR 3681/65, Verfahren gegen Hassebroek, Bl. 9.

33. Höß's testimony of 16 April 1946, quoted in G.M. Gilbert, *Nürnberger Tagebuch* (Frankfurt, 1962), p. 260 f. (Eng., *Nuremburg Diary* [New York, 1947], pp. 268-269. See Rudolf Hoess, *Commandant of Auschwitz: The Autobiography of Rudolf Hoess* (Cleveland and New York, 1959), pp. 205-206 (in German and Martin Broszat (ed.), *Rudolf Höß. Kommandant in Auschwitz. Autobiographische Aufzeichnungen des Rudolf Höß* [13th ed.; Munich, 1992], p. 124). On the point in time when the "Final Solution" was decided upon, see the thematic articles in Vol. 18, *Werkstatt Geschichte*.

34. Hassebroek interrogation (16 March 1967), ZSL, 405 AR 3681/65, Verfahren gegen Hassebroek, Beiheft , Bl. 11.

35. Hoppe interrogation (30 April 1953), NSM, StA Bochum, Bd. 8996, Bl. 88 and Bl. 91R; Hoess, *Commandant*, p. 89.

36. Hassebroek interrogation (21 March 1967), ZSL, 405 AR 3681/65, Verfahren gegen Hassebroek, Beiheft, Bl. 28f. Pister interrogation (2 June 1947), AGB, Buchenwald Prozesse, USA vs. Waldeck et al., roll 11, Bl. 2165.

37. Thus, e.g., the testimony of several German Jews, who were initially deported to Riga, then incarcerated in the Stutthof camp. Most, by far, are found in: NSM, StA Bochum, Bd. 8992 and Bd. 9043.

38. WVHA report (15 August 1944), Nuremburg Tribunal Document NO-399; list of concentration camps and their personnel (1 and 15 January 1945), BAL, Slg, Schumacher/329.

39. Pauly's letter to Hildebrandt (30 December 1944), BAL, Personalakte Pauly, OSS.

40. Höß transcript, Archiv des staatlichen Museums Auschwitz (APMO), Höß-Prozeß, H 21 b, Bl. 25, 234, 242, 248. See Hoess, *Commandant*, pp. 184-185.

41. Hoess, *Commandant*, pp. 191, 197. See Höß manuscript, APMO, Höß-Prozeß, H 21 b, Bl. 197. See Hoppe interrogation (29 December 1953), NSM, StA Bochum, Bd. 9041, Bl. 677R.

42. Hoess, *Commandant*, p. 191. In 1953 Hoppe similarly described Himmler's message; although the distance of eight years was a factor in Hoppe's interrogation by the German Federal State Attorney's office, above all, he intended to make the meeting with the Reich SS leadership seem as banal as possible. Hoppe interrogation (29 December 1953), NSM, StA Bochum, Bd. 9041, Bl. 677R.

43. See Norbert Frei, *Vergangenheitspolitik. Die Anfänge der Bundesrepublik und die NS-Vergangenheit* (2nd ed.; Munich, 1997).

44. No commandant who had been installed during the first phase of the personnel appointment policy, as such, was tried before an Allied and/or German court. Of the commandants condemned to death, eleven were executed (the last one in May 1950); three died while in Allied incarceration. For a more extensive treatment, see Orth, *Konzentrationslager-SS*, pp. 140-142.

45. On the reaction of the American Allies to the liberation of the concentration camps, see Robert H. Abzug, *Inside the Vicious Heart: Americans and the Liberation of Nazi Concentration Camps* (New York and Oxford, 1985); Marcia Feldman (ed.), *Liberation of the Nazi Concentration Camps 1945: Eyewitness Accounts of the Liberators* (Washington, 1987).

46. See Orth, *Konzentrationslager-SS*, p. 141f. Because of active investigations and the initiation of joint trials for some concentration camps, the "gray zone" described above between former inmate functionaries and former concentration camp SS members was to some extent revived.

47. Daniel Jonah Goldhagen, *Hitler's Willing Executioners: Ordinary Germans and the Holocaust* (New York, 1997). For a critique of Goldhagen, see Dieter Pohl, "Die Holocaust-Forschung und Goldhagens Thesen," in *Vierteljahrshefte für Zeitgeschichte* 45 (1997): 1-48; Ruth Bettina Birn, "Revising the Holocaust," in *The Historical Journal*, 40/1 (1997): 195-215.

48. Hans Safrian, *Die Eichmann Männer* (Vienna, 1993).

49. Hofmann testimony (22 April 1959), SLF, Verfahren gegen Mulka u.a., 4 Ks 2/63, Bd. 9, Bl. 1370 (author's emphasis).

50. Höß manuscript, AMPO, Höß-Prozeß, H 21, Bl. 152f., quoted in Manfred Deselaers, "Gott und das Böse. Die Biographie und die Selbstzeugnisse von Rudolf Höß Kommandant von Auschwitz," (Ph.D. Diss., Cracow, 1996),

p. 89f. A revised version has been published as: Deselaers, *"Und Sie hatten nie Gewissensbisse?" Die Biograpfie von Rudolf Höß, Kommandant von Auschwitz, und die Frage nach seiner Verantwortung vor Gott und den Menschen* (Leipzig, 1997).

51. Georg Lilienthal, *Der "Lebensborn e.V. Ein Instrument nationalsozialistischer Rassenpolitik* (Frankfurt, 1993), p. 14.